Lecture Notes in Computer Science

Lecture Notes in Artificial Intelligence   14101

Founding Editor

Jörg Siekmann

Series Editors

Randy Goebel, *University of Alberta, Edmonton, Canada*
Wolfgang Wahlster, *DFKI, Berlin, Germany*
Zhi-Hua Zhou, *Nanjing University, Nanjing, China*

The series Lecture Notes in Artificial Intelligence (LNAI) was established in 1988 as a topical subseries of LNCS devoted to artificial intelligence.

The series publishes state-of-the-art research results at a high level. As with the LNCS mother series, the mission of the series is to serve the international R & D community by providing an invaluable service, mainly focused on the publication of conference and workshop proceedings and postproceedings.

Catherine Dubois · Manfred Kerber
Editors

Intelligent Computer Mathematics

16th International Conference, CICM 2023
Cambridge, UK, September 5–8, 2023
Proceedings

Editors
Catherine Dubois 🆔
ENSIIE
Evry, France

Manfred Kerber
University of Birmingham
Birmingham, UK

ISSN 0302-9743   ISSN 1611-3349 (electronic)
Lecture Notes in Artificial Intelligence
ISBN 978-3-031-42752-7   ISBN 978-3-031-42753-4 (eBook)
https://doi.org/10.1007/978-3-031-42753-4

LNCS Sublibrary: SL7 – Artificial Intelligence

This Springer imprint is published by the registered company Springer Nature Switzerland AG
The registered company address is: Gewerbestrasse 11, 6330 Cham, Switzerland

Preface

This volume contains the papers presented at the 16th Conference on Intelligent Computer Mathematics (CICM 2023), held during 5–8 September 2023, in Cambridge, UK, organized in hybrid mode.

With the continuing, rapid progress of digital methods in communications, knowledge representation, processing, and discovery, the special character and needs of mathematical information require special approaches. Separate communities have developed theoretical and practical solutions for these challenges including computation, deduction, narration, and data management. CICM brings these communities together, offering a venue for discussing and developing solutions to problems posed by the integration of these diverse areas.

CICM was initially formed in 2008 as a joint meeting of communities involved in computer algebra systems, theorem provers, and mathematical knowledge management, as well as those involved in a variety of aspects of scientific document archives. Since then, the conference has been held annually: Birmingham (UK, 2008), Grand Bend (Canada, 2009), Paris (France, 2010), Bertinoro (Italy, 2011), Bremen (Germany, 2012), Bath (UK, 2013), Coimbra (Portugal, 2014), Washington D.C. (USA, 2015), Białystok (Poland, 2016), Edinburgh (UK, 2017), Hagenberg (Austria, 2018), Prague (Czech Republic, 2019), Bertinoro (Italy, 2020, online), Timisoara (Romania, 2021, online) and Tbilisi (Georgia, 2022, hybrid).

CICM 2023 received 31 formal submissions. Each submission was assigned to at least three Program Committee (PC) members and was reviewed in single-blind mode. The committee decided to accept 23 papers including 14 regular ones, two project/survey papers, six short papers describing software systems and datasets, and one paper highlighting the development of systems and tools in the last year.

The reviewing process included a response period in which the authors could respond and clarify points raised by the reviewers. In addition to the main sessions, a doctoral program was organized, providing a forum for PhD students to present their research and get advice from senior members of the community.

The conference featured four invited talks:

- Frédéric Blanqui (Inria):
  "Progress on proof systems interoperability",
- Mateja Jamnik (University of Cambridge):
  "How can we make trustworthy AI?",
- Lawrence C. Paulson (University of Cambridge):
  "Large-Scale Formal Proof for the Working Mathematician - Lessons learnt from the Alexandria Project",
- Martina Seidl (Johannes Kepler University Linz):
  "Never trust your solver: Certificates for SAT and QBF".

Additionally, the following workshops were scheduled:

- the 3rd Workshop on Natural Formal Mathematics (NatFoM 2023),
  organized by Peter Koepke, Adrian De Lon and Dennis Müller,
- the 14th Workshop on Mathematical User Interaction (MathUI 2023),
  organized by Abhishek Chugh and Andrea Kohlhase,
- the 2nd Workshop on Interoperable Knowledge Representation (Tetrapod 2023)
  organized by Katja Bercic, William Farmer, Michael Kohlhase, Dennis Müller and
  Florian Rabe.

The EuroProofNet Workshop on Libraries of Formal Proofs and Natural Mathematical Language, organized by Angeliki Koutsoukou Argyraki and Claudio Sacerdoti Coen, was co-located with CICM 2023. NatFoM 2023 was also affiliated as an EuroProofNet workshop.

We thank the PC members and the additional reviewers for their timely and thorough reviewing work, and for contributing to an animated and informed discussion. Their names are listed on the following pages. The EasyChair conference management system was set up for CICM 2023, supporting submission, review and volume editing processes.

We thank the conference chair James Davenport and his colleagues in Cambridge for the successful organization of the conference. We are grateful to Serge Autexier for his publicity work, Jesús María Aransay Azofra for serving as the doctoral program chair, and Florian Rabe for serving as the workshop chair. We also thank the authors of the submitted papers, the workshop organizers, the invited speakers and the participants of the conference.

August 2023   Catherine Dubois
                                                         Manfred Kerber

Organization

Program Committee Chairs

Catherine Dubois   ENSIIE, France
Manfred Kerber   University of Birmingham, UK

Program Committee

Jesús Aransay	Universidad de La Rioja, Spain
Mauricio Ayala-Rincón	Universidade de Brasilía, Brazil
Haniel Barbosa	Universidade Federal de Minas Gerais, Brazil
Jasmin Blanchette	Ludwig-Maximilians-Universität München, Germany
Kevin Buzzard	Imperial College London, UK
Isabela Drămnesc	West University of Timisoara, Romania
Mădălina Eraşcu	West University of Timisoara, Romania
William Farmer	McMaster University, Canada
John Harrison	Amazon Web Services, USA
Tetsuo Ida	University of Tsukuba, Japan
Moa Johansson	Chalmers University of Technology, Sweden
Fairouz Kamareddine	Heriot-Watt University, UK
Daniela Kaufmann	TU Wien, Austria
Peter Koepke	University of Bonn, Germany
Michael Kohlhase	Friedrich-Alexander-Universität Erlangen-Nürnberg, Germany
Angeliki Koutsoukou-Argyraki	University of Cambridge, UK
Temur Kutsia	Johannes Kepler University Linz, Austria
Micaela Mayero	Université Paris Nord, France
Bruce Miller	NIST, USA
Adam Naumowicz	University of Białystok, Poland
Claudio Sacerdoti Coen	University of Bologna, Italy
Sofiène Tahar	Concordia University, Canada
Olaf Teschke	FIZ Karlsruhe, Germany
Josef Urban	Czech Technical University in Prague, Czech Republic
Stephen Watt	University of Waterloo, Canada
Freek Wiedijk	Radboud University, The Netherlands

Wolfgang Windsteiger   Johannes Kepler University Linz, Austria
Abdou Youssef   George Washington University, USA

Additional Reviewers

Aksoy, Kubra
Arielly de Lima, Thaynara
Barhoumi, Oumaima
Davenport, James H.
Deniz, Elif
Elleuch, Maissa
Gauthier, Thibault
Kameyama, Yukiyoshi
Müller, Dennis
Schaefer, Jan Frederik
Schmidt-Schauss, Manfred
Wong, Thomas

Abstracts of Invited Talks

Progress on Proof System Interoperability

Frédéric Blanqui [ID]

Université Paris-Saclay, ENS Paris-Saclay, LMF, CNRS, Inria, France
frederic.blanqui@inria.fr
https://blanqui.gitlabpages.inria.fr/

Proof system interoperability is a research topic which started about 30 years ago, and received some attention with the formalization of Hales' proof of the Kepler Conjecture in the 2000s as parts of this proof were initially formalized in two different provers. Then, proof system interoperability received new interest in the 2010s with the increasing use of automated theorem provers in proof assistants.

At about the same time a new logical framework appeared, called Dedukti, which extends LF by allowing the identification of types modulo some equational theory. It has been shown that various logical systems can be nicely encoded in Dedukti, and various tools have been developed to actually represent proofs from various provers in Dedukti, and to translate them to other provers.

In this talk, I will review some of these works and tools, and present recent efforts to handle entire libraries of proofs.

Partly supported by the COST action 20111 EuroProofNet.

How Can We Make Trustworthy AI?

Mateja Jamnik(iD)

University of Cambridge, UK
mateja.jamnik@cl.cam.ac.uk
https://www.cl.cam.ac.uk/~mj201/

Not too long ago most headlines talked about our fear of AI. Today, AI is ubiquitous, and the conversation has moved on from whether we should use AI to how we can trust the AI systems that we use in our daily lives. In this talk I look at some key technical ingredients that help us build confidence and trust in using intelligent technology. I argue that intuitiveness, adaptability, explainability and inclusion of human domain knowledge are essential in building this trust. I present some of the techniques and methods we are building for making AI systems that think and interact with humans in more intuitive and personalised ways, enabling humans to better understand the solutions produced by machines, and enabling machines to incorporate human domain knowledge in their reasoning and learning processes.

Contents

Project and Survey Papers

System and Dataset Descriptions

Invited Talks

Large-Scale Formal Proof for the Working Mathematician—Lessons Learnt from the ALEXANDRIA Project

Lawrence C. Paulson[(✉)]

Computer Laboratory, University of Cambridge, Cambridge, UK
lp15@cam.ac.uk
https://www.cl.cam.ac.uk/~lp15/

Abstract. ALEXANDRIA is an ERC-funded project that started in 2017, with the aim of bringing formal verification to mathematics. The past six years have seen great strides in the formalisation of mathematics and also in some relevant technologies, above all machine learning. Six years of intensive formalisation activity seem to show that even the most advanced results, drawing on multiple fields of mathematics, can be formalised using the tools available today.

Keywords: Isabelle · formalisation of mathematics · ALEXANDRIA project

1 Introduction

In the summer of 2017, the Newton Institute at Cambridge held a programme entitled *Big Proof* (BPR) "directed at the challenges of bringing proof technology into mainstream mathematical practice". It was held in recognition of the formalisations that had already been done (which were indeed big). The programme webpage[1] specifically lists the proofs of the Kepler conjecture [19], the odd order theorem [17] and the four colour theorem [16]. That summer also saw the start of my ERC project, ALEXANDRIA. *Big Proof* represented an acknowledgement that the formalisation of mathematics could no longer be ignored, but also an assertion that big problems remain to be solved. These included "novel pragmatic foundations" and large-scale "formal mathematical libraries" and "inference engines", and also the "curation" of formalised mathematical knowledge.

ALEXANDRIA was conceived in part to try to identify those big problems. By hiring professional mathematicians and asking them to formalise advanced mathematics, we would get a direct idea of the obstacles they faced. We would also try to refine our tools, extend our libraries and investigate other technologies. We would have only five years (extended to six due to COVID-19).

The need for formalisation had been stressed by Vladimir Voevodsky, a Fields medallist, who pointedly asked "And who would ensure that I did not forget something and did not make a mistake, if even the mistakes in much more simple

---

[1] https://www.newton.ac.uk/event/bpr/.

© The Author(s), under exclusive license to Springer Nature Switzerland AG 2023
C. Dubois and M. Kerber (Eds.): CICM 2023, LNAI 14101, pp. 3–15, 2023.
https://doi.org/10.1007/978-3-031-42753-4_1

arguments take years to uncover?" [38]. He advocated a new sort of formalism, homotopy type theory, which was the subject of much excitement. However, the most impressive formalisations by that time had been done in Coq (four colour theorem, odd order theorem), HOL Light (Kepler conjecture and much else) or Isabelle/HOL (part of the Kepler proof, and more). Lean, a newcomer, was attracting a user community. Perhaps our project would shed light on the respective values of the available formalisms: calculus of constructions (Coq, Lean), higher-order logic or homotopy type theory. Voevodsky would never find out, due to his untimely death in September 2017.

Since that date, research into the formalisation of mathematics has plunged ahead. Kevin Buzzard, a number theorist at Imperial College London, followed some of the *Big Proof* talks online. This resulted in his adoption of Lean for his Xena Project, with the aim of attracting students to formalisation.[2] Xena has had a huge impact, but here I'd like to focus on the work done within ALEXANDRIA.

2   A Brief Prehistory of the Formalisation of Mathematics

Mathematics is a work of the imagination, and the struggle between intuition and rigour has gone on since classical times. Euclid's great contribution to Greek geometry was the unification of many separate schools through his system of axioms and postulates. Newton and Leibniz revolutionised mathematics, but the introduction of infinitesimals was problematical. During the 19th centuries, the "arithmetisation of analysis" carried out by Cauchy and Weierstrass replaced infinitesimals by rigorous ϵ–δ arguments. (We would not get a consistent theory of infinitesimals until the 1960 s,s, under the banner of non-standard analysis.) Dedekind and Cantor promulgated a radical new understanding of sets and functions that turned out to be inconsistent until Zermelo came up with his axioms. It is notable that Zermelo set theory (which includes the axiom of choice but lacks Fraenkel's replacement axiom) is approximately equal in logical strength to higher-order logic.

Only axiomatic mathematics can be formalised. The first attempt was by Frege, whose work (contrary to common belief) was not significantly impacted by Russell's paradox [1]. Russell and Whitehead in their *Principia Mathematica* [40] wrote out the proofs of thousands of mathematical propositions in a detailed axiomatic form. The work of Bourbaki can also be seen as a kind of formalised mathematics. The philosopher Hao Wang wrote on the topic and also coded the first automatic theorem prover [39] for first-order logic, based on what we would now recognise as a tableau calculus.

This takes us to NG de Bruijn, who in 1968 created AUTOMATH [5], and to his student's formalisation [24] of Landau's *Foundations of Analysis* in 1977. This takes us to the birth of Mizar [18], in which a truly impressive amount of mathematics was formalised in a remarkably readable notation. More recent

---

[2] https://www.ma.imperial.ac.uk/~buzzard/xena/.

history—analysis in HOL Light, the four colour theorem in Coq, etc.—is presumably familiar to readers. But it is appropriate to close this section with a prescient remark by de Bruijn back in 1968:

> As to the question what part of mathematics can be written in AUTOMATH, it should first be remarked that we do not possess a workable definition of the word "mathematics". Quite often a mathematician jumps from his mathematical language into a kind of metalanguage, obtains results there, and uses these results in his original context. It seems to be very hard to create a single language in which such things can be done without any restriction [[4], p. 3].

And so we have two great scientific questions:

- **What sort of mathematics can be formalised?**
- **What sort of proofs can be formalised?**

We would investigate these questions—mostly in the context of Isabelle/HOL—by formalising as much mathematics as we could, covering as many different topics as possible. I expected to run into obstacles here and there, which would have to be recorded if they could not be overcome.

3   ALEXANDRIA: Warmup Formalisation Exercises

The ERC proposal called for hiring research mathematicians, who would bring their knowledge of mathematics as it was practised, along with their *inexperience* of Isabelle/HOL. Their role would be to formalise increasingly advanced mathematical material with the twin objectives of developing formalisation methodologies and identifying deficiencies that might be remedied by extending Isabelle/HOL somehow. The project started in September 2017. We hired Anthony Bordg and Angeliki Koutsoukou-Argyraki. A third postdoc was required to undertake any necessary Isabelle engineering, and Wenda Li was hired.

One of the tasks for the first year was simply to reorganise and consolidate the Isabelle/HOL analysis library, which had mostly been translated from HOL Light. But we were also supposed to conduct pilot studies. The team set to work enthusiastically, and already in the first year they created a number of impressive developments:

- *Irrational rapidly convergent series*, formalising a 2002 proof by J. Hančl [20]
- *Projective geometry*, including Hessenberg's theorem and Desargues's theorem
- The theory of *quantum computing* (which identified a significant error in one of the main early papers)
- *Quaternions, octonions* and several other small exercises
- Effectively counting *real and complex roots of polynomials*, and the Budan-Fourier theorem [30, 31]
- The first formal proof that *every field contains an algebraically closed extension* [37]

Koutsoukou-Argyraki wrote up her reactions to Isabelle/HOL from the perspective of a mathematician in her paper "Formalising Mathematics —in Praxis" [25].

4   Advanced Formalisations

As noted above, Kevin Buzzard had taken an interest in formalisation through participation in *Big Proof*, and by 2019 had marshalled large numbers of enthusiastic students to formalise mathematics using Lean. He had also made trenchant criticisms of even the most impressive prior achievements: that most of it concerned simple objects such as finite groups, or was just 19th-century mathematics. Nobody seemed to be working with sophisticated objects. He expressed astonishment that Grothendieck schemes—fundamental objects in algebraic geometry and number theory—had not been formalised in any tool. His criticisms helped focus our attention on the need to tackle difficult, recent and deep mathematics. Team members proposed their own tasks, but we also contributed to one another's tasks, sometimes with the help of interns or students. We completed three notable projects during this middle period:

- *Irrationality and transcendence criteria for infinite series* [27], extending the Hančl work mentioned above with material from two more papers: Erdős–Straus [13] and Hančl–Rucki [21].
- *Ordinal partition theory* [9]: infinite forms of Ramsey's theorem, but for order types rather than cardinals. We formalised relatively papers by Erdős–Milner [14] and Larson [29], and as a preliminary, the Nash-Williams partition theorem [36]. These were deep results in the context of Zermelo–Fraenkel set theory, involving highly intricate inductive constructions. One of the papers contained so many errors as to necessitate publishing a second paper [15] with a substantially different proof. This material was difficult even for Erdős!
- *Grothendieck Schemes* [3]. Buzzard had formalised schemes in Lean [6] (three times), and even claimed that Isabelle was not up to the job due to its simple type system. We took the challenge and it was straightforward, following a new approach based on locales to manage the deep hierarchies of definitions.

We were aiming for a special issue devoted to formalisation in the journal *Experimental Mathematics*, and were delighted to see these projects take up three of the six papers ultimately accepted.

5   Seriously Deep Formalisation Projects

Inspired by the success of the previous projects—conducted under the difficult circumstances of COVID-19 lockdown—team members continued to propose theorems to formalise, and we continued to collaborate in small groups. By now we had the confidence to take on almost anything. There are too many projects to describe in full, so let's look at some of the highlights.

5.1   Szemerédi's Regularity Lemma and Roth's Theorem on Arithmetic Progressions

Szemerédi's regularity lemma is a fundamental result in extremal graph theory. It concerns a property called the *edge density* of two given sets of vertices X,

$Y \subseteq V(G)$, and a further property of (X, Y) being an ϵ-regular pair for any given $\epsilon > 0$. The lemma itself states that for a given $\epsilon > 0$ there exists some M such that every graph has an ϵ-regular partition of its vertex set into at most M parts. Intuitively, (X, Y) is an ϵ-regular pair if the density of edges between various subsets $A \subseteq X$ and $B \subseteq Y$ is more or less the same for all possible A and B; an ϵ-regular partition enjoys that property for all but an insignificant number of pairs (X, Y) of vertex sets taken from the partition. Intuitively then, the vertices of any graph can be partitioned into most M parts such that the edges between the various parts are uniform in this sense.

We used Szemerédi's regularity lemma to prove *Roth's theorem on arithmetic progressions*, which states that every "sufficiently dense" set of natural numbers includes three elements of the form k, $k + d$, $k + 2d$.

We used a variety of source materials and discovered a good many significant infelicities in the definitions and proofs. These included confusion between $\subset$ and $\subseteq$ (which are often synonymous in combinatorics) and between a number of variants of the lemma statement. One minor claim was flatly incorrect. To make matters worse, the significance of these issues only became clear in the application of the regularity lemma to Roth's theorem. Much time was wasted, and yet the entire formalisation project [10] took under six months.[3] By a remarkable coincidence, a group based in the mathematics department at Cambridge formalised a slightly different version of Szemerédi's regularity lemma, using Lean, around the same time [8].

5.2   Additive Combinatorics

Let A and B be finite subsets of a given abelian group $(G, +)$, and define their *sumset* as
$$A + B = \{a + b : a \in A, b \in B\}.$$

Write nA for the n-fold iterated sumset $A + \cdots + A$. *Additive combinatorics* concerns itself with such matters as the relationship between the cardinality of $A+B$ and other properties of A and B. Angeliki proposed this field as the natural successor to the formalisation of Szemerédi's regularity lemma because it's fairly recent (many results are less than 50 years old) and significant (providing a route to Szemerédi's theorem, a much stronger version of the Roth result mentioned above).

Here's an overview of the results formalised, all within the 7-month period from April to November 2022:

- The *Plünnecke–Ruzsa inequality*: yields an upper bound on the *difference* set $mB - nB$
- *Khovanskii's theorem*: for any finite $A \subseteq G$, the cardinality of nA grows like a polynomial for all sufficiently large n.

---

[3] An email from Angeliki proposing to prove Szemerédi's regularity lemma is dated 8 July 2021. The formalisation was done by 5 November; Roth, 28 December.

– The *Balog-Szemerédi-Gowers theorem* is a deep result bearing on Szemerédi's theorem. The formalisation combines additive combinatorics with extremal graph theory and probability [26].
– *Kneser's theorem* and the *Cauchy-Davenport theorem* yield lower bounds for the size of $A + B$.

These are highly significant results by leading mathematicians. They can all be found in Isabelle's *Archive of Formal Proofs* (AFP).[4]

5.3 Other Formalisation Projects

The members chose a variety of large and small projects with a variety of specific objectives:

– *Combinatorial structures.* This is the PhD project of Chelsea Edmonds, who has used Isabelle's locale system to formalise dozens of varieties of block designs, hypergraphs, graphs and the relationships among them [11]. Results proved include Fisher's inequality [12].
– *Number theory.* We have formalised several chapters of *Modular Functions and Dirichlet Series in Number Theory*, a graduate textbook by Tom M. Apostol.
– *Wetzel's problem* is a fascinating small example, due to Erdős, where the answer to a question concerning complex analysis depends on the truth or falsity of the continuum hypothesis. The formal proof illustrates analysis and axiomatic set theory smoothly combined into a single argument [33].
– *Turán's graph theorem* states a maximality property of Turán graphs. This was a Master's student project.

This is a partial list, especially as regards contributions from interns, students and other visitors.

5.4 On Legibility of Formal Proofs

A proof is an argument, based on logical reasoning from agreed assumptions, that convinces mathematicians that a claim is true. How then do we understand a computer proof? To follow the analogy strictly, a computer proof convinces computers that a claim is true. But computers, even in this age of clever chatbots, are not sentient. We need to convince mathematicians.

Of the early efforts at the formalisation of mathematics, only Mizar aimed for legibility. Even pre-computer formal proofs such as *Principia Mathematica* are unreadable. Isabelle's proof language (Isar) follows the Mizar tradition, as in the following example:

```
lemma deriv_sum_int:
  "deriv (λx. ∑ i=0..n. real_of_int (c i) * x^i) x
    = (if n=0 then 0 else (∑ i=0..n-1. of_int((i+1) * c(Suc i)) *
x^i))"
```

---

[4] https://www.isa-afp.org.

```
(is "deriv ?f x = (if n=0 then 0 else ?g)")
proof -
  have "(?f has_real_derivative ?g) (at x)" if "n > 0"
  proof -
    have "(∑ i = 0..n. i * x ^ (i - Suc 0) * (c i))
        = (∑ i = 1..n. (real (i-1) + 1) * of_int (c i) * x ^ (i-1))"
      using that by (auto simp: sum.atLeast_Suc_atMost intro!: sum.cong)
    also have "... = sum ((λi. (real i + 1) * c (Suc i) * x^i) ∘ (λn.
n-1))
                              {1..Suc (n-1)}"
      using that by simp
    also have "... = ?g"
      by (simp flip: sum.atLeast_atMost_pred_shift [where m=0])
    finally have §: "(∑ a = 0..n. a * x ^ (a - Suc 0) * (c a)) = ?g" .
    show ?thesis
      by (rule derivative_eq_intros § | simp)+
  qed
  then show ?thesis
    by (force intro: DERIV_imp_deriv)
qed
```

Only a little training is required to make some sense of this. The lemma claims that the derivative of a certain summation equals a certain other summation. The proof refers of the variables $?f$ and $?g$, which are defined by the pattern provided in the lemma statement: $?f$ denotes the original summation, and we prove that $?g$ is its derivative. Within that proof we can see summations being manipulated through changes of variable. Since we can see these details of the reasoning, we have reasons to believe that the proof is indeed correct: we do not simply have to trust the computer.

Not all Isabelle proofs can be written in a structured style. Page-long formulas often arise when trying to verify program code, and sometimes just from expanding mathematical definitions. Then we must use the traditional tactic style: long sequences of proof commands. However, most mathematical proofs that humans can write go into the structured style with ease. We have aimed for maximum legibility in all our work.

6   Library Search and Machine Learning Experiments

The focus of this paper is achievements in the formalisation of mathematics, but the ALEXANDRIA proposal also called for investigating supporting technologies. The name of the project refers to the library of Alexandria, and Isabelle's AFP already has nearly 4 million lines of proof text and well over 700 separate entries. How can we take advantage of all this material when developing new proofs?

In May 2019, the team acquired a new postdoc: Yiannos Stathopoulos. He came with the perfect background to tackle these objectives. After much labour, he and Angeliki produced the SErAPIS search engine,[5] which searches both the pre-installed Isabelle libraries and the AFP, offering a great many search strategies based on anything from simple keywords to abstract mathematical concepts [35]. It is not easy to determine the relevance or significance of a formal text to an abstract concept, but a variety of query types can be combined to explore the libraries.

Also mentioned in the proposal was the aim of Intelligent User Support. I had imagined that common patterns of proofs could be identified in the existing libraries and offered up to users, but with no idea how. To generate structured proofs automatically would require the ability to generate intermediate mathematical assertions. Six years of dramatic advances in machine learning have transformed our prospects. Language models can generate plausible texts given a corpus of existing texts. And as the texts we want would be inserted into Isabelle proofs, we can immediately check their correctness.

An enormous amount of work is underway, particularly by a student in our group, Albert Qiaochu Jiang, working alongside Wenda Li and others. It is now clear that language models can generate formal Isabelle proof skeletons [32] and can also be useful for identifying relevant lemmas [22]. We can even envisage *automatic formalisation* [23, 41]: translating informal proofs into formal languages, by machine. Autoformalisation is easier with a legible proof language like ours, because the formal proof can have the same overall structure as the given natural language proof; a project currently underway is to develop the Isabelle Parallel Corpus, pairing natural language and Isabelle texts.[6] The next few years should see solid gains through machine learning.

7   Evaluation

At the start of this paper, I listed two scientific questions: what sort of mathematics, and what sort of proofs, can be formalised? And the answer so far is, everything we attempted, and we attempted a great variety of mathematical topics: number theory, combinatorics, analysis, set theory. The main difficulties have been errors and omissions in proofs. A vignette illustrates this point. Chelsea was formalising a probabilistic argument where the authors wrote "these probabilities are clearly independent, and therefore the joint probability is obtained by multiplying them." The problem is that this multiplication law is the mathematical definition of independent probabilities, which the authors had somehow confused with the real-world concept of unconnected random events. Frequently we have found proofs that are almost right: they need a bit of adjustment, but getting everything to fit takes effort.

Effort remains the main obstacle to the use of verification tools by mathematicians. Obvious claims are often tiresome to prove, which is both discouraging and a waste of an expert's time. But we might already advocate an approach of formalising the definitions and the proofs, stating the obvious claims without

---

[5] https://behemoth.cl.cam.ac.uk/search/.

[6] https://behemoth.cl.cam.ac.uk/ipc/.

proofs (using the keyword **sorry**). Even for this idea to be feasible, much more library material is needed, covering at least all the definitions a mathematician might expect to have available.

Another key scientific question is the role of dependent types. People in the type theory world seem to share the conviction that dependent types are necessary to formalise nontrivial mathematics. But in reality it seems to be Lean users who repeatedly fall foul of *intensional equality*: that $i = j$ does not guarantee that $T(i)$ is the same type as $T(j)$. Falling foul of this can be fatal: the first definition of schemes had to be discarded for this reason. Intensional equality is adopted by almost all dependent type theories, including Coq and Agda: without it, type checking becomes undecidable. But with it, type dependence does not respect equality.

The main limitation of simple type theory is that axiomatic type classes are less powerful than they otherwise would be. Isabelle/HOL has type classes for groups, rings, topological spaces among much else, but they are not useful for defining the theories of groups, rings or topological spaces. Rather they allow us, for example, to define the quaternions, prove a dozen or so laws and immediately inherit entire libraries of algebraic and topological properties. Abstract groups, rings, etc., need to be declared with an explicit carrier set (logically, the same thing as a predicate) rather than using the corresponding type class. It's a small price to pay for a working equality relation.

Having said this, one must acknowledge the enormous progress made by the Lean community over roughly the same period, 2017–now. Lean users, inspired by Buzzard, have taken on hugely ambitious tasks. The most striking is probably the Liquid Tensor Experiment [7]: brand-new mathematics, by a Fields medallist (Peter Scholze) who was concerned about its correctness, formalised over about a year and a half. This one accomplishment, more than anything else, demonstrates that formalisation can already offer real value to professional mathematicians.

We have from time to time looked at type issues directly. De Vilhena [37] describes an interesting technique for defining the n-ary direct product of a finite list of groups, iterating the binary direct product; his trick to avoid type issues involves creating an isomorphism to a suitable type. However, here one could avoid type issues (and handle the infinite case) by defining the direct product of a family in its own right as opposed to piggybacking off of the binary product. Anthony Bordg has done a lot of work on the right way to express mathematics without dependent types [2,3]. Ongoing work, still unpublished, is exploring the potential of the *types-to-sets framework* [28] to allow a smooth transition between type-based and carrier-set based formalisations.

One can also compare formalisms in terms of their logical strength. Higher-order logic is somewhat weaker than Zermelo set theory, which is much weaker than ZFC, which in turn is much weaker than Tarski-Grothendieck set theory:

$$\text{HOL} < \text{Z} \ll \text{ZF} \ll \text{TG}$$

The Calculus of Inductive Constructions, which is the formalism of Lean and Coq, is roughly equivalent to TG. The advantage of a weaker formalism is better automation. The power of ZF set theory, when it is required, can be obtained simply by loading the corresponding library from the AFP [33]. It's highly likely that a similar library could be created for Tarski-Grothendieck. And yet, remarkably, everything we have tried to formalise, unless it refers explicitly to ZF, sits comfortably within HOL alone. Since HOL is essentially the formalism of *Principia Mathematica* [40], we can conclude that Whitehead and Russell were right all along.

The AFP entries contributed by the project authors are too many to list, but they can be consulted via the on-line author indices:

– Anthony Bordg
  https://www.isa-afp.org/authors/bordg/
– Chelsea Edmonds
  https://www.isa-afp.org/authors/edmonds/
– Angeliki Koutsoukou-Argyraki
  https://www.isa-afp.org/authors/argyraki/
– Wenda Li
  https://www.isa-afp.org/authors/li/
– Lawrence C. Paulson
  https://www.isa-afp.org/authors/paulson/

8   Conclusions

We set out to tackle serious mathematics with a combination of hope and trepidation. We were able to formalise everything we set out to formalise and were never forced to discard a development part way through. As Angeliki has pointed out, "we have formalised results by two Fields medalists (Roth and Gowers), an Abel prize winner (Szemerédi) and of course Erdős too!"

We've also seen impressive advances in search and language models to assist users in proof development. Although the effort required to formalise mathematical articles remains high, we can confidently predict that formalisation will be playing a significant role in mathematical research in the next few years.

Acknowledgements. This work was supported by the ERC Advanced Grant ALEXANDRIA (Project GA 742178). Chelsea Edmonds, Angeliki Koutsoukou-Argyraki and Wenda Li provided numerous helpful comments and suggestions.

For the purpose of open access, the author has applied a Creative Commons Attribution (CC BY) licence to any Author Accepted Manuscript version arising from this submission.

References

1. Boolos, G.S.: Saving Frege from contradiction. In: Logic, Logic, and Logic, pp. 171–182. Harvard University Press (1998)
2. Bordg, A., Doña Mateo, A.: Encoding dependently-typed constructions into simple type theory. In: Proceedings of the 12th ACM SIGPLAN International Conference on Certified Programs and Proofs, CPP 2023, pp. 78–89. Association for Computing Machinery (2023). https://doi.org/10.1145/3573105.3575679

3. Bordg, A., Paulson, L., Li, W.: Simple type theory is not too simple: Grothendieck's schemes without dependent types. Exp. Math. **31**(2), 364–382 (2022). https://doi.org/10.1080/10586458.2022.2062073
4. de Bruijn, N.G.: AUTOMATH, a language for mathematics. Tech. Rep. 68-WSK-05, Technical University Eindhoven (Nov 1968)
5. de Bruijn, N.G.: The mathematical language AUTOMATH, its usage, and some of its extensions. In: Laudet, M. (ed.) Proceedings of the Symposium on Automatic Demonstration, pp. 29–61. Springer LNM 125, Versailles, France (Dec 1968)
6. Buzzard, K., Hughes, C., Lau, K., Livingston, A., Mir, R.F., Morrison, S.: Schemes in lean. Experim. Math. **31**(2), 355–363 (2022). https://doi.org/10.1080/10586458.2021.1983489
7. Castelvecchi, D.: Mathematicians welcome computer-assisted proof in 'grand unification' theory. Nature **595**, 18–19 (2021)
8. Dillies, Y., Mehta, B.: Formalizing Szemerédi's regularity lemma in Lean. In: Andronick, J., de Moura, L. (eds.) 13th International Conference on Interactive Theorem Proving, pp. 9:1–9:19. Schloss Dagstuhl - Leibniz-Zentrum für Informatik (2022)
9. Džamonja, M., Koutsoukou-Argyraki, A., Paulson, L.C.: Formalising ordinal partition relations using Isabelle/HOL. Exp. Math. **31**(2), 383–400 (2022). https://doi.org/10.1080/10586458.2021.1980464
10. Edmonds, C., Koutsoukou-Argyraki, A., Paulson, L.C.: Formalising Szemerédi's regularity lemma and Roth's theorem on arithmetic progressions in Isabelle/HOL. J. Autom. Reasoning **67**(1) (2023), https://doi.org/10.1007/s10817-022-09650-2
11. Edmonds, C., Paulson, L.C.: A modular first formalisation of combinatorial design theory. In: Kamareddine, F., Sacerdoti Coen, C. (eds.) CICM 2021. LNCS (LNAI), vol. 12833, pp. 3–18. Springer, Cham (2021). https://doi.org/10.1007/978-3-030-81097-9_1
12. Edmonds, C., Paulson, L.C.: Formalising Fisher's inequality: formal linear algebraic proof techniques in combinatorics. In: Andronick, J., de Moura, L. (eds.) 13th International Conference on Interactive Theorem Proving (ITP 2022), vol. 237, pp. 11:1–11:19. Schloss Dagstuhl - Leibniz-Zentrum für Informatik (2022). https://doi.org/10.4230/LIPIcs.ITP.2022.11
13. Erdős, P., Straus, E.G.: On the irrationality of certain series. Pacific J. Math. 55(1), 85–92 (1974). https://doi.org/pjm/1102911140
14. Erdős, P., Milner, E.C.: A theorem in the partition calculus. Can. Math. Bull. **15**(4), 501–505 (1972). https://doi.org/10.4153/CMB-1972-088-1
15. Erdős, P., Milner, E.C.: A theorem in the partition calculus corrigendum. Can. Math. Bull. **17**(2), 305 (1974). https://doi.org/10.4153/CMB-1974-062-6
16. Gonthier, G.: The four colour theorem: engineering of a formal proof. In: Kapur, D. (ed.) ASCM 2007. LNCS (LNAI), vol. 5081, pp. 333–333. Springer, Heidelberg (2008). https://doi.org/10.1007/978-3-540-87827-8_28
17. Gonthier, G., et al.: A machine-checked proof of the odd order theorem. In: Blazy, S., Paulin-Mohring, C., Pichardie, D. (eds.) ITP 2013. LNCS, vol. 7998, pp. 163–179. Springer, Heidelberg (2013). https://doi.org/10.1007/978-3-642-39634-2_14
18. Grabowski, A., Korniłowicz, A., Naumowicz, A.: Four decades of Mizar. J. Autom. Reasoning **55**(3), 191–198 (Oct 2015). https://doi.org/10.1007/s10817-015-9345-1
19. Hales, T., et al.: A formal proof of the Kepler conjecture. Forum Math. Pi **5**, e2 (2017). https://doi.org/10.1017/fmp.2017.1
20. Hančl, J.: Irrational rapidly convergent series. Rendiconti del Seminario Matematico della Università di Padova **107**, 225–231 (2002). http://eudml.org/doc/108582

21. Hančl, J., Rucki, P.: The transcendence of certain infinite series. Rocky Mountain J. Math. **35**(2), 531–537 (2005). https://doi.org/10.1216/rmjm/1181069744

22. Jiang, A.Q., et al.: Thor: Wielding hammers to integrate language models and automated theorem provers. In: Neural Information Processing Systems (NeurIPS) (2022)

23. Jiang, A.Q., et al.: Draft, sketch, and prove: guiding formal theorem provers with informal proofs. In: Eleventh International Conference on Learning Representations (2023). https://openreview.net/forum?id=SMa9EAovKMC

24. Jutting, L.: Checking Landau's "Grundlagen" in the AUTOMATH System. Ph.D. thesis, Eindhoven University of Technology (1977). https://doi.org/10.6100/IR23183

25. Koutsoukou-Argyraki, A.: Formalising mathematics — in praxis; a mathematician's first experiences with Isabelle/HOL and the why and how of getting started. Jahresbericht der Deutschen Mathematiker-Vereinigung **123**(1), 3–26 (2021). https://doi.org/10.1365/s13291-020-00221-1

26. Koutsoukou-Argyraki, A., Bakšys, M., Edmonds, C.: A formalisation of the Balog-Szemerédi-Gowers theorem in Isabelle/HOL. In: 12th ACM SIGPLAN International Conference on Certified Programs and Proofs, CPP 2023, pp. 225–238. Association for Computing Machinery (2023). https://doi.org/10.1145/3573105.3575680

27. Koutsoukou-Argyraki, A., Li, W., Paulson, L.C.: Irrationality and transcendence criteria for infinite series in Isabelle/HOL. Exp. Math. **31**(2), 401–412 (2022)

28. Kunčar, O., Popescu, A.: From types to sets by local type definition in higher-order logic. J. Autom. Reasoning **62**(2), 237–260 (2019). https://doi.org/10.1007/s10817-018-9464-6

29. Larson, J.A.: A short proof of a partition theorem for the ordinal ω^ω. Annals Math. Logic **6**(2), 129–145 (1973). https://doi.org/10.1016/0003-4843(73)90006-5

30. Li, W., Paulson, L.C.: Counting polynomial roots in Isabelle/HOL: a formal proof of the Budan-Fourier theorem. In: 8th ACM SIGPLAN International Conference on Certified Programs and Proofs, CPP 2019, pp. 52–64. Association for Computing Machinery (2019). https://doi.org/10.1145/3293880.3294092

31. Li, W., Paulson, L.C.: Evaluating winding numbers and counting complex roots through Cauchy indices in Isabelle/HOL. J. Autom. Reasoning (Apr 2019). https://doi.org/10.1007/s10817-019-09521-3

32. Li, W., Yu, L., Wu, Y., Paulson, L.C.: Isarstep: a benchmark for high-level mathematical reasoning. In: 9th International Conference on Learning Representations, ICLR 2021. OpenReview.net (2021). https://openreview.net/forum?id=Pzj6fzU6wkj

33. Paulson, L.C.: Wetzel: formalisation of an undecidable problem linked to the continuum hypothesis. In: Intelligent Computer Mathematics: 15th International Conference, CICM 2022, pp. 92–106. Springer (2022). https://doi.org/10.1007/978-3-031-16681-5_6

34. Peltier, N., Sofronie-Stokkermans, V. (eds.): IJCAR 2020. LNCS (LNAI), vol. 12166. Springer, Cham (2020). https://doi.org/10.1007/978-3-030-51074-9

35. Stathopoulos, Y., Koutsoukou-Argyraki, A., Paulson, L.: Developing a concept-oriented search engine for Isabelle based on natural language: technical challenges. In: 5th Conference on Artificial Intelligence and Theorem Proving (2020). http://aitp-conference.org/2020/abstract/paper_9.pdf

36. Todorčević, S.: Introduction to Ramsey Spaces. Princeton University Press (2010)

37. de Vilhena, P.E., Paulson, L.C.: Algebraically closed fields in Isabelle/HOL. In: Peltier and Sofronie-Stokkermans [34], pp. 204–220
38. Voevodsky, V.: The origins and motivations of univalent foundations. The Institute Letter, pp. 8–9 (Summer 2014). https://www.ias.edu/ideas/2014/voevodsky-origins
39. Wang, H.: Toward mechanical mathematics. IBM J. Res. Dev. **4**(1), 2–22 (1960)
40. Whitehead, A.N., Russell, B.: Principia Mathematica. Cambridge University Press (1962), paperback edition to *56, abridged from the 2nd edition (1927)
41. Wu, Y., et al.: Autoformalization with large language models. In: Neural Information Processing Systems (NeurIPS) (2022)

Never Trust Your Solver: Certification for SAT and QBF

Martina Seidl[(✉)] [iD]

Institute for Symbolic Artificial Intelligence, Johannes Kepler University,
Linz, Austria
martina.seidl@jku.at

Abstract. Many problems for formal verification and artificial intelligence rely on advanced reasoning technologies in the background, often in the form of SAT or QBF solvers. Such solvers are sophisticated and highly tuned pieces of software, often too complex to be verified themselves. Now the question arises how one can one be sure that the result of such a solver is correct, especially when its result is critical for proving the correctness of another system. If a SAT solver, a tool for deciding a propositional formula, returns satisfiable, then it also returns a model which is easy to check. If the answer is unsatisfiable, the situation is more complicated. And so it is for true and false quantified Boolean formulas (QBFs), which extend propositional logic by quantifiers over the Boolean variables. To increase the trust in a solving result, modern solvers are expected to produce certificates that can independently and efficiently be checked. In this paper, we give an overview of the state of the art on validating the results of SAT and QBF solvers based on certification.

Keywords: SAT · QBF · Certification

1 Introduction

Many reasoning tasks depend on the efficiency and the correctness of SAT and QBF solvers. Especially SAT solving, i.e., deciding the decision problem of propositional logic, is a "killer app" in various domains [44] ranging from verification tasks [64], to solving hard mathematical problems [32]. Despite the NP-hardness of SAT and the intractability of this problem, advanced pruning techniques allow SAT solvers to find answers to many SAT encodings of practical interest within a reasonable time frame. The answer "satisfiable" is easy to validate because SAT solvers return a satisfying variable assignment as the solution of the given formula. Then it only needs to be checked if the formula evaluates to true under the assignment. However, when the answer is "unsatisfiable", i.e., the given formula does not have any solution, it is not feasible to enumerate all possible assignments in order to show that none of them satisfies the formula. While several powerful testing techniques have been developed that help to increase the trust

Supported by the LIT AI Lab Funded by the State of Upper Austria

C. Dubois and M. Kerber (Eds.): CICM 2023, LNAI 14101, pp. 16–33, 2023.
https://doi.org/10.1007/978-3-031-42753-4_2

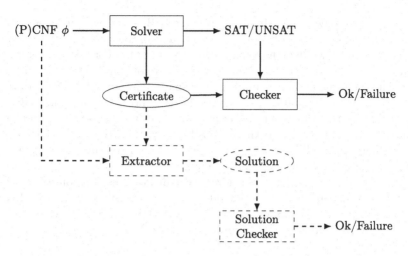

Fig. 1. Certification workflow for SAT and QBF. The dashed part shows the QBF-specific solution extraction.

in a SAT solver implementation [1,13,51], these techniques can never exhaustively guarantee the correctness of a SAT solver. There are fully verified SAT solvers like IsaSAT [11], but such solvers are in general less performant than non-verified solvers as shown in SAT Competition 2022.[1] Fortunately, there is another way of certifying the correctness of an unsatisfiability result: modern SAT solvers are able to produce proofs of unsatisfiability which can be checked efficiently by independent, possibly verified proof checkers. While a SAT solver can still be buggy, proof checking ensures that the result of a specific formula is correct. The general certification workflow is shown in Fig. 1 (for SAT only the upper part with solid lines is relevant). Over the last years, much work has been dedicated to the generation of proofs and nowadays the ability to produce proofs of unsatisfiability is mandatory for the participation at certain tracks at the SAT competition. A detailed discussion of various proof systems and proof formats can be found in [15,30].

Quantified Boolean Formulas (QBFs) extend propositional logic by universal and existential quantification over the Boolean variables [8]. With universal quantifiers, certain problems can be represented more succinctly than it would be possible with propositional logic. Moreover, quantifiers allow for natural encodings of two-player games as found, for example, in the context of reactive synthesis. A recent survey of QBF applications can be found in [60]. In contrast to SAT, the decision problem of QBF is PSPACE-complete. As a consequence, in QBF correctness checking works in a dual manner for true and false formulas. There is no simple case as the checking of satisfying assignments in propositional logic. Furthermore, for QBF, the solving landscape is more heterogeneous as it is in SAT. While conflict-driven clause learning (see Sect. 3 for a short introduction) is

---

[1] https://satcompetition.github.io/2022/.

the predominant solving paradigm in SAT, for QBF several approaches showed to be very successful in the past [50,55]. These approaches rely on different proof systems and are provably orthogonal in their strength [8]. For QBFs, proofs play also an important role for extracting models and counter-models for true and false formulas. These (counter-)models are usually represented as Boolean functions and encode the solutions of the application problem, like the plan of a planning problem or the generated circuit of a hardware synthesis problem. If the functions are plugged into the propositional part of the solved QBF, they can be validated by calling a SAT solver, even more increasing the trust in the solving result (see lower dashed part of Fig. 1).

In this paper, we give an overview of certification in the context of SAT and QBF solving. In Sect. 2, we introduce the necessary preliminaries before discussing certification for SAT in Sect. 3 and for QBF in Sect. 4. We conclude our paper with a summary and an outlook in Sect. 5.

2   Preliminaries

We consider propositional formulas in *conjunctive normal form* (CNF). A formula is in CNF if it is a conjunction of clauses. A *clause* is a disjunction of literals and a *literal* is a possibly negated Boolean variable. If literal $l = x$ or $l = \neg x$, then $\mathsf{var}(l) = x$. Further, $\bar{l} = x$ if $l = \neg x$ and $\bar{l} = \neg x$ if $l = x$. By $\mathsf{var}(\phi)$, we denote the set of variables occuring in CNF ϕ. The empty clause is denoted by $\bot$. Let ϕ be a CNF and $X \subseteq \mathsf{var}(\phi)$. An *assignment* σ is a set of literals such there is no variable x with $x \in \sigma$ and $\neg x \in \sigma$. A CNF ϕ is true under σ if every clause $C \in \phi$ is true under σ. A clause is true under σ if it contains at least one literal l with $l \in \sigma$. Given a propositional formula ϕ and an assignment σ, then ϕ_σ denotes the formula obtained when setting all variables $x \in \mathsf{var}(\sigma)$ to true if $x \in \sigma$ and to false if $\neg x \in \sigma$, respectively. *Boolean Constraint Propagation* (BCP) is an important propagation mechanism that propagates truth values induced by literals in unit clauses, i.e., in clauses of size one. BCP repeats unit propagation until a fixpoint is reached. The fixpoint is denoted by $BCP(\phi))$ and defined as follows: Let $(l) \in \phi$ be a unit clause. Then $BCP(\phi, l)$ is obtained from ϕ by removing all clauses D with $l \in D$ and by removing all occurrences of $\bar{l}$.

Quantified Boolean Formulas extend propositional formulas with a quantifiers and have the form $\Pi.\phi$, where $\Pi = Q_1 X_1 \dots Q_n X_n$ is called *quantifier prefix* (with $Q_i \in \{\forall, \exists\}$, $Q_i \neq Q_{i+1}$, and $X_1, \dots, X_n$ are pairwise disjoint, non-empty sets of Boolean variables). The *matrix* ϕ is a propositional formula in CNF. The prefix Π induces an ordering on the variables: $x_i <_\Pi x_j$ if $x_i \in X_i$, $x_j \in X_j$ and $i < j$. If prefix Π is clear from the context, we just write $x_i < x_j$. A QBF $\forall x \Pi.\phi$ is true iff $\Pi.\phi_{\{x\}}$ and $\Pi.\phi_{\{\neg x\}}$ are true. A QBF $\exists x \Pi.\phi$ is true iff $\Pi.\phi_{\{x\}}$ or $\Pi.\phi_{\{\neg x\}}$ is true. For example, the QBF $\forall x \exists y.(x \leftrightarrow y)$ is true, while the QBF $\exists y \forall x.(x \leftrightarrow y)$ is false.

A *model* F of a true QBF Φ is a set of Boolean functions (called Skolem functions) such that for each existential variable y of Φ, there is a function $f_y(x_1, \dots, x_n) \in F$ where $x_1, \dots, x_n$ are the universal variables of Φ with $x_i < y$. If we take the matrix of Φ and replace all the existential variables by their Skolem

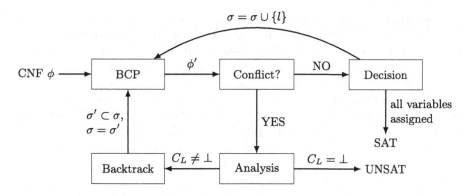

Fig. 2. High-level workflow of a CDCL solver.

functions, we obtain a valid propositional formula over the universal variables of Φ. A model for the true QBF $\forall x \exists y.(x \leftrightarrow y)$ is $\{f_y = x\}$. If we replace y by f_y, we obtain the valid formula $(x \leftrightarrow x)$. For false QBFs, functions for the universal variables (called Herbrand functions) are defined dually.

3   Certification for SAT

In order to explain how a modern SAT solver generates an unsatisfiability proof during the search for a solution, we shortly revisit the *conflict-driven clause learning* solving paradigm (CDCL) [62] which is implemented in most state-of-the-art SAT solvers. In the following, we discuss CDCL only on a higher level and omit many technical details that are not relevant for our purposes. By an example, we illustrate the connection between solving and certification. We refer to [30] for a detailed introduction of CDCL.

3.1   CDCL-Based SAT Solving

The high-level workflow of a CDCL-based SAT solver is shown in Fig. 2. The main concepts involve propagation (BCP), conflict detection (Conflict?), decision making (Decision), conflict analysis and clauses learning (Analysis), and backtracking (Backtrack). In the main loop, all variable assignments are enumerated by decision making and BCP.

First, all unit clauses are removed from the input CNF ϕ by applying BCP as introduced in Sect. 2. Initially, assignment σ is empty, if BCP is applicable, it is updated accordingly. If the resulting formula ϕ' contains the empty clause, i.e., there is a conflict, then the conflict analysis returns the empty clause to be learned ($C_L = \bot$) and the formula is immediately decided to be unsatisfiable. Otherwise, the solver checks if there is a variable that has not been assigned a value. If all variables have been assigned, then the current assignment is a model of the formula, as there was no contradiction. The solver returns satisfiable. If there are unassigned variables, the solver picks one variable according to some branching heuristics [45]. At this point it is also decided whether the variable is set to true or to false. In Fig. 2, this decision is reflected by adding the literal l with $var(l) = x$ to the assignment σ if x is to be assigned next. For setting x to true, x is added to σ, otherwise σ is extended by $\neg x$. Under the updated assignment, BCP is applied again for checking if assignments of further variables are implied. If now a conflict is found, then those decisions are identified which caused the conflict. In order to avoid that unfavorable decisions are made again, a clause C_L is learned that is added to the CNF. This clause also provides information necessary for undoing decisions during backtracking, and for generating a new current assignment. The following example illustrates the concept of clause learning by a small example.

Example 1 (Clause Learning[2]). We consider a CNF ϕ that consists of the following eight clauses:

$$C_1 : (\neg a \vee \neg b \vee \neg c)\ C_3 : (a \vee \neg b \vee \neg c)\ C_5 : (\neg a \vee b \vee \neg c)\ C_7 : (a \vee b \vee \neg c)$$
$$C_2 : (\neg a \vee \neg b \vee c)\quad C_4 : (a \vee \neg b \vee c)\quad C_6 : (\neg a \vee b \vee c)\quad C_8 : (a \vee b \vee c)$$

We now show a possible solver run.

1. Variable a is set to true. Clauses C_1, C_2, C_5, C_6 become binary clauses, the other clauses are removed.
2. Variable b is set to true. By BCP a conflict between C_1 and C_2 is derived. Obviously, $\phi \wedge a \wedge b \models \bot$ and in consequence, $\phi \models \neg(a \wedge b)$. Hence, the clause $(\neg a \vee \neg b)$ can be learned and we get $\phi' = \phi \wedge (\neg a \vee \neg b)$.
3. When undoing the assignment of b, but keeping variable a set to true during backtracking, the newly learned clause becomes a unit clause $(\neg b)$. The application of BCP results in a conflict between clauses C_5 and C_6. Only one variable (namely a) was set by a decision. Following the same argumentation as before, $\neg a$ can be learned and the solver continues with the formula $\phi'' = \phi' \wedge \neg a$.
4. Backtracking undoes setting a to true and by BCP a is set to false. Propagation does not decide the formula, hence a further decision is necessary. Assume that the decision is setting variable c to false. Then BCP results in a conflict between C_4 and C_8. Now the solver learns clause (c).
5. When applying BCP after undoing all decisions, a conflict is derived and the empty clause is learned proving the unsatisfiability of ϕ.

Based on this example, we will now introduce the generation of certificates by CDCL-based SAT solvers.

3.2 Certificates Based on Resolution

One of the best-studied propositional proof systems is *resolution* [57]. Resolution provides the theoretical framework for modern CDCL-based SAT solvers as

---

[2] This example is inspired by an example presented in [10]

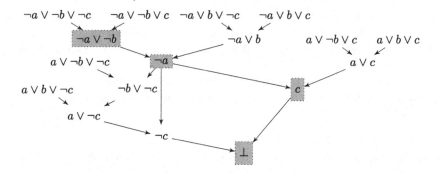

Fig. 3. Derivation of learned clauses (dotted boxes) via propositional resolution.

described above. The two rules of the *Resolution Calculus* are shown in Fig. 4. The *axiom* rule allows to download clauses from the given formula ϕ. With the *resolution* rule a new clause can be derived from two already derived clauses (called antecedents) if one clause contains a literal l and the other clause contains a literal $\bar{l}$. The newly derived clause is also called *resolvent*. Resolution is a sound and complete proof system for propositional logic. An example of a resolution derivation is shown in Fig. 3. For better readability, we represent the proof as a directed acyclic graph (DAG).

If the unsatisfiability of a formula is proven in terms of a resolution proof, the correctness of the result can be checked efficiently. To this end, the proof has to be traversed once, and it has to be shown that the two rules are correctly applied in every derivation step. For the axiom rule, it needs to be shown that the downloaded clause indeed occurs in the input formula. For the resolution rule, the two antecedents

$$\frac{C_1 \cup \{l\} \qquad C_2 \cup \{\bar{l}\}}{C_1 \cup C_2} \quad (\textit{res})$$

$$\frac{}{C} \quad C \in \phi \quad (\textit{axiom})$$

Fig. 4. Rules of the Resolution Calculus (CNF ϕ is the input formula).

need to be clauses that have already been derived, they need to contain l and $\bar{l}$, respectively, and the resolvent has to contain all literals of the antecedents except for l and $\bar{l}$. In the following example, we illustrate how clause learning and resolution are connected.

Example 2 (Clause Learning and Resolution). Consider again the formula of Example 1. The shown run of the CDCL solver enriched the formula with four learned clauses which can also be justified by resolution. The full resolution proof is shown in Fig. 3. The learned clauses are highlighted by dotted boxes.

1. The first learned clause $L_1 = (\neg a \vee \neg b)$ excludes all assignments where a and b are both set to true. In terms of resolution this clause can be derived from C_1 and C_2. Note that c and $\neg c$ of C_1 and C_2 lead to the conflict.

2. Clause $\neg a$ is learned by two applications of the resolution rule. In one resolution step, the previously learned clause L_1 is an antecedent. For the solver, a is set to true by a decision and b is set to false by BCP. This leads to a conflict between C_5 and C_6.
3. Also clause c is derived by two applications of the resolution rule.
4. Finally, $\bot$ can be derived by multiple resolution steps using learned clauses $\neg a$ and c.

Already for early CDCL-based SAT solvers the need to check unsatisfiability results was recognized. Van Gelder showed how to build resolution proofs during solving [20] that can be checked efficiently. Also the SAT solver zchaff was equipped with logging resolution proofs [67]. Both of these approaches provide explicit hints from which antecedents a clause was derived. As such proofs can get very large, a different approach was implemented in the solver Berk-Min [24]. Here a proof is represented as a chronologically ordered set of conflict clauses without any hits. Hence, the checker has to figure out how to derive the clause. Although this can be done in polynomial time, it might become costly in practice.

3.3 Certificates Based on Reverse Unit Propagation

To overcome the restrictions of resolution proofs, *reverse unit propagation* (RUP) was introduced [21]. It exploits the property that for a clause $C_L = (l_1 \vee \ldots \vee l_n)$ that is learned for a formula ϕ, it holds that $BCP(\phi \wedge \bar{C}_L) = \bot$ where $\bar{C}_L$ is the conjunction of unit clauses $\bar{l}_1 \wedge \ldots \wedge \bar{l}_n$ obtained by negating C_L. Formula ϕ is said to *imply* C_L *via unit propagation* (written as $\phi \vdash_1 C_L$) and C_L is a RUP clause. A RUP proof of a formula ϕ is a sequence of clauses $C_1, \ldots, C_n$ such that $\phi \wedge C_1 \wedge \ldots \wedge C_{i-1} \vdash_1 C_i$ for all $1 \leq i \leq n$. Obviously, $C_n = \bot$ for proving unsatisfiability.

Example 3 (RUP Proof). In the following we use the learned clauses of Example 1 in a RUP proof which is shown below.

	RUP proof	**Checking**
input clauses:	$\neg a \vee \neg b \vee c$	
	$\neg a \vee \neg b \vee \neg c$	
	$a \vee \neg b \vee c$	
	$a \vee \neg b \vee \neg c$	
	$\neg a \vee b \vee c$	
	$\neg a \vee b \vee \neg c$	
	$a \vee b \vee c$	
	$a \vee b \vee \neg c$	
learned clauses:	$\neg a \vee \neg b$	BCP $(\phi \wedge a \wedge b) = \bot$
	$\neg a$	BCP $(\phi \wedge (\neg a \vee \neg b) \wedge a) = \bot$
	c	BCP $(\phi \wedge (\neg a \vee \neg b) \wedge \neg a \wedge \neg c) = \bot$
	$\bot$	BCP $(\phi \wedge (\neg a \vee \neg b) \wedge \neg a \wedge c \wedge \top) = \bot$

Using RUP proofs has the advantages that they are compact and that they are easy to generate. To improve checking performance, the solver may annotate clauses that become irrelevant for a proof such that they are not further considered. The proof format that provides a deletion rule is called DRUP.

3.4 Certificates Based on Resolution Asymmetric Tautologies

There are techniques applied in pre- and inprocessing [27] that cannot be efficiently represented with RUP. To overcome this limitation, a more powerful proof system based on *Resolution Asymmetric Tautologies* (RAT) has been introduced [37] leading to a proof system that is equivalent to extended resolution [41]. A clause C is a RAT w.r.t. a CNF ϕ on a literal l if for all clauses $D \in \phi$ with $\bar{l} \in D$, it holds that $\phi \vdash_1 C \setminus \{l\} \cup D \setminus \{\bar{l}\}$, i.e., all possible resolvents upon l are implied by unit propagation. RAT clauses are redundant in the sense that their addition or removal does not affect the truth value of a formula. Moreover, RAT generalizes RUP, because every non-empty RUP clause has the RAT property on every literal. The empty clause is usually considered a RAT clause by definition. Hence, the proof of Example 3 is also a RAT proof. The DRAT proof system as applied in current SAT competitions, allows the deletion of arbitrary clauses. Since those proofs are certificates of unsatisfiability, the removal of arbitrary clauses which are not necessarily redundant does not affect the soundness of the proof. The deletion of clauses is necessary for reasons of efficiency. If the solver marks those clauses not needed for deriving the empty clause, this information is valuable for the proof checker: clauses marked for deletion do not need to be considered for proof checking. For RAT, efficient verified checkers are available [19, 28, 46]. Generalizations of RAT include Propagation Redundancy (PR) [31] and Substitution Redundancy (ST) [16].

4 Certification for QBF

Over the last two decades, several orthogonal solving approaches have been presented for QBFs. These approaches are founded on different proof systems. In the following, we review three of those proof systems that are well investigated in the field of proof complexity and for which proof-producing solvers and proof checkers exist. A recent survey on QBF proof complexity can be found in [5].

4.1 Certificates Based on Q-Resolution

Conflict-driven clause learning which is the most successful solving paradigm for SAT has also been lifted to QBFs [23, 47, 66]. On a higher level, the general workflow is similar as shown in Fig. 2, with the important difference that the QBF variant (usually called QCDCL) derives not only *learned clauses* during the search, but it can also produce *learned cubes* (a cube is a conjunction of literals). Furthermore, there are several technical details to be considered like a redefinition of BCP that takes quantification into account (a detailed example is shown in [8]).

For deriving learned clauses, the underlying proof system for QCDCL is Q-resolution [43], the QBF-specific variant of resolution consisting of the rules shown in Fig. 5. In addition to the axiom and resolution rules, Q-resolution also include the *universal reduction rule* which is necessary for handling universal quantification. It basically says that if the literals of a clause are sorted according to their occurrence in the quantifier prefix, and the last literal is universal, then it can be safely omitted.

Example 4 (Q-Resolution Refutation). Consider the QBF $\exists a \forall b \exists c.\psi$ where ψ contains the following clauses:

$$(\neg a \vee \neg b \vee \neg c) \ (a \vee \neg b \vee \neg c) \ (\neg a \vee b \vee \neg c) \ (a \vee b \vee \neg c)$$
$$(\neg a \vee \neg b \vee c) \quad (a \vee \neg b \vee c) \quad (\neg a \vee b \vee c) \quad (a \vee b \vee c)$$

This formula is the same formula as discussed in the previous examples, but now it is extended by the prefix $\exists a \forall b \exists c$. With the rules of Fig. 5 it is not possible, to resolve over b which can only be eliminated by universal reduction. The Q-resolution refutation is shown in Fig. 6. From the clause $\neg b$, the empty clause is derived by universal reduction.

For proving true QBFs, an almost dual variant of Q-resolution has been introduced. Here, the resolution rule is defined for cubes over a universal literal. Instead of universal reduction, existential reduction is performed on cubes, removing existential literals that are not succeeded by any universal literal when the cube is sorted. The main difference is in the axiom rule, because a formula in PCNF does not contain any cubes. The cubes are obtained from partial assignments that satisfy the matrix of the formula.

Several powerful extensions to Q-resolution have been presented like resolution over universal literals [22], long-distance Q-resolution [3,65], their combination [4], relaxed dependencies for universal reduction [49,54,58], as well as the

$$\frac{C \cup \{l\}}{C} \qquad \begin{array}{l} \{x, \neg x\} \nsubseteq (C \cup \{l\}), \ \mathrm{quant}_\Pi(l) = \forall, \\ \text{and } l' \leq_\Pi l \text{ for all } l' \in C \text{ with } \mathrm{quant}_\Pi(l') = \exists \end{array} \qquad (red)$$

$$\frac{C_1 \cup \{l\} \qquad C_2 \cup \{\bar{l}\}}{C_1 \cup C_2} \qquad \begin{array}{l} \{x, \neg x\} \nsubseteq (C_1 \cup C_2), \\ \bar{l} \notin C_1, \ l \notin C_2, \text{ and } \mathrm{quant}_\Pi(l) = \exists \end{array} \qquad (res)$$

$$\frac{}{C} \quad \{x, \neg x\} \nsubseteq C \text{ and } C \in \psi \qquad (axiom)$$

Fig. 5. Rules of the basic Q-Resolution Calculus for PCNF $\Pi.\psi$.

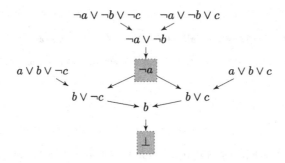

Fig. 6. Refutation via Q-Resolution (a dotted box indicates that the clause has been derived by applying the universal reduction rule).

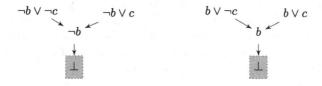

Fig. 7. Rewritten Q-Resolution proof where variable a is set to true (left) and false (right). The dotted box indicates that the clause has been derived by applying the universal reduction rule.

integration of a symmetry rule [38,39,61]. All these extensions result in provably stronger proof systems.

Q-resolution was also the first proof system for which it was shown that Skolem and Herbrand functions can be extracted from proofs. In the round-based approach presented in [25], the prefix is processed from left to right. The Q-resolution refutation of a QBF $\exists X \forall A \exists Y \forall B \exists Z.\psi$ is rewritten based on provided values of the existential variables X of the first quantifier block. The rewritten proof does not contain any variables from X and each variable of A occurs in at most one polarity. This polarity indicates how to set the variable in order to falsify the formula. Then the variables of Y are assigned which induces values for the variables in B. This is repeated until all variables are assigned. The rewritten proofs for the formula of Example 4 is shown in Fig. 7. The proof tree on the left is obtained by setting variable a to true, the proof tree on the right is obtained by setting a to false. An other approach for function extraction was proposed in [3]. Here the Q-resolution proof is traversed in reverse topological order. The functions are build as decision lists from clauses in which universal reduction is applied. Assume that in a proof universal reduction is applied on universal variable x three times in clauses $C_1 \vee x, C_2 \vee \neg x, C_3 \vee x$ (in this order), then the Herbrand function for x is the following if-then-else chain: if C_1 is false then $\bot$ else (if C_2 is false then $\top$ else (if C_3 is false then $\top$ else $*$)) where $*$ denotes a don't care. Note that sub-clauses C_1, C_2, C_3 only contain literals that precede x in the prefix. If for example in Fig. 6 universal literal $\neg b$ is universally

$$\overline{\{l^{[\tau]} \mid l \in C, l \text{ is existential}\} \cup \{\tau(l) \mid l \in C, l \text{ is universal}\}} \quad (axiom)$$

C is a clause from the matrix and τ is an assignment to all universal variables.

$$\frac{C_1 \cup \{x^\tau\} \qquad C_2 \cup \{\neg x^\tau\}}{C_1 \cup C_2} \text{ (Res)} \qquad (res)$$

Fig. 8. The rules of $\forall$Exp+Res (adapted from [8]). The annotation $x^{[\tau]}$ considers only the universal variables that precede x in the prefix.

reduced from clause $\neg a \lor \neg b$, then it is stored in the decision list that b has to be set to true if a is set to true to falsify this clause. This approach works dually for true formulas and cube Q-resolution proofs. The full certification and function extraction workflow is implemented in the QBFCert framework [52]. The efficient checking approach was presented in [53].

4.2 Certificates Based on $\forall$Exp+Res

Expansion-based solver reduce the QBF decision problem to SAT. Consider for example the QBF $\exists X \forall a, b \exists z.\phi$. To eliminate the universal variables it can be expanded to

$$\phi[z/z^{ab}]_{\{a,b\}} \land \phi[z/z^{\bar{a}b}]_{\{\neg a,b\}} \land \phi[z/z^{a\bar{b}}]_{\{a,\neg b\}} \land \phi[z/z^{\bar{a}\bar{b}}]_{\{\neg a,\neg b\}}$$

where each possible assignment of a, b is considered and for each assignment of a and b a fresh variable for z is introduced to take the quantifier dependencies into account. As true formulas could only be proven by full universal expansion which is practically infeasible, existentially quantified variables are partially expanded and the validity of the resulting formula is shown. Early expansion-based solvers fully expanded certain variables and called a SAT solver once [2,9,48]. To avoid a blow-up in memory, refinement-based approaches have been presented, first for 2-QBFs [35], then recursive approaches for arbitrary QBFs [34], and later a non-recursive one [12].

The proof system behind expansion-based solving is $\forall$Exp+Res [36]. This calculus consists of two rules: the axiom rules that assigns values to universal variables and annotates the remaining existential variables with the assignment of the preceding universal variables and the propositional resolution rule. Hence, a $\forall$Exp+Res proof consists of two parts: the expansion part in which the clauses relevant for the proof are expanded to a propositional formula and the resolution part which derives the conflict.

Example 5 ($\forall$Exp+Res Proof). Consider the false QBF

$$\exists a \forall b \exists c.((\neg a \lor b \lor c) \land (\neg a \lor b \lor \neg c) \land (a \lor \neg b \lor c) \land (a \lor \neg b \lor \neg c)).$$

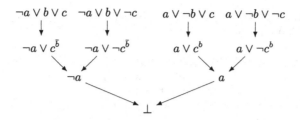

Fig. 9. Example of a ∀Exp+Res proof.

The ∀Exp+Res refutation is shown in Fig. 9. In the first two clauses, b is set to false, hence c and $\neg c$ are annotated with $\bar{b}$. In the last two clauses b is set to true, leading to an annotation of c and $\neg c$ with b. As a has no preceding universal variables, it is not annotated. The empty clause is derived from the annotated clauses by propositional resolution.

Generalizations of ∀Exp+Res have been presented in [7]. The extensions include for example an instantiation rule that allows to extend annotations within the proof. In ∀Exp+Res, fixed annotations can only be introduced with the axiom rule. Another extension introduces a merging rule that allows for the combination of two distinct annotations of a literal. Dynamic instantiation and merging make the proof system stronger than ∀Exp+Res. Round-based strategy extraction for ∀Exp+Res is discussed in [6]. For the example above, the rewritten proof contains only c^b when variable a is set to true. Hence, b has to set to false in order to falsify the formula. If a is set to false, then the rewritten proof contains only c^b, hence b has to be set to true. An algorithm for function extraction is proposed in [59]. A certification and function extraction framework for ∀Exp+Res unsatisfiability proofs is presented in [26].

4.3 Certificates Based on QRAT

The QRAT proof [33] system generalizes propositional RAT (see also Sect. 3.4). To obtain a sound proof system, the quantifiers need to be taken into account. As consequence, QRAT has not only rules for clause addition and removal as RAT, but it also has rules for literal addition and removal. Furthermore, the QRAT proof system also provides an extension of universal reduction that relies on a relaxed notion on quantifier dependencies. Like RAT, redundancy detection in QRAT builds upon implication via unit propagation which is easy to check. While in RAT all literals of a resolvent can be considered for checking if this resolvent is implied via unit propagation, in QBF only a certain subset of the literals may be taken into account. For the full definition of QRAT, we refer to [8, 33] for the details. The following example shows a QRAT proof of satisfiability (clauses that are deleted are marked by letter "d"). Satisfiability is proven by deleting all clauses and obtaining the empty formula.

Example 6 (QRAT Proof). The QBF $\forall a \exists b \exists c.((a \vee \neg b) \wedge (\neg a \vee \neg c) \wedge (b \vee c))$ has the following QRAT proof:

clause	comment
$(a \vee \neg b)$	input clause C_1
$(\neg a \vee \neg c)$	input clause C_2
$(b \vee c)$	input clause C_3
$(a \vee c)$	add clause C_4 (QRAT on c)
d $(a \vee \neg b)$	delete C_1 (QRAT on $\neg b$)
d $(b \vee c)$	delete C_3 (QRAT on b)
d $(\neg a \vee \neg c)$	delete C_2 (QRAT on $\neg c$)
d $(a \vee c)$	delete C_4 (QRAT on c)

Like RAT, QRAT is very powerful, because it can introduce new variables. Originally, it was introduced to capture recent preprocessing techniques, which are crucial for the performance of most state-of-the-art QBF solvers [29] and implemented for the preprocessor Bloqqer together with the proof checker qrat-trim [29]. A BDD-based QBF solver able to produce QRAT proofs was presented in [14]. It turns out that QRAT is able to simulate very strong variants of Q-resolution [40] and also ∀Exp+Res [42]. Function extraction from QRAT satisfiability proofs was shown in [33] which build if-then-else chains from the clauses that are deleted. In [17] it is shown that strategy extraction from QRAT unsatisfiability proofs works only for restricted versions of QRAT [17,18].

5   Conclusion

While it is very hard to fully verify that implementations of modern SAT and QBF solvers are correct, the results for specific formulas can be trusted when independently checkable certificates are provided. For this purpose, powerful propositional proof systems have been presented to witness the correctness of unsatisfiability results even when advanced solving techniques are applied. For SAT, verified proof checkers are available and producing certificates is supported by almost all state-of-the-art SAT solvers. Also in QBFs much work has been done in this direction. Proof systems for QBFs are strongly inspired by their propositional counter-parts. In addition, there are proof systems that are QBF specific, leading to a more heterogeneous proof complexity landscape than in SAT. In QBF solving proofs play also an important role for solution extraction.

Despite the progress made over the last years, proof checking is still expensive. Examples for open challenges concern the reduction of proof sizes and parallelization of proof checking. Furthermore, for QBFs more emphasis needs to be spent on the certification of true formulas and on finding a unified proof format that is supported by all state-of-the-art QBF solvers in a similar manner as DRAT is supported by state-of-the-art SAT solvers. In particular, there are techniques like clausal abstraction as implemented in the successful solver Caqe [56] with a proof system described in [63] that need tighter integration in the proof complexity landscape.

References

1. Artho, C., Biere, A., Seidl, M.: Model-based testing for verification back-ends. In: Veanes, M., Viganò, L. (eds.) TAP 2013. LNCS, vol. 7942, pp. 39–55. Springer, Heidelberg (2013). https://doi.org/10.1007/978-3-642-38916-0_3
2. Ayari, A., Basin, D.: QUBOS: deciding quantified Boolean logic using propositional satisfiability solvers. In: Aagaard, M.D., O'Leary, J.W. (eds.) FMCAD 2002. LNCS, vol. 2517, pp. 187–201. Springer, Heidelberg (2002). https://doi.org/10.1007/3-540-36126-X_12
3. Balabanov, V., Jiang, J.R.: Unified QBF certification and its applications. Formal Methods Syst. Des. **41**(1), 45–65 (2012)
4. Balabanov, V., Widl, M., Jiang, J.-H.R.: QBF resolution systems and their proof complexities. In: Sinz, C., Egly, U. (eds.) SAT 2014. LNCS, vol. 8561, pp. 154–169. Springer, Cham (2014). https://doi.org/10.1007/978-3-319-09284-3_12
5. Beyersdorff, O.: Proof complexity of quantified boolean logic-a survey. In: Mathematics for Computation (M4C), pp. 397–440. World Scientific (2023)
6. Beyersdorff, O., Chew, L., Janota, M.: On unification of QBF resolution-based calculi. In: Csuhaj-Varjú, E., Dietzfelbinger, M., Ésik, Z. (eds.) MFCS 2014. LNCS, vol. 8635, pp. 81–93. Springer, Heidelberg (2014). https://doi.org/10.1007/978-3-662-44465-8_8
7. Beyersdorff, O., Chew, L., Janota, M.: New resolution-based QBF calculi and their proof complexity. ACM Trans. Comput. Theory **11**(4), 26:1–26:42 (2019)
8. Beyersdorff, O., Janota, M., Lonsing, F., Seidl, M.: Quantified boolean formulas. In: Biere, A., Heule, M., van Maaren, H., Walsh, T. (eds.) Handbook of Satisfiability, 2nd edn. Frontiers in Artificial Intelligence and Applications, vol. 336, pp. 1177–1221. IOS Press (2021)
9. Biere, A.: Resolve and expand. In: Hoos, H.H., Mitchell, D.G. (eds.) SAT 2004. LNCS, vol. 3542, pp. 59–70. Springer, Heidelberg (2005). https://doi.org/10.1007/11527695_5
10. Biere, A.: SAT. Tutorial at the 5th Indian SAT and SMT Winter School (2020)
11. Biere, A., Fleury, M.: Gimsatul, IsaSAT and Kissat entering the SAT competition 2022. In: Balyo, T., Heule, M., Iser, M., Järvisalo, M., Suda, M. (eds.) Procedings of SAT Competition 2022 - Solver and Benchmark Descriptions. Department of Computer Science Series of Publications B, vol. B-2022-1, pp. 10–11. University of Helsinki (2022)
12. Bloem, R., Braud-Santoni, N., Hadzic, V., Egly, U., Lonsing, F., Seidl, M.: Two SAT solvers for solving quantified boolean formulas with an arbitrary number of quantifier alternations. Formal Methods Syst. Des. **57**(2), 157–177 (2021)
13. Brummayer, R., Lonsing, F., Biere, A.: Automated testing and debugging of SAT and QBF solvers. In: Strichman, O., Szeider, S. (eds.) SAT 2010. LNCS, vol. 6175, pp. 44–57. Springer, Heidelberg (2010). https://doi.org/10.1007/978-3-642-14186-7_6
14. Bryant, R.E., Heule, M.J.H.: Dual proof generation for quantified boolean formulas with a BDD-based solver. In: Platzer, A., Sutcliffe, G. (eds.) CADE 2021. LNCS (LNAI), vol. 12699, pp. 433–449. Springer, Cham (2021). https://doi.org/10.1007/978-3-030-79876-5_25
15. Buss, S., Nordström, J.: Proof complexity and SAT solving. In: Biere, A., Heule, M., van Maaren, H., Walsh, T. (eds.) Handbook of Satisfiability, 2nd edn. Frontiers in Artificial Intelligence and Applications, vol. 336, pp. 233–350. IOS Press (2021)

16. Buss, S., Thapen, N.: DRAT proofs, propagation redundancy, and extended resolution. In: Janota, M., Lynce, I. (eds.) SAT 2019. LNCS, vol. 11628, pp. 71–89. Springer, Cham (2019). https://doi.org/10.1007/978-3-030-24258-9_5
17. Chew, L., Clymo, J.: The equivalences of refutational QRAT. In: Janota, M., Lynce, I. (eds.) SAT 2019. LNCS, vol. 11628, pp. 100–116. Springer, Cham (2019). https://doi.org/10.1007/978-3-030-24258-9_7
18. Chew, L., Heule, M.J.H.: Relating existing powerful proof systems for QBF. In: Meel, K.S., Strichman, O. (eds.) Proceedings of the 25th International Conference on Theory and Applications of Satisfiability Testing (SAT 2022). LIPIcs, vol. 236, pp. 10:1–10:22. Schloss Dagstuhl - Leibniz-Zentrum für Informatik (2022)
19. Cruz-Filipe, L., Heule, M.J.H., Hunt, W.A., Kaufmann, M., Schneider-Kamp, P.: Efficient certified RAT verification. In: de Moura, L. (ed.) CADE 2017. LNCS (LNAI), vol. 10395, pp. 220–236. Springer, Cham (2017). https://doi.org/10.1007/978-3-319-63046-5_14
20. Gelder, A.V.: Extracting (easily) checkable proofs from a satisfiability solver that employs both preorder and postorder resolution. In: International Symposium on Artificial Intelligence and Mathematics, (AI&M 2002) (2002)
21. Gelder, A.V.: Verifying RUP proofs of propositional unsatisfiability. In: Proceedings of the International Symposium on Artificial Intelligence and Mathematics (ISAIM 2008) (2008)
22. Gelder, A.: Contributions to the theory of practical quantified boolean formula solving. In: Milano, M. (ed.) CP 2012. LNCS, pp. 647–663. Springer, Heidelberg (2012). https://doi.org/10.1007/978-3-642-33558-7_47
23. Giunchiglia, E., Narizzano, M., Tacchella, A.: Learning for quantified boolean logic satisfiability. In: Dechter, R., Kearns, M.J., Sutton, R.S. (eds.) Proceedings of the Eighteenth National Conference on Artificial Intelligence and Fourteenth Conference on Innovative Applications of Artificial Intelligence (AAAI/IAAI 2002), pp. 649–654. AAAI Press/The MIT Press (2002)
24. Goldberg, E.I., Novikov, Y.: Verification of proofs of unsatisfiability for CNF formulas. In: Proceedings of the 2003 Design, Automation and Test in Europe Conference and Exposition (DATE 2003), pp. 10886–10891. IEEE Computer Society (2003)
25. Goultiaeva, A., Gelder, A.V., Bacchus, F.: A uniform approach for generating proofs and strategies for both true and false QBF formulas. In: Walsh, T. (ed.) Proceedings of the 22nd International Joint Conference on Artificial Intelligence (IJCAI 2012), pp. 546–553. IJCAI/AAAI (2011)
26. Hadzic, V., Bloem, R., Shukla, A., Seidl, M.: FERPModels: a certification framework for expansion-based QBF solving. In: Proceedings of the 24th International Symposium on Symbolic and Numeric Algorithms for Scientific Computing (SYNASC 2022), pp. 80–83 (2022)
27. Heule, M., Järvisalo, M., Lonsing, F., Seidl, M., Biere, A.: Clause elimination for SAT and QSAT. J. Artif. Intell. Res. **53**, 127–168 (2015)
28. Heule, M.J.H., Hunt, W.A., Wetzler, N.: Verifying refutations with extended resolution. In: Bonacina, M.P. (ed.) CADE 2013. LNCS (LNAI), vol. 7898, pp. 345–359. Springer, Heidelberg (2013). https://doi.org/10.1007/978-3-642-38574-2_24
29. Heule, M.J.H., Seidl, M., Biere, A.: A unified proof system for QBF preprocessing. In: Demri, S., Kapur, D., Weidenbach, C. (eds.) IJCAR 2014. LNCS (LNAI), vol. 8562, pp. 91–106. Springer, Cham (2014). https://doi.org/10.1007/978-3-319-08587-6_7
30. Heule, M.J.H.: Proofs of unsatisfiability. In: Biere, A., Heule, M., van Maaren, H., Walsh, T. (eds.) Handbook of Satisfiability, 2nd edn., Frontiers in Artificial Intelligence and Applications, vol. 336, pp. 635–668. IOS Press (2021)

31. Heule, M.J.H., Kiesl, B., Biere, A.: Encoding redundancy for satisfaction-driven clause learning. In: Vojnar, T., Zhang, L. (eds.) TACAS 2019. LNCS, vol. 11427, pp. 41–58. Springer, Cham (2019). https://doi.org/10.1007/978-3-030-17462-0_3

32. Heule, M.J.H., Kullmann, O.: The science of brute force. Commun. ACM **60**(8), 70–79 (2017)

33. Heule, M.J.H., Seidl, M., Biere, A.: Solution validation and extraction for QBF preprocessing. J. Autom. Reason. **58**(1), 97–125 (2017)

34. Janota, M., Klieber, W., Marques-Silva, J., Clarke, E.M.: Solving QBF with counterexample guided refinement. Artif. Intell. **234**, 1–25 (2016)

35. Janota, M., Marques-Silva, J.: Abstraction-based algorithm for 2QBF. In: Sakallah, K.A., Simon, L. (eds.) SAT 2011. LNCS, vol. 6695, pp. 230–244. Springer, Heidelberg (2011). https://doi.org/10.1007/978-3-642-21581-0_19

36. Janota, M., Marques-Silva, J.: Expansion-based QBF solving versus q-resolution. Theor. Comput. Sci. **577**, 25–42 (2015)

37. Järvisalo, M., Heule, M.J.H., Biere, A.: Inprocessing rules. In: Gramlich, B., Miller, D., Sattler, U. (eds.) IJCAR 2012. LNCS (LNAI), vol. 7364, pp. 355–370. Springer, Heidelberg (2012). https://doi.org/10.1007/978-3-642-31365-3_28

38. Kauers, M., Seidl, M.: Short proofs for some symmetric quantified boolean formulas. Inf. Process. Lett. **140**, 4–7 (2018)

39. Kauers, M., Seidl, M.: Symmetries of quantified boolean formulas. In: Beyersdorff, O., Wintersteiger, C.M. (eds.) SAT 2018. LNCS, vol. 10929, pp. 199–216. Springer, Cham (2018). https://doi.org/10.1007/978-3-319-94144-8_13

40. Kiesl, B., Heule, M.J.H., Seidl, M.: A little blocked literal goes a long way. In: Gaspers, S., Walsh, T. (eds.) SAT 2017. LNCS, vol. 10491, pp. 281–297. Springer, Cham (2017). https://doi.org/10.1007/978-3-319-66263-3_18

41. Kiesl, B., Rebola-Pardo, A., Heule, M.J.H., Biere, A.: Simulating strong practical proof systems with extended resolution. J. Autom. Reason. **64**(7), 1247–1267 (2020)

42. Kiesl, B., Seidl, M.: QRAT polynomially simulates ∀-Exp+Res. In: Janota, M., Lynce, I. (eds.) SAT 2019. LNCS, vol. 11628, pp. 193–202. Springer, Cham (2019). https://doi.org/10.1007/978-3-030-24258-9_13

43. Kleine Büning, H., Karpinski, M., Flögel, A.: Resolution for quantified boolean formulas. Inf. Comput. **117**(1), 12–18 (1995)

44. Knuth, D.: Handbook of Satisfiability (Quote on Backcover) (2021)

45. Kullmann, O.: Fundaments of branching heuristics. In: Biere, A., Heule, M., van Maaren, H., Walsh, T. (eds.) Handbook of Satisfiability, 2nd edn. Frontiers in Artificial Intelligence and Applications, vol. 336, pp. 351–390. IOS Press (2021)

46. Lammich, P.: Efficient verified (UN)SAT certificate checking. J. Autom. Reason. **64**(3), 513–532 (2020)

47. Letz, R.: Lemma and model caching in decision procedures for quantified boolean formulas. In: Egly, U., Fermüller, C.G. (eds.) TABLEAUX 2002. LNCS (LNAI), vol. 2381, pp. 160–175. Springer, Heidelberg (2002). https://doi.org/10.1007/3-540-45616-3_12

48. Lonsing, F., Biere, A.: Nenofex: expanding NNF for QBF solving. In: Kleine Büning, H., Zhao, X. (eds.) SAT 2008. LNCS, vol. 4996, pp. 196–210. Springer, Heidelberg (2008). https://doi.org/10.1007/978-3-540-79719-7_19

49. Lonsing, F., Biere, A.: Integrating Dependency Schemes in Search-Based QBF Solvers. In: Strichman, O., Szeider, S. (eds.) SAT 2010. LNCS, vol. 6175, pp. 158–171. Springer, Heidelberg (2010). https://doi.org/10.1007/978-3-642-14186-7_14

50. Lonsing, F., Seidl, M., Gelder, A.V.: The QBF gallery: behind the scenes. Artif. Intell. **237**, 92–114 (2016)
51. Manthey, N., Lindauer, M.: SpyBug: automated bug detection in the configuration space of SAT Solvers. In: Creignou, N., Le Berre, D. (eds.) SAT 2016. LNCS, vol. 9710, pp. 554–561. Springer, Cham (2016). https://doi.org/10.1007/978-3-319-40970-2_36
52. Niemetz, A., Preiner, M., Lonsing, F., Seidl, M., Biere, A.: Resolution-based certificate extraction for QBF. In: Cimatti, A., Sebastiani, R. (eds.) SAT 2012. LNCS, vol. 7317, pp. 430–435. Springer, Heidelberg (2012). https://doi.org/10.1007/978-3-642-31612-8_33
53. Peitl, T., Slivovsky, F., Szeider, S.: Polynomial-time validation of QCDCL certificates. In: Beyersdorff, O., Wintersteiger, C.M. (eds.) SAT 2018. LNCS, vol. 10929, pp. 253–269. Springer, Cham (2018). https://doi.org/10.1007/978-3-319-94144-8_16
54. Peitl, T., Slivovsky, F., Szeider, S.: Long-distance q-resolution with dependency schemes. J. Autom. Reason. **63**(1), 127–155 (2019)
55. Pulina, L., Seidl, M.: The 2016 and 2017 QBF solvers evaluations (QBFEVAL'16 and QBFEVAL'17). Artif. Intell. **274**, 224–248 (2019)
56. Rabe, M.N., Tentrup, L.: CAQE: A certifying QBF solver. In: Kaivola, R., Wahl, T. (eds.) Formal Methods in Computer-Aided Design, FMCAD 2015, Austin, Texas, USA, 27–30 September 2015, pp. 136–143. IEEE (2015)
57. Robinson, J.A.: A machine-oriented logic based on the resolution principle. J. ACM **12**(1), 23–41 (1965)
58. Samer, M., Szeider, S.: Backdoor sets of quantified boolean formulas. J. Autom. Reason. **42**(1), 77–97 (2009)
59. Schlaipfer, M., Slivovsky, F., Weissenbacher, G., Zuleger, F.: Multi-linear strategy extraction for QBF expansion proofs via local soundness. In: Pulina, L., Seidl, M. (eds.) SAT 2020. LNCS, vol. 12178, pp. 429–446. Springer, Cham (2020). https://doi.org/10.1007/978-3-030-51825-7_30
60. Shukla, A., Biere, A., Pulina, L., Seidl, M.: A survey on applications of quantified boolean formulas. In: Proceedings of the 31st IEEE International Conference on Tools with Artificial Intelligence (ICTAI 2019), pp. 78–84. IEEE (2019)
61. Shukla, A., Slivovsky, F., Szeider, S.: Short Q-resolution proofs with homomorphisms. In: Pulina, L., Seidl, M. (eds.) SAT 2020. LNCS, vol. 12178, pp. 412–428. Springer, Cham (2020). https://doi.org/10.1007/978-3-030-51825-7_29
62. Silva, J.P.M., Sakallah, K.A.: GRASP - a new search algorithm for satisfiability. In: Rutenbar, R.A., Otten, R.H.J.M. (eds.) Proceedings of the 1996 IEEE/ACM International Conference on Computer-Aided Design (ICCAD 1996), pp. 220–227. IEEE Computer Society/ACM (1996)
63. Tentrup, L.: On expansion and resolution in CEGAR based QBF solving. In: Majumdar, R., Kunčak, V. (eds.) CAV 2017. LNCS, vol. 10427, pp. 475–494. Springer, Cham (2017). https://doi.org/10.1007/978-3-319-63390-9_25
64. Vizel, Y., Weissenbacher, G., Malik, S.: Boolean satisfiability solvers and their applications in model checking. Proc. IEEE **103**(11), 2021–2035 (2015)
65. Zhang, L., Malik, S.: Conflict driven learning in a quantified boolean satisfiability solver. In: Pileggi, L.T., Kuehlmann, A. (eds.) Proceedings of the 2002 IEEE/ACM International Conference on Computer-aided Design (ICCAD 2002), pp. 442–449. ACM / IEEE Computer Society (2002)

66. Zhang, L., Malik, S.: Towards a symmetric treatment of satisfaction and conflicts in quantified boolean formula evaluation. In: Van Hentenryck, P. (ed.) CP 2002. LNCS, vol. 2470, pp. 200–215. Springer, Heidelberg (2002). https://doi.org/10.1007/3-540-46135-3_14

67. Zhang, L., Malik, S.: Validating SAT solvers using an independent resolution-based checker: Practical implementations and other applications. In: Proceedings of the 2003 Design, Automation and Test in Europe Conference and Exposition (DATE 2003), pp. 10880–10885. IEEE Computer Society (2003)

Regular Papers

Evasiveness Through Binary Decision Diagrams

Jesús Aransay[(⊠)], Laureano Lambán, and Julio Rubio

Departamento de Matemáticas y Computación, Universidad de La Rioja,
Logroño, Spain
{jesus-maria.aransay,lalamban,julio.rubio}@unirioja.es

Abstract. In this paper, we explore whether a data structure for representing Boolean functions (namely, Binary Decision Diagrams) can be useful to detect, in an efficient way, the acyclicity of simplicial complexes. This is approached by means of the concept of *evasiveness*, allowing us to study the relation with Alexander duality. Furthermore, as main result, we prove that the (depth) complexity of a kind of acyclic simplicial complexes (*dismantlable* complexes) can be determined by means of Reduced Ordered Binary Decision Diagrams. As the subject has shown itself error prone, we have carried out the proof by using the Isabelle proof assistant, providing a rewarding combination of informal and formal mathematics.

Keywords: Evasiveness · BDD · Alexander dual · Simplicial complex · Dismantlability

1 Introduction

Computational Algebraic Topology, as any other algorithmic discipline, has a direct relation with complexity issues. From the well-known results about the non-computability of homotopy groups (based on the famous unsolvability of the word problem [11,13]; see also [16] for the case of homology groups), several results about the hardness of the computation of combinatorial invariants have been documented in the literature (see, for instance, [1] and [15] dealing with homotopical and homological problems, respectively). Beyond this classical study of the complexity of algorithms, Forman [7], in the context of his successful Discrete Morse Theory [8], described a rather unexpected relation between complexity of Boolean functions and Simplicial Topology.

Forman introduced a deep relationship between non-evasiveness of a monotone Boolean function and the acyclicity of a simplicial complex canonically associated to the Boolean function. A Boolean function is *evasive* when there is an input that requires to evaluate each argument to get the corresponding output of the function. The fact that this concept coming from complexity theory

---

Partially supported by projects PID2020-115225RB-I00 and PID2020-116641GB-I00 financed by MCIN/ AEI /10.13039/501100011033.

C. Dubois and M. Kerber (Eds.): CICM 2023, LNAI 14101, pp. 37–52, 2023.
https://doi.org/10.1007/978-3-031-42753-4_3

could be related with homological issues opens the path to translate ideas from Boolean functions to Topology and vice versa.

From a different point of view, Binary Decision Diagrams (BDDs), and more concretely ROBDDs (Reduced Ordered BDDs) [6], are the preferred data structures to deal with Boolean functions in practical applications. So, it is natural to ask if BDDs could be efficiently used to determine evasiveness (and, then, to get homological information in an optimal manner, from a complexity point of view). This is the problem tackled in this paper. More concretely, we explore whether ROBDDs are sufficient to decide evasiveness. We do not give an answer in the general case, but we prove that for a large class of acyclic simplicial complexes (namely, dismantlable complexes) using ROBDDs is enough.

In order to describe the main contribution of this work, let us recall this well-known chain of implications between simplicial complexes [3,5]:

$$\text{dismantlable} \implies \text{non-evasive} \implies \text{collapsible} \implies \text{contractible} \implies \text{acyclic.}$$

All these implications are known to be strict and none of them is formalised in our work. Instead, in this paper, we introduce a new concept (that is to say, a new class of simplicial complexes) coined *ligneous*, and we enhance the previous chain of implications with:

$$\text{dismantlable} \implies \text{ligneous \& non-evasive} \implies \text{non-evasive,}$$

where the first implication is the main contribution of this paper (the second one being simply a straightforward tautology) and has been formalised in Isabelle/HOL. The first implication is strict, and to know whether it is the case for the second implication is the main open problem of this research line.

Even if this field of research is easy to introduce and very combinatorial in nature, it has been shown to us very error prone. After detecting several faulty steps in our reasoning, we decided to formalise our efforts by using the Isabelle proof assistant. This experience has been quite enlightening and to communicate it is another goal of this paper. When writing this text, we have chosen to keep the standard level of detail in the exposition of the mathematical and algorithmic material, even if the Isabelle code is much more verbose (this fact is dramatically illustrated when comparing Definition 7, of dismantling, with its Isabelle counterpart in Sect. 5). Once the formalisation has been achieved, it is tempting to write a paper mimicking the Isabelle code when introducing the mathematical concepts and results. We consider this (natural) trend a mistake: overwhelming the reader with cumbersome details can, in our humble opinion, discourage the adoption of interactive theorem proving technology among the, let us say, "standard" mathematicians. We attempt in this paper to combine the informal and the formal way of writing, trying to get the best of both worlds.

The paper is organized as follows. We start with preliminaries, and in Sect. 3 we introduced our main working concept, *ligneous Boolean function*, and we explore its behaviour with respect to Alexander duality. In the next section we state our main result (that dismantlable implies ligneous), but its proof is delayed to Sect. 5 where it is carried out formally in Isabelle/HOL. The paper ends with conclusions, future work and the bibliography. The complete Isabelle code is accessible at [2].

2   Preliminaries

2.1   Boolean Functions, BDDs, Evasiveness

In this subsection we recall the main definitions, starting with the first concepts related to Binary Decision Diagrams, and Boolean functions.

Definition 1. *A* binary decision diagram *(BDD) on* $X = \{x_1, \ldots, x_n\}$, X *being its variable set, is a directed acyclic graph with one source and sinks labeled by the constants 0 and 1; furthermore, the source and each internal node is labeled by a variable from X and has two outgoing edges, one labeled by 0 and the other by 1.*

A complete path *in a BDD is a directed path of edges joining the source to a sink.*

An input $b = (b_1, \ldots, b_n) \in \{0, 1\}^n$ activates an edge in a BDD if the edge starts at a node labeled by x_i and the edge is labeled by b_i.

A computation path *for an input b in a BDD is the complete path of edges activated by the input b.*

A computation path *for an input b that leads to the 1-sink is called the* accepting path *for b.*

A BDD represents *the Boolean function f (on n variables) for which $f(b) = 1$ if and only if there exists an accepting path in the BDD for the input b.*

The depth *of a BDD is the maximum of the lengths of complete paths in the BDD. The* (BDD) depth *of a Boolean function f is the minimum of the depths of the BDDs representing f.*

Now, we specialize the BDD notion to several variants, which are important in practical applications.

Definition 2. *(i) A* free binary decision diagram *(FBDD) is a BDD where each complete path contains for each variable at most one node labeled by this variable.*

(ii) An ordered binary decision diagram *(OBDD) is a BDD where on each complete path the node labels of the internal nodes are a subsequence of a given variable ordering $x_{\pi(1)}, x_{\pi(2)}, \ldots, x_{\pi(n)}$, where π is a permutation on $\{1, \ldots, n\}$.*

Note that each OBDD is, in particular, a FBDD.

It is not difficult to design an algorithm removing a repetition of a variable in a complete path, representing the same Boolean function and keeping or decreasing the depth of the output BDD. Therefore, the depth of a Boolean function can be *realised* through a FBDD; that it to say, there exists a FBDD ϕ representing f such that $\text{depth}(f) = \text{depth}(\phi)$.

In its full generality the problem explored in this paper is whether the depth of a Boolean function can be realised (in the previous sense) through OBDDs.

It is clear, too, that if depth can be realised through OBDDs it can also be realised through ROBDDs, *reduced* OBDDs, the hegemonic data structure to encode efficiently Boolean functions [6]. We introduce the notion of ROBDD by means of the classical Knuth approach [10]. Given a permutation of the variable set X of a Boolean function f, we can identify the *truth table* of f (with respect to the global ordering of variables defined by the initial permutation) with a 2^n-tuple $tt \in \{0,1\}^{2^n}$, where n is the number of variables, the cardinality of X (the tuple tt is obtained by sorting the inputs $b = (b_1, \ldots, b_n) \in \{0,1\}^n$ in lexicographical order). According to Knuth, a 2^m-tuple τ is a *bead* if it can be written as a concatenation $\tau = \tau_1 \tau_1$ (this implies that τ_1 is a 2^{m-1}-tuple). Then, fixing an ordering of X, we can build a canonical OBDD where each node is associated to a non-bead in the truth table tt (see a formalisation of this idea in Sect. 5). This kind of OBDDs are the ROBDDs, the *reduced* OBDDs.

Instead of focusing on the question of whether the depth of a Boolean function can be realised through OBDDs (or, equivalently, ROBDDs), we study the problem in the particular case of evasiveness.

Definition 3. *A Boolean function on n variables is called* evasive *if its depth is n.*

Evasiveness is important in complexity theory, because it measures when it is needed to know the value of every variable for obtaining the output of a Boolean function (see, for instance, [12]). In addition, when the Boolean function is monotone, the concept has, rather surprisingly, deep topological outcomes.

To finish this subsection, let us remark that a ROBDD has maximal depth, n, if and only if there is an entry in the corresponding truth table not contained in any bead. Such an entry is called an *evader*. Let us also note that evaders appear in pairs: an entry b is an evader if and only if the entry obtained from b by negating the value of x_n (the last variable in the global ordering) is an evader, too. Furthermore, if a ROBDD ϕ has no evaders, then the Boolean function represented by ϕ is non-evasive. We collect this fact in the following theorem, because it is the terminology used in our Isabelle formalisation in Sect. 5.

Theorem 1. *If a Boolean function f has a ROBDD with no evaders, then f is non-evasive.*

2.2   Alexander Dual, Dismantling

A Boolean function over a variable set X can be interpreted as a *test (or characteristic)* function of a set of sets of X: an input $b = (b_1, \ldots, b_n) \in \{0,1\}^n$ denotes a subset $S(b)$ of X ($b_i = 1$ if and only if the variable x_i is in the subset $S(b)$); then the value of the Boolean function on the input b is 1 if and only if the set $S(b)$ belongs to the set of sets of X being specified. Thus, there is a canonical bijection between Boolean functions over X and the set $\mathcal{P}(\mathcal{P}(X))$ (where $\mathcal{P}(Y)$ denotes the power set of a set Y). The elements of $\mathcal{P}(\mathcal{P}(X))$ are called *hypergraphs* [4] (since the case of *graphs* can be recovered by means of $\mathcal{P}(\mathcal{P}_2(X))$, where $\mathcal{P}_2(-)$ denotes the family of sets with 2 elements). Now, a *simplicial complex* is a hypergraph which is closed by the operation "taking the subsets of a set". When returning to the corresponding Boolean functions, it turns out that the functions defining simplicial complexes are exactly the monotone decreasing

Boolean functions (where the inputs are ordered lexicographically considering $0 < 1$). That is to say, each monotone decreasing Boolean function on variables X defines canonically a simplicial complex where the set of vertices is X (if the function is monotone *increasing*, it is also possible to get from it a simplicial complex; see [17] for details). Reciprocally, each simplicial complex over X defines a decreasing Boolean function (or increasing, depending on our choice), producing a canonical bijection between the set of decreasing Boolean functions and the set of simplicial complexes over the same variable set X.

Thus, when working with monotone Boolean functions, we can inherit concepts and techniques from combinatorial topology and apply them to algorithms and complexity in Boolean logic. The next definition is a typical example.

Definition 4. *The* Alexander dual *of a Boolean function $f(x_1, \ldots, x_n)$ is the Boolean function f^d defined by:*

$$f^d(x_1, \ldots, x_n) := \neg f(\neg x_1, \ldots, \neg x_n).$$

When f is monotone and then determines a simplicial complex, this definition corresponds to the notion of simplicial Alexander duality.

In the same vein, it is well-known that if a monotone Boolean function is non-evasive, then the corresponding simplicial complex is collapsible (then contractible, then acyclic; see Sect. 1). In addition, the concept of non-evasive monotone Boolean function (or non-evasive simplicial complex) can be layered by a notion of m-collapsibility [3]. In the case $m = 0$, the complexes are called *dismantlable*. Before introducing this definition, we need to recall the notions of *link* and *co-star*.

Definition 5. *The* link *of a Boolean function $f(x_1, x_2, \ldots, x_n)$ with respect to the variable x_1 is the Boolean function $f^{\mathrm{lnk}(x_1)}$ defined by:*

$$f^{\mathrm{lnk}(x_1)}(x_2, \ldots, x_n) := f(1, x_2, \ldots, x_n).$$

The co-star *of a Boolean function $f(x_1, x_2, \ldots, x_n)$ with respect to the variable x_1 is the Boolean function $f^{\mathrm{cost}(x_1)}$ defined by:*

$$f^{\mathrm{cost}(x_1)}(x_2, \ldots, x_n) := f(0, x_2, \ldots, x_n).$$

Let us note that in the previous definitions the variable set of $f^{\mathrm{lnk}(x_1)}$ and $f^{\mathrm{cost}(x_1)}$ is $\{x_2, \ldots, x_n\}$ (that is to say: their variable set is $X \setminus \{x_1\}$ if X is the variable set of f).

These two functions are the well-known *projections* giving rise to the *Shannon decomposition*:

$$f(x_1, x_2, \ldots, x_n) = x_1 f(1, x_2, \ldots, x_n) + \neg x_1 f(0, x_2, \ldots, x_n).$$

Nevertheless, we have chosen to call them *link* and *co-star* because, when the function f is monotone (and then $f^{\mathrm{lnk}(x_1)}$ and $f^{\mathrm{cost}(x_1)}$ are monotone, too), the constructions over the corresponding simplicial complexes coincide with the *simplicial* link and co-star. Along the same line, we define the notion of *cone* over Boolean functions, emulating the definition on simplicial complexes.

Definition 6. *A Boolean function* $f(x_1, x_2, \ldots, x_n)$ *is a* cone *with respect to the variable* x_1 *if* $f^{\mathrm{lnk}(x_1)} = f^{\mathrm{cost}(x_1)}$.

Let us note that this property is equivalent to the fact that the output of f does not depend on the value of the argument x_1.

The definitions of link, co-star and cone can be generalized in the obvious way to any other variable x_i, with $1 < i \leq n$, and then we can talk about link, co-star or cone with respect to any variable $x \in X$, the variable set of the Boolean function f.

Now, we are ready to introduce the concept of dismantlable (or 0-collapsible) Boolean function.

Definition 7. *A Boolean function* f *over a variable set* X *is* dismantlable *if either* $X = \{x\}$, *a singleton, and* $f(x) = 1$, *a tautology, or there exists a variable* $x \in X$ *such that* $f^{\mathrm{lnk}(x)}$ *is a cone and* $f^{\mathrm{cost}(x)}$ *is dismantlable.*

The previous definition mimics the following well-known characterisation (see [3], for instance) of non-evasiveness for simplicial complexes.

Theorem 2. *A monotone Boolean function* f *is non-evasive if and only if either* $X = \{x\}$, *a singleton, and* $f(x) = 1$, *a tautology, or there exists a variable* $x \in X$ *such that* $f^{\mathrm{lnk}(x)}$ *and* $f^{\mathrm{cost}(x)}$ *are both non-evasive.*

In Sect. 5 we prove formally that a cone is non-evasive (applying Theorem 1). Then, the fact that dismantlable implies non-evasive, in the monotone case, follows from the very definition.

3   Ligneous Boolean Functions

We focus now on monotone Boolean functions where the evasiveness can be determined by means of OBDDs. This idea is covered by the following formal definition. But, first, let us observe that the depth of an OBDD may depend on the ordering of the variables: there are monotone Boolean functions where two different orderings of variables produce ROBDDs of different depth. Figure 1 shows two ROBDDs for the monotone decreasing Boolean function $f(x_1, x_2, x_3, x_4) = x_1 x_2 + x_2 x_3 + x_3 x_4$. The first one, on the left (Fig. 1a), corresponds to the ordering $x_1 < x_2 < x_3 < x_4$ and its depth is 4. The second one, on the right (Fig. 1b), corresponds to the ordering $x_2 < x_3 < x_1 < x_4$ and its depth is 3. In this kind of figure, the sinks are denoted by a boxed 0 or 1, and from each source or internal node (circled variables) the right (solid) edges are labeled with 1 and the left ones with 0.

Definition 8. *A Boolean function* f *over* n *variables is* ligneous *if* f *is monotone and either* f *is evasive or there exists a permutation of the* n *variables and an OBDD* ϕ *with respect to that permutation representing* f *and such that* $\mathrm{depth}(\phi) < n$.

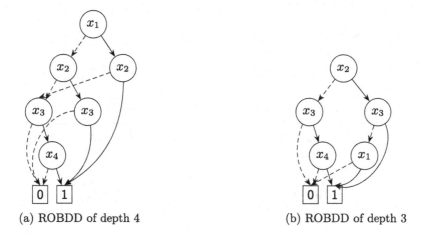

(a) ROBDD of depth 4   (b) ROBDD of depth 3

Fig. 1. Two ROBDDs of different length for the same monotone Boolean function.

The previous definition imposes the constraint of being monotone because we know that there are Boolean functions f on n variables where every OBDD representing f has depth n but there is a FBDD representing f and with depth strictly less than n. As an example, in Fig. 2 we show two BDDs for the non-monotone Boolean function

$$f(x_1, x_2, x_3, x_4) = \neg x_1 \neg x_2 x_3 + \neg x_1 x_2 x_4 + x_1 \neg x_3 x_4 + x_1 x_2 x_3.$$

The one on the left (Fig. 2a) is a ROBDD corresponding to the ordering $x_1 < x_2 < x_2 < x_4$ and has depth 4. The one on the right (Fig. 2b) is a FBDD of depth 3. A small Lisp program allows us to check that for any of the 24 possible orderings of $\{x_1, x_2, x_3, x_4\}$ the corresponding ROBDDs for this function are of depth 4. Thus, this example proves that, in the non-monotone case, the depth of a Boolean function cannot be realised through OBDDs.

Let us now explore how the ligneous notion is related to Alexander duality. First, we place ourselves in the general case of a BDD ϕ representing a Boolean function f. Then, we can construct a new BDD ϕ^d from ϕ with the following procedure:

– In the source and in each internal node of ϕ, the 0-branch and the 1-branch are swapped.
– In the sink nodes, 0 and 1 are swapped.

It is clear that this new BDD ϕ^d represents the Alexander dual f^d. In addition, by construction, depth(ϕ) = depth(ϕ^d). From this observation the next theorem follows. Furthermore, let us remark that this construction is robust with respect to the different classes of BDD; that is to say, the dual of a FBDD is a FBDD, the dual of an OBDD is an OBDD with respect to the same variable ordering, and so on.

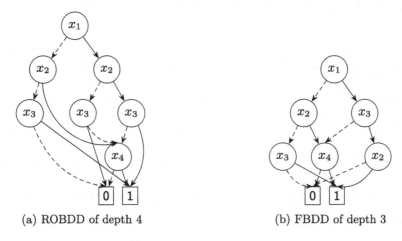

(a) ROBDD of depth 4   (b) FBDD of depth 3

Fig. 2. Two BDDs of different length for a non-monotone Boolean function.

Theorem 3. *The depth of a Boolean function is equal to the depth of its Alexander dual.*

Corollary 1. *A Boolean function is ligneous if and only if its Alexander dual is ligneous.*

The corollary is not really a consequence of Theorem 3 but of its *proof*. Effectively, since the dual of a ROBDD has the same depth (the structure of the dual of a ROBDD admits a neat reading from its truth table: the beads in the truth table are in canonical bijection with the beads in the dual truth table; it is, in particular, a ROBDD too), it is clear that the ligneous properties are preserved when passing to the Alexander dual (since it is simple to check that a Boolean function is monotone if and only if its Alexander dual is monotone).

4   Dismantlable Implies Ligneous

Since in the definition of *ligneous* Boolean function we have imposed the monotonicity condition, we can export the concept to the topological setting and consider *ligneous simplicial complexes*, too. Once the concept of *ligneous* Boolean function (or simplicial complex) is introduced, one can wonder if there are enough instances of it. The following theorem describes that, in the non-evasive case (several large classes of non-evasive simplicial complexes are known [3]), there are many ligneous functions.

Theorem 4. *If a Boolean monotone function is dismantlable, then it is ligneous.*

Let us stress here that, since we have already observed that dismantlable implies non-evasive, the proof of the previous theorem consists in building an ordering of the variables such that the corresponding truth table has no evaders.

As the topic is very error-prone (as explained in the introduction), it was undertaken in a formal setting, and it is described in the following section. In fact, this error-prone nature was confirmed when trying to formalise our arguments in Isabelle/HOL: namely, the two concepts of *external* and *internal* links were missing in our paper&pencil approach, and the very definition of *dismantlable* was refined interactively by using the proof assistant.

From a methodological point of view, we try to delay the introduction of the constraint of being monotone and develop the proof in a set-theoretic manner. This implies that instead of working with simplicial complexes, we deal with *hypergraphs*. So, proofs flow more naturally, and just in the last steps we impose the monotonicity of the Boolean functions.

5 Formalisation in Isabelle/HOL

In this section we introduce the Isabelle formalisation of part of the results presented in the previous sections. In order to make it clear which parts have been formalised, let us enumerate the meta-theoretical results we are assuming and the concrete scope of our formalisation:

- The bijection between Boolean functions and hypergraphs is not formalised, and we work directly over hypergraphs.
- Theorem 1 is not formalised. It is used to explain the result that we prove in Isabelle/HOL (that is to say, that a dismantlable complex can be defined through a ROBDD without evaders, implying it is non-evasive). In fact, we didn't define in Isabelle/HOL a general notion of non-evasiveness.
- Theorems 2 and 3 are not formalised, the first one being well-known [3,5], and the second one, being original from this paper and feasible in Isabelle/HOL, requires the general definition of *depth* of a Boolean function, which is not included in our formalisation.
- Theorem 4 is fully formalised, with the hypergraph language and with the notion of non-evasiveness evoked in the statement of Theorem 1.

In Definition 5, we introduced the notion of *link* of a variable in a Boolean function and we explained there that this notion corresponds to the *simplicial link* from Algebraic Topology. Nevertheless, it is only true when we are working with *monotone* Boolean functions. In the non-monotone case, the case of hypergraphs, two possible definitions of link appear.

Definition 9. *Let $\mathcal{K}$ be a hypergraph over a variable set X (that is: $\mathcal{K} \in \mathcal{P}(\mathcal{P}(X))$) and let x be a variable from X.*

- *The* external link *of $\mathcal{K}$ over the variable x is the hypergraph:* $\mathrm{lnk}^{\mathrm{ext}}(\mathcal{K}, x) := \{S \in \mathcal{P}(X) \mid x \notin S \ \wedge \ S \cup \{x\} \in \mathcal{K}\}$.
- *The* internal link *of $\mathcal{K}$ over the variable x is the hypergraph:* $\mathrm{lnk}^{\mathrm{int}}(\mathcal{K}, x) := \{S \in \mathcal{K} \mid x \notin S \ \wedge \ S \cup \{x\} \in \mathcal{K}\}$.

Let us note that for the *co-star* only a definition is possible (namely: $\text{cost}(\mathcal{K}, x) := \{S \in \mathcal{K} \mid x \notin S\}$). Definition 5 of $f^{\text{lnk}(x)}$ corresponds, in the general case, to the *external* link.

The Isabelle definitions of the *external link*, the *internal link* (or simply *link*) and the *co-star* of a hypergraph follow:

definition `link_ext :: "nat ⇒ nat set ⇒ nat set set ⇒ nat set set"`
  where `"link_ext x X K = {s. s ∈ powerset X ∧ x ∉ s ∧ insert x s ∈ K}"`

definition `link :: "nat ⇒ nat set ⇒ nat set set ⇒ nat set set"`
  where `"link x X K = {s. s ∈ powerset (X - {x}) ∧ s ∈ K ∧ insert x s ∈ K}"`

definition `cost :: "nat ⇒ nat set ⇒ nat set set ⇒ nat set set"`
  where `"cost x X K = {s. s ∈ powerset (X - {x}) ∧ s ∈ K}"`

We also introduce the notion of *simplicial complex* (over a vertex set A), which can be seen as a particular case of *hypergraph* satisfying the condition of being *closed* under the operation *parts of any set* that belongs to the simplicial complex (a property that we have introduced in *pow-closed*):

definition `pow_closed :: "'a set set ⇒ bool"`
  where `"pow_closed S ≡ (∀s∈S. ∀s'⊆s. s'∈ S)"`

inductive_set `cc_s :: "(nat set × nat set set) set"`
  where `"({}, {}) ∈ cc_s"`
  | `"(A, {}) ∈ cc_s"`
  | `"A ≠ {} ⟹ K ⊆ powerset A ⟹ pow_closed K ⟹ (A, K) ∈ cc_s"`

Simplicial complexes can be characterised also as *hypergraphs* where lnk^{ext} and lnk^{int} (or simply *link* in our Isabelle code) coincide:

lemma `cc_s_link_eq_link_ext:`
  assumes `cc: "(X, K) ∈ cc_s"`
  shows `"link x X K = link_ext x X K"`

lemma `link_eq_link_ext_cc_s:`
  assumes `v: "X ≠ {}"`
    and `f: "finite X"`
    and `k: "K ⊆ powerset X"`
    and `l: "∀x∈X. link x X K = link_ext x X K"`
  shows `cc: "(X, K) ∈ cc_s"`

The definition of a *cone* of a hypergraph follows:

definition `cone :: "nat set ⇒ nat set set ⇒ bool"`
  where `"cone X K = ((∃x∈X. ∃T. T ⊆ powerset (X - {x})`

$$\wedge\ K\ =\ T\ \cup\ \{s.\ \exists t{\in}T.\ s\ =\ \mathit{insert}\ x\ t\}))"$$

It can be noted that the previous definition does not mimic the one introduced for Boolean functions in Definition 6. The following lemmas show the equivalence between the definition formalised in Isabelle and Definition 6:

lemma `cone_impl_cost_eq_link_ext:`
  assumes x: `"x ∈ X"`
    and cs: `"T ⊆ powerset (X - {x})"`
    and kt: `"K = T ∪ {s. ∃t∈T. s = insert x t}"`
  shows `"cost x X K = link_ext x X K"`

lemma `cost_eq_link_ext_impl_cone:`
  assumes c: `"cost x X K = link_ext x X K"`
    and x: `"x ∈ X"` **and** p: `"K ⊆ powerset X"`
  shows `"cone X K"`

Now we can introduce the notion of 0-*collapsible* (or dismantlable) hypergraph (see Definition 7). It is worth mentioning that the Isabelle formalisation has to consider various cases that do not show up in the mathematical definition, since Isabelle/HOL does not have dependent types and we must define explicitly how the predicate *zero_ collapsible* behaves for a set K whose elements are not sets over V:

function `zero_collapsible ::` `"nat set ⇒ nat set set ⇒ bool"`
  where
  `"V = {} ⟹ zero_collapsible V K = False"`
  `| "V = {x} ⟹ K = {} ⟹ zero_collapsible V K = True"`
  `| "V = {x} ⟹ K = {{},{x}} ⟹ zero_collapsible V K = True"`
  `| "V = {x} ⟹ K ≠ {} ⟹ K ≠ {{},{x}} ⟹ zero_collapsible V K =`
`False"`
  `| "2 ≤ card V ⟹ zero_collapsible V K =`
    `(∃x∈V. cone (V - {x}) (link_ext x V K) ∧ zero_collapsible (V - {x})`
`(cost x V K))"`
  `| "¬ finite V ⟹ zero_collapsible V K = False"`

Our main formalised results will be to prove that both cones and 0-collapsible hypergraphs are non-evasive. First we must introduce the notions that permit us to present our formalisation of *evasiveness*. In order to evaluate a Boolean function for a given set of variables, we introduce *sorted-variables*, that represents an ordering over a given set of variables (variables are represented by natural numbers):

inductive_set `sorted_variables ::` `"(nat set × nat list) set"`
  where `"({}, []) ∈ sorted_variables"`
  `| "(A, l) ∈ sorted_variables ⟹ x ∉ A ⟹ (insert x A, Cons x l) ∈`
`sorted_variables"`

Two relevant results about *sorted-variables* are that the length of the list of variables and the cardinality of the set of variables are equal, and also that the list contains the same elements as the set:

```
lemma sorted_variables_length_coherent:
  assumes a1: "(A, 1) ∈ sorted_variables" shows "card A = length l"
```

```
lemma sorted_variables_coherent:
  assumes a1: "(A, 1) ∈ sorted_variables" shows "A = set l"
```

If we are now interested in *computing* or *evaluating* the result of a given Boolean function for a particular ordering of variables, we can do so as follows. Do note that the Boolean function is encoded by means of its associated *hypergraph* K and the definition is done by induction over the list of variables. For a given list containing n variables, its evaluation will contain 2^n Boolean values:

```
function evaluation :: "nat list ⇒ nat set set ⇒ bool list"
  where "evaluation [] {} = [False]"
  | "K ≠ {} ⟹ evaluation [] K = [True]"
  | "evaluation (x # l) K =
          (evaluation l (link_ext x (set (x # l)) K)) @
          (evaluation l (cost x (set (x # l)) K))"
```

Finally, we have to state what we consider for an evaluation not to contain evaders, and thus (Theorem 1) being non-evasive. A function will be non-evasive whenever it contains *beads*.

```
inductive_set not_evaders :: "(bool list) set"
  where  "l1 = l2 ⟹ l1 @ l2 ∈ not_evaders"
  | "l1 ∈ not_evaders ⟹ l2 ∈ not_evaders ⟹ length l1 = length l2
⟹ l1 @ l2 ∈ not_evaders"
```

From the previous definitions we can now state and prove in Isabelle that the evaluation of a list of vertexes over a hypergragh which is also a *cone* does not contain any pair of evaders, and thus (Theorem 1) *cones are non-evasive*:

```
lemma evaluation_cone_not_evaders:
  assumes k: "K ⊆ powerset X" and c: "cone X K" and X: "X ≠ {}"
    and f: "finite X" and x1: "(X, l) ∈ sorted_variables"
  shows "evaluation l K ∈ not_evaders"
```

The proof proceeds by induction on the cardinality of the vertex set X. The case where card X is equal to 0 can be automatically discarded since X is not empty. Then, when card X is equal to suc n, we use our Isabelle definition of cone to obtain T and a vertex x such that:

```
"K = T ∪ {s. ∃t∈T. s = insert x t}"
```

Accordingly, and making use of the previous result *obdt-list-length-coherent* we also obtain a decomposition of the list l.

obtain y 1' **where** l: "l = y # l'" **and** y: "y ∈ X"

The proof now distinguishes the cases where $x = y$ or $x \neq y$. If $x = y$ we take advantage of the fact that, since we are in a cone, $\mathrm{cost}\, x\ X\ K$ is equal to link-ext $x\ X\ K$ and thus both parts of the evaluation are equal, and therefore there are no evaders.

If x and y are distinct, we use two intermediary results that state that the *cost* of a cone over a given vertex x and vertex set X is also a cone for a vertex y and vertex set $X \setminus \{x\}$, and so is the *link-ext*:

lemma cost_cone_eq:
  assumes x: "x ∈ X" **and** xy: "x ≠ y"
    and cs: "T ⊆ powerset (X - {x})"
    and kt: "K = T ∪ {s. ∃t∈T. s = insert x t}"
  shows "cost y X K =
    (cost y (X - {x}) T) ∪ {s. ∃t∈(cost y (X - {x}) T). s = insert x t}"

lemma link_ext_cone_eq:
  assumes x: "x ∈ X" **and** xy: "x ≠ y"
    and cs: "T ⊆ powerset (X - {x})"
    and kt: "K = T ∪ {s. ∃t∈T. s = insert x t}"
  shows "link_ext y X K =
    (link_ext y (X - {x}) T) ∪
    {s. ∃t∈(link_ext y (X - {x}) T). s = insert x t}"

Incidentally, the previous equality also holds for the internal link.

The crucial point here is that the cones obtained have one vertex fewer than the original ones, and thus we can take advantage of the induction hypothesis to prove that *link-ext* over y and the vertex set $X \setminus \{x\}$ and *cost* over y and the vertex set $X \setminus \{x\}$ do not contain evaders, and since their evaluations both have the same length, thanks to the definition of *no-evaders*, appending them also does not produce any evaders.

The same property of not containing pairs of evaders also holds for *0-collapsible* hypergraphs:

theorem
  zero_collapsible_implies_not_evaders:
  assumes k: "K ⊆ powerset X"
    and x: "X ≠ {}" **and** f: "finite X" **and** cc: "zero_collapsible X K"
  shows "∃l. (X, l) ∈ sorted_variables ∧ evaluation l K ∈ not_evaders"

The proof again proceeds by induction on the cardinality of the set of vertexes X. The case where the number of vertexes is 0 can be automatically discarded. For $\mathrm{card}\, X = \mathrm{suc}\, n$ we first consider the case where $K = \emptyset$. Then, we obtain a *list of variables* for the (finite, and not empty) set of vertexes X and we make use of the following result (based on the fact that both *cost* and the *link-ext* of the empty set are empty):

```
lemma evaluation_empty_set_not_evaders:
  assumes a: "l ≠ []" shows "evaluation l {} ∈ not_evaders"
```

If $K \neq \emptyset$, we have to distinguish the case where X is a singleton. Let $X = \{x\}$. Then we have to prove that 'evaluation $[x]$ K' does not contain evaders. In this case there are only three possible hypergraphs, namely $K = \{\{\}\}$, $K = \{\{x\}\}$, and $K = \{\{\}, \{x\}\}$. The first and second cases are proven obtaining a contradiction with the fact that $[x]$ and K are 0-collapsible. In the third case we obtain the evaluation $[True, True]$, which is not an evader. For the case where $\operatorname{card} X > 1$, we can obtain some vertex x satisfying that:

```
obtain x where x: "x ∈ X" and cl: "cone (X - {x}) (link_ext x X K)"
  and ccc: "zero_collapsible (X - {x}) (cost x X K)" and xxne: "X - {x}
≠ {}"
```

With the previous facts we use the induction hypothesis to obtain some list l' such that:

```
obtain l' where xxb: "(X - {x}, l') ∈ sorted_variables"
  and ec: "evaluation l' (cost x X K) ∈ not_evaders" by auto
```

Now we make use of the fact that link-ext x X K is a cone over the vertex set $X \setminus \{x\}$ (labelled as *cl* in the code snippet above) and therefore its evaluation over l' neither has evaders (thanks to the previous lemma *evaluation-cone-not-evaders*).

Finally, we are now ready to prove that there exists a list $l = x\#l'$ such that (X, l) is a *sorted-variables* element and the evaluation of K over l does not contain evaders. The proof is completed by using the second introduction rule in definition *not-evaders*, since the evaluation of both cones (cost x X K and link-ext x X K) do not contain evaders and moreover both lists have the same length.

Now, because we have proved in Isabelle/HOL that when we are working with simplicial complexes (equivalently, with monotone Boolean functions), the external and internal links coincide, we get the proof of Theorem 4.

6   Conclusions and Further Work

In this paper, the notion of *ligneous* Boolean function has been introduced. It is a decreasing monotone Boolean function (so defining canonically a simplicial complex) such that a ROBDD is a witness for its non-evasiveness. We prove that a function is ligneous if and only if it is the case for its Alexander dual. Our main result is: dismantlable implies ligneous. Furthermore, and we consider it as a major achievement of our research, the proof of this main result is implemented in the Isabelle/HOL proof assistant.

In relation to our future work, let us repeat that the main concern has not been solved: whether the depth of a Boolean function can be realised through OBDDs (in fact, the notion of *ligneous* complex is simply a technical tool that allowed us to state the main properties we detected around this problem). To complete the research, it would be necessary to prove that if all the ROBDDs of a monotone Boolean function are of maximal depth n (the number of variables) then the Boolean function is evasive, or to find a counterexample: a monotone Boolean function such that all its ROBDD are of depth n but there is a FBDD of depth less than n. We have heuristics to make both cases plausible:

- To lean towards the first case:
  - The canonical examples of m-collapsible complexes that are not $(m-1)$-collapsible [3] are ligneous (but, turning the argument around, we have not been able to prove that every 1-collapsible complex is ligneous; it seems there is some obstruction to pass from the 0-collapsible or dismantlable case, to the 1-collapsible one).
  - The statistical argument: in 1976, Rivest and Vuillemin [14] proved that almost all Boolean functions are evasive, in the sense that the number of functions on n variables that are non-evasive goes very rapidly to 0, as $n \to \infty$. Then, one can wonder that imposing the tight constraint that all the ROBDDs are of depth n one could escape from the rare case of non-evasiveness (but then let us remark that *monotonicity* would be essential in this case, because of our counterexample displayed in Fig. 2).
- In favour of the existence of a counterexample: we could follow the technique used in several papers (see [9], for instance) to construct ROBDDs of exponential *size* (the *size* is the number of nodes in a BDD) but with FBDDs of polynomial size. The technique consists in building two ROBDDs of polynomial size but with incompatible orderings, in such a way that adding a fresh source variable produces a polynomial size FBDD, but any re-ordering of variables produces an exponential ROBDD. Nevertheless, we have not been capable of translating to the *depth* of a BDD this argument relative to the *size* of BDDs.

Unfortunately, it seems that the counterexamples, if they exist, would have a number of variables that excludes the possibility of making an exhaustive computer search (as the mentioned one about the counterexample of Fig. 2: generating all the ROBDDs to compute their depths).

Another line of further research is to continue with the formalisation efforts in proof assistants inside this area where complexity, Boolean functions and topology interplay, since our preliminary work illustrate the benefits of this approach.

References

1. Anick, D.J.: The computation of rational homotopy groups is $\#\mathcal{P}$-hard. Comput. Geome. Topol. Lect. Notes Pure Appl. Math. **114**, 1–56 (1989)
2. Aransay, J.: Isabelle code for "Evasiveness through Binary Decision Diagrams". https://github.com/jmaransay/morse/blob/Isabelle_2022/BDT.thy

3. Barmak, J.A., Minian, E.G.: Strong homotopy types, nerves and collapses. Discrete Comput. Geom. **47**(2), 301–328 (2012)
4. Berge, C.: Graphs and Hypergraphs. Elsevier Science Ltd. (1985)
5. Björner, A.: Topological methods. In: Handbook of Combinatorics, pp. 1819–1872. Elsevier (1995)
6. Bryant, R.E.: Graph-based algorithms for Boolean function manipulation. IEEE Trans. Comput. **35**, 677–691 (1986)
7. Forman, R.: Morse theory for cell complexes. Adv. Math. **134**(1), 90–145 (1998)
8. Forman, R.: Morse theory and evasiveness. Combinatorica **20**(4), 489–504 (2000)
9. Hayase, K., Imai, H.: OBDDs of a monotone function and its prime implicants. Theory Comput. Syst. **31**, 579–591 (1998)
10. Knuth, D.E.: The Art of Computer Programming, vol. 4, fascicle 1, Bitwise Tricks & Techniques; Binary Decision Diagrams. Addison-Wesley (2009)
11. Markov, A.A.: Unsolvability of homeomorphy problem. In: Proceedings International Congress of Mathematicians 1958, pp. 300–306. Cambridge University Press (1960)
12. Milner, E.C., Welsh, D.J.A.: On the computational complexity of graph theoretical properties. In: Proceedings Fifth British Combinatorial Conference, Congressus Numerantium XV, pp. 471–487 (1975)
13. Novikov, P.S.: Algorithmic unsolvability of the word problem in group theory. J. Symb. Log. **23**(1), 50–52 (1958)
14. Rivest, R.L., Vuillemin, J.: On recognizing graph properties from adjacency matrices. Theor. Comput. Sci. **3**(3), 371–384 (1976)
15. Roune, B.H., Sáenz-de-Cabezón, E.: Complexity and algorithms for Euler characteristic of simplicial complexes. J. Symb. Comput. **50**, 170–196 (2013)
16. Rubio, J., Sergeraert, F.: Computing with locally effective matrices. Int. J. Comput. Math. **2**(10), 1177–1189 (2005)
17. Scoville, N.A.: Discrete Morse theory. Student Mathematical Library, vol. 90. American Mathematical Society (2019)

Nominal AC-Matching

Mauricio Ayala-Rincón[1], Maribel Fernández[2], Gabriel Ferreira Silva[1(✉)],
Temur Kutsia[3], and Daniele Nantes-Sobrinho[1,4]

[1] University of Brasília, Brasília, Brazil
`ayala@unb.br, gabrielfsilva1995@gmail.com`
[2] King's College London, London, UK
`maribel.fernandez@kcl.ac.uk`
[3] Johannes Kepler University Linz, Linz, Austria
`kutsia@risc.jku.at`
[4] Imperial College London, London, UK
`dnantess@ic.ac.uk`

Abstract. The nominal syntax is an extension of the first-order syntax that smoothly represents languages with variable bindings. Nominal matching is first-order matching modulo alpha-equivalence. This work extends a certified first-order AC-unification algorithm to solve nominal AC-matching problems. To our knowledge, this is the first mechanically-verified nominal AC-matching algorithm. Its soundness and completeness were verified using the proof assistant PVS. The formalisation enriches the first-order AC-unification algorithm providing structures and mechanisms to deal with the combinatorial aspects of nominal atoms, permutations and abstractions. Furthermore, by adding a parameter for "protected variables" that cannot be instantiated during the execution, it enables nominal matching. Such a general treatment of protected variables also gives rise to a verified nominal AC-equality checker as a byproduct.

Keywords: Nominal Matching · Nominal AC-Matching · Formal Methods · PVS

1 Introduction

The nominal approach to the specification of systems with binders [20, 25] extends first-order syntax with notions of name and binding that allow us to represent systems with binders smoothly. Such systems frequently appear in the formalisation of mathematics and when reasoning about the properties of programming languages. Taking into account α-equivalence is essential to represent bindings correctly. For example, the formulas $\forall x : x + 1 > 0$ and $\forall y : y + 1 > 0$ should be considered equivalent despite being syntactically different. From the user point of view it is easier to use systems with variable names than systems with indices. Hence, instead of using indices to represent bound variables, as in explicit substitution calculi à la de Bruijn, the nominal theory uses atoms, atom permutations and freshness constraints to represent binders more naturally [19, 25].

C. Dubois and M. Kerber (Eds.): CICM 2023, LNAI 14101, pp. 53–68, 2023.
https://doi.org/10.1007/978-3-031-42753-4_4

Given terms t and s, syntactic unification is the problem of finding a substitution σ such that $\sigma t = \sigma s$ and syntactic matching is the problem of finding a substitution σ such that $\sigma t = s$. Algorithms to solve matching problems are an essential component of functional languages and equational theorem provers: matching is used to decide if an equation can be applied to a term. The problem of syntactic matching can be generalised to consider an equational theory E. In this case, called E-matching, we must find a substitution σ such that σt and s are equal modulo E, which we denote $\sigma t \approx_E s$. For example, if the system includes associative and commutative (AC) operators, such as $+$ in the example above, then the matching algorithm should consider the AC axioms. Furthermore, equational programming languages, such as Maude, require efficient implementations of AC-matching to deal with AC-theories (see [16]).

If the system under study includes binders and AC operators, then α-equivalence should also be considered: for example, $\forall x : x + 1 > 0$ should be considered equivalent to $\forall y : 1 + y > 0$. This paper focuses on the matching problem for languages that include binders and AC operators.

Nominal matching is the extension of first-order matching to the nominal syntax, replacing the notion of syntactic equality by α-equivalence. It has applications in rewriting, functional programming, and metaprogramming. For instance, various versions of matching modulo α-equivalence are used in functional programming languages that provide constructs for manipulating abstract syntax trees involving binders (e.g. [26,29]). In this work, we specify a nominal matching algorithm modulo AC function symbols (nominal AC-matching, for short) and prove its correctness and completeness using the proof assistant PVS.

Related Work. Nominal syntactic (i.e. modulo α-equivalence) equality-check, matching and unification were solved since the beginning of the development of the nominal approach; more than twenty years ago, Urban et al. [34] developed the first rule-based algorithm for nominal syntactic unification and further, Urban mechanised its correctness and completeness in Isabelle/HOL as part of the formalisation of the nominal approach in this proof assistant [32,33]. Furthermore, different approaches were designed to deal with nominal syntactic unification efficiently. Calvès and Fernández [11,12] and Levy and Villaret [22,23] developed efficient nominal syntactic unification algorithms to solve nominal unification problems. Furthermore, Ayala-Rincón et al. [6] developed a nominal syntactic unification algorithm specified as a functional program and verified it in the proof assistant PVS. Enriching the nominal equational analysis with equational theories started with developing rule-based techniques for commutative operators. Such developments were initially checked in the proof assistant Coq and further in PVS [1,4]. Remarkable differences between nominal unification and nominal C-unification were discovered, such as the fact that when expressing solutions as pairs consisting of a freshness context and substitutions, nominal unification is unitary whereas nominal C-unification is not finitary [2,3].

Avoiding freshness constraints through a fixed-point approach was also studied as a mechanism to obtain finite complete sets of solutions [5]. Such fixed-point equations also appear in nominal techniques designed to deal with higher-order recursive let operators [27,28].

First-order AC-unification algorithms were proposed almost half a century ago, when Stickel [30,31] showed the connection between solving this problem and computing solutions to linear Diophantine equations until a certain bound. Almost a decade later, Fages [17,18] fixed a mistake in Stickel's proof of termination. Since then, ideas to obtain more efficient AC-unification algorithms have been proposed, either by using a smaller bound when computing the solutions to the linear Diophantine equation [14], or by solving those equations more efficiently [14], or even by solving whole systems of linear Diophantine equations and using suitable data structures to represent the problem [8,10]. First-order AC-unification algorithms were not formalised until recently when a version of Fages' AC-unification algorithm was proved correct and complete using the proof assistant PVS [7]. This mechanisation applies the linear-Diophantine AC unification method discovered and fixed in works by Stickel and Fages [17,18,30,31], and can easily be adapted to deal with AC-equality and AC-matching problems as well. It is important to stress that such mechanisation was not a routine-formalisation effort; before this formalisation, only a formalisation of AC-matching (which has simpler combinatorics) was reported in the proof assistant Coq [15].

Contributions. Adapting first-order syntactic AC unification to the nominal setting is challenging since the new variables included in the Diophantine systems (used to generate new possible AC combinations) give rise to new AC-unification problems of the same complexity as the input problems. This paper shows that such cyclicity is not possible when only nominal AC-matching problems are considered. We present a novel nominal AC-matching algorithm adapted from the Stickel-Fages linear-Diophantine approach and prove its termination, correctness and completeness in the proof assistant PVS.

Organisation. Section 2 recalls the main concepts and notations needed in the paper. In Sect. 3, we present and explain the pseudocode for the algorithm specified in PVS. Section 4 discusses the main features of the formalisation, while Sect. 5 discusses the challenges in adapting our approach to nominal AC-unification. Finally, in Sect. 6, we conclude the paper and suggest possible paths for future work. We assume familiarity with PVS (see [24]) and include hyperlinks (with the ↗ icon) to specific points of interest of the PVS formalisation. An extended version of this paper is available at https://www.mat.unb.br/ayala/publications.html.

2 Background

2.1 Nominal Terms, Permutations and Substitutions

Assume disjoint countable sets of atoms $\mathbb{A} = \{a, b, c, \ldots\}$ and of variables $\mathbb{X} = \{X, Y, Z, \ldots\}$, and a signature Σ of function symbols which contains associative-commutative function symbols. A permutation π is a bijection of the form π :

$\mathbb{A} \rightarrow \mathbb{A}$ such that the domain of π (i.e., the set of atoms modified by π) is finite. Permutations are usually represented as a list of swappings, where the swapping $(a\ b)$ exchanges atoms a and b and fixes all the other atoms. Therefore, a permutation is represented as $\pi = (a_1\ b_1) :: ... :: (a_n\ b_n) :: nil$. The inverse of this permutation, denoted by π^{-1}, can be computed simply by reversing the list. The identity permutation is denoted by id.

Definition 1 (*Nominal Terms* ☑). *The set $\mathcal{T}(\Sigma, \mathbb{A}, \mathbb{X})$ of nominal terms is generated according to the grammar:*

$$s, t ::= \quad a \mid \pi \cdot X \mid \langle\rangle \mid [a]t \mid \langle s, t\rangle \mid f\ t \mid f^{AC}\ t \qquad (1)$$

where $\langle\rangle$ is the unit, a is an atom term, $\pi \cdot X$ is a moderated variable or suspension (the permutation π is suspended on the variable X), $[a]t$ is an abstraction (a term with the atom a abstracted), $\langle s, t\rangle$ is a pair, $f\ t$ is a function application and $f^{AC}\ t$ is an associative-commutative function application.

Remark 1. We represent moderated variables of the form $id \cdot X$ simply as X. We follow Gabbay's name convention, which says that atoms differ in their names. Therefore, if we consider atoms a and b, it is redundant to say $a \neq b$.

Definition 2 (*Well-formed Terms* ☑). *We say that a term t is well-formed if t is not a pair and every AC-function application that is a subterm of t has at least two arguments.*

As was done in [7], we have restricted the terms that our algorithm receives to well-formed terms to ease our formalisation (more details in the extended version). Excluding pairs is a natural decision since they are used to encode a list of arguments to a function.

Definition 3 (Permutation Action). *The action of permutations on atoms ☑ is defined recursively: $nil \cdot c = c$ and $((a\ b) :: \pi) \cdot c = a$, if $\pi \cdot c = b$; $((a\ b) :: \pi) \cdot c = b$, if $\pi \cdot c = a$; $((a\ b) :: \pi) \cdot c = \pi \cdot c$ otherwise. The action of permutations on terms ☑ is defined recursively:*

$$\pi \cdot \langle\rangle = \langle\rangle \qquad \qquad \pi \cdot (\pi' \cdot X) = (\pi :: \pi') \cdot X \qquad \pi \cdot [a]t = [\pi \cdot a]\pi \cdot t$$
$$\pi \cdot \langle s, t\rangle = \langle \pi \cdot s, \pi \cdot t\rangle \qquad \pi \cdot f\ t = f\ \pi \cdot t \qquad \qquad \pi \cdot f^{AC}t = f^{AC}\pi \cdot t$$

Notation 1. *When convenient, we may mention that a function symbol f is an AC-function symbol, omit the superscript and write simply f instead of f^{AC}.*

A substitution σ is a function from variables to terms, such that $\sigma X \neq id \cdot X$ only for a finite set of variables, called the domain of σ and denoted as $dom(\sigma)$. The image of σ is then defined as $im(\sigma) = \{\sigma X \mid X \in dom(\sigma)\}$. We denote the identity substitution by id. From now on, when composing substitution σ with δ we may omit the composition symbol and write $\sigma\delta$ instead of $\sigma \circ \delta$.

A well-formed substitution ☑ only instantiates variables to well-formed terms. In the proofs of soundness and completeness of the algorithm, we restrict ourselves to well-formed substitutions. Let V be a set of variables. If $dom(\sigma) \subseteq V$ and $Vars(im(\sigma)) \subseteq V$ we write $\sigma \subseteq V$. In our PVS code, substitutions are represented by a list, where each entry of the list is called a *nuclear substitution* and is of the form $\{X \to t\}$.

Definition 4 (*Nuclear substitution action on terms* ☐). *A nuclear substitution* $\{X \to t\}$ *acts over a term by induction as shown below:*

$$\{X \to t\}\langle\rangle = \langle\rangle \qquad\qquad \{X \to t\}\langle s_1, s_2\rangle =$$
$$\{X \to t\}([a]s) = [a](\{X \to t\}s) \qquad \langle\{X \to t\}s_1, \{X \to t\}s_2\rangle$$
$$\{X \to t\}(f\ s) = f\ (\{X \to t\}s) \qquad \{X \to t\}\pi \cdot Y = \begin{cases} \pi \cdot Y & \text{if } X \neq Y \\ \pi \cdot t & \text{otherwise} \end{cases}$$
$$\{X \to t\}a = a \qquad\qquad \{X \to t\}(f^{AC}\ s) = f^{AC}\ (\{X \to t\}s)$$

Definition 5 (*Substitution acting on terms* ☐). *Since a substitution* σ *is a list of nuclear substitutions, the action of a substitution is defined as:*

- NIL $t = t$, *where* NIL *is the null list, used to represent the identity substitution.*
- CONS($\{X \to s\}$, σ) $t = \{X \to s\}(\sigma t)$.

Remark 2. The notion of substitution used here differs from the more traditional view of a substitution as a simultaneous application of nuclear substitutions, although both are correct. The way we defined substitution here is closer to triangular substitutions [21]. In the definition of action of substitutions the nuclear substitution in the head of the list is applied last. This lets us, given substitutions σ and δ, obtain the substitution $\sigma \circ \delta$ in our code simply as APPEND(σ, δ).

2.2   Freshness and α-Equality

Freshness and α-equality are two valuable notions in nominal theory and are represented by the predicates $\#$ and $\approx_\alpha$. Intuitively, $a\#t$ means that if a occurs in t then it does so under an abstractor $[a]$, and $s \approx_\alpha t$ means that s and t are α-equivalent, that is, they are equal modulo the renaming of bound atoms. These concepts are given in Definitions 6 and 7.

Definition 6 (*Freshness* ☐). *A freshness context* ∇ *is a set of constraints of the form* $a\#X$. *We denote contexts by letters* $\Delta, \Gamma, \nabla, \ldots$ *An atom* a *is said to be fresh on* t *under a context* ∇, *denoted by* $\nabla \vdash a\#t$, *if it is possible to build a proof using the rules:*

$$\frac{}{\nabla \vdash a\#\langle\rangle}\ (\#\langle\rangle) \qquad \frac{}{\nabla \vdash a\#b}\ (\#atom) \qquad \frac{(\pi^{-1} \cdot a\#X) \in \nabla}{\nabla \vdash a\#\pi \cdot X}\ (\#X)$$

$$\frac{}{\nabla \vdash a\#[a]t}\ (\#[a]a) \qquad \frac{\nabla \vdash a\#t}{\nabla \vdash a\#[b]t}\ (\#[a]b) \qquad \frac{\nabla \vdash a\#s \quad \nabla \vdash a\#t}{\nabla \vdash a\#\langle s,t\rangle}\ (\#pair)$$

$$\frac{\nabla \vdash a\#t}{\nabla \vdash a\#f\ t}\ (\#app) \qquad \frac{\nabla \vdash a\#t}{\nabla \vdash a\#f^{AC}\ t}\ (\#AC)$$

Definition 7 (*α-equality with AC operators* ✂). *Let* f *be an AC function symbol,* $S_n(f\,t)$ *be an operator that selects the nth argument of* $f\,t$ *(considering the flattened form) and* $D_n(f\,t)$ *be an operator that deletes the nth argument of* $f\,t$ *(considering the flattened form). If there exist i and j such that* $\Delta \vdash S_i(f^{AC}s) \approx_\alpha S_j(f^{AC}t)$ *and* $\Delta \vdash D_i(f^{AC}s) \approx_\alpha D_j(f^{AC}t)$, *then* $\Delta \vdash f^{AC}s \approx_\alpha f^{AC}t$. *In other words, the rule of α-equality for an AC-function application is:*

$$\frac{\Delta \vdash S_i(f^{AC}s) \approx_\alpha S_j(f^{AC}t) \quad \Delta \vdash D_i(f^{AC}s) \approx_\alpha D_j(f^{AC}t)}{\Delta \vdash f^{AC}s \approx_\alpha f^{AC}t} \;(\approx_\alpha AC)$$

Two terms t *and* s *are said to be α-equivalent under the freshness context* Δ *(*$\Delta \vdash t \approx_\alpha s$*) if it is possible to build a proof using rule* $(\approx_\alpha AC)$ *and the rules:*

$$\frac{}{\Delta \vdash \langle\rangle \approx_\alpha \langle\rangle}\;(\approx_\alpha \langle\rangle) \qquad\qquad \frac{}{\Delta \vdash a \approx_\alpha a}\;(\approx_\alpha atom)$$

$$\frac{\Delta \vdash s \approx_\alpha t}{\Delta \vdash f\,s \approx_\alpha f\,t}\;(\approx_\alpha app) \qquad\qquad \frac{\Delta \vdash s \approx_\alpha t}{\Delta \vdash [a]s \approx_\alpha [a]t}\;(\approx_\alpha [a]a)$$

$$\frac{\Delta \vdash s \approx_\alpha (a\ b)\cdot t,\ \ \Delta \vdash a\#t}{\Delta \vdash [a]s \approx_\alpha [b]t}\;(\approx_\alpha [a]b) \qquad \frac{ds(\pi,\pi')\#X \subseteq \Delta}{\Delta \vdash \pi \cdot X \approx_\alpha \pi' \cdot X}\;(\approx_\alpha var)$$

$$\frac{\Delta \vdash s_0 \approx_\alpha t_0,\ \ \Delta \vdash s_1 \approx_\alpha t_1}{\Delta \vdash \langle s_0, s_1\rangle \approx_\alpha \langle t_0, t_1\rangle}\;(\approx_\alpha pair)$$

Notation 2. *We define the difference set between two permutations* π *and* π' *as* $ds(\pi, \pi') = \{a \in \mathcal{A}|\pi\cdot a \neq \pi'\cdot a\}$. *By extension,* $ds(\pi, \pi')\#X$ *is the set containing every constraint of the form* $a\#X$ *for* $a \in ds(\pi, \pi')$.

2.3   Solution to Quintuples and Additional Notation

For the proofs of soundness and completeness of the algorithm, we need the notion of a solution to a quintuple (Definition 8). This definition depends on a parameter $\mathcal{X}$, a set of "protected variables", i.e., variables that cannot be instantiated.

Let P be a finite set of equational constraints. We denote the left-hand side of P by $lhs(P)$ ✂ and the right-hand side of P by $rhs(P)$ ✂. The set of variables in $t \approx_? s$ is denoted as $Vars(t, s)$ ✂. Finally, if Γ is a context then we denote by $Vars(\Gamma)$ ✂ the set $\{X \mid a\#X \in \Gamma, \text{for some atom } a\}$.

Notation 3. *Let* ∇ *and* ∇' *be freshness contexts and* σ *and* σ' *substitutions. We need the following notation to define a solution to a quintuple:*

- $\nabla' \vdash \sigma\nabla$ *denotes that* $\nabla' \vdash a\#\sigma X$ *holds for each* $(a\#X) \in \nabla$.
- $\nabla \vdash \sigma \approx_V \sigma'$ *denotes that* $\nabla \vdash \sigma X \approx_\alpha \sigma'X$ *for all* X *in* V. *When* V *is the set of all variables* $\mathbb{X}$, *we write* $\nabla \vdash \sigma \approx \sigma'$.

Definition 8 (*Solution for a Quintuple* ✂). *Suppose that* Γ *is a context,* P *is a set of freshness constraints (of the form* $a\#_? t$*) and equational constraints (of the form* $t \approx_? s$*),* σ *is a substitution,* V *is a set of variables and* $\mathcal{X}$ *is a* set of protected variables that cannot be instantiated. A solution for a quintuple $(\Gamma, P, \sigma, V, \mathcal{X})$ is a pair (Δ, δ), where the following conditions are satisfied:

1. $\Delta \vdash \delta\Gamma$.
2. if $a\#_? t \in P$ then $\Delta \vdash a\#\delta t$.
3. if $t \approx_? s \in P$ then $\Delta \vdash \delta t \approx_\alpha \delta s$.

4. there exists λ such that
   $\Delta \vdash \lambda\sigma \approx_V \delta$.
5. $dom(\delta) \cap \mathcal{X} = \emptyset$.

Remark 3. Note that if (Δ, δ) is a solution of $(\Gamma, \text{NIL}, \sigma, \mathbb{X}, \mathcal{X})$ this corresponds to the notion of (Δ, δ) being an instance of (Γ, σ) that does not instantiate variables in $\mathcal{X}$.

Definition 9 (Solution for an AC-unification/matching/equality problem). *A solution for an AC-unification problem with protected variables $(\Gamma, P, \mathcal{X})$ is a solution for the associated quintuple $(\Gamma, P, id, Vars(P), \mathcal{X})$. When $\mathcal{X} = Vars(rhs(P))$, we have the definition for an AC-matching problem and when $\mathcal{X} = Vars(P)$ we have the definition of solution to an AC-equality checking problem.*

3   Algorithm

We present the algorithm's pseudocode instead of the actual PVS code for readability. We developed a nominal algorithm (Algorithm 1 ⬚) for matching terms t and s. The algorithm is recursive and needs to keep track of the current context Γ, the equational constraints P that we have to unify, the substitution σ computed so far, the set of variables V that are/were in the problem and the set of protected variables $\mathcal{X}$. Hence, its input is a quintuple $(\Gamma, P, \sigma, V, \mathcal{X})$. The output is a list of solutions, each of the form (Γ_1, σ_1). The freshness constraints are treated by auxiliary functions (see Sect. 3.1), and the equational constraints P are represented as a list in our PVS code, where each element of the list is a pair (t_i, s_i) that represents an equation $t_i \approx_? s_i$. The first call to the algorithm, in order to match t to s, is done with $P = \{t \approx_? s\}$; $\Gamma = \emptyset$ and $\sigma = id$ (because we have not computed any freshness constraint or substitution yet); $V = Vars(t, s)$ and $\mathcal{X} = Vars(s)$.

Although extensive, Algorithm 1 is simple. It starts by analysing the list P of terms to match. If it is empty (line 2), it has finished and can return the answer computed so far, a list with a unique element: (Γ, σ). Otherwise, the algorithm calls the auxiliary function CHOOSEEQ (line 4), which returns a pair (t, s) and a list of equational constraints P_1 such that $P = \{t \approx_? s\} \cup P_1$. Then, P is updated by simplifying $\{t \approx_? s\}$ and it does so by seeing the form of t (an atom, a moderated variable, a unit, and so on).

3.1   Functions CHOOSEEQ and DECOMPOSE

The function CHOOSEEQ(P)⬚ selects an equational constraint $t \approx_? s$ in P, picking the equation with the biggest size. This heuristic aims to aid us in the proof of termination (see Sect. 4.2).

Algorithm 1. Nominal AC-Matching Algorithm 1 ⟐

1: **procedure** ACMATCH($\Gamma, P, \sigma, V, \mathcal{X}$)
2:     **if** nil?(P) **then** $cons((\Gamma, \sigma), \text{NIL})$
3:     **else**
4:         **let** $((t, s), P_1) = \text{CHOOSEEQ}(P)$ **in**
5:         **if** t matches a and s matches a **then** ACMATCH($\Gamma, P_1, \sigma, V, \mathcal{X}$)
6:         **else if** t matches $\pi \cdot X$ and $X \notin Vars(s)$ and $X \notin \mathcal{X}$ **then**
7:             **let** $\sigma_1 = \{X \mapsto \pi^{-1}s\}$,
8:                 $(\Gamma_1, \mathit{flag}) = \text{FRESHSUBS?}(\sigma_1, \Gamma)$ **in**
9:             **if** flag **then** ACMATCH($\Gamma_1 \cup \Gamma, \sigma_1 P_1, \sigma_1 \sigma, V, \mathcal{X}$)
10:             **else** NIL
11:         **else if** t matches $\pi \cdot X$ and s matches $\pi' \cdot X$ **then**
12:             **let** $\Gamma_1 = ds(\pi, \pi')\#X \cup \Gamma$ **in** ACMATCH($\Gamma_1, P_1, \sigma, V, \mathcal{X}$)
13:         **else if** t matches $\langle \rangle$ and s matches $\langle \rangle$ **then** ACMATCH($\Gamma, P_1, \sigma, V, \mathcal{X}$)
14:         **else if** t matches $f\ t_1$ and s matches $f\ s_1$ **then**
15:             **let** $(P_2, \mathit{flag}) = \text{DECOMPOSE}(t_1, s_1)$ **in**
16:             **if** flag **then** ACMATCH($\Gamma, P_2 \cup P_1, \sigma, V, \mathcal{X}$)
17:             **else** NIL
18:         **else if** t matches $[a]\ t_1$ and $s = [a]\ s_1$ **then**
19:             **let** $(P_2, \mathit{flag}) = \text{DECOMPOSE}(t_1, s_1)$ **in**
20:             **if** flag **then** ACMATCH($\Gamma, P_2 \cup P_1, \sigma, V, \mathcal{X}$)
21:             **else** NIL
22:         **else if** t matches $[a]\ t_1$ and $s = [b]s_1$ **then**
23:             **let** $(\Gamma_1, \mathit{flag}1) = \text{FRESH?}(a, s_1)$,
24:                 $(P_2, \mathit{flag}2) = \text{DECOMPOSE}(t_1, (a\ b) \cdot s_1)$ **in**
25:             **if** $\mathit{flag}1$ and $\mathit{flag}2$ **then** ACMATCH($\Gamma \cup \Gamma_1, P_2 \cup P_1, \sigma, V, \mathcal{X}$)
26:             **else** NIL
27:         **else if** t matches $f^{AC}\ t_1$ and s matches $f^{AC}\ s_1$ **then**
28:             **let** $InputLst = \text{APPLYACSTEP}\ (\Gamma, cons((t, s), P_1), \sigma, V, \mathcal{X})$,
29:                 $LstResults = \text{MAP}(\text{ACMATCH}, InputLst)$ **in** FLATTEN($LstResults$)
30:         **else** NIL

The function DECOMPOSE ⟐ (lines 15, 19 and 24) receives two terms t and s, and if they are both pairs, it recursively tries to decompose them, returning a tuple (P, flag), where P is a list of equational constraints and flag is a boolean that is *True* if the decomposition was successful. This function guarantees that only well-formed terms are in the matching problem.

Example 1. Examples of the function DECOMPOSE are given below.

- DECOMPOSE($\langle a, \langle b, c\rangle\rangle, \langle c, \langle X, Y\rangle\rangle$) = ($\{a \approx_? c,\ b \approx_? X,\ c \approx_? Y\}$, *True*).
- DECOMPOSE(a, Y) = ($\{a \approx_? Y\}$, *True*).
- DECOMPOSE($X, \langle c, d\rangle$) = (NIL, *False*).

3.2 Handling Freshness Constraints - Functions FRESHSUBS? and FRESH?

Following the approach of [6], freshness constraints are handled separately by the auxiliary functions FRESH? ⟐ and FRESHSUBS? ⟐. These functions were already implemented in [6], and extending them to handle AC-functions is straightforward. FRESHSUBS?(σ, Γ) returns the minimal context (Γ_1 in Algorithm 1) in which $a\#_?\sigma X$ holds, for every $a\#X$ in the context Γ. FRESH?(a, t) computes and returns the minimal context (Γ_1 in Algorithm 1) in which a is fresh for t. Both functions also return a boolean (*flag* in Algorithm 1), indicating if it was possible to find the aimed context.

3.3   The Function APPLYACSTEP

The function APPLYACSTEP ⬚ was adapted from the formalisation of first-order AC-unification (see [7]). It handles equations $t \approx_? s$, where t and s are rooted by the same AC function symbol. This function returns a list (*InputLst* in line 28 of Algorithm 1) with each entry in this list corresponding to a branch ACMATCH will explore. ACMATCH explores every branch generated by calling itself recursively on every input in *InputLst* (line 29 of the algorithm). The algorithm's output is a list of solutions of the form (Γ, σ), where Γ is a context and σ is a substitution. In addition, the result of calling MAP(ACMATCH, *InputLst*), *LstResults* in line 29 of Algorithm 1, is a list of lists of solutions. Hence, *LstResults* is flattened and then returned.

Remark 4 (SOLVEAC and INSTANTIATESTEP). APPLYACSTEP relies on two functions: SOLVEAC ⬚ and INSTANTIATESTEP ⬚, which are fully described in [7]. In synthesis, the function SOLVEAC finds the linear Diophantine equational system associated with the AC-matching equational constraint, generates the basis of solutions, and uses these solutions to generate the new AC-matching equational constraints. The function INSTANTIATESTEP instantiates the moderated variables that it can.

3.4   An Example of First-Order AC-Unification and How We Adapted It to the Nominal Setting

We give a very high-level example (taken from [31] and more detailed in the extended version) of how we would solve the first-order AC-unification problem $\{f(X, X, Y, a, b, c) \approx_? f(b, b, b, c, Z)\}$. The first step is to eliminate common arguments. Next we associate our unification problem with a linear Diophantine equation ($2U_1 + U_2 + U_3 = 2V_1 + V_2$ in our case) and generate a basis of solutions to this equation, associating a new variable ($Z_1, Z_2, \ldots, Z_7$ in our case) to each solution. The algorithm may branch into (possibly) many unification problems and these new variables will be the building blocks for these unification problems. Finally, before proceeding to unify the new unification problems, we can drop the cases where a variable term is paired with an AC-function application. In the end, the solutions computed are:

$$\sigma_1 = \{Y \mapsto f(b,b), Z \mapsto f(a,X,X)\} \quad \sigma_2 = \{Y \mapsto f(Z_2,b,b), Z \mapsto f(a,Z_2,X,X)\}$$
$$\sigma_3 = \{X \mapsto b, Z \mapsto f(a,Y)\} \quad\quad \sigma_4 = \{X \mapsto f(Z_6,b), Z \mapsto f(a,Y,Z_6,Z_6)\}$$

With this example in mind, there are four main modifications (more details in the extended version) when moving from first-order AC-unification to nominal AC-matching. When eliminating common arguments we do not eliminate arguments t_i and s_j of t and s if they are equal modulo AC, we eliminate them if they are α-equivalent (modulo AC) under the context Γ that we are working with. Regarding the new variables introduced: the permutation suspended on them is always the identity. Additionally, we drop the cases where a moderated variable $\pi \cdot X$, with $X \in \mathcal{X}$, is paired with an AC-function application. Finally, we must guarantee that the new variables Z_is introduced by the algorithm can be instantiated, i.e. $Z_i \notin \mathcal{X}$.

4   Formalisation

As is done in [7], to help us in the proofs of termination (Sect. 4.2), soundness (Sect. 4.3) and completeness (Sect. 4.4) we define the notion of a *nice input* (Sect. 4.1).

4.1   Nice Inputs

Nice inputs are invariant under the action of the ACMATCH function with valuable properties. Notice that Item 7 of Definition 10 would need to be removed for the proofs of termination, soundness, and completeness to be used in unification.

Definition 10 (*Nice input*☑).   *An input* $(\Gamma, P, \sigma, V, \mathcal{X})$ *is said to be nice if:*
1. σ *is idempotent.*
2. $Vars(P) \cap dom(\sigma) = \emptyset$.
3. $\sigma \subseteq V$.
4. $Vars(P) \subseteq V$.
5. $Vars(\Gamma) \subseteq V$.
6. $\mathcal{X} \subseteq V$.
7. $Vars(rhs(P)) \subseteq \mathcal{X}$.

4.2   Termination

For the lexicographic measure used in the proof of termination, we need the definition of the size of an equational constraint $t \approx_? s$ (Definition 11).

Definition 11 (*Size of an Equational Constraint*☑).   *The size of an equational constraint* $t \approx_? s$ *is* $size(t) + size(s)$, *where the size of a term* t☑ *is recursively defined as follows:*

- $size(a) = 1$.
- $size(\pi \cdot X) = 1$.
- $size(\langle\rangle) = 1$.
- $size(\langle t_1, t_2 \rangle) = 1 + size(t_1) + size(t_2)$.
- $size(f\ t_1) = 1 + size(t_1)$.
- $size(f^{AC}\ t_1) = 1 + size(t_1)$.
- $size([a]t_1) = 1 + size(t_1)$.

Although the nominal AC-matching algorithm is based on the first-order AC-unification algorithm ([7]), the proof of termination was much easier for nominal AC-matching than for first-order AC-unification. Instead of the intricate lexicographic measure used in [7] (which came from the work of [17]), it was possible to prove that for the particular case of matching (unlike unification) all the new moderated variables introduced by SOLVEAC are instantiated by INSTANTIATESTEP.

Hence, the lexicographic measure used has as its first component the number of variables in the equational constraints P and as a second component the multiset order of the size of each equation $t \approx_? s \in P$. Although PVS does not directly implement multiset orders, this part can be emulated easily by analysing the maximum size n of all equations $t \approx_? s$ in P and the number of equations $t \approx_? s$ in P with maximal size (in this order). The algorithm selects an equation with maximal size to simplify (the heuristic selection is enforced by the function CHOOSEEQ).

4.3 Soundness

As mentioned, to match terms t and s we first call the Algorithm 1 with parameters $\Gamma = \emptyset$, $P = \{t \approx_? s\}$, $\sigma = id$, $V = Vars(t,s)$ and $\mathcal{X} = Vars(s)$. However, since the parameters of ACMATCH change after recursive calls, the proof of soundness (Corollary 1) cannot be done directly by induction, and we must instead prove first the Theorem 1 with generic parameters Γ, P, σ, V and $\mathcal{X}$. Once the Theorem 1 is proved, it is also immediate to adapt the algorithm to solve nominal AC-equality checking and to prove its soundness (Corollary 2).

Theorem 1 (*Soundness for Nice Inputs* ✔). *Let the pair* (Γ_1, σ_1) *an output of* ACMATCH$(\Gamma, P, \sigma, V, \mathcal{X})$ *and suppose that* $(\Gamma, P, \sigma, V, \mathcal{X})$ *is a nice input. If* (Δ, δ) *is a solution to* $(\Gamma_1, \text{NIL}, \sigma_1, \mathbb{X}, \mathcal{X})$ *then* (Δ, δ) *is a solution to* $(\Gamma, P, \sigma, \mathbb{X}, \mathcal{X})$.

Corollary 1 (*Soundness for AC-Matching* ✔). *Let the pair* (Γ_1, σ_1) *an output of* ACMATCH$(\emptyset, \{t \approx_? s\}, id, Vars(t,s), Vars(s))$. *If* (Δ, δ) *is an instance of* (Γ_1, σ_1) *that does not instantiate the variables in s, then* (Δ, δ) *is a solution to* $(\emptyset, \{t \approx_? s\}, id, \mathbb{X}, Vars(s))$.

Corollary 2 (*Soundness for AC-Equality Checking* ✔). *Let* (Γ_1, σ_1) *be an output of* ACMATCH$(\emptyset, \{t \approx_? s\}, id, Vars(t,s), Vars(t,s))$. *If* (Δ, δ) *is an instance of* (Γ_1, σ_1) *that does not instantiate the variables in t or s, then* (Δ, δ) *is a solution to* $(\emptyset, \{t \approx_? s\}, id, \mathbb{X}, Vars(t,s))$.

Remark 5. An interpretation of Corollary 1 is that if (Δ, δ) is an AC-matching instance to one of the outputs of ACMATCH, then (Δ, δ) is an AC-matching solution to the original problem. Corollary 2 has a similar interpretation, replacing AC-matching with AC-equality checking.

4.4 Completeness

Completeness of Algorithm 1 is given by the Corollary 3 and similarly to the soundness proof, it is derived easily after proving the Theorem 2.

Theorem 2 (*Completeness for Nice Inputs* ☑). *Let* $(\Gamma, P, \sigma, V, \mathcal{X})$ *be a nice input. Suppose that* (Δ, δ) *is a solution to* $(\Gamma, P, \sigma, \mathbb{X}, \mathcal{X})$, *that* $\delta \subseteq V$ *and that* $\mathit{Vars}(\Delta) \subseteq V$. *Then, there exists* $(\Gamma_1, \sigma_1) \in \mathrm{ACMATCH}(\Gamma, P, \sigma, V, \mathcal{X})$ *such that* (Δ, δ) *is an instance (restricted to the variables of V) of* (Γ_1, σ_1) *that does not instantiate the variables in* $\mathcal{X}$.

Corollary 3 (*Completeness for AC-Matching* ☑). *Suppose that* (Δ, δ) *is a solution to* $(\emptyset, \{t \approx_? s\}, id, \mathbb{X}, \mathit{Vars}(s))$, *that* $\delta \subseteq V$ *and that* $\mathit{Vars}(\Delta) \subseteq V$. *Then, there exists* $(\Gamma_1, \sigma_1) \in \mathrm{ACMATCH}(\emptyset, \{t \approx_? s\}, id, V, \mathit{Vars}(s))$ *such that* (Δ, δ) *is an instance (restricted to the variables of V) of* (Γ_1, σ_1) *that does not instantiate the variables of s.*

Corollary 4 (*Completeness for AC-equality Checking* ☑). *Suppose* (Δ, δ) *is a solution to* $(\emptyset, \{t \approx_? s\}, id, \mathbb{X}, \mathit{Vars}(t, s))$ *satisfying* $\delta \subseteq V$ *and* $\mathit{Vars}(\Delta) \subseteq V$. *Then, there exists* $(\Gamma_1, \sigma_1) \in \mathrm{ACMATCH}(\emptyset, \{t \approx_? s\}, id, V, \mathit{Vars}(t, s))$ *such that* (Δ, δ) *is an instance (restricted to the variables of V) of* (Γ_1, σ_1) *that does not instantiate the variables of t or s.*

Remark 6. An interpretation of Corollary 3 is that if (Δ, δ) is an AC-matching solution to the initial problem, then (Δ, δ) is an AC-matching instance of one of the outputs of ACMATCH. Corollary 4 has a similar interpretation, replacing AC-matching with AC-equality checking.

As was the case for first-order AC-unification (see [7]), the hypothesis $\delta \subseteq V$ in the proof of completeness is merely a technicality that was put in order to guarantee the new variables introduced by the algorithm in the AC-part do not clash with the variables in $dom(\delta)$ or in the terms in $im(\delta)$. This mechanism could be replaced by a different one that assures that the variables introduced by the AC-part of ACMATCH are indeed new. When going from the first-order setting to the nominal setting, we go from having a unifier δ to a pair (Δ, δ) and hence we must add the hypothesis $\mathit{Vars}(\Delta) \subseteq V$.

Remark 7. (*High-level description of how to remove hypotheses* $\delta \subseteq V$ *and* $\mathit{Vars}(\Delta) \subseteq V$). The critical step to prove a variant of Corollary 3 with $V = \mathit{Vars}(t, s)$ and without the hypothesis $\delta \subseteq V$ and $\mathit{Vars}(\Delta) \subseteq V$ is to prove that the outputs computed when we call ACMATCH with input $(\Gamma, P, \sigma, V, \mathcal{X})$ "differ only by the name of the new variables" from the outputs computed when we call ACMATCH with input $(\Gamma, P, \sigma, V', \mathcal{X})$. However, this cannot be proved directly by induction because if V and V' differ and ACMATCH enters in the AC-part, the new variables introduced for each input may "differ only by a renaming" and once we instantiate those variables, it may happen that the substitutions computed so far (the third component in the input quintuple) will also "differ only by the name of the new variables". Similar to what was done in first-order AC-unification, the solution is to prove the more general statement that if the inputs $(\Gamma, P, \sigma, V, \mathcal{X})$ and $(\Gamma, P, \sigma', V', \mathcal{X}')$ "differ only by the name of the new variables", then the output of ACMATCH with the first input "differ only by the name of the new variables" from the output of ACMATCH with the second input.

5   Towards a Nominal AC-Unification Algorithm

Stickel's AC-unification algorithm relies on solving Diophantine equations where new variables are used to represent arguments of AC operators. Using the same approach to solve nominal AC-unification problems leads to non-termination in cases where the same variable occurs as an argument of an AC operator multiple times with *different* suspended permutations.

As an example, suppose that we are working under an empty context (i.e. $\Gamma = \emptyset$) and want to solve the equational constraint $f(X, W) \approx_? f(\pi \cdot X, \pi \cdot Y)$, with $\mathcal{X} = \emptyset$. Additionally, assume that we apply Stickel's AC-unification algorithm to this equational constraints and let Z_1, W_1, Y_1, X_1 be the name of the new variables introduced (we choose these names deliberately to make the loop in nominal AC-unification clearer). Then, 7 branches (more details in the extended version) are generated and one of them is:

$$\{X \approx_? Y_1 + X_1, W \approx_? Z_1 + W_1, \pi \cdot X \approx_? W_1 + X_1, \pi \cdot Y \approx_? Z_1 + Y_1\}$$

After instantiating the variables we obtain

$$\sigma = \{X \mapsto f(Y_1, X_1), \ W \mapsto f(Z_1, W_1), Y \mapsto f(\pi^{-1} \cdot Z_1, \pi^{-1} \cdot Y_1)\}$$

and one equational constraint remain: $f(X_1, W_1) \approx_? f(\pi \cdot X_1, \pi \cdot Y_1)$. Notice that our final problem is essentially a renaming of our initial problem:

$$f(X, W) \approx_? f(\pi \cdot X, \pi \cdot Y)$$
$$f(X_1, W_1) \approx_? f(\pi \cdot X_1, \pi \cdot Y_1)$$

This problem does not arise in first-order AC-unification because, in the corresponding first-order problem, we would not have two different permutations (*id* and π in this case) suspended on the same variable (X in this case). Instead, we would have the same variable X as an argument to both terms and eliminate it. Finally, this problem also does not arise in nominal AC-matching because X would be a protected variable. Hence, we would not compute the substitution $\sigma = \{X \mapsto f(Y_1, X_1), W \mapsto W_1, Y \mapsto \pi^{-1} \cdot Y_1\}$, we would instead discard this branch. In future work, we will consider the alternative approach to AC-unification proposed by Boudet, Contejean and Devie [8,10], which was used to define AC higher-order pattern unification [9]. To our knowledge, this AC unification approach has not been formalised yet. However, it has the advantage of generating simpler Diophantine systems, which could simplify the task of nominal AC-unification.

6   Conclusion and Future Work

We propose the first (to the best of our knowledge) nominal AC-matching algorithm, together with proofs of its termination, soundness and completeness. All proofs were formalised in the proof assistant PVS. As a byproduct, we also obtained a formalised nominal AC-equality checking algorithm. Nominal AC-matching has applications for nominal AC-rewriting, being the first step towards a nominal AC-unification algorithm.

Our formalisation extends the formalisation of first-order AC-unification by Ayala-Rincón et al. [7] to nominal terms and uses the functions that deal with freshness constraints from [6], extending them to deal with AC-function symbols. Furthermore, by adding a parameter $\mathcal{X}$ for protected variables, it enables both AC-matching and AC-equality checking, according to whether $\mathcal{X}$ is the set of variables in the right-hand side of the problem or the set of variables in the problem. The .pvs files have a combined size of 290 KB and contain the specification of functions and the statements of the theorems. The .prf files contain the proofs of the theorems and have a combined size of 22 MB.

Future work will explore ways to define a nominal AC-unification algorithm, avoiding the loop described in Sect. 5. We will consider alternative AC-unification algorithms as a starting point [9,10] and explore the connection between higher-order pattern unification and nominal unification (e.g., [13,23]).

A nominal AC-unification algorithm would have applications in logic programming languages that employ the nominal paradigm, such as α-Prolog. A second possible future work path is to use this formalisation to formalise a more efficient nominal AC-matching algorithm. Finally, a third future work path would be formalising matching/unification algorithms for different equational theories and a fourth path would be investigating if/how nominal unification algorithms can be used for term indexing.

Acknowledgments. Partially supported by the Austrian Science Fund (FWF) Project P 35530, Brazilian FAP-DF Project DE 00193.00001175/2021-11, Brazilian CNPq Project Universal 409003/2021-2, and Georgian Rustaveli National Science Foundation Project FR-21-16725. First author was partially funded by a CNPq productivity research grant 313290/2021-0.

References

1. Ayala-Rincón, M., de Carvalho-Segundo, W., Fernández, M., Nantes-Sobrinho, D.: Nominal C-unification. In: Fioravanti, F., Gallagher, J.P. (eds.) LOPSTR 2017. LNCS, vol. 10855, pp. 235–251. Springer, Cham (2018). https://doi.org/10.1007/978-3-319-94460-9_14
2. Ayala-Rincón, M., de Carvalho-Segundo, W., Fernández, M., Nantes-Sobrinho, D.: On solving nominal fixpoint equations. In: Dixon, C., Finger, M. (eds.) FroCoS 2017. LNCS (LNAI), vol. 10483, pp. 209–226. Springer, Cham (2017). https://doi.org/10.1007/978-3-319-66167-4_12
3. Ayala-Rincón, M., de Carvalho Segundo, W., Fernández, M., Nantes-Sobrinho, D., Oliveira, A.C.R.: A formalisation of nominal α-equivalence with A, C, and AC function symbols. Theor. Comput. Sci. **781**, 3–23 (2019). https://doi.org/10.1016/j.tcs.2019.02.020
4. Ayala-Rincón, M., de Carvalho Segundo, W., Fernández, M., Silva, G.F., Nantes-Sobrinho, D.: Formalising nominal C-unification generalised with protected variables. Math. Struct. Comput. Sci. **31**(3), 286–311 (2021). https://doi.org/10.1017/S0960129521000050

5. Ayala-Rincón, M., Fernández, M., Nantes-Sobrinho, D.: On nominal syntax and permutation fixed points. Log. Methods Comput. Sci. **16**(1) (2020). https://doi.org/10.23638/LMCS-16(1:19)2020

6. Ayala-Rincón, M., Fernández, M., Oliveira, A.C.R.: Completeness in PVS of a nominal unification algorithm. In: Proceedings of the 10th Workshop on Logical and Semantic Frameworks, with Applications, LSFA. ENTCS, vol. 323, pp. 57–74. Elsevier (2015). https://doi.org/10.1016/j.entcs.2016.06.005

7. Ayala-Rincón, M., Fernández, M., Silva, G.F., Sobrinho, D.N.: A certified algorithm for AC-unification. In: 7th International Conference on Formal Structures for Computation and Deduction, FSCD. LIPIcs, vol. 228, pp. 8:1–8:21. Schloss Dagstuhl - Leibniz-Zentrum für Informatik (2022). https://doi.org/10.4230/LIPIcs.FSCD.2022.8

8. Boudet, A.: Competing for the AC-unification race. J. Autom. Reasoning **11**(2), 185–212 (1993). https://doi.org/10.1007/BF00881905

9. Boudet, A., Contejean, E.: AC-unification of higher-order patterns. In: Smolka, G. (ed.) CP 1997. LNCS, vol. 1330, pp. 267–281. Springer, Heidelberg (1997). https://doi.org/10.1007/BFb0017445

10. Boudet, A., Contejean, E., Devie, H.: A new AC unification algorithm with an algorithm for solving systems of diophantine equations. In: Proceedings of the 5th Annual Symposium on Logic in Computer Science, LICS, pp. 289–299. IEEE Computer Society (1990). https://doi.org/10.1109/LICS.1990.113755

11. Calvès, C.F., Fernández, M.: Matching and alpha-equivalence check for nominal terms. J. Comput. Syst. Sci. **76**(5), 283–301 (2010). https://doi.org/10.1016/j.jcss.2009.10.003

12. Calvès, C., Fernández, M.: A polynomial nominal unification algorithm. Theor. Comput. Sci. **403**(2–3), 285–306 (2008). https://doi.org/10.1016/j.tcs.2008.05.012

13. Cheney, J.: Relating nominal and higher-order pattern unification. In: Proceedings of the 19th International Workshop on Unification, UNIF, pp. 104–119 (2005)

14. Clausen, M., Fortenbacher, A.: Efficient solution of linear Diophantine equations. J. Sym. Comput. **8**(1–2), 201–216 (1989). https://doi.org/10.1016/S0747-7171(89)80025-2

15. Contejean, E.: A certified AC matching algorithm. In: van Oostrom, V. (ed.) RTA 2004. LNCS, vol. 3091, pp. 70–84. Springer, Heidelberg (2004). https://doi.org/10.1007/978-3-540-25979-4_5

16. Eker, S.: Associative-commutative rewriting on large terms. In: Nieuwenhuis, R. (ed.) RTA 2003. LNCS, vol. 2706, pp. 14–29. Springer, Heidelberg (2003). https://doi.org/10.1007/3-540-44881-0_3

17. Fages, F.: Associative-commutative unification. In: Shostak, R.E. (ed.) CADE 1984. LNCS, vol. 170, pp. 194–208. Springer, New York (1984). https://doi.org/10.1007/978-0-387-34768-4_12

18. Fages, F.: Associative-commutative unification. J. Sym. Comput. **3**(3), 257–275 (1987). https://doi.org/10.1016/S0747-7171(87)80004-4

19. Fernández, M., Gabbay, M.J.: Nominal rewriting. Inf. Comput. **205**(6), 917–965 (2007). https://doi.org/10.1016/j.ic.2006.12.002

20. Gabbay, M.J., Pitts, A.M.: A new approach to abstract syntax with variable binding. Formal Aspects Comput. **13**(3), 341–363 (2002). https://doi.org/10.1007/s001650200016

21. Kumar, R., Norrish, M.: (Nominal) unification by recursive descent with triangular substitutions. In: Kaufmann, M., Paulson, L.C. (eds.) ITP 2010. LNCS, vol. 6172, pp. 51–66. Springer, Heidelberg (2010). https://doi.org/10.1007/978-3-642-14052-5_6

22. Levy, J., Villaret, M.: An efficient nominal unification algorithm. In: Proceedings of the 21st International Conference on Rewriting Techniques and Applications, RTA. LIPIcs, vol. 6, pp. 209–226. Schloss Dagstuhl - Leibniz-Zentrum für Informatik (2010). https://doi.org/10.4230/LIPIcs.RTA.2010.209
23. Levy, J., Villaret, M.: Nominal unification from a higher-order perspective. ACM Trans. Comput. Log. **13**(2), 10:1–10:31 (2012). https://doi.org/10.1145/2159531.2159532
24. Owre, S., Shankar, N.: The formal semantics of PVS. Technical report. 97-2R, SRI International Computer Science Laboratory, Menlo Park CA 94025 USA (1997, revised 1999)
25. Pitts, A.M.: Nominal Sets: Names and Symmetry in Computer Science. Cambridge University Press, Cambridge (2013)
26. Pottier, F.: An overview of CαML. In: Benton, N., Leroy, X. (eds.) Proceedings of the ACM-SIGPLAN Workshop on ML, ML. Electronic Notes in Theoretical Computer Science, vol. 148, pp. 27–52. Elsevier (2005). https://doi.org/10.1016/j.entcs.2005.11.039
27. Schmidt-Schauß, M., Kutsia, T., Levy, J., Villaret, M.: Nominal unification of higher order expressions with recursive let. In: Hermenegildo, M.V., Lopez-Garcia, P. (eds.) LOPSTR 2016. LNCS, vol. 10184, pp. 328–344. Springer, Cham (2017). https://doi.org/10.1007/978-3-319-63139-4_19
28. Schmidt-Schauß, M., Kutsia, T., Levy, J., Villaret, M., Kutz, Y.D.K.: Nominal unification and matching of higher order expressions with recursive let. Fundam. Informaticae **185**(3), 247–283 (2022). https://doi.org/10.3233/FI-222110
29. Shinwell, M.R., Pitts, A.M., Gabbay, M.: FreshML: programming with binders made simple. In: Proceedings of the 8th ACM SIGPLAN International Conference on Functional Programming, ICFP, pp. 263–274. ACM (2003). https://doi.org/10.1145/944705.944729
30. Stickel, M.E.: A complete unification algorithm for associative-commutative functions. In: Advance Papers of the Fourth International Joint Conference on Artificial Intelligence, IJCAI, pp. 71–76 (1975). https://ijcai.org/Proceedings/75/Papers/011.pdf
31. Stickel, M.E.: A unification algorithm for associative-commutative functions. J. ACM **28**(3), 423–434 (1981). https://doi.org/10.1145/322261.322262
32. Urban, C.: Nominal techniques in Isabelle/HOL. J. Autom. Reason. **40**(4), 327–356 (2008). https://doi.org/10.1007/s10817-008-9097-2
33. Urban, C.: Nominal unification revisited. In: Proceedings of the 24th International Workshop on Unification, UNIF. EPTCS, vol. 42, pp. 1–11 (2010). https://doi.org/10.4204/EPTCS.42.1
34. Urban, C., Pitts, A.M., Gabbay, M.: Nominal unification. Theor. Comput. Sci. **323**(1–3), 473–497 (2004). https://doi.org/10.1016/j.tcs.2004.06.016

Category Theory in Isabelle/HOL as a Basis for Meta-logical Investigation

Jonas Bayer[1]([✉]), Alexey Gonus[1]([✉]), Christoph Benzmüller[2,1], and Dana S. Scott[3,4]

[1] Freie Universität Berlin, Berlin, Germany
`jonas.bayer@fu-berlin.de`
[2] Otto-Friedrich-Universität Bamberg, Bamberg, Germany
[3] University of California, Berkeley, CA, USA
[4] Topos Institute, Berkeley, CA, USA

Abstract. This paper presents meta-logical investigations based on category theory using the proof assistant Isabelle/HOL. We demonstrate the potential of a free logic based shallow semantic embedding of category theory by providing a formalization of the notion of elementary topoi. Additionally, we formalize symmetrical monoidal closed categories expressing the denotational semantic model of intuitionistic multiplicative linear logic. Next to these meta-logical-investigations, we contribute to building an Isabelle category theory library, with a focus on ease of use in the formalization beyond category theory itself. This work paves the way for future formalizations based on category theory and demonstrates the power of automated reasoning in investigating meta-logical questions.

Keywords: Formalization of mathematics · Category theory · Proof assistants · Formal methods · Shallow embeddings

1 Introduction

Category theory is a very abstract and general theory of mathematical structures [15] that next to being used for organizing mathematical theories can also serve as an axiomatic basis of mathematics. It has a myriad of use cases in fields ranging from topology and algebra to the foundations of mathematics.

A good understanding of categorical notions and methods can provide a mathematician with a generic framework to unify and describe concepts. The results obtained on a category theoretical level might later be applied to particular mathematical objects collected under a specific categorical setting. By this approach, many findings and ideas in one theory of mathematical structures can possibly be translated to the other.

Formalizing Category Theory. Given its special standing in mathematics it is only natural to ask for a formalization of category theory, hoping that the benefits of the categorical perspective will carry over to formal mathematics.

J. Bayer and A. Gonus—Contributed equally.

C. Dubois and M. Kerber (Eds.): CICM 2023, LNAI 14101, pp. 69–83, 2023.
https://doi.org/10.1007/978-3-031-42753-4_5

Concretely, one would not only wish to be able to formally use certain theorems from category theory but also utilize its power in the organization of formal mathematical libraries.

Yet, the formalization of category theory poses significant challenges. Many experts consider first-order logic and the Zermelo-Fraenkel axioms of set theory as a suitable foundation for mathematics. However, e.g., topologists often work with the (large) category of topological spaces, which cannot be easily represented within this system of axioms, since large categories in standard formalizations within such a system are (obviously) not sets. It is thus not immediately clear how category theory should best be done formally.

Next to this, significant challenges in the formalization of category theory stem from the double position that it carries in mathematics. Ideally, a formalization of category theory would not only lend itself to use cases in algebra but also enable meta-logical investigations that use categories as a foundation of mathematics. We refer to [8,16,17] for a deeper discussion on category-theoretic versus set-theoretic foundations of mathematics.

Meta-logical Investigations. In this paper we intend to demonstrate the potential of a (shallow semantical embeddings based) formalization of category theory for the investigation of meta-logical questions. This will be done using the proof assistant Isabelle/HOL which is naturally suited for such work due to its strong support for automation.

Concretely, we give a formalization of the notion of elementary topoi that carry an important role in fundamental mathematics. We build up category theoretical concepts in order to eventually provide an elegant definition of a topos. Moreover, we formalize all necessary concepts allowing for future work that could implement the internal language of a topos.

As a second meta-logical result, we present a formalization of linear logic (LL). Linear logic carries the idea of treating mathematical "truths" as information resources and has found a large number of theoretical and practical applications, ranging from computer science to linguistics. Categories come with the inherent property of representing denotational semantical models for different logics. We develop symmetrical monoidal closed categories that express the denotational semantical model of intuitionistic multiplicative linear logic (IMLL).

In addition, at an orthogonal, methodological level, we study the scalability of an approach to universal meta-logical reasoning [7], that is based on shallow semantical embeddings of (layers of) object logics in classical higher-order logic, aka Church's simple type theory.

Further Contributions. Next to our main focus on meta-logical investigation, we aim at contributing to the build up of a category theory library in Isabelle. At the time of writing, we are not aware of cases where the existing formalizations in the Isabelle Archive of Formal Proofs [13,21,26,30] have been used for the purpose of verification in other fields of mathematics. Our work cannot (yet) compete with the extent of concepts verified in the aforementioned AFP entries.

However, we pay a lot of attention to closely mimicking mathematical notation, cleanly organizing our theories, and giving examples of how to use the concepts we provide. Thereby, we hope to facilitate the use of category theoretical notions in future formalizations in other fields, too. Moreover, the paper is embedded in a larger project context, namely the exploration of the Benzmüller and Scott [6] approach to the axiomatic modeling (in the tradition also of the early work of Saunders Mac Lane, although with more emphasis on Dana Scott, Freyd an Scedrov works) of category theory based on free-logic using the LogiKEy meta-logical/logico-pluralistic KR&R [4] methodology. It was important for us to study the scalability, advantages and disadvantages of this distinguished approach. In the end, we obtain a high degree of automation and a high level of abstraction.

2   Category Theory from a Free Logic Perspective

Our work exploits a shallow semantic embedding of free logic in Isabelle/HOL (or, more generally, in Church's simple type theory [3] aka. classical higher-order logic HOL), that is subsequently used for defining a notion of category theory, which then provides the basis for further formalization studies on top of it.

2.1   Free Logic and Its SSE into Isabelle/HOL

Free Logic (FL) is a logic that comes with less existential assumptions than its classical counterpart. Terms in free logic might denote so-called *non-existent objects*, i.e., terms that refer to objects outside the domain of discourse [24]. Existential and universal quantifiers are assumed to range over the *existent terms*, i.e., those that denote objects within the domain of discourse. Such a logic is particularly interesting because it helps to reason about partiality.

Therefore, free higher-order logic (FHOL) is ideal for an axiomatization of category theory since the composition of morphisms in a category is a partial function. In order to distinguish existent and non-existent objects we use the dual domain approach, i.e., we consider a domain D of all objects which has a subset E of objects that are considered to be the existent objects. Alternatively, one could consider two disjoint sets for the non-existent and existent objects. We will follow the first approach as has been previously discussed by Cocchiarella [22] and also in the early work of Scott [28]. The issue of properly defining free (higher-order) logic within the simple theory of types has been addressed in the works of Schütte [27] and Farmer [9] whose approach we follow with some modifications. It should also be noted that free logic could be implemented with exactly one undefined value (Benzmüller and Scott have also shown that before [5]). Here we decided to go without this additional requirement (of having one undefined value) and to focus more on the "existence" part of the category theory without carrying about "non-existing" area.

Shallow Semantical Embedding. In order to reason formally and interactively within free logics without building a new theorem prover from scratch, a translation of logics is necessary. In Isabelle/HOL one can implement alike using a shallow semantical embedding (SSE), which is based on logic translation approaches as discussed by Gabbay, Nonnengart, Ohlbach and de Rijke [11,25] for translating e.g. propositional modal logics to first-order logic. Exploiting the expressivity and compositionality of the simply typed λ-calculus in HOL, the SSE approach encodes such logic translations directly in HOL itself, which makes external translation mechanisms superfluous. This HOL-internal translation approach has been successfully extended for various quantified non-classicals logics and applied, under the name *universal meta-logical reasoning* [7], amongst others, to encode free first-order logic [5] in Isabelle/HOL. This approach was then further extended to embed FHOL in HOL [18] which, in this paper, we will rely on to implement our higher-level categorical constructions.

In SSE, the semantics of the language of interest, e.g. (positive) FHOL[1] is mapped to the corresponding syntax constructs of the target language. It may be viewed as a translation between the logics, where only semantical differences are targeted, for example, these could be the existential features of free semantics. The SSE approach showed itself as a readily available way for implementing the translation of a variety of nonclassical logics. It also enables the use of automation from the target system which is not as well supported with a deep semantical embedding.

A shallow semantic embedding is to be contrasted with a deep semantic embedding, in which the syntax of the target language is represented using an inductive data structure (e.g., following the BNF of the language) and the semantics of a formula is evaluated by recursively traversing the data structure. Shallow semantic embeddings, by contrast, define the syntactic elements of the target logic while reusing as much of the infrastructure of the meta-logic as possible; cf. also [14]. In particular, the degree of proof automation that can be achieved is much better in the case of shallow semantic embeddings, since e.g. inductive proofs on the structure of the embedded logic are omitted.

Formalization in Isabelle/HOL. Concretely, we represent the domain of objects $\mathcal{D}$ through a type α in Isabelle/HOL. The notion of existence is then given through a predicate $\mathsf{E} : \alpha \to$ bool. Therefore, every function will be total when viewed on the level of Isabelle terms. However, from the free logic perspective non-partial maps can still be observed as such since they are modelled as functions that map some objects to "non-existent" objects outside E.

At the level of free logic, one can immediately define several notions of equality, which are used in the definition of categories and reappear in the course of the development of the formalizations.

Definition 1 (Equalities with Existence).   *Given $x, y \in D$ define three notions of equality as follows:*

---

[1] Positive FHOL refers to a semantics for FHOL where formulas built from non-existing objects are allowed to be true [18].

1. *We write $x \simeq y$ if and only if $x = y \wedge \mathsf{E}x \wedge \mathsf{E}y$ (Existing Identity).*
2. *We also write $x \cong y$ if and only if $(\mathsf{E}x \vee \mathsf{E}y) \longrightarrow x = y$ (Kleene Equality).*
3. *Finally, we write $x \geq y$ precisely when $\mathsf{E}x \longrightarrow x = y$ (Directed equality).*

2.2 Formalization of Axiomatic Category Theory

In Isabelle/HOL, concepts from category theory have been formalized as early as 2005 [26]. The original formalization could be improved and extended significantly as indicated by subsequent research [13,21,30].

In addition to these, Benzmüller and Scott presented an alternative approach for formalizing category theory in Isabelle/HOL [6], which is based on an axiom system in free logic originally proposed by Scott [29]. This work models on one-sorted categories, i.e., it only refers to morphisms without mentioning objects. This approach was first expanded upon by Tiemens who defined inverse categories in order to generalize so-called modeloids [31].

Categories. Our formalization of categories follows the approach by Benzmüller and Scott [6] with slight modifications[2]. Firstly, when declaring the categorical notions of domain, codomain and composition, polymorphic types are employed which allow the use of higher-level constructions later. Secondly, an additional axiom is added that states the existence of a "non-existent object". This means that $\mathcal{D}$ is required to be a strict superset of E which is advantageous in the definition of certain concepts as it enables referring to an explicit non-existent element. On the implementation side, we represent categories through an Isabelle locale.

Functors. Functors are the morphisms between categories. The next definition is slightly adapted from Freyd and Scedrov's textbook [10]:[3]

Definition 2 (Functor). *A functor $\mathbf{F}$ between two categories $\mathcal{C}$ and $\mathcal{D}$ is a function $\mathbf{F} : \mathcal{C} \longrightarrow \mathcal{D}$ which satisfies the following axioms: (1) $\mathsf{E}x \longrightarrow \mathsf{E}(F(x))$, (2) $\neg \mathsf{E}x \longrightarrow \neg \mathsf{E}(F(x))$, (3) $\mathbf{F}(dom_{\mathcal{C}}(x)) \cong dom_{\mathcal{D}}(\mathbf{F}(x))$, (4) $\mathbf{F}(cod_{\mathcal{C}}(x)) \cong cod_{\mathcal{D}}(\mathbf{F}(x))$, (5) $\mathbf{F}(x \cdot_{\mathcal{C}} y) \geq \mathbf{F}(x) \cdot_{\mathcal{D}} \mathbf{F}(y)$.*

Natural Transformations. Morphisms between functors are called natural transformations. There can be two different formulations, resp. formalizations, of this notion, and both are used in our work. The first definition is taken from [23] (the one which is directly based on the idea of one-sorted categories and is heavily

---

[2] It should be noted that all categories considered in this paper are one-sorted categories and, therefore, all free variables appearing in the definitions refer to "morphisms", although, they might be seen as "objects" in a usual sense when they satisfy specific (identity) predicates.

[3] The first and second axioms result from the totality of functions in Isabelle/HOL and are used for the separation of existing and non-existing morphisms. This part of the paper, where we have to deal with the proper preservation of existence, has been one of the main difficulties in the subsequent formulation of the concepts.

exploited in this formalization) and modified according to the equalities that were introduced earlier:

Definition 3 (Natural Transformation). *A natural transformation η between the functors* $\mathbf{F}\colon \mathcal{C} \longrightarrow \mathcal{D}$ *and* $\mathbf{G}\colon \mathcal{C} \longrightarrow \mathcal{D}$ *is a function* $\eta : \mathcal{C} \longrightarrow \mathcal{D}$ *such that: (1)* $\mathbf{E}x \longrightarrow \mathbf{E}(\eta(x))$, *(2)* $\neg \mathbf{E}x \longrightarrow \neg\mathbf{E}(\eta(x))$, *(3)* $dom_{\mathcal{D}}(\eta(x)) \cong dom_{\mathcal{D}}(\mathbf{F}(x))$, *(4)* $cod_{\mathcal{D}}(\eta(x)) \cong cod_{\mathcal{D}}(\mathbf{F}(x))$, *(5)* $\mathbf{E}x \cdot y \longrightarrow \eta(x) \cdot_{\mathcal{D}} \mathbf{F}(y) \simeq \mathbf{G}(x) \cdot_{\mathcal{D}} \eta(y)$.

The monoidal category characterization is partly based on the notion of *inverse natural transformation*, which is more naturally described with the following second definition:

Definition 4 (Natural Transformation through Identities). *A natural transformation* $\eta : \mathbf{F} \Rightarrow \mathbf{G}$ *between the functors* $\mathbf{F}\colon \mathcal{C} \longrightarrow \mathcal{D}$ *and* $\mathbf{G}\colon \mathcal{C} \longrightarrow \mathcal{D}$ *assigns to every object A a morphism* $\eta(A) : \mathbf{F}(A) \longrightarrow \mathbf{G}(A)$, *such that for any morphism* $x : A \longrightarrow B$ *in* $\mathcal{C}$ $\mathbf{G}(x) \cdot_{\mathcal{D}} \eta(dom_{\mathcal{C}}(x)) \cong \eta(cod_{\mathcal{C}}(x)) \cdot_{\mathcal{D}} \mathbf{F}(x)$.

This second definition can be (and was) extended to the former via a specification of how this function operates in the more general case for all morphisms, i.e. for $x : A \longrightarrow B$ we have $\eta(x) = \mathbf{G}(x) \cdot_{\mathcal{D}} \eta(dom_{\mathcal{C}}(x))$. Starting with these definitions we proceed further to define *natural isomorphisms* and *inverse natural transformations*. The later concept might be an example of a module system advantage as it is easily defined as a locale built on top of the natural isomorphism locale with the specification of the inverse mapping. Invoking Isabelle's `unfold_locales` method during proving then allows to split the conditions into simpler parts.

3   Formalization of Elementary Topoi

In order to perform the intended meta-logical investigations it is necessary to define additional structures on top of categories. In particular, we formalize notions like categories with binary (co)products, exponential categories and cartesian closed categories. Our implementation makes heavy use of Isabelle's locales that allow to elegantly model the layered character of these definitions. To validate the correctness of the implementation we also formalize certain examples including the category of categories and the category of sets. The Isabelle code of all concepts that will be presented in this section can be found in a gitlab repository.[4] Our formalization of elementary topoi generally follows the book "Elementary categories, elementary topoi" by Colin McLarty [19].

Formalization of Elementary Notions. To build up the necessary constructions, we first formalize various elementary structures that can be defined within a category. This includes initial and final objects, (co)products, equalizers, a generic implementation of limits, monomorphisms and epimorphisms, and pullbacks.

---

[4] https://permalink.jonasbayer.de/bachelorthesis.

Not only do we define these notions, but we also formalize the elementary equivalences and relations between them. Each of these categorical structures received their own Isabelle theory in order to increase clarity, with definitions made in a multi-layered style and custom notation introduced for ease of use.

As an example, consider the beginning of the theory on pullbacks shown in Fig. 1. There, we first introduce the preliminary notions of is_corner and is_pullback before defining pullback diagrams. The latter is given in custom syntax that allows a presentation in diagram format. Although such syntax can become cluttered during proving and therefore is not the most useful representation in that context, it still allows for a very readable presentation of results within the theorem prover. This approach is continued throughout the formalization, further examples include product diagrams or even commutative diagrams with multiple squares.

```
definition is_corner :: "'a ⇒ 'a ⇒ bool" where
  "is_corner f g = cod f ≃ cod g"

definition is_pullback :: "'a ⇒ 'a ⇒ 'a ⇒ 'a ⇒ bool" where
  "is_pullback f g p1 p2 ≡ (f · p1 ≃ g · p2
       ∧ (∀h k. f·h ≃ g·k ⟶ (∃!u. p1 · u ≃ h ∧ p2 · u ≃ k)))"

text ‹cf. the Picture on page 41 of McLarty's book ›
abbreviation is_pullback_diagram :: "'a ⇒ 'a ⇒ 'a ⇒ 'a ⇒ bool"
("is'_pullback'_diagram // □ −_→ □ // _↓  ↓_ // □ −_→ □"
   [120, 120, 120, 120] 120) where
  "is_pullback_diagram □ −p2→ □
                    p1↓          ↓g
                    □ − f→ □
     ≡ is_pullback f g p1 p2"
```

Fig. 1. The implementation of pullbacks in Isabelle

Next to these constructions, we also give an implementation of several basic categories. Most notably, this includes the category of sets, the category of categories and the poset category. All these examples are formalized following the same scheme of first defining a custom type which will correspond to the type α in the category definition. Consequently, the existence predicate E followed by definitions for (co)domain and composition can be declared. In all three cases, the instance proof can essentially be handled by Isabelle's automatic tools. When using Isabelle2021 (February 2021), which is the version this development started with, occasional help is only necessary for proving associativity of composition. In Isabelle2022 even this part can be tackled by automated tools within less than 5 s when employed on an average personal computer.

Categories with Additional Structure. Refering back to the elementary structures defined previously, we implement categories that have additional structures. We start with categories that have binary products and/or binary coproducts. To validate these definitions, it is also formalized that the poset category has binary products and coproducts when the poset is a lattice. In this case, products correspond to meets and coproducts correspond to joins.

Having defined binary products one can continue to declare exponential objects and exponential evaluation maps in a category which we collect into an Isabelle record. Exponentials are then used to specify cartesian closed categories after having defined cartesian categories. For the precise mathematical definitions, we refer the reader to McLarty [19] whose presentation we follow closely.

Formalization of Topoi. With all these preliminary notions at hand, the definition of a topos can finally be formalized (Fig. 2):

```
locale topos = cartesian_closed_category +
    fixes subobjectClassifier :: "'a" ("Ω") and
          true :: "'a" ("t")
    assumes
          trueMap: "t:1→Ω" and
          toposProperty: "is_monic s ⟶
          (∃!χ. χ:dom s→Ω ∧ is_pullback_diagram □ −!1 (dom s)→ □
                                                        s↓              ↓t
                                                        □      − χ→     □ )"
```

Fig. 2. The implementation of an elementary topos in Isabelle

A topos is a special case of a cartesian closed category that also has a so-called subobject classifier and a designated object t representing the boolean value true. Here we make use of the aforementioned custom syntax to present the pullback diagram in a very intuitive form. Moreover, we formalize that in a topos all monomorphisms are equalizers, which does not hold in arbitrary categories.

To conclude, the formalization we give provides a basis for further meta-logical investigations related to category theory. In particular, an interesting continuation of this work would be the implementation of the internal language of an elementary topos including topos axioms.

4   Formalization of the Categorical Model of IMLL

Another direction that has been explored in the proposed approach to categorical formalizations is the one laying down a translation layer between the HOL/FHOL and *intuitionistic multiplicative linear logic* (IMLL) semantics. The motivation behind the IMLL formalization (or its semantics, to be more precise) was to investigate practical capabilities of Isabelle/HOL in the field of meta-logical questions, i.e., to derive tools that would formulate IMLL theorems and proofs through its encoded semantical language that talk about morphisms. It is important to emphasize the word "practical" in this context, since it is of course generally possible to model a wide range of constructions with the help of a proof assistant such as Isabelle/HOL. However, it is not a priori clear if this can be done with a reasonable effort with respect to the logic "translations" as exploited in our SSE approach. In this paper we have chosen (a fragment of) linear logic as our object of study, since it has a plethora of applications in various domains. The Isabelle implementation and certification of all constructions presented in this section (which make use of the "locales" feature of Isabelle/HOL) can be found in a GitHub repository.[5]

4.1   IMLL and Its Categorical Model

Linear Logic (LL) was proposed by Girard in 1987 [12] as a refinement of classical as well as intuitionistic logic. Within LL the two different notions of conjunction and disjunction are introduced together, i.e., *multiplicative* and *additive* types of connectives. They behave distinctly in derivations (through inference rules), but their intrinsic difference can be revealed with a computational interpretation of proofs [2]. Within this work we deal with a particular fragment of LL, which is *intuitionistic multiplicative linear logic* (IMLL), by restricting the syntax and adapting inference rules.

The categorical denotational model of IMLL is built around the notion of a *monoidal category*.[6] The key part of a semantical translation is a function $[\![\cdot]\!]$ that assigns some categorical construct to a proof-theoretical piece. Moreover, the construction of categories using only one sort of objects, i.e., morphisms, determines our main interest in modeling proofs (rather than formulas) with categorical denotational semantics. In order to briefly present the general idea, one assigns a morphism $f : [\![A]\!] \longrightarrow [\![B]\!]$ to a proof of a sequent $A \vdash B$.[7] Here, $[\![A]\!]$ means an identity morphism. The final goal within this part of the work is to translate all the inference rules we have in IMLL to theorems about morphisms in a special category, i.e., *symmetrical monoidal closed category* (SMCC), and to show practical feasibility of these meta-logical translations.

4.2   Isabelle/HOL Formalization of the IMLL Categorical Model

To fully represent IMLL connectives, such as linear intuitionistic implication and multiplicative conjunction, we need to incorporate their corresponding inference rules into our categorical setting. These rules describe the connectives' behavior as well as their structural and non-logical inference rules. To do so, we must make use of monoidal categories, braidings and symmetries, and closed structures.

---

[5] https://github.com/HaskDev0/Linear-Logic-Cat-semantics.

[6] For more information, see Mellies [20]. It provides a thorough description of the topic as well as lists all the inference rules for IMLL that are formalized and proved within our framework.

[7] All the translations of proofs are carried out under proof-theoretic normalization invariance.

The shift towards monoidal categories for modeling IMLL semantics is crucial due to the necessity to move away from diagonal maps in categories which allow the duplication of the objects, or, equivalently, resources [1].[8] Moreover, the *locales* environments of Isabelle/HOL are used to develop formalizations of translated IMLL concepts for their convenience of presentation and of working with algebraic theories.

Definition 5 (Monoidal Category). *A monoidal category $\mathcal{C}$ is a category $\mathcal{C}$ equipped with: (1) a bifunctor $\otimes : \mathcal{C} \times \mathcal{C} \longrightarrow \mathcal{C}$, (2) a natural isomorphism[9] $\alpha_{A,B,C} : (A \otimes B) \otimes C \longrightarrow A \otimes (B \otimes C)$, (3) a special identity morphism, or object in our meaning, $\mathbf{e}$, which is a unit, and (4) two natural isomorphisms $\mathbf{e} \otimes A \longrightarrow A$ and $\rho_A : A \otimes \mathbf{e} \longrightarrow A$, which satisfy the triangular identity $(\mathcal{C}.Id\ A) \wedge (\mathcal{C}.Id\ B) \longrightarrow (A \otimes \lambda_B) \cdot \alpha_{A,\mathbf{e},B} \simeq \rho_A \otimes B$ and the pentagonal identity $(\mathcal{C}.Id\ A) \wedge (\mathcal{C}.Id\ B) \wedge (\mathcal{C}.Id\ C) \wedge (\mathcal{C}.Id\ D) \longrightarrow (A \otimes \alpha_{B,C,D}) \cdot (\alpha_{A,B \otimes C,D} \cdot \alpha_{A,B,C} \otimes D) \simeq \alpha_{A,B,C \otimes D} \cdot \alpha_{A \otimes B,C,D}.$[10]*

Here it is essential to understand that the natural isomorphism α acts between functors $(\bullet \otimes \bullet) \otimes \bullet : \mathcal{C} \times \mathcal{C} \times \mathcal{C} \longrightarrow \mathcal{C}$ and $\bullet \otimes (\bullet \otimes \bullet) : \mathcal{C} \times \mathcal{C} \times \mathcal{C} \longrightarrow \mathcal{C}$ of domain $\mathcal{C} \times \mathcal{C} \times \mathcal{C}$ and codomains $\mathcal{C}$. There exist similar interpretations for the other two isomorphisms occurring in the definition.

Definition 6 (Braided Monoidal Category). *A braided monoidal category is a monoidal category $\mathcal{C}$ equipped with a braiding, i.e. a natural isomorphism $\gamma_{A,B} : A \otimes B \longrightarrow B \otimes A$, making two hexagonal axioms hold: (1) $(\mathcal{C}.Id\ A) \wedge (\mathcal{C}.Id\ B) \wedge (\mathcal{C}.Id\ C) \longrightarrow \alpha_{B,C,A} \cdot (\gamma_{A,B \otimes C} \cdot \alpha_{A,B,C}) \simeq (B \otimes \gamma_{A,C}) \cdot (\alpha_{B,A,C} \cdot (\gamma_{A,B} \otimes C))$, and (2) $(\mathcal{C}.Id\ A) \wedge (\mathcal{C}.Id\ B) \wedge (\mathcal{C}.Id\ C) \longrightarrow \alpha_{C,A,B}^{-1} \cdot (\gamma_{A \otimes B,C} \cdot \alpha_{A,B,C}^{-1}) \simeq (\gamma_{A,C} \otimes B) \cdot (\alpha_{A,C,B}^{-1} \cdot (A \otimes \gamma_{B,C})).$*

Definition 7 (Symmetric Monoidal Category). *A symmetric monoidal category is a braided monoidal category $\mathcal{C}$, whose braiding is a symmetry, i.e. $(\mathcal{C}.Id\ A) \wedge (\mathcal{C}.Id\ B) \longrightarrow \gamma_{A,B} \simeq \gamma_{B,A}^{-1}.$*

These notions already allow one to reason about the multiplicative conjunction and exchange inference rules in IMLL, and the final step is to properly describe *closed structures*. There are three equivalent definitions of these terms, and the way to define one chooses depends on the goals and the frame one works in due to the ease of use in some cases. We will give two variations here and we will provide some comments on their connection. The first one was chosen since it will directly be used in further developments of IMLL semantics, and the second one will deliver a clearer view of the notion and the understanding of why we introduced an evaluation morphism *eval* later (see Definition 10) to describe the translation of formulas to categorical constructs.

---

[8] The definitions that are needed to describe the model of IMLL are taken from Mellies [20] and adopted to our framework.

[9] A family of natural isomorphisms.

[10] $\mathcal{C}.Id$ denotes an identity morphism predicate.

Definition 8 (Left Closed Monoidal Category). *A left monoidal closed category is a monoidal category $\mathcal{C}$ endowed with a left closed structure, i.e. with a data of: (1) a bifunctor $-\!\!\circ: \mathcal{C}^{op} \times \mathcal{C} \longrightarrow \mathcal{C}$, and (2) a bijection $\mathcal{C}(A \otimes B, C) \cong_b \mathcal{C}(B, A \multimap C)$, which is natural in A, B and C.*[11]

The second point in the definition should be understood as the natural transformation between the functors $\mathcal{C}(\_ \otimes_{ex} \_, \_)$ and $\mathcal{C}(\_, \_ \multimap \_)$ which act between categories $\mathcal{C}^{op} \times \mathcal{C}^{op} \times \mathcal{C}$ and *Set*. Therefore, the encoding of *Hom*-functors should have been encoded first, which would have added additional layer of complexity. Instead, we decided to translate it to the language of sets directly with the help of two function Φ and Ψ acting as inverses of each other and having more inputs than just one, namely, the morphism itself. The functions, thus, have the following types:

$$\Phi::'a \Rightarrow' a \Rightarrow' a \Rightarrow' a \text{ and } \Psi::'a \Rightarrow' a \Rightarrow' a \Rightarrow' a.$$

The reason we are using two functions describing the bijection lies in the fact that in the Isabelle/HOL system functions are total, but in our framework we are working with the so-called existent morphisms which constitute only a subdomain of some type. Moreover, two additional arguments need to be specified when we want to apply the mentioned bijection, in order to know the exact structure of the domain of the input morphism for the bijection going right in the Definition 8 (2) and the same for the codomain of the input morphism for the bijection going left. In other words, given some morphism f, and a necessity to check whether the domain of f is exactly $A \otimes B$, we cannot merely apply the *dom* function to find the hidden parts. Therefore, this additional information recovers the missing data. The same reasoning clarifies the equivalent features of Ψ. This encoding process also reveals the actual compressed information that is needed to talk about IMLL semantical constructs within Isabelle/HOL. Therefore, formalization of this definition in Isabelle/HOL looks as follows:

Definition 9 (Left Closed Monoidal Category in Isabelle/HOL). *A left monoidal closed category is a monoidal category $\mathcal{C}$ endowed with a bifunctor $-\!\!\circ: \mathcal{C}^{op} \times \mathcal{C} \longrightarrow \mathcal{C}$ and functions Φ and Ψ, that satisfy:*
(1) $(f : A \otimes B \to C) \wedge (\mathcal{C}.IdEx\ A) \wedge (\mathcal{C}.IdEx\ B) \longrightarrow \Phi(A, B, f) : B \to (A \multimap C)$,
(2) $(g : B \to A \multimap C) \wedge (\mathcal{C}.IdEx\ A) \wedge (\mathcal{C}.IdEx\ B) \longrightarrow \Psi(A, C, g) : A \otimes B \to C$,
(3) $(f : A \otimes B \to C) \wedge (\mathcal{C}.IdEx\ A) \wedge (\mathcal{C}.IdEx\ B) \longrightarrow \Psi(A, C, \Phi(A, B, f)) \simeq f$,
(4) $(g : B \to A \multimap C) \wedge (\mathcal{C}.IdEx\ A) \wedge (\mathcal{C}.IdEx\ B) \longrightarrow \Phi(A, B, \Psi(A, C, g)) \simeq g$,
   and the requirement for Ψ for being natural in f:
(5) $(f : A \otimes B \to C) \wedge (\mathcal{C}.IdEx\ A) \wedge (\mathcal{C}.IdEx\ B) \wedge (cod\ x = A) \wedge (cod\ y = B) \wedge$
   $(dom\ z = C) \longrightarrow \Phi(dom\ x, dom\ y, z \cdot (f \cdot (x \otimes y))) \simeq (z \multimap y) \cdot (\Phi(A, B, f) \cdot y).$

We have proved (in our formalization) that this function Ψ is a natural transformation. As was pointed out above, the other definition of *left closed structure* is the following:

---

[11] The sign $\cong_b$ here means the bijection between the sets and we introduced it in order to distinguish it from the Kleene duality.

Definition 10 (Left Closed Structure). *A left closed structure in a monoidal category* $\mathcal{C}$ *is composed of: (1) an identity morphism* $A \multimap B$, *and (2) a left evaluation morphism* $eval_{A,B} : A \otimes (A \multimap B) \longrightarrow B$, *for every identity morphisms* A *and* B. *The* $eval_{A,B}$ *morphism satisfies the following universal property:* $\forall f : A \otimes X \longrightarrow B.(\exists! h : X \longrightarrow A \multimap B) \wedge (f \simeq eval_{A,B} \cdot (A \otimes h))$.[12]

The evaluation morphism *eval* is a translation of the elimination rule for $\multimap$ if the proof system is designed with it instead of the *left* rule for $\multimap$. The former definition entails the latter for a left closed structure (this is formalized as a theorem in Isabelle/HOL). In the same way, with slight modifications, one may define the *right closed structure*.

At this point we are able to describe the categorical model of IMLL.

Definition 11 (Symmetric Monoidal Closed Category). *A symmetric monoidal closed category (SMCC) is a monoidal category* $\mathcal{C}$ *equipped with a symmetry* γ *and a left closed structure* $\multimap$.

We proved in our formalization that in any such monoidal category there is also a *right closed structure* as well, which confirms theoretical expectations. To demonstrate this, define the functions $\bullet \multimap_r \bullet = \bullet \multimap \bullet$, $\Phi_r(f) = \Phi(f \cdot \gamma_{A,B})$ and $\Psi_r(g) = \Psi(g) \cdot \gamma_{B,A}$ for morphisms $f : B \otimes A \longrightarrow C$ and $g : B \longrightarrow A \multimap C$, which would exhibit the desired properties.[13] Provided that we described through locales tensor product T, left closed structure Impl, natural isomorphisms α, μ, ρ, natural isomorphisms between *Hom*-functors via Φ, Ψ and a symmetry γ, the corresponding encoding of a SMCC inside Isabelle/HOL would look as in Fig. 3:

At this point we are ready to give the formalization of IMLL formulas in SMCC. For that, we start with the discussion of the well-known principle in intuitionistic logic, which in particular holds in IMLL, that every formula A implies its double negation $\neg\neg A$. For this purpose there should be some formula $\perp$, which helps to define the negation of a formula as $A \multimap \perp$ [20]. Thus, the mentioned principle translates to the fact in SMCC as:

Proposition 1 (Existence of Double Negation Morphism). *There is always a morphism* $\delta_A : A \longrightarrow (A \multimap \perp) \multimap \perp$ *for every identity* A *in any SMCC.*

Note that this is not a new result, but a proposition that we used to test our encoding with and which we certified within the Isabelle/HOL SSE framework.

It is worth mentioning that in a sequent style proof there is no difference how we derive the formula $(A_2 \multimap \perp) \multimap \perp$ given a formula A_1 and a derivation π of $A_1 \vdash A_2$. In other words, we could have derived to it via double negating A_1 and then applying the derivation π translated for double negation, or we double negate A_2. In SMCC this fact corresponds to:

---

[12] Here, we exploited a new abbreviation $\exists! h.P(h)$ for unique existence, which means $\exists h.(P(h) \wedge (\forall t.P(t) \rightarrow t = h))$.

[13] That is exactly the place where we use in the encoding those additional first two parameters of Φ and Ψ to specify the morphisms.

```
locale SymmetricMonClosedCat =
LM: LeftClosedMonCatBifunctor domain codomain
        composition nonex T α μ ϱ e Impl Φ Ψ +
Sym: Symmetry domain codomain composition nonex T α γ
for
    domain::"'a⇒'a" ("dom _") and
    codomain::"'a⇒'a" ("cod _") and
    composition::"'a⇒'a⇒'a" (infix "·" 110) and
    nonex :: "'a" ("*") and
    T :: "'a * 'a ⇒ 'a" and
    α :: "'a * 'a * 'a ⇒ 'a" and
    μ :: "'a ⇒ 'a" and
    ϱ :: "'a ⇒ 'a" and
    e :: "'a" and
    γ :: "'a * 'a ⇒ 'a" and
    Impl :: "'a * 'a ⇒ 'a" and
    Φ :: "'a ⇒ 'a ⇒ 'a ⇒ 'a" and
    Ψ :: "'a ⇒ 'a ⇒ 'a ⇒ 'a" +
fixes
    FalseM :: "'a" ("⊥m")
assumes
    FM: "LM.A.IdEx (⊥m)"
```

Fig. 3. The implementation of a symmetric monoidal closed category

Proposition 2 (Double Negation as a Natural Isomorphism). *In every SMCC the constructed morphism δ_A is, in fact, a natural transformation.*

Propositions 1, 2 already quite firmly indicate the possibility of applying the chosen categorical axiomatization and formalization approach to logical questions expressed in a denotational (categorical) framework. As long as everything above is formalized in Isabelle/HOL, it is now possible to translate all the inference rules of IMLL as theorems about the morphisms in SMCC. For this step one has to be slightly creative in terms of finding the most appropriate translations, i.e., relying only on automated tools for this step would be a very naive way, leading to an explosion of "search space", while human interference with "reasonable" assumptions and ideas solves the problem of finding suitable morphisms that represent specific IMLL sequents. The task was successfully accomplished, as can be seen in the full encoding. This provides some evidence for the practical feasibility of using readily available higher-order theorem provers to support even very abstract and complex meta-logical investigations for IMLL within a categorical language suitably encoded in free logic embedded in HOL.

5   Conclusions

This article has outlined an option for, and the potential of, formalizing category theory in higher-order logic to investigate meta-logical questions. The

Isabelle/HOL proof assistant was used to formalize the notion of elementary topoi and to subsequently develop and formalize symmetrical monoidal closed categories expressing the denotational semantical model of intuitionistic multiplicative linear logic. This was carried out on the basis of (layered) shallow semantical embeddings, exploiting at the base layer a shallow semantical embedding of positive free higher-order logic in classical higher-order logic.

In addition to these meta-logical investigations, we outline with our work a possible way of building-up a category theory library in Isabelle to support reuse and application. We optimized our formalization to closely resemble mathematical notation and provided examples of how to use our formalized concepts. We hope that this will facilitate the future use of category theoretical notions in formalizations beyond just category theory itself.

References

1. Abramsky, S., Tzevelekos, N.: Introduction to categories and categorical logic. In: Coecke, B. (ed.) New Structures for Physics, pp. 3–94. Springer, Heidelberg (2011). https://doi.org/10.1007/978-3-642-12821-9_1
2. Beffara, E.: Introduction to linear logic, August 2013. https://hal.archives-ouvertes.fr/cel-01144229, lecture
3. Benzmüller, C., Andrews, P.: Church's type theory. In: Zalta, E.N. (ed.) The Stanford Encyclopedia of Philosophy, Summer 2019 edn., pp. 1–62 (in pdf version). Metaphysics Research Lab, Stanford University (2019). https://plato.stanford.edu/entries/type-theory-church/
4. Benzmüller, C., Parent, X., van der Torre, L.: Designing normative theories for ethical and legal reasoning: LogiKEy framework, methodology, and tool support. Artif. Intell. **287**, 103348 (2020). https://doi.org/10.1016/j.artint.2020.103348
5. Benzmüller, C., Scott, D.: Automating free logic in Isabelle/HOL. In: Greuel, G.-M., Koch, T., Paule, P., Sommese, A. (eds.) ICMS 2016. LNCS, vol. 9725, pp. 43–50. Springer, Cham (2016). https://doi.org/10.1007/978-3-319-42432-3_6
6. Benzmüller, C., Scott, D.S.: Automating free logic in HOL, with an experimental application in category theory. J. Autom. Reason. **64**(1), 53–72 (2020). https://doi.org/10.1007/s10817-018-09507-7
7. Benzmüller, C.: Universal (meta-)logical reasoning: recent successes. Sci. Comput. Program. **172**, 48–62 (2019). https://doi.org/10.1016/j.scico.2018.10.008
8. Ernst, M.: Category theory and foundations. In: Categories for the Working Philosopher, pp. 69–89. Oxford University Press (2017). https://doi.org/10.1093/oso/9780198748991.003.0005
9. Farmer, W.M.: A partial functions version of church's simple theory of types. J. Symb. Logic **55**(3), 1269–1291 (1990). https://www.jstor.org/stable/2274487
10. Freyd, P., Scedrov, A.: Categories, Allegories, North-Holland Mathematical Library, vol. 39. Elsevier Science (1990). https://books.google.de/books?id=fCSJRegkKdoC
11. Gabbay, D.M.: Introduction to labelled deductive systems. In: Gabbay, D.M., Guenthner, F. (eds.) Handbook of Philosophical Logic, vol. 17, pp. 179–266. Springer, Dordrecht (2014). https://doi.org/10.1007/978-94-007-6600-6_3
12. Girard, J.Y.: Linear logic. Theoret. Comput. Sci. **50**(1), 1–101 (1987). https://doi.org/10.1016/0304-3975(87)90045-4

13. Katovsky, A.: Category theory. Arch. Formal Proofs 2010 (2010)
14. Kirchner, D., Benzmüller, C., Zalta, E.N.: Computer science and metaphysics: a cross-fertilization. Open Philos. **2**(1), 230–251 (2019). https://doi.org/10.1515/opphil-2019-0015
15. MacLane, S.: Categories for the Working Mathematician. Graduate Texts in Mathematics, vol. 5. Springer, New York (1971)
16. Maddy, P.: Set-theoretic foundations. Contemp. Math. **690**, 289–322 (2017)
17. Maddy, P.: What do we want a foundation to do? In: Centrone, S., Kant, D., Sarikaya, D. (eds.) Reflections on the Foundations of Mathematics. SL, vol. 407, pp. 293–311. Springer, Cham (2019). https://doi.org/10.1007/978-3-030-15655-8_13
18. Makarenko, I., Benzmüller, C.: Positive free higher-order logic and its automation via a semantical embedding. In: Schmid, U., Klügl, F., Wolter, D. (eds.) KI 2020. LNCS (LNAI), vol. 12325, pp. 116–131. Springer, Cham (2020). https://doi.org/10.1007/978-3-030-58285-2_9
19. McLarty, C.: Elementary Categories. Elementary Toposes. Clarendon Press, New York (1992)
20. Melliès, P.A.: Categorical semantics of linear logic, pp. 1–196. No. 27 in Panoramas et Synthèses, Société Mathématique de France (2009)
21. Milehins, M.: Category theory for ZFC in HOL I: Foundations: Design patterns, set theory, digraphs, semicategories. Archive of Formal Proofs, September 2021. https://isa-afp.org/entries/CZH_Foundations.html, Formal proof development
22. Morscher, E., Simons, P.: Free logic: a fifty-year past and an open future. In: Morscher, E., Hieke, A. (eds.) New Essays in Free Logic. In Honour of Karel Lambert, pp. 1–34. Springer, Dordrecht (2001). https://doi.org/10.1007/978-94-015-9761-6_1
23. nLab authors: single-sorted definition of a category, April 2021. https://ncatlab.org/nlab/show/single-sorted+definition+of+a+category
24. Nolt, J.: Free logic. In: Zalta, E.N. (ed.) The Stanford Encyclopedia of Philosophy, Winter 2020 edn. Metaphysics Research Lab, Stanford University (2020)
25. Ohlbach, H.J., Nonnengart, A., de Rijke, M., Gabbay, D.M.: Encoding two-valued nonclassical logics in classical logic. In: Robinson, J.A., Voronkov, A. (eds.) Handbook of Automated Reasoning (in 2 volumes), pp. 1403–1486. Elsevier and MIT Press (2001). https://doi.org/10.1016/b978-044450813-3/50023-0
26. O'Keefe, G.: Category theory to yoneda's lemma. Archive of Formal Proofs, April 2005. https://isa-afp.org/entries/Category.html, Formal proof development
27. Schütte, K.: Syntactical and semantical properties of simple type theory. J. Symb. Logic **25**(4), 305–326 (1960). https://www.jstor.org/stable/2963525
28. Scott, D.: Existence and description in formal logic. In: Schoenman, R., Russell, B. (eds.) Philosopher of the Century, pp. 181–200. George Allen & Unwin, London (1967). Reprinted with additions. In: Lambert, K. (ed.) Philosophical Application of Free Logic, pp. 28–48. Oxford University Press (1991)
29. Scott, D.: Identity and existence in intuitionistic logic. In: Fourman, M., Mulvey, C., Scott, D. (eds.) Applications of Sheaves. LNM, vol. 753, pp. 660–696. Springer, Heidelberg (1979). https://doi.org/10.1007/BFb0061839
30. Stark, E.W.: Category theory with adjunctions and limits. Archive of Formal Proofs, June 2016. https://isa-afp.org/entries/Category3.html, Formal proof development
31. Tiemens, L., Scott, D.S., Benzmüller, C., Benda, M.: Computer-supported exploration of a categorical axiomatization of modeloids. In: Fahrenberg, U., Jipsen, P., Winter, M. (eds.) RAMiCS 2020. LNCS, vol. 12062, pp. 302–317. Springer, Cham (2020). https://doi.org/10.1007/978-3-030-43520-2_19

Learning Support Systems Based on Mathematical Knowledge Management

Marc Berges[1], Jonas Betzendahl[1], Abhishek Chugh[2],
Michael Kohlhase[1], Dominic Lohr[1], and Dennis Müller[1(✉)]

[1] Computer Science, FAU Erlangen Nürnberg, Erlangen, Germany
dennis.mueller@fau.de
[2] Sophize Foundation, Bangalore, India

Abstract. To cater to the increasingly diverse student bodies, higher education has to personalize education. In times of stagnant educational budgets and staffing problems, this can only be achieved via adaptive, interactive learning support services. In this paper we show how these can be generated by modeling the domain, the learner competencies, and the rhetoric and didactic relations among learning objects, re-using existing technologies and systems of mathematical knowledge management.

This paper uses $\mathcal{S}T_EX3$. The semantically annotated XHTML version of this paper is available at https://url.mathhub.info/CICM23ALEA

1 Introduction

STEM education in universities and high-schools faces the problem that *i*) the student population becomes more and more diverse – and thus we can less and less rely on a uniform educational background – and *ii*) students expect to be able to learn everything, anytime, anywhere, ideally on their mobile devices. Ideally, each student would have their personal, online teacher/tutor/mentor (we will use the shorthand "educator" and analogous for this in the following text), but this is not something the education system can provide due to funding and staffing constraints. Instead institutions of higher education are increasingly turning to online delivery of course materials and video lectures even though this is often ill-suited for coping with individual student needs.

In this paper we want to explore the possibility of automating – relevant abilities of – a personal educator as a possible solution to the situation described above using and critically profiting from methods and systems from mathematical knowledge management.

We contend that a good educator relies on and maintains four models (see Fig. 1) that inform the interactions with the educatee:

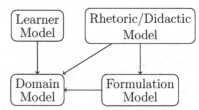

Fig. 1. Models for Teaching.

C. Dubois and M. Kerber (Eds.): CICM 2023, LNAI 14101, pp. 84–97, 2023.
https://doi.org/10.1007/978-3-031-42753-4_6

1. A fine-grained domain model that contains detailed knowledge about the concepts, objects, and their relations relevant to the domain of discourse,
2. a collection of ready-made "formulations"[1] of this knowledge – they are often called learning objects[2] – that can be assembled/adapted into a tutorial dialogue,
3. a didactic model that classifies the formulations wrt. their rhetoric role (where can they go into a structured text) and didactic potential (how can they change competencies) and how they are related to each other.
4. a learner model that estimates the educatee's competency distribution by monitoring their interaction with the learning objects and the educator.

Following [Ull08] we posit that constructing e.g. an educating dialogue is an online planning process assembling suitably adapted learning objects based on the competency predictions by the learner model. We further posit that this process must optimize the epistemic constraints from the domain model and the rhetoric/didactic constraints from the didactic model. We observe that the three models involved in the generation of educational materials profit from the structure of the domain model, which serves as the – enabling – foundation of the four models (see the arrows representing the "references/uses" relation in Fig. 1). Note that even though we cast such a dialogue as a directed interaction where knowledge flows from teacher to student, it applies to nearly all academic communication, only that the role of teacher/student can fluctuate in every dialogue turn.

Contribution. We present the ALEA system (Adaptive Learning Assistant), which is realized as an extension of the MMT system which supplies mathematical knowledge management functionality based on a domain model expressed as a MMT/OMDOCtheory graph. We show how a surprising variety of user-adaptive and interactive teaching materials with embedded learning support services can be realized from the information in the three remaining models and remark that the heavy lifting in all of this is provided by CICM technologies.

Overview. In Sect. 2 we evaluate how the 4-models idea from Fig. 1 contributes to the automated assembly of an educational dialogue. In Sect. 3 we present the architecture of the ALEA system which implements this approach. This is followed by an elaboration on the rhetoric/didactic model in Sect. 4. Finally, Sect. 5 concludes this paper, evaluates the approach and discusses ongoing and future work.

The design of the ALEA system shares/inherits a lot of the intuitions from the ActiveMath/LeActiveMath system [Mel+01] (∼2000–2010), which was

---

[1] Note that we use the concept of a "formulation of knowledge" very inclusively: it should cover any modality: textual representations – in any language – as well as images, and even – say – a ballet choreography of the concept of "spring".

[2] As a note of caution: while in the didactic literature a learning object is defined as *anything that is useful in the context of education*, for the purposes of the ALEA system we will understand learning object as semantically annotated formulation in the sense of footnote 1.

based on a very early version of OMDoc [Koh06], which turned into $\mathcal{S}$TEX and MMT/OMDOC over the last two decades. So the ALEA system and approach presented in this paper can be thought of as a successor of ActiveMath system based on more evolved mathematical knowledge management technology, but lacking the educational scope that massive EU grants bring about.

2   Assembling an Educational Dialogue

We will now evaluate the 4-models analysis introduced in the introduction via a Gedankenexperiment: can it be used to explain an educational dialogue – a key task to automate in the envisioned personalized learning environment? We will use this dialogue as a running example in the rest of the paper; a more complete version of the dialogue below is at https://courses.voll-ki.fau.de/exp/pp_dialogue_tour.

Say a learner using the system would like to know about the Pythagorean Theorem[3]. A dialogue with the system about that might look like the following:

> My records show that you are already familiar with triangles and angles. The Pythagorean Theorem concerns right triangles. Do you already feel comfortable with that topic?

Here, we assume that the learner model already indicates a sufficient familiarity with some of the prerequisites for the educational target, but it does not have any data on the learner's competency of right triangles, so the dialogue defers to the user's self-evaluation.

> I'm not sure...

> Okay. Let's find out! Please solve the following problem:

As the learner indicated uncertainty about their competency, the system opens a short tangent to evaluate it empirically by selecting one of the available problems that test this knowledge.

> In a right triangle, one of the angles at the longest side is 60°. What would that make the other angle on the longest side?

> 30°

> That is correct! Let's talk about the Pythagorean Theorem then.

The prerequisite is met, so the system moves on. At this point the learner model would also have been updated to include the demonstrated knowledge. If the learner had answered incorrectly, the system would refocus on understanding right triangles first. So it is time to move to the statement of the Pythagorean Theorem:

---

[3] We have chosen this example for general familiarity, its simplicity does not restrict the scope of the analysis.

Theorem (Pythagoras). In a right triangle, the square of the hypotenuse is equal to the sum of the squares of the other two sides. Often, this is expressed as the formula $a^2 + b^2 = c^2$.

Again, the learner model does not have an indication whether the learner knows about the proof, so it appeals to their self-assessment again.

Do you see why this is true?

No

No problem! There are multiple proofs of this theorem. Here is one of them:

Here we present a geometric proof of the theorem[4]. This learning object has been selected because it is annotated to be relevant to the current educational goal of understanding the Pythagorean Theorem.

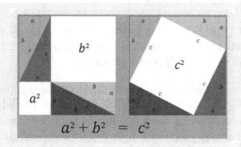

Did that help you understand?

Yes

It would also be possible to further differentiate what the educational goal of such a dialogue would be. In this example, we want the learner to gain a working understanding of the Pythagorean Theorem, but – to that end – also present them with materials showing why exactly it is true. In a different context or at a later date we might also want to insist they are able to recreate the steps of a proof. Ultimately, the system can make recommendations, but users have final say about what topics and what aspects thereof they choose to learn about.

Good. Let's put it to the test. Please solve the following problem:

In a right triangle, the hypotenuse is 5 units long. One of the shorter sides is 4 units long. Using the Pythagorean Theorem, calculate the length of the remaining side.

---

[4] In the interactive version of the dialogue, the diagram is actually an animation, which is much easier to understand for the learner. The diagram is licensed CC-BY, attribution William B. Faulk.

3 units

You're right! Seems like you understand the Pythagorean Theorem well enough now. What do you want to do next?

Here, the user asserts that they understand the theorem statement, so the system asks them to solve another problem (demonstrating that the student knows how to apply their asserted competence) that needs to be solved before it updates the learner model to include knowledge about the Pythagorean Theorem.

In conclusion, this dialogue shows us that all the material in the dialogue can be traced either to a dialogue template (that corresponds to the rhetorical/didactic model) or content from one of the other three models. In the following we will see how we can build on these ideas to realize a concrete learning assistant system.

3   The VoLL-KI ALeA System

In the VoLL-KI project (Von Lernenden Lernen mit KI – Learning from Learners with AI) we have instantiated the 4-models approach from Fig. 1 with concepts developed in the CICM and EdTech communities:

1. The domain model is realized as an MMT/OMDOCtheory graph,
2. the formulation model by the OMDoc/STEX document model,
3. the learner model as a function from the symbols in the theory graph into a six-dimensional probability distribution, keyed by a revised Bloom taxonomy! [AK09]. We use this to classify both a learner's competency and the objectives of learning objects with respect to a given subject matter along the cognitive dimensions remember, understandard, apply, analyze, evaluate and create.
4. the rhetoric/didactic model classifies learning objects and domain model concepts by the role they can play in a (to be generated) educational discourse; see Sect. 4 for details.

For the dialogue we will employ the active documents paradigm [Koh+11] (see Fig. 2) where the part of the content commonsis played by the domain model, that of the document commons by the formulation model from Fig. 1 and the active document player is implemented by the ALeA front-end with the help of the MMT system [MMT].

Concretely, this translates into the ALeA system architecture in Fig. 3:

1. The information from the domain-, formulation-, and rhetoric/didactic models and the knowledge management algorithms pertaining to them are combined into a learning object server (LOS; see Subsect. 3.1) that serves learning objects – both atomic ones like individual statements or problems and aggregated ones like guided tours (aggregated mini-courses that lead up to a particular topic).

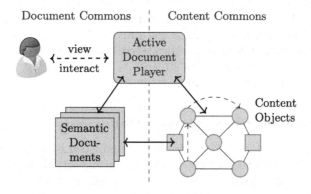

Fig. 2. The Active Documents Paradigm

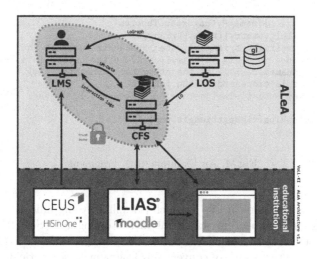

Fig. 3. The ALeA System Architecture

2. The course fragment server (CFS; see Subsect. 3.3) serves as the front-end to the ALEA application, it serves course fragments directly to the educatee, hosts all learning support services, and monitors all interactions. In a standalone version of ALEA, the CFS serves the course fragments directly to learners. Alternatively ALEA can be embedded into institutional learning management systems like Moodle or Ilias.
3. The learner model server (LMS; see Subsect. 3.2) encapsulates the learner model, it receives and logs interaction information from the CFS and informs the LOS about competency levels, needed for the learner-adapted learning object generation.

In the scope of the VoLL-KI project, the ALeAv system interfaces with the infrastructure of the participating universities. The CEUS system is a joint Bavarian data warehousing system that manages all curriculum, cohort, and eventually also exam grade data, and the CFS integrates into Moodle/Ilias learning management systems. All these systems can provide data about learners that can e.g. inform the learner model. But the system can also be used in a stand-alone fashion without these learner data streams.

We will now look at the components in detail.

3.1   The Learning Object Server (LOS)

Both the domain and formulation models are provided by sTeX document fragments [KM,KM22]. The symbols, modules, and imports therein constitute the theory graph of the domain model, whereas the individual definitions, examples, theorem statements and problems constitute the learning objects.

```
 1 \begin{sassertion}[name=Pythagorean Theorem]
 2   \importmodule[geometry]{right-triangle}
 3   In a \symname{right triangle}, the \symname{square} of the
 4   \symname{hypotenuse} is \symname{equal} to the \symref{plus}{sum}
 5   of the \symnames{square} of the other two \symnames{side}.
 6   Often, this is expressed as the formula
 7   $\definiens{\equal{\plus{\square \a, \square \b}, \square \c}}$.
 8
 9   \includegraphics{right_triangle.png}
10 \end{sassertion}
```

Fig. 4. An Example sTeX Fragment

Consider the fragment in Fig. 4, which is a (slightly simplified) version of the sTeX sources for the theorem statement in the dialogue in Sect. 2. It declares a new symbol "Pythagorean Theorem", and provides it with a (flexiformal) definiens. The MMT system can convert this fragment to semantically annotated HTML and extract the symbols declared therein as MMT/OMDOC [MK22]. Additionally, the HTML corresponding to the theorem statement (via the sassertion environment) is extracted as a learning object "defining" the symbol. The semantically marked up concepts occurring in the statement (using the \symname and \symref macros that mark up references to symbols) are known to be direct dependencies of the learning object. Additionally, the symbols occurring in the definiens are known to be direct dependencies of the symbol itself.

Note that as a consequence, we obtain *two* knowledge graphs: The theory graph of symbols with the usual relations from the MMT/OMDOC ontology, and a separate graph of learning objects consisting of whole documents, chapters/sections, slides (in a presentation) and document snippets, but also (semantically annotated) definitions, theorems, statements, problems, examples, etc. learning objects are connected with each other via relations from the *Upper Library Ontology (ULO)* [Con+19] such as occurs-in or references, but also relate to the MMT/OMDOctheory graph via relations such as defines or is-an-example-for or ⟨theorem⟩concerns⟨symbol⟩. Notably, while the ULO was previously only used for *formal* libraries, we are now in the process of extending it to (flexi-)formal libraries of natural language document fragments.[5]

To *test* a learner's competency with respect to some concept, we can provide *problems* and semantically annotate them with *i*) *learning objectives* (the concepts and competencies tested by the problem) and *ii*) (known – fully or partially, correct or wrong – answers learners typically give), that we can associate with particular competency levels.   learning objectives are pairs $\langle D, S \rangle$, where S is a symbol and D a cognitive dimension in the revised Bloom taxonomy. Importantly, problems and other learning objects can have multiple objectives. For example, we can annotate the first problem in the dialog above with the objectives $\langle$remember, right triangle$\rangle$ and $\langle$apply, triangle angle sum$\rangle$.

Particularly for the kinds of problems that can be evaluated automatically (e.g. single/multiple choice), the answer classes can provide us with updates to the learner model corresponding to the answer, and, in case of a wrong answer, the likely cause and missing competency.

To interface with the remaining component of the architecture, MMT provides a REST API to query the system for symbols and learning objects; both in general as well as restricted to those being introduced in a specific course document or sections therein. The ALEA frontend uses this API *via* the learner model server to restrict functionality to the relevant learning objects both with respect to a certain *context* (e.g. a university course) and the current state of a user's learner model.

The Dialogue Planner. This is sufficient to realize the dialogue above: Upon a user wanting to learn about the symbol "Pythagorean Theorem" (and not knowing anything about it yet), the MMT system can retrieve all known learning objects defining it from the formulation model. It can determine the dependencies of those learning objects, select the one with the smallest number of concepts predicted to be still unknown by the learner from the learner model, and then ask them about their familiarity with the dependencies (basically recursing into them). Analogously, we can mark up and retrieve *proofs*, if, when, and where desired.

When subsequently wanting to test a user's competency with respect to a symbol (e.g. right triangles or Pythagorean Theorem), we can query MMT specifically for problems with the corresponding learning objective. From the list of problems, we filter those with the minimal dependencies known to be (sufficiently well) known by the learner. In our running example, both problems are multiple choice exercises, so the system can automatically evaluate the provided answers. Upon answering, the learner model is updated accordingly.

3.2   The Learner Model Server (LMS)

Learner Model structure and semantics. At the core of the learner model lies a server component that can interface with both the front- and backend of the

---

[5] The precise relational ontology is subject to ongoing research and experimentation.

system. Part of this Learner Model Server (LMS) is a database that stores all explicit knowledge about (estimated) learnercompetencies. For a given element of the theory graph and a given learner (identified only by a token), the data that is stored is a sextuple of numerical values between 0 and 1, inclusive. Every value is representative of the system's current best guess as to the competencies along a certain cognitive dimension (see Sect. 3)[6].

The intended semantics for these values are of a statistical nature which enables an empirical process for evaluation and correction: For a given element of the theory graph, a learner, and a cognitive dimension, the stored value represents the (system's estimate of the) probability that the student will be able to successfully solve a randomly selected problem from the pool of problems that are annotated to require both the given symbol and the cognitive dimension. A score of 0 would indicate that we expect them to be able to solve none of them and a score of 1, all of them.

Interaction Logs. Beyond the explicit current state of the learner model as described above, the LMS also keeps a detailed log about every meaningful learner interaction with the system. This includes learners giving self-evaluations on specific symbols, taking guided tours, answering questions (no matter if their answers are correct or not) and can be extended if another feature becomes available. The data we store includes all educationally relevant information (e.g. the learning object that was interacted with or precise answers that were given) as well as which learner was involved in the interaction and when exactly it happened.

Keeping the aforementioned records in addition to just the explicit state at any given time allows us to experiment, even retroactively, with different ideas of what exactly every interaction means (or should mean) for the learner model– after all, the exact effects of an interaction are not given a priori. It is clear that answering a difficult question correctly should increase the relevant scores in the learner model. Additionally, we can exploit the structure of the underlying theory graph to update learner model values for *related* symbols as well for various relations. But by how much exactly and which ones? Should competency values stay constant in the absence of interaction or decay over time?

There is a multitude of different approaches to these questions and finding the "best" or even just a good one is subject to ongoing research. Hence, we use the interaction logs to be able to re-create a version of the learner model with a new learning function that we can then compare with the previous model (say, on their ability to accurately predict students' exam scores at the end of a semester).

---

[6] It should be noted that not every cognitive dimension necessarily plays well with every type of learning object. For example, it would be difficult to coherently assign a student a competency in `create`-ing for Pythagorean Theorem. But in this case, the value will simply not be used.

Given the required data (in future work), we can also use *latent trait analysis* to identify relevant clusters of symbols whose values should be updated in concert, if their competencies can be found to be sufficiently correlated.

3.3   The Course Fragment Server (CFS)

The ALEA frontend is realized as lightweight, responsive, client-side web application via the React library/framework. The CFS serves the educational content – which it receives from the LOS– as JSON to the browser. The CFS has three main purposes: establishing the ALEAtrust zone, packaging/theming the learning objects received from the LOS into learning situations, and integrating learning support services into these.

Personally Identifiable Information and Data Privacy. Learner model data and learner interaction logs are highly sensitive personal data, therefore the LMS and the CFS are enclosed in a trust zone(the yellow bubble in Fig. 3) operationalized by a single sign on regime: when a learner logs into the ALEA system[7], they also authorize the LMS to log interactions (e.g. answers to problems in the education dialogue) and provide the CFS with (personal) competency data. The learning support services hosted by the CFS pass competency data – but without personal data – to the LOS, which then assembles the course fragments, which the CFS then passes on to the learner. Thus personally identifiable information never leaves the trust zone.

Storing data securely is, however, not enough by itself. We also strive to give all learners a high degree of control over their data. This includes functionality to easily access, visualize, and download (in JSON format) their current learner model. Every learner can also at any time initiate a purge of their data, resetting their learner model to zero and deleting all saved interaction logs. The only thing that remains is a record of the purge itself. Of course a purge will negatively affect personalization and the overall quality of the learning experience in ALEA.

Learning Support Services. We have already seen the most ubiquitous learning support services in Sect. 2 above: a guided tour– a generated, user-adaptive course dialogue leading up to a particular competency given a learner model state. In the ALEA system, every content term (any phrase annotated by a \symname macro in STEX) directly induces a target competency.

Another learning support service is modeled on the time-tried technique of writing definitions (and associated knowledge) for concepts on the back of file cards and drilling them by eliminating "known" cards. In ALEA, all learning objects directly induce flash cards from existing semantic annotations. learners can select a scope (e.g. a selection of sections in the course notes) and a competency target (a 6-tuple of competency values) up to which cards should be selected, and then learners can drill, assessing competency – and updating the learner model. Note that – like most other learning support services – the drill

---

[7] We employ eduGAIN authentication for global academic authentication and access.

cards feature are generated from the same $\mathcal{S}$TEX representations and therefore basically "come for free" for the educator's authoring course materials.

4   The Rhetoric/Didactic Model

The Rhetoric/Didactic model consists of classifications and relational annotations to and between symbol from the domain model and learning objects from the formulation model.

For the rhetoric part we follow the idea of the Rhetorical Structure Theory (RST) [MT88], but specialize the relations and classes to the mathematical/educational setting. Following the general $\mathcal{S}$TEX setup, we allow RST annotations as optional arguments.

```
1 \begin{sparagraph}[type=introduction,to=Pythagorean Theorem]
2   One of the most useful theorems in geometry is the following:
3 \end{sparagraph}
```

RST is traditionally used in natural language generation for (hierarchically) planning coherent documents. The paragraph marked as an introduction to the Pythagorean theorem might – not in a dialogue as the one in Sect. 2 but e.g. in course notes – be used to make more naturally flowing text.

For didactic information we use the Y-model classifications and relations [Loh+22]. A very simple example is

```
1 \objective{apply}{Pythagorean Theorem}
```

in the source of the problem about the length of the remaining side posed in the dialogue from Sect. 2. This $\mathcal{S}$TEX annotation states that this problem "tests" the learner's competency of applying the theorem. This information can be used by the dialogue planner to ensure that a prerequisite $\langle$apply, pythagorean theorem$\rangle$ is actually met. Such prerequisites can often be derived from the $\mathcal{S}$TEX sources of a learning object: if a learning object with cognitive dimension D contains a symbol reference S (e.g. via \symname{S}), then we know (at the very least) that $\langle$remember, $S\rangle$ is a prerequisite. Additional prerequisites can be provided as annotations to the learning object.

But the didactic relations are not restricted to learning objects. Consider the situation in Fig. 5, where the lower part consists of a theory graph in the domain model and the upper part of a "occurs-in graph" of learning objects from the formulation model (a lecture structured into slides sl_i with fragments n_i). In Fig. 5 the lecture introduces a new concept via the didactic trick of a "strawman": it first introduces a naive, reduced approximation $\mathcal{N}$ of the real theory $\mathcal{F}$, only to show an example $\mathcal{E}_\mathcal{N}$ of where this is insufficient. Then it proposes a first (straw-man) solution $\mathcal{S}$, and show an example $\mathcal{E}_\mathcal{S}$ of why this does not work either. Based on the information gleaned from this failed attempt, it builds the eventual version $\mathcal{F}$ of the concept or theory and demonstrates that this works on $\mathcal{E}_\mathcal{F}$. The (lower) domain theory graph and the straw-man relation shown as the thick arrow in Fig. 5 can be thought of as a didactic pattern that can be registered in the rhetoric/didactic model. Given a sufficiently expressive relational ontology, the dialogue planner could automatically generate the learning object structure

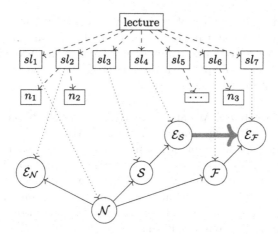

Fig. 5. Introducing a Concept via a Straw-Man Theory

in the upper part; resulting in didactically more sophisticated learning materials in the future.

5   Conclusion, Evaluation, and Future Work

We have presented the ALEA system, an adaptive learning assistant based largely on existing MKM technologies. The method feeds on semantic annotations of (mathematical) knowledge in existing learning materials, and employs the induced theory graph – the centerpiece of the domain model– and the learner model to guide the didactic algorithms. The ALEA system is open source and is deployed to over 1000 students in 6 courses at FAU; see https://courses.voll-ki.fau.de.

Note that user-adaptive features that make use of learner models require a user to be logged into the system, which can be done using eduGAIN.

Evaluation of the 4-Models Concept. The system development and deployment in active courses has informed the 4-models conceptualization. Initially, the domain, formulation, and didactic models were just sTeX annotations to the sources of existing course materials – slides, problems, and course notes. But the use of the definitions in slides as sources of dependency information for guided tours led to an increasing "formalization" of the course materials, sometimes to the detriment of didactic concerns – e.g. overloading students with "everything, all at once" rather than gently easing them into understanding. Separating the learning objects (fragments in course materials, that are optimized for playing a particular didactic role there) from ontological definitions (a "platonic" representation of the underlying domain knowledge) has allowed to collect and curate the "full story" in the domain model in a unique location and reference it as "the underlying meaning" in many learning objects that may only give didactically condensed versions of "the story". Separating out the rhetorical/-didactical classifications and relations out from the learning objects make the latter into much more re-usable components that can be automatically assembled into learner/cohort-adapted learning materials along the former, as we have seen in the thought experiment in Sect. 2.

Ongoing and Future Work. We are currently working on shaping the semantic annotations of the initial six courses currently in the ALᴇA system (covering AI, logic, and CS tools for humanities and social sciences) more fully into the 4-models concept, mainly by separating out the domain model. At the same time we are expanding the course repertoire to cover more of the CS curriculum: currently we are working on the canonical courses: Programming, Algorithms & Data structures, and Theoretical CS. Again, the separation of domain and formulation models starts paying off: there is considerable overlap in the domain models between the courses, even though the learning objects are quite distinct due to the progression of overall student competency. One of the bottlenecks in this endeavour is the provisioning of "quiz questions" like the two in the dialogue above – simple problems that can be solved in less than a minute – where we can determine the answer class automatically, which in turn can be used for feedback and learner model updates. We have the markup format, but literally need thousands of them per course.

The further development of the rhetoric/didactic model and its influence on the automated generation of guided tours, quizzes, exam preparation materials will be the next big step; we expect that the current learning support services – which have been very positively evaluated by students who used them – are just a first step towards more complete, data-driven, personalized tutoring support.

Finally, we have only concentrated on tutoring individual learners so far. But there is no reason why the learning support services cannot be tailored to cohorts of learners based on aggregated learner data and – based on this – be extended to "instructor support services", giving instructors up-to-date information on the state of learning in a course or even degree program – rather than only the grade averages after the exams.

Acknowledgements. The work reported in this article was conducted as part of the VoLL-KI project (see https://voll-ki.de) funded by the German Research/Education Ministry under grant 16DHBKI089.

References

[AK09] Anderson, L.W., Krathwohl, D.R.: A Taxonomy for Learning, Teaching, and Assessing: A Revision of Bloom's Taxonomy of Educational Objectives. Longman, New York (2009)

[CICM22] Kamareddine, F., Sacerdoti Coen, C. (eds.): CICM 2021. LNCS (LNAI), vol. 12833. Springer, Cham (2022). https://doi.org/10.1007/978-3-030-81097-9

[Con+19] Condoluci, A., Kohlhase, M., Müller, D., Rabe, F., Sacerdoti Coen, C., Wenzel, M.: Relational data across mathematical libraries. In: Kaliszyk, C., Brady, E.,

Kohlhase, A., Sacerdoti Coen, C. (eds.) CICM 2019. LNCS (LNAI), vol. 11617, pp. 61–76. Springer, Cham (2019). https://doi.org/10.1007/978-3-030-23250-4_5. https://kwarc.info/kohlhase/papers/cicm19-ulo.pdf

[KM] Kohlhase, M., Müller, D.: The STEX3 package collection. https://github.com/slatex/sTeX/blob/main/doc/stex-doc.pdf. Visited 24 Apr 2022

[KM22] Kohlhase, M., Müller, D.: System description: STEX3 -A LATEX based ecosystem for semantic/active mathematical documents. In: Buzzard, K., Kutsia, T. (eds.) Intelligent Computer Mathematics. LNAI, vol. 13467, pp. 184–188. Springer, Cham (2022). https://doi.org/10.1007/978-3-031-16681-5_13. https://kwarc.info/people/dmueller/pubs/cicm22stexsd.pdf

[Koh+11] Kohlhase, M., et al.: The planetary system: web 3.0 & active documents for STEM. Procedia Comput. Sci. 4 (2011). Sato, M., Matsuoka, S., Sloot, P.M., van Albada, G.D., Dongarra, J. (eds.) Special Issue: Proceedings of the International Conference on Computational Science (ICCS). Finalist at the Executable Paper Grand Challenge, pp. 598–607. https://doi.org/10.1016/j.procs.2011.04.063. https://kwarc.info/kohlhase/papers/epc11.pdf

[Koh06] Kohlhase, M.: OMDoc - An Open Markup Format for Mathematical Documents [Version 1.2]. LNAI 4180. Springer, Heidelberg (2006). https://doi.org/10.1007/11826095. http://omdoc.org/pubs/omdoc1.2.pdf

[Loh+22] Lohr, D., Berges, M., Kohlhase, M., Müller, D., Rapp, M.: The Y model - formalization of computer-science tasks in the context of intelligent tutoring systems (2022). https://kwarc.info/kohlhase/submit/kali22.pdf

[Mel+01] Melis, E.: The ActiveMath learning environment. Artif. Intell. Educ. **12**(4) (2001)

[MK22] Müller, D., Kohlhase, M.: Injecting formal mathematics into LaTeX. In: Buzzard, K., Kutsia, T. (eds.) Intelligent Computer Mathematics. LNAI, vol. 13467, pp. 168–183. Springer, Cham (2022). https://doi.org/10.1007/978-3-031-16681-5_12. https://kwarc.info/people/dmueller/pubs/cicm22stexmmt.pdf

[MMT] MMT - Language and System for the Uniform Representation of Knowledge. Project web site. https://uniformal.github.io/. Visited 15 Jan 2019

[MT88] Mann, W.C., Thompson, S.A.: Rhetorical structure theory: toward a functional theory of text organization. Text - Interdisc. J. Study Discourse **8**(3), 243–281 (1988). https://doi.org/10.1515/text.1.1988.8.3.243. https://doi.org/10.1515/text.1.1988.8.3.243

[Ull08] Ullrich, C.: Pedagogically Founded Courseware Generation for Web-Based Learning. LNCS. Springer, Heidelberg (2008). https://doi.org/10.1007/978-3-540-88215-2. https://link.springer.com/book/10.1007/978-3-540-88215-2

Isabelle Formalisation of Original Representation Theorems

Marco B. Caminati[✉]

School of Computingm and Communications, Lancaster University in Leipzig,
Nikolaistrasse 10, 04109 Leipzig, Germany
m.caminati@lancaster.ac.uk

Abstract. In a recent paper, new theorems linking apparently unrelated mathematical objects (event structures from concurrency theory and full graphs arising in computational biology) were discovered by cross-site data mining on huge databases, and building on existing Isabelle-verified event structures enumeration algorithms. Given the origin and newness of such theorems, their formal verification is particularly desirable. This paper presents such a verification via Isabelle/HOL definitions and theorems, and exposes the technical challenges found in the process. The introduced formalisation completes the verification of Isabelle-verified event structure enumeration algorithms into a fully verified framework to link event structures to full graphs.

1 Introduction

In [4], the first machine-verified contribution to the *Online Encyclopedia of Integer Sequences* (*OEIS*) [22] was presented, through an Isabelle/HOL-verified algorithm enumerating all labeled *prime event structures* (or just event structures, or even only *ES's*). In [7], a mining technique over massive sets of documents permitted to unearth unforeseen connections between apparently unrelated mathematical domains. One particular connection was, in the same paper, explored, linking event structures (via the algorithm from [4]) to *full graphs* (*FGs*). Event structures are originated in the study of concurrent computational systems, while full graphs arise in the field of computational biology [12]. In [7], the deeper motivation of this connection was found as being given rise by a new representation theorem for event structures and a set of derived results, cross-fertilising between the two fields and permitting to obtain new theorems for both the related objects (ES's and FGs). The two papers [4] and [7], therefore, complement each other to provide enumerating algorithms and new connections found using the former. However, only the results from [4] have been mechanically checked. The present paper completes the work by providing a Isabelle/HOL (from now on, just Isabelle) [18] formalisation of the representation theorem, the theorem connecting ES's and FGs, a number of related Isabelle definitions and tools, and a computable Isabelle isomorphism providing the connection between ES's and FGs.

© The Author(s), under exclusive license to Springer Nature Switzerland AG 2023
C. Dubois and M. Kerber (Eds.): CICM 2023, LNAI 14101, pp. 98–112, 2023.
https://doi.org/10.1007/978-3-031-42753-4_7

Section 2 introduces the subjects of the discourse (e.g., event structures and full graphs), Sect. 3 provides the pen-and-paper version of the theorems formalised, Sect. 4 illustrates the main formalised theorems and definitions, Sects. 5 and 6, respectively, illustrate the formalisation of the two main theorems, while Sect. 7 contains overall consideration about the formalisation process. Section 8 concludes.

2   Event Structures and Full Graphs

This section formally introduces the objects of our theorems. To make this paper self-contained, it summarises, together with the subsequent one, the main elements of Sections IV and VI of [7].

2.1   Event Structures

A prime event structure (or simply event structure, ES) describes a concurrent computation by identifying the computational events that are causally related and those that exclude one another. According to the following definition, this is achieved via two relations: $\leq$ (causality) and $\#$ (conflict).

Definition 1. *An event structure is a pair of relations* $(\leq, \#)$ *where* $\leq$ *is a partial order,* $\#$ *is irreflexive and symmetric,* (fie $\leq$) $\supseteq$ (fie $\#$) *is called the set of events, and for any three events* x_0, x_1, y: $x_0 \# y \wedge x_0 \leq x_1 \rightarrow x_1 \# y$.

The last condition is referred to as conflict propagation. In Definition 1, fie denotes the field of a relation: that is, the union of its domain (dom) and range (ran). The usual infix notation for the relations in Definition 1 can become inconvenient, therefore we also introduce an additional notation representing the relations with letters, writing, e.g., $(x, y) \in D$ instead of $x \leq y$ and $(x, y) \in U$ in lieu of $x \# y$. We will typically use the letters D and U as above to suggest the reader what they encode: D stands for "directed" and U for "undirected". Indeed, $\leq$, as a partial order, is naturally viewable as a directed graph and $\#$, being symmetric, as an undirected graph. See also the comment immediately after Definition 2. Since any finite relation is a graph having its vertices (or nodes) coinciding with the field of the relation, and since, for any finite partial order, that graph can be naturally made a directed graph, it is easy to represent any finite ES via diagrams such as the one in Fig. 1.

2.2   Full Graphs

Any family of sets can be used to build a graph where each vertex represents a set of the family, an undirected edge connects overlapping sets, and a directed edge connects a superset to a subset. Such a construction occurs when studying the following problem: given n subsets of a given set of m elements, is there a way of labeling the elements with natural numbers such that the element

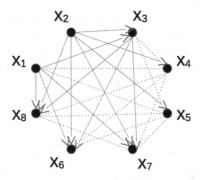

Fig. 1. An example event structure, with eight events related by causality (denoted by an arrow standing for $\leq$) and conflict (denoted by a dashed line).

occur consecutively (with respect to this labeling) in each subset? One practical application of this labeling problem arises in bioinformatics, where the elements of subsets represent observed blemishes to parts of a gene, which are supposed to be more likely to affect parts of the gene which are connected: therefore, finding such a labeling can provide essential information about the topology of a gene [2,12]. The graphs that can be created in this way are specified by Definition 2.

Definition 2. *A* full graph *(FG) is a mixed, unweighted, simple[1] graph over vertices V, of directed edges D, and undirected edges T such that there is an injective function f on V yielding non-empty sets and with the property*

$$\forall x, \ y \in V. \ ((x,y) \in D \leftrightarrow f \ x \supseteq f \ y \ ) \wedge \tag{1}$$

$$((x,y) \in T \leftrightarrow f \ x \ and \ f \ y \ overlap) \, ; \tag{2}$$

here, we say that two sets A and B overlap *(written $A \between B$) when $A \cap B \notin \{A, B, \emptyset\}$. We call f an* fg-representation *of the full graph (D, T). Alternatively, we will say that T* makes a full graph *of D (through f) when such an fg-representation f exists.*

Having insisted in Definition 2 in encoding T via ordered pairs, even though is an undirected graph, makes that encoding redundant; however, this is convenient because we can then regard T as a (symmetric) relation, as all the other components in the definitions of ES's and FGs, also thanks to the fact that all these components are simple graphs, making the encoding as relations adequate.

3   Connecting ES's and FGs

In [7], a systematic way of looking for matches between entries in the OEIS and free text search results across Google and Google Scholar is introduced,

---

[1] Recall that a graph is *simple* when it has no self loops and no multi-edges; it is *mixed* when it has both directed and undirected edges. See [13, Section 1.1].

producing thousands of unexplored and potentially interesting matches. One of them relates the enumerations of ES's (introduced in OEIS by [4]) and of FGs (in [9, Section 4]): the number of (labeled) ES's and of FGs over a fixed number of vertices n coincide for small n. In the same paper [7], this connection is explored, motivated and proven by providing a one-to-one map between ES's and FGs, which is an isomorphism once framed as a mapping between representations of ES's and FGs.

To introduce the ideas in the latter paper, we start by looking at the evaluation, through this isomorphism, of the ES in Fig. 1, giving the FG in Fig. 2.

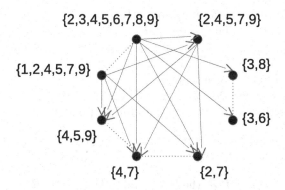

Fig. 2. The full graph isomorphic to the event structure of Fig. 1. This is the full graph example originally featured in Section 3 of [12]. Here, the arrows represent $\supseteq$, and the dashed lines the overlapping relation.

To make more precise the similarity between the figures, we must understand how they are generated: in Fig. 2, the edges are determined by looking at operations on sets associated to each node. In this sense, we have a representation of the FG in terms of set-theoretical notions, indirectly dictating the structure of the FG itself by definition. In the case of event structures, however, such a representation is absent in the definition, which dictates the property of the structure directly by imposing relationships between $\leq$ and $\#$. To formally link the connection we are looking at, we must find a representation for the ES as well, through a suitable definition of ES-representation and a *representation theorem* establishing that an equivalent definition of ES can be given in terms of such a representation, as done with FGs. This is an interesting endeavour in general, not limited to the specific task of finding connections between different domains: see [7, Section III], which also discusses and details the notion of representation.

The following definition will turn out to yield adequate representations for ES's.

Definition 3. *Given two binary relations D and U, the set-valued function f is a representation for (D, U) if*

$$\forall x\, y \in \operatorname{dom} f.\ ((x, y) \in D \leftrightarrow f(x) \supseteq f(y)) \ \wedge \tag{3}$$

$$\forall x\, y \in \operatorname{dom} f.\ ((x, y) \in U \leftrightarrow f(x) \cap f(y) = \emptyset). \tag{4}$$

Here, we say that, given D and any U with $\operatorname{fie} U \subseteq \operatorname{fie} D$, any such a f (if it exists) is called admissible.

And by adequate we mean that the following representation theorem holds.

Theorem 1 (Representation theorem). *Consider two binary relations D and U, with D finite and $\operatorname{fie} U \subseteq \operatorname{fie} D$. Then (D, U) is an event structure if and only if there is an injective representation $f : \operatorname{fie} D \to \overline{2}^{\mathbb{N}} \setminus \{\emptyset\}$ for (D, U),*

where $\overline{2}^{X}$ denotes the finite subsets of X.

Our second representation theorem for event structures, Theorem 2, offers a bijective construction connecting them to full graphs.

Theorem 2. *Consider a finite relation D and a function F_D mapping working as follows on its argument R:*

$$F_D := R \mapsto (\operatorname{fie} D \times \operatorname{fie} D) \setminus (D \cup D^{-1}) \setminus R.$$

A bijection between
$X := \{T | T$ makes a full graph of $D\}$ and
$Y := \{U | U$ is admissible for $D\}$
is given by $F_D|_X$.

Figure 3 attaches a representation (always existing, according to Theorem 1) to the ES of Fig. 1. Using F_D as in Theorem 3, one can now promptly relate that ES to the FG of Fig. 2.

4   Formalisation and Verification: Introduction

We start from the top level, that is, the Isabelle renditions of the main theorems. Theorem 1 is stated as

Listing 1.1. Isabelle rendition of Theorem 1

```
theorem representation: assumes "finite D"
        "Field U ⊆ Field D" shows
"(isLes D U) = (∃ f. isInjection f & Domain f = Field D &
        ({}::nat set)∉Range f & finite ((Union o Range) f)
        & isRepresentation f D U)",
```

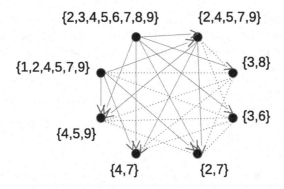

Fig. 3. A representation for the event structure of Fig. 1. Now, the arrows represent ⊇ and the dashed lines the disjointness relation. Theorem 1 states that any set of events is an event structure if and only if such a representation is constructible.

while Theorem 2 reads

Listing 1.2. Isabelle rendition of Theorem 2

```
theorem bijection: assumes "finite D"
"F=(λR. ((Field D × Field D) - (D ∪ D^-1)- R))"
"X={T|T. Field T ⊆ Field D & (∃ f. isInjection f &
    ({}::nat set)∉Range f & Domain f=Field D &
    isFgRepr f D T)}"
"Y={U|U. Field U ⊆ Field D & (∃ f. isInjection f &
    ({}::nat set)∉Range f & Domain f=Field D &
    isRepresentation f D U)}" shows
"F'X=Y & F'Y=X & inj_on F X & inj_on F Y & card X=card Y",
```

where `inj_on F X` returns true when the total function `F` is injective over the set `X`, while the notation `^-1` denotes the converse of a relation.

The reader might have noticed a subtle difference between `f` occurring in Listing 1.1 and `F` occurring in Listing 1.2: while both are functions, they are implemented very differently within Isabelle/HOL. Indeed, `F` is a standard HOL function, a primitive notion in higher order logic [16]; on the other hand, `f` is implemented as a set of ordered pairs, in the way standard set theory (e.g., ZF, Zermelo-Fraenkel set theory [11]) represents functions. The verification presented here extensively exploits this duality, choosing one construct or the other depending on the particular function at hand and on the theorem it appears in. There are several reasons for this approach: one is that the totality of functions imposed by HOL is sometimes an inconvenience [16] which can be worked around by choosing the second construct; another one is that set theoretical operations on functions, such as union, subtraction, conversion (`^-1`) are sometimes useful, and are unavailable with the first construct; as an example of this usefulness, let us take the `+<` infix operator, which grows a relation `P` with another one `Q`, performing overriding if necessary, and is defined as

```
(P - (Domain Q × Range P)) ∪ Q.
```

One advantage of this definition is that it works for any pair of relations P and Q, and at the same time preserves right-uniqueness if P and Q are right-unique (that is, functions). Additionally, existing facts about the building blocks of +< (-, ×, Domain, Range, ∪) typically makes proofs about +< easier, helped by the simplicity of its definition. This operator can be conveniently overloaded to the point-wise special case:

```
abbreviation singlepaste where "singlepaste f pair ==
f +< {(fst pair, snd pair)}"
notation singlepaste (infix "+<" 75)
```

Note that the type of g in f+<g avoids ambiguity for the overloaded +< operator.

On the other hand, set-theoretical functions are actually relations and, as such, need to be shown to be right unique (by showing they satisfy a dedicated Isabelle predicate runiq) before they can be treated as functions. Overall, keeping both constructs has the upside of being able to take advantage of the best of both worlds [8].

The price to pay for this upside is that we have duplicated versions of most operations on functions, one for each construct. For example, if F is a standard HOL function and f is a set theoretical function, then the application operation on an argument x is written F x for F and f,,x for f; the operation yielding the image of a set X through the function is F'X versus f''X, the range operation is range F versus Range f; the property of injectivity is inj_on versus isInjection, etc. Other operations, such as union, intersection, domain, ^-1, restriction (denoted ||), and others, only make sense for set-theoretical functions, although a restriction operating on HOL functions (and denoted |||) was also introduced. In this case, naturally, the result is a set-theoretical functions, since in HOL all functions are total and cannot therefore be restricted directly [16].

In practice, the reader needs not to worry about these subtle differences deriving from the duality between HOL functions and set-theoretical functions, which were nevertheless discussed in the digression above to prevent confusion.

The first theorem above, in Listing 1.1, equates the definition of being an event structure (isLes) to the existence of a representation (whose definition is contained in isRepresentation), while the second theorem shows that F (the Isabelle rendition of F_D occurring in Theorem 2) is indeed a bijection between the set Y of admissible conflicts for D and the set X of undirected graphs making D a full graph. Since this holds for all finite Ds, we have a verified proof of the mined matches illustrated in Sect. 1 and in [7].

isLes, isRepresentation, isFgRepr are all straightforward from the pen-and-paper definitions, with the first already used in previous formalisations regarding event structures [4–6]:

```
definition "isLes causality conflict =
propagation conflict causality & sym conflict &
irrefl conflict & trans causality &
antisym causality & reflex causality",
```

```
definition "isRepresentation f D U = ∀x∈Domain f.
       (∀y∈Domain f. ((((x, y)∈D)=(f,,x ⊇ f,,y)) &
       (((x,y)∈U) = ((f,,x ∩ f,,y)={})))))"

definition "isFgRepr f D T = ∀x∈Domain f.
       (∀y∈Domain f. ((((x, y)∈D)=(f,,x ⊇ f,,y)) &
       (((x,y)∈T) = ((f,,x) overlaps (f,,y)))))",
```

with the definition of overlapping also very close to the paper version and taking advantage of the infix notation definition capabilities of Isabelle:

```
definition "Overlap X Y = (X ∩ Y ∉ {X, Y, {}})"
notation "Overlap" ("_ overlaps ")
```

Moreover, `propagation` is a synonym for the following:

```
definition "isMonotonicOver conflict causality =
∀ x y. (x,y) ∈ causality → conflict''{x} ⊆ conflict''{y}",
```

while `reflex` was introduced as follows:

```
definition "reflex P = refl_on (Field P) P",
```

where `refl_on A R` returns true when the relation `R` is reflexive over a subset `A` of its domain and range.

All the other Isabelle objects occurring above are part of Isabelle's standard library.

5   Formalisation and Verification: Proof Structure for `bijection`

We start from the second theorem introduced above, which is the simpler of the two, in that it relates full graphs to sets of admissible conflict relations for a given partial order, while the link between ES representations and ES's is provided by `representation`.

The idea for the proof is simple: we just note that the definition of fg-representation (Definition 2) and of event structure representation (Definition 3) are very similar, mainly differing by the substitution of the overlapping relation with that of disjointness; therefore, we introduce the following operator to map between them:

```
λR. (unRel' D - R),
```

where the helper `unRel'` takes the complement of a relation:

```
abbreviation "unRel' D==(Field D × Field D) - (D ∪ D^-1)".
```

Now, the idea is to show that we can pass from event structures to full graphs by applying the above operator to the conflict relation. To show that, it suffices to show that the set of valid undirected edges for a given `D` can be obtained from the set of valid conflict relations for `D` by applying the operator above: this is exactly the thesis `F'X=Y & F'Y=X` appearing in the `bijection` theorem's thesis. By bijectivity, it suffices to show the weaker relations `F'X ⊆ F'Y` and `F'Y ⊆ F'X`, which is done by `153a` and `153b` below, respectively:

```
lemma 153a: assumes "F=(λR. (unRel' D - R))" shows
"F'{T|T. Field T ⊆ Field D & (∃ f. isInjection f
      & ({}::nat set)∉Range f & Domain f=Field D
      & isFgRepr f D T)} ⊆
{U|U. Field U ⊆ Field D & (∃ f. isInjection f &
      ({}::nat set)∉Range f & Domain f=Field D
      & isRepresentation f D U)}"

lemma 153b: assumes "F=(λR. (unRel' D - R))" shows
"F'{U|U. Field U ⊆ Field D & (∃ f. isInjection f &
      ({}::nat set)∉Range f & Domain f=Field D &
      isRepresentation f D U)} ⊆
{T|T. Field T ⊆ Field D & (∃ f. isInjection f &
      ({}::nat set)∉Range f & Domain f=Field D &
      isFgRepr f D T)}"
```

153a and 153b are sufficient to draw the thesis of bijection thanks to the following general propositions (the latter provided by Isabelle's standard library):

```
proposition 152a: assumes "finite (X ∪ Y)" "inj_on f X"
"inj_on f Y" "f'X ⊆ Y" "f'Y ⊆ X" shows "f'X=Y & f'Y=X"

lemma card_image:
  assumes "inj_on f A"
  shows "card (f ' A) = card A"
```

Finally, the hypotheses inj_on f X and inj_on f Y can be deduced when X and Y are, respectively, the sets appearing in 153b by another general result:

```
proposition 155: "inj_on (λX. Y-X) (Pow Y)"
```

(where Pow takes the power set), which applies when X and Y take the particular values above thanks to

```
lemma 154bb: assumes "isFgRepr f D T" "Domain f = Field D"
"Field T ⊆ Field D" shows "T ⊆ (Field D × Field D)-(D∪D^-1)"
```

and

```
lemma 154aa: assumes "isRepresentation f D U"
"({}::nat set)∉Range f" "runiq f" "Domain f = Field D"
"Field U ⊆ Field D" shows "U ⊆ (Field D × Field D)-(D∪D^-1)",
```

where the runiq predicate was introduced in the discussion after Listing 1.2.

6   Formalisation and Verification: Proof Structure for representation

The proof is in the two directions; that is, having a representation implies being an event structure (theorem main1) and being an event structure implies having a representation (theorem main2):

```
theorem main1: assumes "runiq f"
"Field D ∪ Field U ⊆ Domain f"
"isRepresentation' f D U"
        shows
"isPreorder D & isMonotonicOver U D & sym U &
(luniq f → antisym D) & ({}∉(Range f) → irrefl U)"

theorem main2: assumes "finite D" "isLes D U" obtains
f::"('a × nat set)set" where "Domain f=Field D &
        isInjection f & {}∉Range f &
        finite ((Union o Range) f) & isRepresentation f D U"
```

6.1 Proof of main2

The proof for main2 is arguably among the most complex in the project, since it needs to provide a representation for any given ES. It is done by induction on the cardinality of D, starting with the base case which can be proved by Sledgehammer [3]:

```
proposition 1150a: assumes "f={}" "D={}" shows
"isRepresentation f D U & Domain f=Field D &
isInjection f & runiq f & {}∉Range f"
```

The induction step now requires to somehow pass from a representation f of a D' smaller than a given D to a representation for D itself. This requires to determine two things:

1. in which sense D' is smaller than D;
2. how to construct the new representation from f.

For (1), we set D' and D to differ by exactly one *terminal* event: that is, D' is obtained from D by removing one event s with no children in D.

For (2), we obtain the new representation for D by just growing f with one new set RA representing s; this growth is done by the +< operator seen in Sect. 4. Note that this growth does not affect the values f has on the old events. Theorem extension2 below does exactly that, showing that the function resulting from the +< operation is still a representation for D. However, for this thesis to hold, there are three fundamental requirements on RA, the set representing the new event s; these requirements must hold for any existing event x, and appear in the hypotheses of extension2 labeled as hypOverlap, hypCausality and hypConflict. The remaining hypotheses are merely technical, expressing obvious requirements such as f needing to be a function, s having no children, s being fresh, etc.

```
theorem extension2: assumes "runiq f" "(s,s)∈D"
"D''{s}⊆{s}" "s∉Domain f" assumes
hypOverlap: "∀x∈Domain f. ¬(f,,,x ⊆ RA)" assumes
hypCausality: "∀x∈Domain f. RA ⊆ f,,,x = (x∈D^-1''{s}-{s})"
assumes
hypConflict: "∀x∈Domain f. ((f,,,x)∩RA={})=(x∈U^-1''{s})"
```

```
"∀x∈Domain f. ((x,s)∈U) = ((s,x)∈U)"
"isRepresentation f (D---s s) (U---s s)"
"F=f+<(s,RA)" "RA≠{}" "(s,s)∉U"
         shows
"isRepresentation' F D U"
```

extension2 presents a couple of new constructs: first, the operator --- allows
to remove a pair from a relation, so that, in this case, D and U are extensions
of D---s s and U---s s. Secondly, the operator ,,, is very similar to ,, seen
in Sect. 4, but with a slightly more general definition which is technically more
convenient in some cases. Let us start with the definition of ---:

```
definition "bouthside P X Y =
        P - ((X×Range P) ∪ ((Domain P)×Y))"
notation "bouthside" ("_\\")
definition "singlebouthside P x y = bouthside P {x} {y}"
notation "singlebouthside" ("_---")
```

This definition uses a special case of \\, which merely removes portions of
domain and range from any relation using elementary set-theoretical operations.

extension2 is what we need to obtain our representation theorem. However, as we mentioned above, it dictates three conditions on RA (hypOverlap,
hypCausality and hypConflict) for its validity. We therefore need to build a set
RA satisfying them. The following result, one of the most technical, builds a suitable RA, by transforming the representation f occurring in extension2 into an
intermediate representation g before inducting.

```
lemma 146: assumes "isRepresentation f (D---s s) (U---s s)"
"runiq f & D''{s}={s} & sym U &
(let dm=Domain in let R=Range in {}∉R f &
finite ((Union o R) f) & (Domain D)-{s} ⊆ dm f &
        (let d=D---s s in dm f ⊆ Range d & trans d))"
"let d=D---s s in let sparents=d^-1''(D^-1''{s}) in
let sconfl=U^-1''{s} in
let sconcurs=Range d-(sparents ∪ sconfl) in
  finite sconcurs & sconcurs⊆fixPts D &
  sparents=D^-1''{s}-{s} &
  irrefl (U||(sconcurs ∪ Domain f)) &
  sconfl ∩ D^-1''{s}={} &
  d''sconfl⊆sconfl &
  isMonotonicOver U (D|^(D^-1''{s} ∪ (Range d - sconfl)))"
shows
  "∃ l. let N=Max ((Union o Range) f)+1+size l in
  let d=Domain in let R=Range in
  let RA=(Union o set)((map (Union o R) l)@[{N}]) in
  let g=foldl pointUnion f (l@[(D^-1''{s}-{s})×{{N}}]) in
  let h=g+<(s,RA) in d g=d f & d h=d f∪{s} & {}∉R g &
  {}∉R h & isRepresentation g (D---s s) (U---s s) &
  isRepresentation h D U & runiq g & runiq h &
  (Union o R) h ⊆ {0..<1+N} &
  (luniq f → (isInjection g & isInjection h))"
```

Although harder to read than `extension2`, `146` has the advantage of having moved all the requirements on `RA` back to the given event structure (D, U). This comes at the price of passing through `g`, which is obtained from `f` by repeatedly applying the following operator `pointUnion` to the given `f` over a suitable list of sets, through the standard functor `foldl`:

```
definition "pointUnion ff A =
        ff +< ((λx. ff,,,x ∪ A,,,x)|||(Domain A))".
```

Recall that `|||` is the restriction operator, see Sect. 4.

6.2 Proof of `main1`

The proof of theorem `main1` is less technical, and is nicely broken into sublemmas each providing a part of the thesis. The following lemma takes care of the transitivity:

```
lemma 149a: assumes "runiq f" "Field D ⊆ Domain f"
"∀x0∈Domain f. (∀x1∈Domain f. (((x0, x1)∈D)=(f,,x0⊇f,,x1)))"
shows "Field D ⊆ fixPts D & trans D",
```

(where `definition "fixPts P=Domain(Id∩P)"`), while this other proposition takes care of conflict propagation:

```
proposition 149bb: assumes "Field D ∪ Range U ⊆ Domain f"
"∀x∈Domain f. (∀y∈Domain f. ((((x, y)∈D)→(f,,x ⊇ f,,y)) &
        (((x,y)∈U) = ((f,,x ∩ f,,y)={})))))"
shows "isMonotonicOver U D"
```

The reflexivity is then granted by combining `149a` with this simple but useful fact:

```
proposition 145e: "(∀x∈Field P. (x,x)∈P)=reflex P".
```

When writing the formalisation, a guiding principle was to always try to derive particular results from weaker results (whether the latter already exist in some library or not) applicable to more general objects, which can be strengthened to be applied to more particular objects needed in the specific formalisation one is carrying out. This resulted in over 300 lemmas, propositions and theorems, and around 50 new objects defined.

Isabelle was also used to work out minimal requirements for particular results. For example, in `main1`, no finiteness is required over `D`, and the particular irreflexivity property is explicitly bound to the additional requirement of `f` not yielding the empty set as a representation. Similarly, in theorem `main1` the antisymmetry property of event structures is linked to the representation being an injection. These details add proof-theoretical information to any development, and are usually hard to keep track of manually with a pen-and-paper proof.

7   The Formalisation Process

The code is available at[2] https://gitlab.com/users/mbc8/contributed. The formalisation of the mathematical objects and results introduced above is roughly 2.7kSLOC and 151Kb (36Kb gzipped) of Isabelle code; a bit more due to spawned additions to the theories created for event structures for previous papers such as [4–6]. To quantitatively assess the formalisation, the length of the mathematical parts appearing in [7] was computed by converting the relevant pdf to text, obtaining 21502 bytes (8229 gzipped) as a result. This gives an apparent de Bruijn factor of 7, and an intrinsic one of 4.3. There are about 4 pages of mathematical content in [7], whereas the time spent to formalise it has been estimated in around two weeks of work, giving a formalisation cost of 0.5 weeks per page. All these numerical parameters are approximate, but help giving an idea of the process itself [1,17]. It should also be noted that, although Isabelle/HOL implementations of graph theory abound [15,19–21], the present formalisation used none of them, for two reasons: first, although the theorems relate event structures and full graphs, they don't really need much graph theory. Not even basic notions as walks, paths, etc. are even mentioned. Secondly, our formalisation deals with mixed graphs (i.e., having both directed and undirected edges), thus restricting the available libraries. The theorem `representation` uses 141 facts (including lemmas, propositions, theorems and definitions) included in the file `fullGraph.thy`. The proofs can be divided into automatically generated ones and one with an explicit Isar proof (starting with the `proof` keyword). A minority of those explicit proofs were generated by Sledgehammer's `isar_proof` feature, but most of them were manually written. In general, the preference is to have small general facts with simple, usually automatic proofs, which are then put together for the more complex, manual proofs. This yields a proliferation of lemmas which are hopefully reusable. This approach goes hand-in-hand with the one providing definitions built in blocks on top of more general definitions. For example, `pointUnion` is defined in terms of ||| and +<, which are in turn defined in terms of elementary set theoretical operations (cartesian product, union, intersection, set difference, etc.). One of the longest proof is that of `146` (see Sect. 6.1), which is 139 lines and about 10Kb. About 10 results have proof longer than 20 lines, usually substantially longer, and a number of them has to do with the problem of suitably constructing `RA` using a reiterated (via `foldl`) `pointUnion` operation (see Sect. 6.1). Most proofs are non-constructive; for example, they do not provide an algorithm to build representations. However, the operator `F` appearing in theorem `bijection` and allowing to pass from representations to fg-representations and vice-versa is computable.

8   Conclusions

This paper has presented a rare instance of original theorems having been formalised natively: they were born formalised. More than that, they were

---

[2] The link requires a reasonably recent browser.

discovered thanks to existing formalisations. Such theorems provide new representations for event structures and unexpectedly link the latter to the unrelated field of computational biology through the notion of full graphs. This permits to apply results from one domain to another to immediately obtain new theorems (some such examples are reported in [7]) Therefore, an obvious idea for future work is to formally verify these new theorems, which would imply a formalisation for the domain which is currently not formalised: that of full graphs. Indeed, while event structures have now a reasonable amount of results formalised, no formalisation exists for more advanced results applicable to full graphs, for example those in [9,14].

Looking at automated theorem proving, the origin of the presented results (obtained via data mining, as explained in [7]), can provide avenues to both develop new techniques and test existing ones: thousands of potentially interesting matches similar to the one giving rise to the results presented here were found.

Another future work direction will seek the generalisation of the original theorems presented here: one natural idea is the extension of Theorem 1 to infinite event structures, which is comparable to how Priestley's representation theorem generalises (in a by no means trivial manner!) Birkhoff's [10, Theorem 11.23].

Acknowledgements. I wish to thank the anonymous reviewers and the shepherd for their time and useful input.

References

1. Asperti, A., Sacerdoti Coen, C.: Some considerations on the usability of interactive provers. In: Intelligent Computer Mathematics: 10th International Conference, AISC 2010, 17th Symposium, Calculemus 2010, and 9th International Conference, MKM 2010, Paris, France, 5–10 July 2010, Proceedings, p. 147 (2010)
2. Benzer, S.: On the topology of the genetic fine structure. Proc. Natl. Acad. Sci. **45**(11), 1607–1620 (1959)
3. Blanchette, J.C., Böhme, S., Paulson, L.C.: Extending sledgehammer with SMT solvers. J. Autom. Reason. **51**(1), 109–128 (2013)
4. Bowles, J., Caminati, M.B.: A verified algorithm enumerating event structures. In: Geuvers, H., England, M., Hasan, O., Rabe, F., Teschke, O. (eds.) CICM 2017. LNCS (LNAI), vol. 10383, pp. 239–254. Springer, Cham (2017). https://doi.org/10.1007/978-3-319-62075-6_17
5. Bowles, J.K.F., Caminati, M.B.: Balancing prescriptions with constraint solvers. In: Liò, P., Zuliani, P. (eds.) Automated Reasoning for Systems Biology and Medicine. CB, vol. 30, pp. 243–267. Springer, Cham (2019). https://doi.org/10.1007/978-3-030-17297-8_9
6. Bowles, J.K., Caminati, M.B., Cha, S.: An integrated framework for verifying multiple care pathways. In: Eleventh International Symposium on Theoretical Aspects of Software Engineering (TASE). IEEE Computer Society, United States (2017)
7. Caminati, M.B., Bowles, J.K.F.: Representation theorems obtained by mining across web sources for hints. In: 6th International Conference on Information and Computer Technologies (ICICT). IEEE (2023, in press). https://eprints.lancs.ac.uk/id/eprint/185196/

8. Watt, S.M., Davenport, J.H., Sexton, A.P., Sojka, P., Urban, J. (eds.): CICM 2014. LNCS, vol. 8543. Springer, Cham (2014). https://doi.org/10.1007/978-3-319-08434-3

9. Cowen, L.J., Kleitman, D.J., Lasaga, F., Sussman, D.: Enumeration of full graphs: onset of the asymptotic region. Stud. Appl. Math. **96**(3), 339–350 (1996)

10. Davey, B., Priestley, H.: Introduction to Lattices and Order. Cambridge Mathematical Textbooks. Cambridge University Press, Cambridge (2002)

11. Enderton, H.B.: Elements of Set Theory. Academic Press, Cambridge (1977)

12. Fulkerson, D., Gross, O.: Incidence matrices and interval graphs. Pac. J. Math. **15**(3), 835–855 (1965)

13. Gross, J.L., Yellen, J.: Handbook of Graph Theory. CRC Press, Boca Raton (2003)

14. Kleitman, D.J., Lasaga, F.R., Cowen, L.J.: Asymptotic enumeration of full graphs. J. Graph Theory **20**(1), 59–69 (1995)

15. Koutsoukou-Argyraki, A., Bakšys, M., Edmonds, C.: A formalisation of the Balog-Szemerédi-Gowers theorem in Isabelle/HOL. In: Proceedings of the 12th ACM SIGPLAN International Conference on Certified Programs and Proofs, pp. 225–238 (2023)

16. Müller, O., Slind, K.: Treating partiality in a logic of total functions. Comput. J. **40**(10), 640–651 (1997)

17. Naumowicz, A.: An example of formalizing recent mathematical results in Mizar. J. Appl. Log. **4**(4), 396–413 (2006)

18. Nipkow, T., Paulson, L.C., Wenzel, M.: Isabelle/HOL: A Proof Assistant for Higher-Order Logic. Springer, London (2002). https://doi.org/10.1007/3-540-45949-9

19. Nordhoff, B., Lammich, P.: Dijkstra's shortest path algorithm. Archive of Formal Proofs (2012)

20. Noschinski, L.: Proof pearl: a probabilistic proof for the girth-chromatic number theorem. In: Beringer, L., Felty, A. (eds.) ITP 2012. LNCS, vol. 7406, pp. 393–404. Springer, Heidelberg (2012). https://doi.org/10.1007/978-3-642-32347-8_27

21. Noschinski, L.: A graph library for Isabelle. Math. Comput. Sci. **9**(1), 23–39 (2015)

22. Sloane, N.J.A.: The on-line encyclopedia of integer sequences. In: Annales Mathematicae et Informaticae, vol. 41, pp. 219–234 (2013)

Teaching Linear Algebra in a Mechanized Mathematical Environment

Robert M. Corless[1] , David J. Jeffrey[1] , and Azar Shakoori[2]([⊠])

[1] University of Western Ontario, London, ON, Canada
{rcorless,djeffrey}@uwo.ca
[2] Ontario Tech University, Oshawa, ON, Canada
Azar.Shakoori@ontariotechu.ca

Abstract. This paper outlines our ideas on how to teach linear algebra in a mechanized mathematical environment, and discusses some of our reasons for thinking that this is a better way to teach linear algebra than the "old fashioned way". We discuss some technological tools such as Maple, Matlab, Python, and Jupyter Notebooks, and some choices of topics that are especially suited to teaching with these tools. The discussion is informed by our experience over the past thirty or more years teaching at various levels, especially at the University of Western Ontario.

Keywords: mechanization · linear algebra · teaching

1 Overview

"Linear algebra is the first course where the student encounters algebra, analysis, and geometry all together at once."

—William (Velvel) Kahan,
to RMC at the 4th SIAM Linear Algebra Conference in Minneapolis 1991

This paper describes the current state of our ongoing practice of teaching linear algebra in mechanized environments. We report our thoughts, arrived at after several decades of history in differing technological and administrative support structures. Some of our teaching philosophy is laid out in [2] and the references therein (especially for *active* teaching), but to keep this paper self-contained we will give a precis of our approach in Sect. 1.1.

We believe that this paper will be of interest for this conference both for its use of various computational environments (Jupyter notebooks, Maple, Matlab, and historically the HP48 series of calculators) and for its recommendations of what is needed for future environments for mechanized mathematics.

Linear algebra as a mathematical subject is second only to Calculus in terms of overall teaching effort at secondary institutions, accounting for many millions

---

Supported in part by NSERC and by the MICINN.

of dollars spent every year. There are those who believe that we should devote even more money and effort to it, because linear algebra is foundational for so many applications: optimization (linear programming), scientific computing, and analysis of data, for examples.

We take as fundamental that the vast majority of people taking these enormous numbers of courses are *not* going to choose careers as pure mathematicians. Rather, they are going to become engineers, biologists, chemists, physicists, economists, computer scientists, or something else[1]. They will likely need probability, and methods to solve linear equations, and the understanding of what an eigenvalue is (and perhaps what a singular value is). By and large they will not need to reason their way out of tricky artificial problems. They will need graph theory, and how to solve algebraic equations. They will need to learn how to use computers to help with the drudgery of the computations involved, so that they can be free to think about what the answers mean, instead of how they are arrived at. They will need to learn when they can rely on computers to help, and when they should be suspicious.

Our favourite *introductory* textbook—out of the myriad possible choices—arose from an NSF-funded educational project, namely [6]. The book is [14]. Yet this choice is not uncontroversial, and the book is not an especially good match for a mechanized environment. We see a need for a specialized textbook to support active learning of linear algebra in a mechanized environment.

1.1   Active Learning in a Mechanized Environment

Within the mathematics mechanization community, it is uncontroversial to assert that the tools available and being developed will make the learning and practice of mathematics better. In theory, this is obvious. In practice, there are devils in the details. For one thing, students (and researchers in industrial environments) must be trained in the use of the new tools, and the time spent learning these tools cannot also be spent on learning the mathematical topics. For this reason, we advocate at least some "re-use" of tools, namely that teaching of mechanized mathematics should use tools that will also be used for something else in the student's or researcher's career.

Nowadays this largely means Jupyter notebooks and Python, which are both very popular in data science and neuroscience. In a few years this might mean a replacement for Jupyter together with Julia (perhaps). The one thing that we can say about the software environment for mathematics is that it is changing as rapidly now as it ever has been.

However, it will not be surprising to the attendees of this conference that there are lessons to be learned from attempts to use mechanized mathematics in teaching in the past. Indeed the "deep structure" of Python is not so different

---

[1] The diversity of where our students go afterwards makes it tricky to choose motivating applications. Network flow problems will appeal to a subset of people; electrical circuits might appeal to another subset. Markov chains are fun for some. Very few applications are interesting to *everybody*.

from that of Maple, and many aspects of programming in the one language transfer readily to the other (for instance, dictionaries in Python are analogous to tables in Maple). More to the point, learning to program in *any* language exercises some of the same mental muscles that writing a mathematical proof does. The analogy between recursion and mathematical induction is very close, indeed. So, at least some of the material that has been developed with older technology can be given some syntactic re-sugaring and used in much the same way. We will give examples.

The most important use of technology, however, is to increase the activity level of the student. One needs to engage the student's attention, and get them to do more than just passively read a text, attend a lecture, watch a video, or regurgitate on an exam. In some ways, fashion helps with this. The students are more likely to want to learn Python than (say) C.

1.2   How to Teach with Technology

There are many papers, and indeed books, written on how to teach with technology. We mention the influential paper [3], which introduced the "White Box"/"Black Box" model, which we have used with some success. The idea there is that when teaching a particular technique (for instance, what a determinant is) the student is not allowed to use the `Determinant` command; but after they have understood that topic, whenever they are *using* determinants in a future topic (say, Cramer's Rule) they are allowed to use it. The psychological and pedagogical point is that people need a certain amount of human action with a concept before it is internalized. We tend to say that at that point, the concept has become an *answer* to the student instead of a *question*. At that point, the students can use the technology with assurance, and the feeling that they know what is going on.

This rule can be used in other ways, and even backwards: use a tool as a mysterious Black Box for a while, probing its output by giving it various inputs until some sense of what is going on arises. We have used this reverse strategy with some success, as well, most commonly with the Singular Value Decomposition (SVD). See [2] for more strategies for teaching with technology that have been tested in practice.

1.3   What to Teach, When Technology Is Involved

A much more interesting question arises when one considers that the curriculum must be continually curated as new tools come available. New topics may be added (for instance, the SVD), and old topics dropped (for instance, condensation, or perhaps Gauss–Seidel iteration). Indeed a certain amount of room must be made in the course for instruction in the responsible use of the new tools. This is by no means easy, and the students will resist such instruction if they are not also assessed on the use of the tools. The fact that they will be expected to use these tools later in life as a matter of course is sometimes not enough to encourage the students to learn them now. However, society appears to expect that we as instructors will be teaching the students the best way to actually use the material we teach, and (as a matter of course) this means that we must be teaching the students to use the tools of modern mechanized mathematics. Those of us who are actually in the classroom know that sometimes compromises are necessary.

1.4   Outline of the Paper

In Sect. 2, we discuss some of the tools that are available. In Sect. 3 we mention a few necessary topics that work well with these tools (we do not give a full syllabus, because of space limitations). In Sect. 4 we discuss methods of assessment. In Sect. 5 we discuss some reactions from colleagues and students to these changes from a traditional syllabus, and then conclude.

2   Tools

The members of this community will have their own preferred computational tools, which may not be the same as ours. We will not fully justify our choices here, but instead sketch only some of the reasons for our choices.

2.1   Proprietary Tools

We do use some proprietary tools, namely Maple and Matlab. Our Universities have site licences for these, and we have a significant body of experience with using these tools both for research and for teaching. Many engineering students will graduate into work environments that have Matlab, and by the usual feedback mechanism from other students and other professors, most engineering students are well-motivated to learn Matlab. Matlab has some especially nice tools for sparse matrices, and its live scripts are quite usable.

Maple is less well-used in industry, but in some countries it does have a presence; nonetheless it is a harder "sell" to students, and if the course does not explicitly give marks for knowing how to use Maple, students are sometimes reluctant to spend time learning it. But it is powerful enough that students do appreciate it, once they have made the effort.

There are other proprietary products which also could be used. Maple Learn is a new one, for instance; but we do not yet have experience with it.

Other places will use Mathematica instead of Maple, but the concerns and affordances are similar.

2.2   Free Software

Within the free software ecosystem, Python and Jupyter stand out as tools of choice for a lot of scientists and engineers. For linear algebra, Matlab and Maple are both superior in terms of capability and in terms of ease of use (in our opinion), especially for sparse matrices, but there is no doubt whatever that Python and Jupyter are more popular.

Python is remarkable for its support for long integer arithmetic (although its quiet casting of types behind the scenes can cause problems, especially when things unexpectedly contain 32 bit unsigned integers instead of the expected long integers). Learning to program in Python is perhaps easier in the beginning than is learning any other language (we are aware that opinions differ in this regard, but surely the statement "the easy parts of Python are easy to learn" would be uncontroversial).

Julia is newer, more exciting, and extremely impressive for its speed as well as its ease of use. We anticipate that use of Julia will eclipse that of Python.

2.3   Visualization

Linear algebra might not seem to need visualization tools as much as Calculus does, but there are several instances where we have found dynamic visualizations to be extremely helpful. One is exemplified by the old Matlab command `eigshow` (which, curiously, has been deprecated and moved into a relatively obscure location inside the Matlab environment) which is extremely effective in giving students "aha!" moments about both eigenvalues and singular values. One of the keys to that tool's effectiveness is (was) the kinesthetic use of the mouse, by the student, to move the input vectors around. The immediate visual feedback of where the output eigenvectors (and singular vectors) move to in response is, in our experience, *much* more effective than simple animations (or static pictures).

More simply, getting the students to plot eigenvalue distributions, or to plot eigenvector components, is valuable as an action.

An opportunity, neglected in most courses and textbooks, is the making of a connection between equation solving and linear transformations. Typically, a course or book opens with an algebraic account of equation solving. The question of how many solutions an equation has is answered by row reduction and the defining of column space. When transformations are introduced, equation solving is not reconsidered. The equation $Ax = b$ is a transformation of the unknown x, in the domain of A, to the range, containing b. The reverse journey is equation solving, and can be the subject of visualization. In 2-D, everything is rather trivial[2], so software allowing 3-D interactive plotting is much better. Transforming a cube using a singular matrix, we observe that the cube is squashed flat. An equation, or the reverse transform, is solvable only if b lies in the plane. See Fig. 1.

2.4   Programming

One of the most venerable introductory programming tasks is to write code for LU factoring. One can then add partial pivoting, complete pivoting, or rook pivoting. The topic is accessible, but difficult enough that students will really feel a sense of accomplishment when they have succeeded.

---

[2] We resisted the temptation to call it "2" trivial.

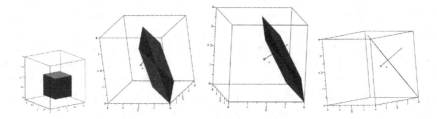

Fig. 1. Transformation of the cube with a singular matrix. The three images are an attempt to show in a static medium a student rotating the plot to see that the cube is now flat. $Ax = b$ has no solution because b is not in the plane. We show, however, a projection of b onto the plane, if least-squares is part of the course.

The hard part is to get them *actually to do it* and not to copy someone else's code. This is especially true in engineering classes, where the students are so heavily pressured that they feel that they *must* cut corners wherever they can. One needs to be creative, here, in finding ways to encourage them not to cheat themselves.

One method that we have found effective is to allow them to work in small groups, and to allow them to use code that they find on the internet or copy from other groups *provided* that they give proper credit and cite where they found it. Students are frequently surprised that their instructors know about Stack Overflow or Chegg as well; but then, in a work environment, any and all tools will be allowed. With some creativity in problem assignment, enough novel features can be used so that the online resources will only help, not solve the complete problem for them. That's unless they use the outright cheating resources where the students post the problems and pay other people to give them the solutions, of course. To combat that, you have to encourage a culture of honesty by being honest yourself and by actually punishing people caught cheating in that way, so that the honest students feel that they can benefit more by remaining honest. However, that's a very hard problem to deal with.

It is however something that people in the mathematics mechanization community need to be aware of. For some decades now, some fully automatic servers have been giving step-by-step solutions to math homework problems. This is only going to get harder for educators to deal with. The statement "if anything can be automated, it should be automated" ignores the need for the "White Box" part of education. Some concepts need human manual work to be internalized.

Remark 1. Many students are only comfortable using computers where they simply enter the data into prescribed fields, and push buttons to achieve pre-programmed aims. One of the things that we want them to do is to get their "keyboards dirty" and engage with a programming language. Doing this at the same time as teaching them the concepts of linear algebra is a stretch. One should expect only minimal success with getting them to write programs, and then only if you assess them (give them marks) on their ability to do so. Time spent on that is time that cannot be spent on linear algebra topics. The topics that we discuss below are chosen in part for their aptness to programming.

3   Topics

In this section we sketch some of the topics that we feel should be encountered in a modern, mechanized, first course in linear algebra, together with how we think that some of the described tools can help with the concepts.

3.1   The Language of Matrices

There is a nontrivial transition from systems of equations such as

$$3x + 4y = 7$$
$$2x - 8y = 1 \tag{1}$$

to the equivalent matrix equations, and most mechanized systems do not have features to help with this transition. Matlab, for instance, expects the user to enter the matrices. We spend some time on this transition, and the conventions that lead to the natural rules for matrix-vector multiplication and thence to matrix-matrix multiplication. The use of elementary matrices to encode operations on equations (especially elimination of a variable) is a crucial feature.

With beginning students, this takes time. Hand manipulation is best for this at the beginning, but after experiencing a certain amount of tedium, the students begin to appreciate the ability to construct and manipulate equations through the algebraic rules of matrix multiplication[3]. The simple syntax of Matlab is likely the most appreciated: `A*b` for matrix-vector multiplication is close to $\mathbf{A} \cdot \mathbf{b}$, a common human notation; omitting the $\cdot$ seems natural. Maple's `A.b` is somewhat less natural.

Python's notation is similar, except for one thing. The issue is *transpose*. Some linear algebra approaches are very snobbish, and insist that there is no such thing as a row vector or column vector, only abstract vectors. Python is like this. This can be very confusing for students. We have found it best to be explicit and consistent about dimensions in our teaching, and to treat vectors normally as column vectors and to treat these as basically indistinguishable from $n \times 1$ matrices (even that convention needs to be taught: one of our colleagues memorably put it as "you *row* with columns (oars) when you row a boat").

The "four ways" of interpreting matrix-matrix multiplication is something we explicitly teach. For instance, in one of these four ways, the matrix-matrix product $\mathbf{AB}$ can be usefully thought of by first thinking of $\mathbf{B} = [\mathbf{b}_1, \mathbf{b}_2, \ldots, \mathbf{b}_n]$

---

[3] They quite like Maple's `GenerateMatrix` command, which transforms linear equations with variables into matrix-vector equations. We try to be careful to introduce this only after the students have some experience in doing the transformation by hand.

as a collection of columns, and then $\mathbf{AB} = [\mathbf{Ab}_1, \mathbf{Ab}_2, \ldots, \mathbf{Ab}_n]$ is then a collection of the column vectors $\mathbf{Ab}_k$. Technological support for this can be as simple as asking the students to construct the matrix on the right hand side explicitly, and verifying that the internal matrix multiplication routine produces the same result. An advanced question is to consider parallelism in matrix-matrix multiplication using this partition.

We also *begin* with complex numbers. They will be needed, so we introduce them first thing. Without technological support, students hate complex numbers. With technological support, complex numbers become routine.

3.2   Parametric Linear Algebra

One important feature of our course is that it is not purely numerical. Mathematical modelling frequently involves unknown parameters. One wants the solution in terms of those parameters (if possible) to make it possible to identify those parameters by comparing to experimental data. There is also the pedagogical value of strengthening student's understanding of formulas, when the answers are not numbers but instead are formulas.

As is well-known in the computer algebra community, this can make computations much more costly and indeed some problems are known to have exponential cost or, worse, combinatorial cost. There is significant literature on the topic, starting with [19]. Recent work includes [4,8,10] and [11]. We will address this issue as it comes up in the various topics. The paper [11] raises the important point that for many practical problems with only a few parameters, perhaps only one or two, and for problems with structure or low dimension or both, solutions are perfectly feasible using modern computers and infrastructure.

3.3   Factoring Matrices

Factoring matrices, whether it is the Turing factoring $\mathbf{PA} = \mathbf{LDUR}$ which gives the reduced row echelon form [9], or $\mathbf{A} = \mathbf{QR}$ into an orthogonal factor $\mathbf{Q}$ and upper (right) triangular factor $\mathbf{R}$, or any of several other factorings, is fundamental for modern linear algebra. There is the Schur factoring $\mathbf{A} = \mathbf{QTQ}^H$ which gives the eigenvalues in a numerically stable way.

We teach the notion of factoring matrices as a method of solving linear systems of equations (and of eigenvalue problems). This represents a conceptual advance over Gaussian Elimination, and has several important consequences in a symbolic context [9,13]. The most important feature in a symbolic context is that a factoring preserves special cases.

Students can factor matrices by hand (and in the beginning, they should). This gives them something useful to *do*. Elementary matrices encoding row operations, column operations, and row exchanges are all useful to teach because they consolidate students' knowledge into a modern framework of understanding of linear algebra, and they do so in a way that allows the student to be *active*.

Then one can introduce *block* matrix manipulation and *block* factoring, with noncommuting elements. This gives the Schur complement and the Schur determinantal formula.

Interestingly, Maple has recently begun to support matrices over noncommuting variables via the Physics package by Edgardo Cheb–Terrab. This allows students to manipulate block matrices with technology, although they still have to think about dimensions. This is apparently also possible in SageMath. Here is an example, showing the Schur complement, in Maple.

> *with*(*Physics*):
> *Setup*(*mathematicalnotation* = *true*):
> *Setup*(*noncommutativeprefix* = {*B*}):
> *with*(*LinearAlgebra*):
> $A := Matrix([[B[1,1], B[1,2]], [B[2,1], B[2,2]]])$

$$A := \begin{bmatrix} B_{1,1} & B_{1,2} \\ B_{2,1} & B_{2,2} \end{bmatrix} \tag{2}$$

> $L := Matrix([[1,0], [B[2,1] \cdot B[1,1]^{-1}, 1]])$

$$L := \begin{bmatrix} 1 & 0 \\ B_{2,1}B_{1,1}{}^{-1} & 1 \end{bmatrix} \tag{3}$$

> $U := Matrix([[B[1,1], B[1,2]], [0, B[2,2] - B[2,1] \cdot B[1,1]^{-1} \cdot B[1,2]]])$

$$U := \begin{bmatrix} B_{1,1} & B_{1,2} \\ 0 & B_{2,2} - B_{2,1}B_{1,1}{}^{-1}B_{1,2} \end{bmatrix} \tag{4}$$

> $L \cdot U$

$$\begin{bmatrix} B_{1,1} & B_{1,2} \\ B_{2,1} & B_{2,2} \end{bmatrix} \tag{5}$$

This *illustrative* usage of simple noncommuting scalar variables to represent blocks inside matrices, where 1 represents an appropriately-sized identity matrix and 0 represents a zero block, might disconcert people intent on formalizing the computations involved. One of the things that would be necessary to properly formalize this would be a notion of dimension of each block; in practice one would want the dimensions to be *symbolic* but to match appropriately. We are not aware of any widely-available system at present that can deal properly with this, although there has been research in the area, such as [17,18]. Making a package widely available that could do such computations correctly would be very welcome.

122 R. M. Corless et al.

3.4 Determinant

Approaching linear algebra via the determinant is a historically valid approach. It is pedagogically valid, also, because the students are happier (and better off) with having something to *do*, not just think about. We feel that it is "fair game" that the students be required to memorize the formulas for the determinant and the inverse of a 2×2 matrix (and in fact this memorization is surprisingly useful for them, later). Laplace expansion (determinant by minors) can be costly and numerically dubious but is extremely useful for sparse symbolic matrices. More, it is crucial in the one "gem" proof that we include in the course simply because it is so pretty, namely the proof of Cramer's Rule[4] which we learned from [5].

Asking them to memorize a formula for a three-by-three determinant serves no useful purpose, in our opinion, and letting them use technology for computation of third or higher-order determinants seems perfectly justified.

We also demonstrate combinatorial growth by showing the determinant of fully symbolic matrices, for a few small dimensions. Asking them to program Laplace expansion recursively is also useful for this. One can also ask them to program the recursive computation of determinant by the Schur determinantal formula $\det \mathbf{A} = \det \mathbf{B}_{11} \det(\mathbf{B}_{22} - \mathbf{B}_{21}\mathbf{B}_{11}^{-1}\mathbf{B}_{12})$. Explicit computation of the inverse of $\mathbf{B}_{11}$ should be avoided, and can be, by using a suitable factoring. The end result can be significantly more efficient than Laplace expansion.

We spend time on the geometry of determinant and its relationship to how area transforms under linear transformations; this is needed in calculus, and can be motivating for the students as well because it makes a connection to something that they already know. Computer visualizations help, here. The ones freely available on YouTube, especially the very professionally produced ones by 3Blue1Brown such as https://youtu.be/Ip3X9LOh2dk, are hard to compete with. So, we do not compete, and instead share our favourites (such as that one) with the student.

With determinant in hand, the students have a worthwhile test for linear dependence. We extend this using the SVD because in the context of data error (which our clientele will surely encounter), the notion of exact singularity or dependence is less useful than that of ill-conditioning or near-dependence.

Least Squares. Matlab will silently return a least-squares solution to overdetermined problems. Or, even, inconsistent problems. Therefore it is incumbent on us as instructors to teach least squares solutions, in order that the user may understand and appreciate what the system has done.

3.5 Eigenvalues and Floating-Point

We teach eigenvalues more by the "Black Box"/"White Box" approach, because computing eigenvalues by first computing the determinant of $\lambda \mathbf{I} - \mathbf{A}$ and then

---

[4] One of us teaches Cramer's Rule only because of this beautiful proof. Cramer's Rule itself is not particularly useful computationally nowadays, except in very special situations. But that proof is so beautiful. The students seem to like it, too.

solving the polynomial is a pretty brutal hand computation for anything more than 2×2 matrices. We show them what eigenvalues and eigenvectors *are* by the use of `eigshow` or similar, and then set them to compute eigenvalues by the technology. For instance in Fig. 2 we see how to do this using Maple (from inside a Jupyter notebook). This requires a discussion of floating-point arithmetic and backward error analysis, which we do not shy away from. Again, our clientele will encounter data error and they must learn tools such as the condition number (which is really just the derivative) to deal with it; putting numerical error on the same footing as data error gives them the tools to deal with that, as well. The computation of eigenvalues of small matrices (say, of dimension less than 1000) is a solved problem nowadays.

Indeed we view eigenvalues as answers nowadays because the algorithms are so good in practice (and have recently been shown to be globally convergent in theory, as well [1]). We have had units (in some of our courses) where we talk about companion matrices of various kinds, as tools for solving polynomial equations and systems of polynomial equations. We discuss this in Sect. 3.6.

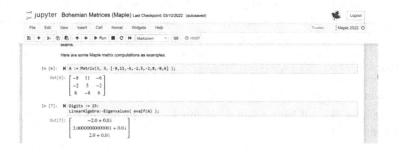

Fig. 2. Using Maple from a Jupyter notebook

Eigenvalues of *parametric* matrices are important, for instance in dynamical systems, and their study leads directly to bifurcation theory. We do not include many such problems, but we have used one in particular, namely a perturbation of Matlab's `gallery(3)` matrix to examine the sensitivity of its eigenvalues to perturbations. This is an advanced topic, however, and occurs only toward the end of the first course (and much more frequently in the second or later course).

3.6   Special Matrices

There are countless kinds of special matrices. Likely the most important in practice are symmetric (Hermitian) positive definite matrices; others include orthogonal (unitary) matrices, triangular matrices, banded matrices, circulant matrices, Toeplitz matrices, Hankel matrices, and totally positive matrices. Getting the students to write programs that generate some of these, or factor some of these in special ways, is quite interesting. The Cayley transform is quite important

nowadays (see e.g. [15]) in control theory and in some kinds of scientific computing, and getting students to parameterize orthogonal matrices using symmetric
matrices and the Cayley transform may teach several lessons.

While this course should include some of the most common and useful kinds
of special matrices, we feel it is also important to let the students invent some
of their own kinds of matrices. Examples of student-generated matrices include
"checkerboard" matrices which alternate nonzero entries with zero entries and
"anti-tridiagonal" matrices. We have found it fun to let the students play, as
they program. Sometimes even their bugs give rise to interesting developments.

Symmetric Positive Definite Matrices

"Symmetric positive definiteness is one of the highest accolades to which
a matrix can aspire."

—Nicholas J. Higham, in [12, p. 196]

Symmetric Positive Definite (SPD) matrices arise very often in practice. For an
enlightening discussion of just why this is so, see [20]. The inductive proof of
unicity of the Cholesky factoring for SPD matrices (see e.g. [12, p. 196]) can
be turned into a recursive program for its computation, and this is a useful
programming exercise for the students. The many applications of SPD matrices
can be motivating for students, but having the technology to solve them is clearly
essential.

Companion Matrices

"What does this all have to do with matrices? The connection is through
the *companion* matrix."

—Cleve Moler, in [16].

Another thing technology really makes possible is the use of companion matrices
and resultants in the solution of polynomial equations. The topic is surprisingly
rich, not just useful. Algebraically, companion matrices for a monic polynomial
$p(z)$ are matrix representations of multiplication by z in the ideal generated by
$p(z)$. Companion matrices are not unique, and indeed there are open problems as
to which is the "best" companion for a given polynomial $p(z)$, as we will discuss.
Extending the idea to non-monic polynomials leads to generalized eigenvalue
problems $p(z) = \det(\lambda \mathbf{B} - \mathbf{A})$ where now $\mathbf{B}$ is not necessarily the identity matrix
(or of full rank). Using other polynomial bases (e.g. Chebyshev, Bernstein, or
Lagrange interpolational bases) leads again to surprisingly deep waters. Given a
(monic) polynomial over the integers, one can ask which companion matrix over
the integers has minimal height? The "height" of a matrix is the infinity norm
of the matrix made into a vector; that is, the largest absolute value of any entry.
No good algorithms for this problem are known [7]. In the case of Mandelbrot
polynomials $p_0 = 0$ and $p_{n+1}(z) = zp_n^2(z) + 1$ there are companions of height 1,
while the maximum coefficient of $p_n(z)$ is exponential in the degree of $p_n(z)$ (and
therefore doubly exponential in n). Smaller height matrices seem to be easier to
compute eigenvalues for.

3.7   Proof and Formal Methods

"I have absolutely no interest in proving things that I know are true."

—the American physicist Henry Abarbanel, at a conference in 1994

Entering students in North America have long since been deprived of an introductory course on proof (which was, classically, Euclidean geometry). Typically the first course in which they encounter "proof" nowadays is their first linear algebra class. For the clientele described previously, we feel it is more important to *motivate* proof at this stage. Students who are asked to listen to a proof of something they consider obvious (or for which they would be happy to take the professor's word, such as $\det \mathbf{AB} = \det \mathbf{A} \cdot \det \mathbf{B}$) do not learn much. Ed Barbeau put it thus: "there should be no proof without doubt" (on the part of the student).

Asking students to write programs is, we believe, a useful intermediate step. In addition to developing the necessary habit of precise thinking, writing programs makes students receptive to the idea of proving their programs correct (after they have witnessed a few failures, which are somehow always surprising to beginning programmers).

4   Assessment

Assessment is critical for the success of a course. Students want bribes (marks) in order to spend time on any particular topic. If a topic is not assessed, then it can be safely skipped and the student can rationally spend their effort on topics that actually will be assessed.

The recent introduction of chat AIs that generate plausible-sounding answers has thrown a further monkey wrench into assessment of courses by project, a method that we have heretofore favoured. It is even the case that these chat AIs can, perhaps by plagiarising GitHub and other software sources, provide readable (and sometimes even working) software to students. We may have to go back to individual exams with direct supervision: essentially, oral examinations. This is so labour intensive that it seems impractical for the very large linear algebra classes that our Universities want us to teach, however.

There are several strategies for written exams that still may be of interest, however, and we give some of them here. The first is the venerable multiple-choice exam. Constructing good multiple-choice exams is a skill that can be taught, and there is significant research on it.

A second assessment strategy is to use computer-generated individual questions, where the student is expected to work at their computer (or at a locked-down lab computer) and provide full notes on their work. These kinds of exams are very stressful for students, however. They are even more stressful if intrusively-monitoring software is involved (and there may be human rights abuses committed by those pieces of software which the instructor or administration will be responsible for).

Since we want to include the use of mechanized tools into the assessment, testing in a computational environment is quite natural. If the students know that they will be tested on their competence in (say) Python, then they will spend some effort to learn it. Incorporating personalized questions into such exams then becomes both feasible and informative.

5 Promoting Agreement on Syllabus Change

Some of our colleagues and administrative structures have been very support- ive of innovation along these lines. Others have been, well, reactionary. Using technology is more labour intensive than is re-using the same old linear algebra textbooks, problem sets, and exam questions. Using technology also requires con- tinual re-training because the technologies keep changing. Some people resent being told that they have to change in order to do their jobs well in a changing environment.

We give an example here of a suboptimal linear algebra exam question, taken from last year's multi-section course at Western[5], taught both by progressive and regressive colleagues. The exam took place without notes, books, calculators, or computers. Students are allowed by law (in some parts of the world) to have access to their phones, but many universities will attempt to restrict that, too. The exams at Western typically have quite alarming language on the cover sheet saying that students caught with a cell phone will be given a zero. We feel that this is a lamentable state.

The question was: Find the inverse of the matrix

$$\mathbf{A} = \begin{bmatrix} 2 & 1 & 0 \\ 1 & 0 & -1 \\ 0 & 1 & 1 \end{bmatrix}. \tag{6}$$

This question does have a few virtues. For one, it is something the students can *do*. It was worth three marks, which the students could grind out.

But it also has some serious flaws. Probably the most serious is that it does not test anything that the students will really need in their future use of linear algebra. There were calculators thirty years ago that could solve this problem in under a second. No one is going to invert 3×3 matrices by hand any more, unless there is something special about it. [There *is* something special about this matrix; it is unimodular, so that the elements of the inverse are all integers. That didn't happen by chance, so we suspect the examiners chose the question so as not to strain the student's arithmetic overmuch.]

More, not only will students not need to invert by hand, they usually will not need to invert at all. The *inversion of matrices* is really only of very specialized concern nowadays. There are statistical applications where the elements of the inverse are what is wanted; but for the most part, "Anything that you can do

---

[5] A simple web search for "Math 1600 Western" brings the entire exam up, if you wish to see the entire context.

with the matrix inverse can be done without it." Matrix factorings are much more important.

Students are rational creatures. If this is the kind of question that they have to answer in order to pass, then they will spend their time trying to find strategies to give good answers to this kind of question. They will do that at the expense of time spent learning to program (for instance).

This represents a significant lost opportunity for the student and for this University. Indeed, the absolute explosion in on-line courses (for instance, at brilliant.org, where they claim that interactive learning is six times more effective than lectures) is a direct response to the failure of many universities to adapt their courses. Students resent having to pay twice to get the knowledge they actually want and need. The next few years are going to be "interesting."

One way to repair that particular question might be to ask if the matrix factors into a lower triangular and upper triangular factor, without pivoting. The matrix is tridiagonal, so this variation has fewer computations, although this time involving fractions (just $1/2$ though). This is something that could be asked even if the student has access to technology during the exam. The details of the computation are not that important—it is just arithmetic—but the question of whether or not the factoring can be done without pivoting would require some understanding of the process involved.

6   Concluding Remarks

The state of the art for learning linear algebra is, to our minds, unsatisfactory, though getting better. Technological platforms are split: some are proprietary, while some others are unsupported at the level needed for reliable use. Methods and syntax are not standardized (or, rather, there are too many standards). The textbooks largely do not integrate mechanized mathematical tools into the learning process. [A very notable exception is [21], which uses Matlab extensively.] Yet failing to use a mechanized approach does a true disservice to students who will go on to practice linear algebra in some kind of mechanized environment.

The role of technology, including formal methods, is therefore multiplex. We believe that people must be trained in its use. In particular, people must be trained to want proof, and to want formal methods. We feel that having students write their own programs plays a motivating role in that training as well as a developmental role. The first linear algebra course is important not only because its tools and concepts are critical for science, but also as a venue for teaching the responsible use of mathematical technology.

Acknowledgements. This work was partially supported by NSERC under RGPIN-2020-06438 and RGPIN-2018-06670 and by the grant PID2020-113192GB-I00 (Mathematical Visualization: Foundations, Algorithms and Applications) from the Spanish MICINN. We also acknowledge the support of the Rotman Institute of Philosophy. We thank the referees for their thoughtful and constructive comments.

References

1. Banks, J., Garza-Vargas, J., Srivastava, N.: Global convergence of Hessenberg shifted QR I: Dynamics (2022)
2. Betteridge, J., Chan, E.Y.S., Corless, R.M., Davenport, J.H., Grant, J.: Teaching programming for mathematical scientists. In: Richard, P.R., Vélez, M.P., Van Vaerenbergh, S. (eds.) Mathematics Education in the Age of Artificial Intelligence, vol. 17, pp. 251–276. Springer, Cham (2022). https://doi.org/10.1007/978-3-030-86909-0_12
3. Buchberger, B.: Should students learn integration rules? ACM SIGSAM Bull. **24**(1), 10–17 (1990)
4. Camargos Couto, A.C., Moreno Maza, M., Linder, D., Jeffrey, D.J., Corless, R.M.: Comprehensive LU factors of polynomial matrices. In: Slamanig, D., Tsigaridas, E., Zafeirakopoulos, Z. (eds.) MACIS 2019. LNCS, vol. 11989, pp. 80–88. Springer, Cham (2020). https://doi.org/10.1007/978-3-030-43120-4_8
5. Carlson, D., Johnson, C.R., Lay, D., Porter, A.D.: Gems of exposition in elementary linear algebra. Coll. Math. J. **23**(4), 299–303 (1992). https://doi.org/10.1080/07468342.1992.11973473
6. Carlson, D., Johnson, C.R., Lay, D.C., Porter, A.D.: The linear algebra curriculum study group recommendations for the first course in linear algebra. Coll. Math. J. **24**(1), 41–46 (1993)
7. Chan, E.Y., Corless, R.M.: Minimal height companion matrices for Euclid polynomials. Math. Comput. Sci. **13**, 41–56 (2019)
8. Corless, R.M., Giesbrecht, M., Rafiee Sevyeri, L., Saunders, B.D.: On parametric linear system solving. In: Boulier, F., England, M., Sadykov, T.M., Vorozhtsov, E.V. (eds.) CASC 2020. LNCS, vol. 12291, pp. 188–205. Springer, Cham (2020). https://doi.org/10.1007/978-3-030-60026-6_11
9. Corless, R.M., Jeffrey, D.J.: The Turing factorization of a rectangular matrix. ACM SIGSAM Bull. **31**(3), 20–30 (1997)
10. Corless, R.M., Moreno Maza, M., Thornton, S.E.: Jordan canonical form with parameters from Frobenius form with parameters. In: Blömer, J., Kotsireas, I.S., Kutsia, T., Simos, D.E. (eds.) MACIS 2017. LNCS, vol. 10693, pp. 179–194. Springer, Cham (2017). https://doi.org/10.1007/978-3-319-72453-9_13
11. Deng, S., Reid, G., Jeffrey, D.: Parametric linear algebra in maple: reduced row echelon form. In: Proceedings of SYNASC, pp. 33–36. IEEE (2021)
12. Higham, N.J.: Accuracy and Stability of Numerical Algorithms, 2nd edn. SIAM, Philadelphia (2002)
13. Jeffrey, D.J., Corless, R.M.: Linear algebra in maple®. In: Hogben, L. (ed.) Handbook of Linear Algebra, 2nd edn., pp. 89–1. Chapman and Hall/CRC, Boca Raton (2013)
14. Lay, D.C., Lay, S.R., McDonald, J.: Linear Algebra and Its Applications. Pearson Education, New York (2016)
15. Mehrmann, V.: A step toward a unified treatment of continuous and discrete time control problems. Linear Algebra Appl. **241**, 749–779 (1996)
16. Moler, C.: Roots–of polynomials, that is (1991). https://www.mathworks.com/company/newsletters/articles/roots-of-polynomials-that-is.html
17. Sexton, A., Sorge, V.: Abstract matrices in symbolic computation. In: Proceedings of ISSAC. ACM, July 2006. https://doi.org/10.1145/1145768.1145820
18. Sexton, A.P., Sorge, V., Watt, S.M.: Computing with abstract matrix structures. In: Proceedings of ISSAC, pp. 325–332 (2009)

19. Sit, W.Y.: An algorithm for solving parametric linear systems. J. Symb. Comput. **13**(4), 353–394 (1992)
20. Strang, G.: Introduction to Applied Mathematics. Wellesley-Cambridge Press, Wellesley (1986)
21. Van Loan, C.F., Fan, K.Y.D.: Insight Through Computing - A MATLAB Introduction to Computational Science and Engineering. SIAM, Philadelphia (2010)

Highlighting Named Entities in Input for Auto-formulation of Optimization Problems

Neeraj Gangwar[(✉)] and Nickvash Kani

Electrical and Computer Engineering, University of Illinois Urbana-Champaign,
Urbana, IL, USA
{gangwar2,kani}@illinois.edu

Abstract. Operations research deals with modeling and solving real-world problems as mathematical optimization problems. While solving mathematical systems is accomplished by analytical software, formulating a problem as a set of mathematical operations has been typically done manually by domain experts. Recent machine learning methods have shown promise in converting textual problem descriptions to corresponding mathematical formulations. This paper presents an approach that converts linear programming word problems into mathematical formulations. We leverage the named entities in a problem description and augment the input to highlight these entities. Our approach achieves the highest accuracy among all submissions to the NL4Opt competition, securing first place in the generation track.

1 Introduction

Operations research deals with modeling and solving real-world problems as mathematical optimization problems [1,2,8,14]. There exist optimization solvers powered by efficient algorithms [5,9] that can be used to solve these problems. However, these solvers do not directly take problem descriptions as input, and domain experts are required to model a problem into a mathematical formulation. Ramamonjison et al. [12] described an interactive system that can suggest a formulation based on the natural language description of a linear programming problem. Their system consists of two main components – an *entity tagger* to tag the named entities in an input problem description and a *formulation generator* to generate a mathematical formulation. They also published a dataset of linear programming problems with two tasks – named entity tagging and mathematical formulation generation.

In this paper, *we focus on formulation generation*. Figure 1 shows an overview of the task. The input to formulation generation consists of a word problem, labeled semantic entities, and the order mapping of variables. We propose a novel approach that leverages the labeled semantic entities. In particular, we highlight the named entities in a problem description using XML-like start and end tags. Our results show that a sequence-to-sequence (SEQ2SEQ) model, like BART [6], can leverage this information while generating a mathematical formulation. Our approach achieves the highest accuracy among all submissions to the

C. Dubois and M. Kerber (Eds.): CICM 2023, LNAI 14101, pp. 130–141, 2023.
https://doi.org/10.1007/978-3-031-42753-4_9

generation track of the NL4Opt competition.[1] Unlike the NL4Opt Generation dataset, labeled named entity information is not available in most applications. We show that these applications may still benefit by using an existing named entity recognition (NER) system to predict and highlight the named entities in an input. Lastly, we present an ablation study, highlighting the impact of different components of our model. Though our approach fails in certain cases, the results indicate that deep learning methods may prove helpful in automating the formulation generation process. Furthermore, it may be used to provide suggestions to users, reducing manual effort, similar to a system described in Ramamonjison et al. [12]. Our source code is available on GitHub.[2]

2   Related Work

The problem of identifying the named entities in linear programming word problems and generating their mathematical formulation was proposed by Ramamonjison et al. [12]. In their work, they provided a baseline model for the formulation generation task, which used a two-step mapping approach. They used BART-base with copy mechanism [6,13] to generate an intermediate representation of the problem, which was then parsed into a canonical formulation. Jang [4] used entity tag embeddings with BART-large [6] to leverage the named entity information and introduced data augmentation in their approach. Ning et al. [10] used prompt-guided inputs along with adversarial learning. Their approach used BART-base and achieved competitive performance compared to the approaches utilizing BART-large. On the other hand, He et al. [3] used multitask learning and input pre-processing. They augmented the input problem description by encapsulating the named entities in tags corresponding to their labels. Their approach used prompt-guided inputs and generated either an objective or a constraint at a time. Prasath and Karande [11] used CodeT5-base [17] to generate an intermediate representation and a custom beam search with rule-based scoring. They trained their model on auxiliary tasks, such as predicting the number of constraints, variable names, parameter values, and objective direction, in addition to the primary task.

Our approach utilizes named entity information and augments the input problem description by encapsulating the named entities in tags corresponding to their labels. We use BART with copy mechanism to generate an intermediate representation, which is then parsed into a canonical formulation. Differing from He et al. [3], Ning et al. [10], and Ramamonjison et al. [12], we use "all-at-once" strategy and generate the objective and constraints for an input problem at once. We do not use multitask learning or adversarial learning in our approach. Unlike Jang [4], our approach does not have an additional hyperparameter. Despite its simplicity, our approach achieves better results than the more complex approaches, suggesting all that is needed for optimal performance is well-tagged data and a large model.

---

[1] https://nl4opt.github.io.
[2] https://github.com/mlpgroup/nl4opt-generation.

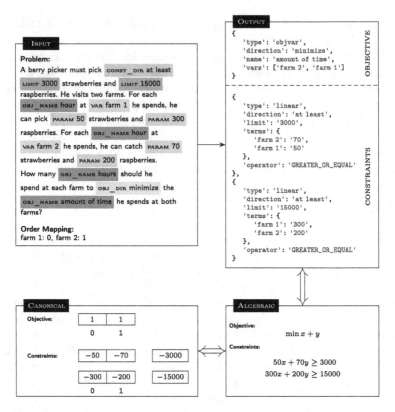

Fig. 1. *(Top)* An example input-output pair from the dataset consists of a problem statement, labeled named entities, and the order mapping of variable mentions. *(Bottom)* The algebraic and the corresponding canonical formulations are shown on the right and left, respectively. We use the canonical formulation to represent a mathematical formulation in our implementation for evaluation. In a canonical formulation, it is assumed that the objective is always minimized, and the constraints are upper bounds. For a maximization objective or a lower bound constraint, the signs of the parameters are inverted.

3   Proposed Approach

Named entities carry important semantic information. For generating mathematical formulations from linear programming word problems, the highlighted named entities can be utilized to form the objective and constraints for an input problem (Fig. 1). We leverage this information and hypothesize that this additional information can help a SEQ2SEQ model in generating mathematical formulations. In our proposed approach, we highlight the named entities in an input problem description before passing it to a SEQ2SEQ model.

Named Entity-Based Augmentation. We use XML-like start and end tags to highlight the named entities in an input problem description. We create XML-

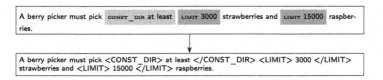

Fig. 2. An example of the named entity-based augmentation. In an input problem description, the named entities are encapsulated inside XML-like start and end tags of their respective types.

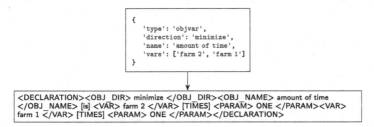

Fig. 3. Objectives and constraints are converted to an XML format to form intermediate representations. This figure shows the conversion for an objective.

like tags for all named entity labels and encapsulate each entity in the input within these tags. Figure 3 shows an example of this augmentation.

Output. Similar to Ramamonjison et al. [12], we follow a two-stage approach for generating a canonical representation. We use BART to generate an intermediate representation, which is then parsed into a canonical representation for evaluation. The intermediate representation consists of a set of declarations in an XML format, where a declaration corresponds to either an objective or a constraint. Figure 3 shows an example of converting an objective to an intermediate representation. A similar approach is followed for constraints.

The canonical form always minimizes an objective. In the case of a maximization objective, the sign of each objective parameter is inverted. Similarly, inequality constraints are always assumed to have a "$\leq$" operator. In the case of a "$\geq$" operator, the sign of each constraint parameter is inverted.

Model. Our model is similar to the one presented in Ramamonjison et al. [12]. We use BART with copy mechanism in our experiments. The copy mechanism is useful in cases where certain tokens in the input need to be directly copied to the output. The mechanism allows for the preservation of specific information, for example, parameters, limits, etc. in the formulation generation task. The model uses the mean of the cross attention weights to generate a probability distribution over the input tokens, P_{input}, and combines it with the output distribution, P_{vocab}, to compute the final distribution of a token as

$$P = p_{\text{gen}}P_{\text{vocab}} + (1 - p_{\text{gen}})P_{\text{input}} \tag{1}$$

Table 1. Different constraint types and their mathematical form. Here, x and y are variables and a, b, and c are constants. Refer to Table 4 in Ramamonjison et al. [12] for details.

Constraint Type	Mathematical Form
SUM	$x + y \leq c,\ x + y \geq c$
UPPER BOUND	$x \leq c$
LOWER BOUND	$x \geq c$
LINEAR	$ax + by \leq c,\ ax + by \geq c$
RATIO	$x \leq c(x + y),\ x \geq c(x + y)$
XY	$x \leq y,\ x \geq y$
XBY	$x \leq by,\ x \geq by$

Here, $p_{\text{gen}} \in [0, 1]$ is a soft switch to decide between generating a token from the vocabulary or copying it from the input. It is computed using other learnable parameters of the model. We find that the copy mechanism has a small impact on the performance when the input problem description is augmented to highlight the named entities.

Lastly, we add new tokens, corresponding to the XML tags for the named entity labels, to the tokenizer and initialize their weights randomly at the time of training. At inference, we use greedy decoding to generate an output.

4   Experiments

4.1   Dataset

We use the NL4Opt Generation dataset for our experiments.[3] This dataset consists of 1101 examples, divided into the train, dev, and test splits composed of 713, 99, and 289 examples, respectively. Each example consists of a linear programming word problem, labeled semantic entities, and the order mapping of named variables. These problems are from the advertising, investment, sales, production, science, and transportation domains. The training split consists of problems from the first three domains. The dev and test splits contain problems from all six domains to evaluate the model's ability to generalize for domains it has not seen during training. The dataset divides constraints into different categories. Table 1 shows different constraint types and their mathematical form. Refer to Ramamonjison et al. [12] for more details.

4.2   Training Details

The PyTorch transformers library implementation of the base and large versions of BART is used [18]. We use the AdamW optimizer [7] with a learning rate of

---

[3] Available at https://github.com/nl4opt/nl4opt-competition.

Table 2. Accuracy achieved by our approach on the test set and a comparison with the existing approaches. For our approach, we report the best and mean (shown in brackets) accuracy values. The values for our approach are with greedy decoding.

APPROACH	ACCURACY
JANG [4]	0.878
NING ET AL. [10]	0.867
HE ET AL. [3]	0.780
PRASATH AND KARANDE [11]	0.896
OUR APPROACH	
w/ BART-BASE	0.834 (0.812 ± 0.019)
w/ BART-LARGE	0.929 (0.896 ± 0.025)

5×10^{-5} and a weight decay of 10^{-5}. Batch sizes of 16 with gradient accumulation for two steps and 32 with no gradient accumulation are used for BART-large and BART-base, respectively. The models are fine-tuned for 400 epochs and are evaluated at the end of every epoch. We use a learning rate schedule with a linear warm-up for the first five epochs and a linear decay after that. The experiments are run on one A100 40 GB GPU.

4.3 Evaluation Metrics

The model is evaluated on declaration-level accuracy [12]. The accuracy is defined as

$$\text{Accuracy} = 1 - \frac{\min\left\{\sum_{i=1}^{N} FP_i + FN_i, D_i\right\}}{\sum_{i=1}^{N} D_i} \qquad (2)$$

where N is the number of test examples. For i^{th} example, D_i is the number of ground truth declarations, FP_i is the number of non-matched predicted declarations and FN_i is the number of excess ground truth declarations.

4.4 Results

Table 2 shows the accuracy achieved by our approach. We initialize the training using five seeds and report the best and mean accuracies achieved by our models on the test set. Our approach achieves the best accuracy among approaches that use SEQ2SEQ models and fine-tune them on the generation dataset.

4.5 Error Analysis

To understand the errors made by our model, we analyze examples from the test set for which our best model makes a mistake in either an objective, a constraint, or both. For a few examples, the ground truth output is not correct, hence we do not consider them for the analysis. It should be noted that the model predicts the output correctly for half of these examples.

The model makes a mistake in predicting the objective for 11 examples. While these errors are caused by incorrect parameter predictions, for five examples, the model considers all variables as part of the objective, even though the objective is defined only on a subset of the variables. The train set contains a very small number of such examples, which may explain the model's inability to handle these cases during evaluation.

For 41 examples, the model makes an error while predicting one or multiple constraints. These errors fall into different buckets:

– The predicted constraint operators are incorrect. For example, the $\leq$ operator is predicted instead of the $\geq$ operator or vice versa.
– The model does not generate all constraints or generates excess constraints.
– The predicted constraint type is incorrect. For example, SUM is predicted instead of LINEAR.
– The constraint parameters are incorrect. For example, $2x + 3y \leq 100$ is predicted instead of $x + y \leq 100$.

Almost half the errors are caused by an incorrect constraint operator prediction. It is interesting that these errors stem from the model predicting the "$\leq$" operator instead of the "$\geq$" operator. We only notice one example for which the model outputs the "$\geq$" operator instead of the "$\leq$" operator, and it is not part of the 41 examples due to a missing constraint in the ground truth output. Furthermore, the majority of the constraint operator errors are in XY and LINEAR constraints. It may be attributed to the fact that the "$\leq$" operator occurs in 693 LINEAR and 45 XY constraints, whereas the "$\geq$" operator occurs in 323 LINEAR and 4 XY constraints in the train set. But this imbalance is present for other constraint types. Another possible reason for this behavior may be the overall imbalance in the train set which contains 1245 constraints with the "$\leq$" operator and 743 constraints with the "$\geq$" operator, causing the model to lean more towards the former.

4.6   Ablation Study

This section discusses the impact of the named entity-based augmentation, copy mechanism, and model size on the model performance. We experiment with BART-base and BART-large and fine-tune the models by removing the named entity-based augmentation and copy mechanism one at a time. We fix the other hyperparameters, initialize the training with five seed values, and report the best and mean accuracies. The results of the ablation study are shown in Table 3.

It can be observed from these results that the named entity-based augmentation plays a major role in improving the performance of both BART-base and BART-large. This shows that highlighting named entities in the input text helps the model generate output formulations correctly. Furthermore, while the copy mechanism improves the best accuracy, it does not have a positive effect on the

Table 3. Results of the ablation study. We report the best and mean accuracy values achieved by the models with greedy decoding on the test set. Here, NEA and CM stand for the named entity-based augmentation and copy mechanism, respectively.

	BART-BASE	BART-LARGE
w/o CM	0.827 (0.812 ± 0.012)	0.908 (0.902 ± 0.007)
w/o NEA	0.681 (0.663 ± 0.016)	0.863 (0.849 ± 0.015)
w/o NEA AND CM	0.681 (0.657 ± 0.015)	0.865 (0.839 ± 0.021)

mean accuracy. It should also be noted that the performance improves significantly by adding the named entity-based augmentation and copy mechanism on top of BART-base, making its performance comparable to the vanilla version of BART-large. These results indicate that data pre-processing and specialized architectures may offset the need for a larger architecture.

5   Datasets Without Labeled Named Entities

In most applications, the labeled named entities are not available with the datasets. For these datasets, NER systems may be used to identify the named entities. The state-of-the-art NER systems achieve >90% accuracy on the CoNLL 2003 and NL4Opt NER tasks [3,12,15,16]. In this section, we investigate whether using these systems to label the named entities can be helpful in formulation generation.

5.1   Noisy Named Entities

The existing NER systems can identify the named entities with a certain accuracy. The errors from these systems fall into one of the following buckets:

1. A named entity span is missed by the system.
2. A named entity span is identified correctly but labeled incorrectly.
3. An excess named entity span is identified by the system.

To simulate this behavior, for a fraction of labeled spans, p, we either drop the span, mislabel it, or change its start and end positions, with an equal mix. We ensure that no two spans overlap. For our experiments, two datasets with noisy named entities are generated for $p = 0.2$ and $p = 0.5$. To quantify the extent of the noise, we use the micro-averaged F1 score to compare the named entities in the generated and original datasets. Table 4 shows these scores, and Fig. 4 shows an example from the noisy datasets.

Table 4. Comparison of noisy named entities with the original ground-truth labels (micro-averaged F1).

p	TRAIN	DEV	TEST
0.2	0.8333	0.8397	0.8353
0.5	0.5783	0.5742	0.5822

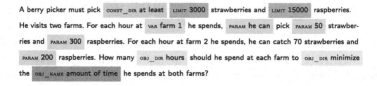

Fig. 4. An example of the input from the noisy dataset generated using $p = 0.5$. See Fig. 1 for the ground truth named entity spans and their labels.

5.2 Results

We train and evaluate our approach on the noisy datasets generated through the process mentioned in the previous section. Table 5 shows the results of this experiment for $p = 0.2$ and $p = 0.5$. It can be observed that the named entity-based augmentation improves the performance even with a noisy named entity tagging compared to the vanilla BART models (See Sect. 4.6 for the vanilla BART results). BART-base is affected more by the noise compared to BART-large. This is expected as BART-base also benefits more from the named entity-based augmentation.

5.3 Generality of the Proposed Approach

The experiments with noisy datasets indicate that the named entity-based augmentation may prove helpful even with noisy named entity labels. However, the noise introduced in Sect. 5.1 may not reflect the true behavior of an imperfect named entity recognition (NER) system. To understand this behavior further, we train an NER model from Ramamonjison et al. [12] on the NL4Opt NER dataset and use it to predict the named entity spans and their labels.[4] As the NL4Opt NER dataset contains the same linear programming problems as the generation dataset, the model predictions are almost perfect for the training set. It achieves F1 scores of 0.9871, 0.8796, and 0.9049 on the train, dev, and test sets for named entity prediction. A near-perfect named entity tagging for the train set and a noisy one for the dev and test sets may not represent a real-world NER system trained independently of the NL4Opt dataset. To alleviate this issue, we drop a fraction of the predicted named entities from the train set

---

[4] Refer to https://github.com/nl4opt/nl4opt-subtask1-baseline for training an NER model. We use the default configuration for training.

Table 5. Accuracy achieved by our approach on the datasets with noisy named entities. A lower value of p implies more accurate named entity labeling.

	BART-BASE	BART-LARGE
SYNTHETIC NOISE		
$p = 0.2$	0.771 (0.746 ± 0.015)	0.900 (0.887 ± 0.015)
$p = 0.5$	0.724 (0.711 ± 0.011)	0.902 (0.887 ± 0.010)
PREDICTED NERs		
TRAIN SET (F1 = 0.9871)	0.670 (0.663 ± 0.007)	0.844 (0.827 ± 0.021)
TRAIN SET (F1 = 0.9062)	0.703 (0.684 ± 0.012)	0.885 (0.860 ± 0.022)

so that the resulting F1 score for the train set becomes 0.9062. This simulates an independent NER tagger that has not seen examples from the NL4Opt dataset during training.

The results of this experiment are shown in Table 5. It is evident that a disparity between the F1 scores for the predicted named entities in the train and test sets plays a crucial role in the final performance of the model. The advantage of the named entity-based augmentation diminishes when a model is trained on a dataset with near-perfect named entities and evaluated on a dataset with noisy named entities. In this case, the model fails to outperform a model that does not use named entities. However, if the F1 scores of the train and test sets are made comparable, the model benefits from the named entity-based augmentation. These results indicate that the proposed approach may not benefit the datasets where an NER predictor behaves differently for the training and test sets. Furthermore, they support the hypothesis that the proposed approach may be helpful even with the noisy named entities but with an NER predictor that exhibits similar behavior across train and test sets. However, the experimental setting has some bias as the NER predictor is trained on the examples that are present in the generation dataset, and synthetic noise is introduced in the predicted named entities of the train set to make the F1 score comparable to the dev and test sets. To substantiate these findings, an NER model must be trained independently of the generation dataset.

6   Conclusion

In this paper, we proposed a novel approach based on highlighting the named entities in the input text to generate the mathematical formulations of linear programming word problems. Our approach produced the highest accuracy among all submissions to the generation track of the NL4Opt competition. We also found that the "all-at-once" strategy works well with the named entity-based augmentation. Lastly, we showed that applications without labeled named entities might use the proposed approach by first identifying named entities using an existing NER system. We believe that this augmentation may prove useful in other natural language processing applications. However, these findings must be investigated further to establish the generality of the proposed approach. We leave these avenues for future work.

Acknowledgements. We thank Prof. Shaloo Rakheja (University of Illinois Urbana-Champaign) for providing computing resources for this work. This work also utilizes resources supported by the National Science Foundation's Major Research Instrumentation program, grant #1725729, as well as the University of Illinois Urbana-Champaign. We also thank the CICM reviewers for their insightful comments.

References

1. Beairsto, J., Tian, Y., Zheng, L., Zhao, Q., Hong, J.: Identifying locations for new bike-sharing stations in glasgow: an analysis of spatial equity and demand factors. Annals GIS **28**(2), 111–126 (2022)
2. Bitran, G., Caldentey, R.: An overview of pricing models for revenue management. IEEE Eng. Manage. Rev. **44**(4), 134–134 (2016)
3. He, J., Mamatha, N., Vignesh, S., Kumar, D., Uppal, A.: Linear programming word problems formulation using ensemblecrf ner labeler and t5 text generator with data augmentations. ArXiv abs/2212.14657 (2022)
4. Jang, S.: Tag embedding and well-defined intermediate representation improve auto-formulation of problem description. ArXiv abs/2212.03575 (2022)
5. Karmarkar, N.: A new polynomial-time algorithm for linear programming. In: Proceedings of the Sixteenth Annual ACM Symposium on Theory of Computing, pp. 302–311 (1984)
6. Lewis, M., et al.: BART: denoising sequence-to-sequence pre-training for natural language generation, translation, and comprehension. In: Proceedings of the 58th Annual Meeting of the Association for Computational Linguistics, pp. 7871–7880, Association for Computational Linguistics, July 2020. https://doi.org/10.18653/v1/2020.acl-main.703, https://aclanthology.org/2020.acl-main.703
7. Loshchilov, I., Hutter, F.: Decoupled weight decay regularization. arXiv preprint arXiv:1711.05101 (2017)
8. Ma, Y., Qin, X., Xu, J., Zou, X.: Research on pricing method of public bicycle service: a case study in guangzhou. In: 2016 IEEE International Conference on Service Operations and Logistics, and Informatics (SOLI), pp. 156–161, IEEE (2016)
9. Nash, J.C.: The (dantzig) simplex method for linear programming. Comput. Sci. Eng. **2**(1), 29–31 (2000)
10. Ning, Y., et al.: A novel approach for auto-formulation of optimization problems. arXiv preprint arXiv:2302.04643 (2023)
11. Prasath, G., Karande, S.: Synthesis of mathematical programs from natural language specifications. arXiv preprint arXiv:2304.03287 (2023)
12. Ramamonjison, R., et al.: Augmenting operations research with auto-formulation of optimization models from problem descriptions. arXiv preprint arXiv:2209.15565 (2022)
13. See, A., Liu, P.J., Manning, C.D.: Get to the point: summarization with pointer-generator networks. In: Proceedings of the 55th Annual Meeting of the Association for Computational Linguistics (Volume 1: Long Papers), pp. 1073–1083, Association for Computational Linguistics, Vancouver, Canada, July 2017. https://doi.org/10.18653/v1/P17-1099, https://aclanthology.org/P17-1099

14. Tao, D.Q., Pleau, M., Akridge, A., Fradet, O., Grondin, F., Laughlin, S., Miller, W., Shoemaker, L.: Analytics and optimization reduce sewage overflows to protect community waterways in kentucky. INFORMS J. Appl. Anal. **50**(1), 7–20 (2020)
15. Tjong Kim Sang, E.F., De Meulder, F.: Introduction to the CoNLL-2003 shared task: language-independent named entity recognition. In: Proceedings of the Seventh Conference on Natural Language Learning at HLT-NAACL 2003, pp. 142–147 (2003). https://aclanthology.org/W03-0419
16. Wang, X., et al.: Automated concatenation of embeddings for structured prediction. In: Proceedings of the 59th Annual Meeting of the Association for Computational Linguistics and the 11th International Joint Conference on Natural Language Processing (Volume 1: Long Papers), pp. 2643–2660, Association for Computational Linguistics, August 2021. https://doi.org/10.18653/v1/2021.acl-long.206, https://aclanthology.org/2021.acl-long.206
17. Wang, Y., Wang, W., Joty, S., Hoi, S.C.: Codet 5: identifier-aware unified pretrained encoder-decoder models for code understanding and generation. arXiv preprint arXiv:2109.00859 (2021)
18. Wolf, T., et al.: Transformers: state-of-the-art natural language processing. In: Proceedings of the 2020 Conference on Empirical Methods in Natural Language Processing: System Demonstrations, pp. 38–45, Association for Computational Linguistics, October 2020. https://doi.org/10.18653/v1/2020.emnlp-demos.6, https://aclanthology.org/2020.emnlp-demos.6

Formalization Quality in Isabelle

Fabian Huch[1]([⊠])[iD] and Yiannos Stathopoulos[2]

[1] Technische Universität München, Boltzmannstraße 3, 85748 Garching, Germany
huch@in.tum.de
[2] Department of Computer Science and Technology, University of Cambridge,
Cambridge, UK
yas23@cam.ac.uk

Abstract. Little is known about the quality of formalizations in interactive theorem proving. In this work, we analyze the relationship between static analysis warnings (lints) and maintenance effort for 6470 Isabelle theories, create models to predict lints based on structural features, and compare the results to a small ground-truth dataset collected with the help of domain experts. We find that for the majority of lints, there is a significant but low-strength correlation between frequency of occurrence and churn in maintenance change-sets. In particular, for proofs using tactic methods (which can be brittle), the Spearman correlation is highest with a strength of 0.16, $p < 0.005$. Furthermore, when classifying theories as lint-prone based on their formal entity graphs (which capture the dependencies between underlying logical entities), random forests outperform even deep learning models on our data, achieving 58 % precision and 21 % recall. Finally, in our ground-truth dataset of 35 good and 35 problematic theories, our pre-defined criterion that identifies theories with more than one lint every 100 lines achieves 95 % precision and 51 % recall. Remarkably, this is very close to the optimal criterion, which we observe at one lint every 109 lines. Moreover, the random forest model trained for lint-proneness even achieves perfect accuracy at 43 % recall, providing additional evidence of its effectiveness.

Keywords: Isabelle · Formalization quality · Static analysis · Linter · Code smell · Change frequency · Machine learning · Deep learning

1 Introduction

Interactive theorem proving is a powerful technique for verifying the correctness of mathematical proofs and software systems. In this field, the quality of the resulting formalization code is crucial for several reasons. Firstly, understandability is essential to ensure that practitioners can use existing material, as code that is easy to understand is more likely to be helpful in proofs and employable as a building block for further constructions. Secondly, maintainability is important, particularly for large libraries such as the Isabelle Archive of Formal Proofs (AFP). As those grow in size, more and more maintenance effort is required to

C. Dubois and M. Kerber (Eds.): CICM 2023, LNAI 14101, pp. 142–157, 2023.
https://doi.org/10.1007/978-3-031-42753-4_10

ensure that all the existing material remains interoperable with updated Isabelle and AFP versions. Hence, developments that are less prone to break decrease the amount of maintenance required, and understandable material is easier to adapt. Thirdly, while in theorem proving the traditional notion of a software error is not applicable, errors in another sense can still occur: for instance, a library might not be usable because its assumptions are too strict.

While various tools and techniques have been developed to improve code quality in other fields, such as software engineering, there is currently little research that addresses formalization quality in interactive theorem proving. On one hand, most systems employ style guides, but those do not help much in the context of large libraries as they lack automation. On the other hand, there are static analysis tools (called linters) which detect common anti-patterns, but they are available for few systems and limited in scope.

Problem. While currently linters only exist for the Isabelle and Lean systems, they have the potential to be very effective. However, it is still unclear how much of an impact linters have on formalization quality in practice.

Solution. The effectiveness of linters can be judged by analyzing the relationships between lint results and ground-truth for various aspects of formalization quality. This also allows to develop more comprehensive metrics and models for formalization quality.

Contribution. In this work, we devise several quality models based on syntactical and dependency graph features, and compare results with ground-truth data for change frequencies as well as hand-derived quality estimates.

Organization. In Sect. 2, we give an overview of software engineering concepts related to code quality and discuss approaches and findings of the related work in that field. In Sect. 3, we discuss how methods in software quality can be adapted to theorem proving and present our analysis and findings.

2   Code Quality in Software Engineering

Code quality in software engineering is the measure of how well-designed, efficient, and maintainable the code is, and whether it meets its intended purpose. The topic has been subject to a vast amount of research, but most work is focused on *software defects*—observable errors in executed software.

In contrast, *Code smells* are specific patterns or structures in the source code that indicate the existence of deeper problems such as poor design, lack of maintainability, or potential faults [8, Ch. 3]. Code smells are more direct indicators of quality than actual faults in the code, which can usually only be identified by observing defects from the program behaviour.

In software engineering, much effort is put into measuring the effect of code smells and defects by quantifiable project and source code characteristics. For instance, the number of changes to a source file in a given time (*change frequency*) or the amount of lines changed (*churn*) are considered to be important characteristics of interest [12]. They are usually measured by analyzing the change-sets (also called *commits*) from the underlying version control system.

In systematic literature reviews, Amancio et al. analyzed 64 studies on the effects of code smells [19], and Kaur later analyzed 74 studies on the effect on software quality attributes [11]. Both reviews observed that findings are divergent and results largely depend on the exact smells considered.

However, many investigations on the effect of code smells on change frequency and manual maintenance effort find positive correlations, but do not control for file size [3–5, 12, 15, 18, 27], or consider size only (log-)transformed [25]. Decoupling these variables from file size is important because larger bodies of code will exhibit more occurrences of those phenomena, thus it is important to untangle the variables of interest from file size. In fact, when size is controlled for in the correlation, most code smells do not reflect on change frequency and size [21] or maintenance effort [16, 26] in a significant way, and the few that do only do so weakly. Still, Khomh et al. as well as Palomba et al. conclude that size alone also does not explain the relationship between code smells and change frequencies [13, 17], but do not compute strength of the correlations with size accounted for. When separating maintenance effort into different tasks, Soh et al. found that file size impacted maintenance effort more than code smells for reading and searching activities, whereas code smells affected it more for editing and navigation tasks (though change size of tasks performed had the most impact) [22]. Lastly, Bessghaier et al. found that change size is connected to smells but not class size [6].

As for the prediction of code smells using machine learning approaches, Azeem et al. give an excellent overview over the vast field in their systematic literature review. Importantly, they find that research achieves F_1-score (i.e., harmonic mean of precision and recall) of 0.81 on average, the dependent variables used play a major role in performance, and that overall, random forests are the most reliable models [2]. However, it is important to note that some of the best results (F_1-scores of up to 0.97 [1]) were found not to generalize well in a replication study by Nucci et al. [7], which might skew the results of the review.

3   Analysis of Formalization Quality

In our previous work, we did not find metrics for detecting defects in software systems suitable to detect lints in formalizations [10]. However, the concept of code smells in software is more closely related to formalization code, because the concept of code anti-patterns is transferable to formalizations. In fact, the Isabelle linter offers detection for a wide range of different anti-patterns [14], but not all of them are universally agreed on to have a detrimental effect on quality—for instance, some are specifically designed for certain styles. With the editors of the AFP, we discussed which of the available lints should be executed on new submissions. A few checks were suitable only for new submissions (e.g., the use of phased-out Isabelle commands), and the following subset was agreed on to indicate actual quality problems (even for existing material)[1]:

---

[1] Some of those criteria are checked by a combination of multiple lints.

1. *Switch between apply-style and Isar* as such proofs are "hacked together" and not written down properly (and hence hard to read).
2. *Counter-example and proof-finder commands* which are left over from inter-active use, and only affect the proof-checking speed in the archive.
3. *Diagnostic commands* which are left over as well, though sometimes intentionally for documentation purposes.
4. *Changes of global lemma attributes* as such changes should only be made in a local context so as not to affect users of the formalization.
5. *Unnamed lemmas in prover collections* (e.g., the simplification set), as without a name to address them, those lemmas can't be disabled.
6. *Use of auto-style methods as non-terminal proof methods*, which makes the following proof steps brittle as they rely on goals generated by aggressive rewriting.
7. *Structured proof starting with an auto-style method* which is an especially bad version of the former, as then the entire proof structure can change.
8. *Overly complex methods* as they make it very hard to read and follow a proof.
9. *Tactic proofs* since they allow to refer to system-generated names which are arbitrary and could change at any point, so they should not be explicitly referenced.

These lints have been adopted in the AFP submission process and appear to be useful, but there is no quantifiable proof of their effectiveness yet.

To account for file size, we define *lint frequency* to be the number of lints reported per line of Isabelle source code (without whitespace or comments). Hence, lint frequency is independent of file size. To classify theories as good or problematic, we use a pre-defined threshold of one lint per 100 lines. While this threshold is a bit arbitrary, it seems appropriate given our previous experience with lints in Isabelle and the AFP, where we found that one lint occurred every 200 lines in HOL and four times more often in other sessions [14] (albeit with a different selection of lints).

Change-sets and churn can easily be measured for the Isabelle and AFP repositories[2]. Of course, not all changes are due to maintenance problems—many authors contribute further additions and improvements (e.g., better naming) to their developments. We consider change-sets affecting more than a *single* development to represent maintenance effort, assuming that developers generate coherent change-sets that don't put the codebase into an inoperable state—under that assumption, change-sets affecting *multiple* developments correspond to changes that break other entries which then need to be repaired, which is maintenance effort by definition. It should be noted that maintenance effort is not necessarily caused by poor maintainability of a theory: some edits induced by upstream changes might be unavoidable, e.g., re-naming of a lemma that is later explicitly mentioned. Still, change frequency should be a reasonable measure to approximate maintainability.

We quantify the above metrics over the Isabelle and AFP libraries to answer the following specific research questions:

---

[2] Merge commits are omitted as they only exist for technical reasons.

RQ1: Which of the problems uncovered by lints actually increase maintenance effort?

RQ2: Are formalizations where many lints occur structurally different from others?

RQ3: How much do lints reflect on perceived quality? Do other models?

Our data are based on the Isabelle2022 release, excluding tools as they are mostly not written in Isabelle/Isar (and hence not covered by the Linter), example theories since they could differ a lot from regular material, and particularly slow developments due to computation time considerations. A total of 6470 theory files remain. In the sections that follow we address each research question individually.

3.1 Maintenance Effort

Since we rely on the notion of single or multiple AFP developments for change frequencies, we do not consider theories of the Isabelle distribution itself here, leaving us 6160 AFP theories. On average, such a theory file is changed every 506 days, and 139 lines are edited in a change. Figure 1 shows violin plots for the distribution of change frequencies, separated by whether or not lints occur frequently (more often than one lint every 100 lines) in the theory. The distributions for change-sets affecting a single development (i.e., possibly improvement changes), and multiple developments (i.e., maintenance changes), are shown separately. The change frequency for maintenance change-sets is centered around zero, whereas it is greater than zero for those affecting only a single development. Also, while overall the distributions for frequent and infrequent lints are quite similar, the peak at zero for maintenance change-sets is far more pronounced for theories with infrequent lints.

Both the number of lints in a theory file and its change frequency are dependent on the theory size (as measured in source lines of code) since larger theories contain more code that can contain problems and can break. Hence, we need to control for size when measuring the relationship between change frequency (or churn) and number of lints. We do a partial analysis with Spearman correlation (i.e., measuring how much one variable increases as the other increases, while accounting for the third). Table 1 shows the result. The observed relationships are not very strong, but the results are significant at the $p < 0.01$ level or below (i.e., the likelihood of the variables being independent is less than 1%). When all change-sets are considered (where maintenance and improvements are mixed), there is almost no significant correlation. For change-sets affecting multiple entries (i.e., maintenance), most lints correlate positively with the frequency of changes. Out of the three anti-patterns that would *cause* maintenance incidents, both auto as initial method and tactic proofs are positively correlated—tactic proofs have the strongest relationship with change frequency we observed with a value of 0.125—but auto as non-terminal method has no significant impact. It is noteworthy that during the discussion with the AFP editors, Paulson, who built auto, objected that the pattern would be problematic, arguing that the usage was as designed (though his vote was overruled).

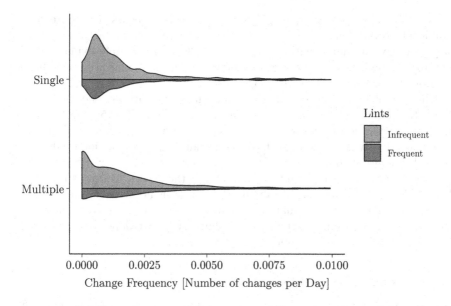

Fig. 1. Probability density of change frequencies for change-sets affecting single and multiple developments. Density functions are separated by lint frequency (more than one lint every 100 lines is considered *frequent*), and scaled by count.

Table 1. Lint count and Spearman correlation with change and churn frequency for all change-sets as well as change-sets affecting only multiple or single entries. Correlations are only shown for $p < 0.01$, values significant at the $p < 0.005$-level are printed bold.

	Count	Change Frequency			Churn Frequency		
		All	Multi	Single	All	Multi	Single
Apply Isar Switch	1366	–	–	–	–	–	–
Counterexample/Proof Finder	263	–	–	–	–	–	.053
Diagnostic Commands	1426	–	–	–	–	–	–
Global Attribute Changes	44	–	–	–	–	–	–
Unnamed Lemma in Collection	872	–	.044	–	–	.045	-.045
Non-terminal Auto	9087	–	–	.041	–	-.038	.059
Auto as Initial Proof Method	4863	–	.041	–	–	.043	–
Complex Methods	4585	–	.058	–	–	.055	-.041
Tactic Proofs	15338	**-.074**	**.125**	**-.136**	**-.074**	**.159**	**-.136**
Bad Style	140	–	.046	-.033	–	.045	-.043
Lemma-transforming Attribute	1015	–	.033	-.056	–	.042	-.052
Short Name	425	–	-.058	.067	–	-.070	.078
Implicit Rule	2735	–	.065	–	–	.058	-.051
Apply Style	190838	–	.044	-.042	–	–	-.051

For the change-sets concerning only single developments, there are fewer significant correlations, of which most are negative. Again, tactic proofs are most strongly correlated with a value of -0.136. One possible explanation is that authors replace tactics as part of their improvements—this is even explicitly mentioned four times in the AFP commit log.

Churn frequency is quite similar to change frequency overall, and the correlation with tactic proofs is even a bit stronger with a value of 0.159. On the other hand, the correlation to non-terminal auto calls is negative, which could be due to the fact that when such a proof breaks, usually only a single line needs to be touched. We also computed correlations for other lints not covered in our selection (in the bottom half of the table), and while the overall picture is the same, the correlation with the warning about short names is negative for maintenance change-sets. A possible explanation is that such identifiers are commonly used when logical foundations are formalized, which is mostly done by experts who usually produce high-quality and robust formalizations.

3.2   Lints and Formalization Structure

The advantage of lints as quality indicators is that they can be extracted directly from source code, and the uncovered problems are easy to understand. Still, to establish more metrics for formalization quality, it is important to know how poor-quality formalizations are structurally different from good ones. In particular, we are interested to see whether code quality also reflects on the dependency graph such that it can be detected without syntax. Hence, in our previous work we analyzed graph metrics, such as number of neighbours, centrality scores, etc., computed over the Isabelle *formal entity graph* (the dependency graph of logically relevant entities in a formalization). Although graph metrics are used successfully as quality indicators in software systems, we found that these metrics are not good indicators of lint frequency for Isabelle code [10].

In this work, we investigate the feasibility of using these metrics with machine learning models to differentiate between formalizations with frequent and infrequent lints. In our investigation, we consider nearest neighbours, multilayer perceptron, decision tree, gradient-boosted tree, and random forest, as representatives of classical models. Feature inputs for these models are produced per theory and include size and aggregated formal entity graph properties, such as node degree and centrality. Additionally, we consider graph neural networks as representatives of deep learning models, motivated by successes for similar tasks [20]. We used graph convolutional networks, the GraphSAGE model [9], and graph attention networks [24], trained purely on the underlying formal entity graphs (node degree as single feature).

We consider two scenarios: treating the task as binary classification (i.e., using a binary label that stands for frequent or infrequent lints), and as a regression task (i.e., fitting the model directly to the lint frequency). We use 70 % of our data for training, 15 % for validation (hyper-parameter tuning and model selection) and 15 % final testing (to evaluate generalizability). Hyper-parameters (i.e., additional parameters of the models) were tuned by random search on appropriate parameter grids, which can be found in our published source code[3]. We evaluate all models in the classification setting by computing the average precision (AP) over all thresholds for each model. To evaluate how well the final model performs for different thresholds (i.e., the decision cut-off points of a model), we analyze the curve of precision (how many of the theories predicted as problematic were actually problematic) and recall (how many problematic theories were found).

Figure 2 shows the validation performance of our trained models. It is evident that the deep learning models do not perform better than classical models on our dataset, which is not uncommon for a dataset of this size (6470 data points), especially as we would expect quite some noise in the data given the scenario. Overall, the random forest model trained as a classifier is the best model with

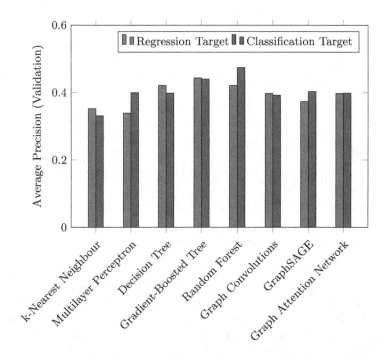

Fig. 2. Average precision values of different models on validation data when classifying theories as problematic, for both regression (for lint frequency) and classification training targets.

[3] https://github.com/Dacit/isabelle-formalization-quality.

a validation AP of 0.47. Its precision-recall curve on the test data is shown in Fig. 3. With a test AP of 0.51, the model generalizes quite well—for example, 58 % precision and 21 % recall can be reached at a default threshold of 0.5, and the model is far better than random on the whole range. This shows that while lints cannot be predicted very accurately, they do reflect strongly on the formal entity graphs.

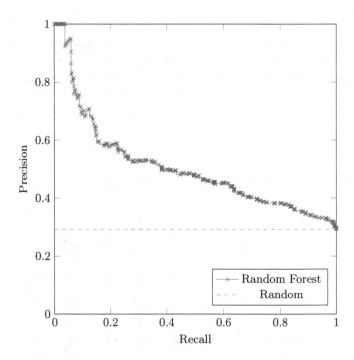

Fig. 3. Precision-recall curve for random forest model, with values for precision and recall on test data plotted for varied thresholds.

To find out which features are most important, we perform an ablation study with the random forest model, i.e., we iteratively re-train the model, removing the feature that leads to the smallest decrease in validation AP. An explanation of the features can be found in Appendix 1. Figure 4 shows the result. Initially, the score fluctuates slightly, until it takes a steep decline when the features betweenness centrality (median and max), out-degree (max), closeness centrality (mean), and in-degree (mean) are removed.

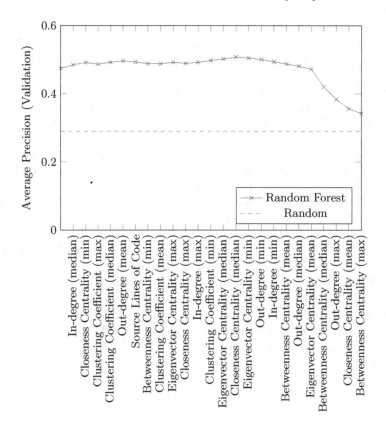

Fig. 4. Average precision for best random forest model after tuning, when cumulatively removing features with the least contribution to average precision (name of the removed feature is on the x-axis). In-degree (median) is the first feature removed, In-degree (mean) remains as last feature.

3.3   Comparison with Perceived Quality

Obtaining a dataset for perceived quality is quite difficult, since often only domain experts are capable of judging the quality of a given formalization, especially when it comes to quality problems that are not obvious. By inquiring Isabelle experts in various domains about theories or AFP developments they would consider good and bad quality, we obtained a sample of 70 labelled theories (35 good and bad each). Importantly, we did not give a definition of quality (relying on the experts' intuition) nor did we contribute any data ourselves, so as not to skew the dataset in any way. As an example, one expert classified a theory as problematic because the assumptions on the main theorem were stronger than needed, making it unusable to them. The sample can hence be considered ground-truth for theory quality.

While 70 examples is not enough data to train any models on, the sample is sufficiently large to evaluate both the lint results and our other machine learning model discussed previously. In addition, we evaluated the un-tuned capabilities of a large language model: By prompting the pre-trained LLAMA (7 billion parameters) transformer [23] about the quality of chunks of formalization code (on a scale from 1 to 10) and averaging the scores for each theory, we obtained quality predictions for the whole AFP. Even though we did not fine-tune the model due to the prohibitive hardware requirements, we did get mostly coherent results—an in-depth description of the prompting as well as qualitative analysis can be found in Appendix 2.

For predicting poor-quality theories in our sample, the LLAMA model does not have a pre-defined threshold, but we can analyze its precision-recall curve where the threshold is varied. In contrast, the simple lint threshold approach of one lint every 100 lines achieved 95 % precision and 51 % recall. The random forest model scored 43 % precision and 100 % recall at its default threshold. Figure 5 shows the full precision-recall curves for all three classifiers. The simple lint frequency remains an excellent estimator even for high thresholds where recall goes up to 77 % (at 79 % precision), and is outperformed by the random forest model only in the low-recall regions (where the latter attains perfect precision for up to 43 % recall). The large language model performs well in the low-recall regions, which is surprising given that it has not been trained on Isabelle quality at all, suggesting that textual structure alone (which is what the model understands) can give a hint about overall quality. However, for higher thresholds, it is close to random.

4   Discussion

We analyzed the relationship between warnings of the Isabelle linter and other aspects of formalization quality, and found that frequency and churn of change-sets affecting more than one AFP entry (which we assume connected to maintenance) were positively correlated with many lints. However, the effect was rather weak when we controlled for file size, and there was almost no significant effect when all change-sets were considered. In software engineering, there are divergent findings regarding the influence of code smells on change frequency and maintenance effort, though it appears that only few smells are (weakly) correlated when size is taken into account as well [16,21,26]. The performance we obtained when predicting lints based on graph and source code features (F_1-score of 0.31) is much lower than what can be achieved when predicting code smells from source code metrics (0.81 on average over multiple studies [2]), which leads us to believe that other source code metrics would need to be derived for this task on formalization code. Still, random forests performed best on our dataset, which is in line with the results from code smell prediction. Finally, both the linter and our prediction model can classify theories as good or problematic quite well (F_1-score of 0.66/0.60 without any fine-tuning to the task), and even an un-tuned large language model can achieve better-than-random classification accuracy. We found that when using the linter, a threshold of one lint every 109 lines was optimal.

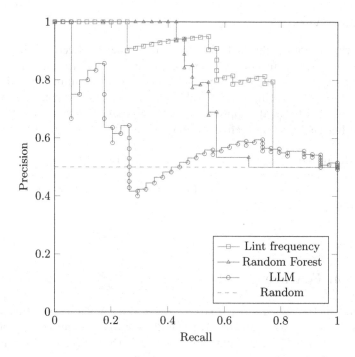

Fig. 5. Precision-recall curves on ground truth data set for different models.

4.1 Limitations

Our study has several potential threats to its validity that must be considered. Regarding internal validity, there is a risk that unknown factors may have influenced our correlation analysis, thereby affecting our results. As a consequence, the correlations we observed may not provide accurate representations of the true relationships between the variables we examined. Our construct is also slightly inaccurate in that lints were measured on the current Isabelle version (for technical reasons), whereas frequently changed parts that were problematic could have been improved in some of the changes, but those previous problems might not be detected by the linter any more. Regarding external validity, the use of only a single dataset limits the generalizability of our findings. However, the AFP contains many heterogeneous developments, which mitigates the risk somewhat. Another limitation is that the manual evaluation dataset we used is relatively small, which increases the risk of obtaining biased results that do not accurately represent the larger population. To reduce this risk, we obtained the classifications from experts and did not contribute our own data. Finally, there is a possibility that better areas of the model and parameter space exist in the machine learning aspect of our study. As such, our findings may not be fully optimized or representative of the best possible results that could be obtained.

4.2 Future Work

In this work, we found the Isabelle linter to be highly effective. Hence, more effort should be spent into developing a larger number of appropriate lints, for example by instrumenting proof terms to find unused assumptions. Moreover, other than lints, there still are no good metrics for formalization quality. More research is needed to create appropriate code metrics for formalizations and to assess whether they can be useful in judging quality.

Acknowledgements. A large part of this work would not have been possible without the help of many Isabelle experts, who contributed to our ground-truth quality dataset. The second author is supported by the ERC Advanced Grant ALEXANDRIA (Project 742178).

Appendix

1   Graph Features

As a general metric, we use the *Source lines of code* in the theory file, without comments and whitespace. Moreover, the following metrics (further explained in our previous work [10]) were aggregated for each theory (using the minimum, maximum, median, and mean value):

1. *In-degree* counts the number of incoming edges (how often the entity is used).
2. *Out-degree* is the number outgoing edges (how many other entities are used).
3. *Clustering coefficient* represents the likelihood that a node's neighbours are also connected.
4. *Closeness centrality* captures the average distance to all other reachable nodes in the graph.
5. *Betweenness centrality* corresponds to the number of shortest paths through the graph in which the node is contained.
6. *Eigenvector centrality* captures transitive importance in the graph.

2   Large Language Model Analysis

We used LLAMA [23] as a large language model (LLM) to obtain quality predictions for Isabelle snippets. We generated the snippets from AFP theories (without comments) such that they start with a command, truncated to a length that fits into the context size (2048 tokens). As LLAMA is a raw transformer model not fine-tuned on question answering tasks, we devised the following prompt that the model should complete:

> When assessing the quality of an Isabelle formalization, we can always be totally assured that it is correct. However, quality can vary: Formalizations need to be understandable, maintainable, and easy to use. Unclear definitions, proofs that are too hard to follow, and proofs that are likely

to break with future changes are all problematic and should be avoided. Let us take the following snippet as an example:
SNIPPET end
Of course some definitions and lemmas are missing as this is just a snippet. It works and is correct. As for the quality, on a scale of 1 to 10, I would give it a

A proper response from LLAMA would be to complete this prompt starting with a numeric score (hence, at most two characters need to be predicted). All 261207 snippets of the AFP yielded a response of this form, though some gave a score not on the scale.

To evaluate the answers qualitatively, we generate longer responses for a sample of 100 snippets, truncate them to the first few full sentences, and categorized them as shown in Table 2 (multiple categories possible).

Table 2. Categorization of LLM replies by manual interpretation of first few sentences for 100 examples. Multiple categories are possible.

Category	Count	Example Snippet
Answering about snippet quality	51	[...] the lemma 'equivclp_least[OF hash]' is a bit cryptic and I would prefer something more explicit [...]
Discussing general quality	9	It is difficult to write a good formalization that is both clear and maintainable [...]
Concern with elements missing from snippet	7	[...] the function 'hash_blindable' is not introduced, and therefore its type is not defined.
Questioning correctness	10	[...] it does not provide any indication of its correctness.
No category	32	The Isabelle formalization of the above snippet was verified by formalverification.org [...]

The majority of replies (51) answered the quality prompt. Of those, only 8 justifications were inconsistent with their scores (e.g., "10. The proof is quite hard to follow."). A total of 26 answers (in similar parts) either discussed general quality, wrote about elements missing from the snippet, or questioned correctness of the formalization—those could potentially be improved by further prompt tuning. 32 answers did not fit any of the categories, i.e., failed the prompt completely.

References

1. Arcelli Fontana, F., Mäntylä, M.V., Zanoni, M., Marino, A.: Comparing and experimenting machine learning techniques for code smell detection. Empirical Softw. Eng. **21**(3), 1143–1191 (2015). https://doi.org/10.1007/s10664-015-9378-4

2. Azeem, M.I., Palomba, F., Shi, L., Wang, Q.: Machine learning techniques for code smell detection: a systematic literature review and meta-analysis (2019). https://doi.org/10.1016/j.infsof.2018.12.009

3. Bán, D.: The Connection between antipatterns and maintainability in firefox. In: Acta Cybernetica, vol. 23, pp. 471–490. University of Szeged (2017). https://doi.org/10.14232/actacyb.23.2.2017.3

4. Bán, D., Ferenc, R.: Recognizing antipatterns and analyzing their effects on software maintainability. In: Murgante, B., et al. (eds.) ICCSA 2014. LNCS, vol. 8583, pp. 337–352. Springer, Cham (2014). https://doi.org/10.1007/978-3-319-09156-3_25

5. Bessghaier, N., Ouni, A., Mkaouer, M.W.: On the diffusion and impact of code smells in web applications. In: Wang, Q., Xia, Y., Seshadri, S., Zhang, L.-J. (eds.) SCC 2020. LNCS, vol. 12409, pp. 67–84. Springer, Cham (2020). https://doi.org/10.1007/978-3-030-59592-0_5

6. Bessghaier, N., Ouni, A., Mkaouer, M.W.: A longitudinal exploratory study on code smells in server side web applications. Softw. Q. J. **29**(4), 901–941 (2021). https://doi.org/10.1007/s11219-021-09567-w

7. Di Nucci, D., Palomba, F., Tamburri, D.A., Serebrenik, A., De Lucia, A.: Detecting code smells using machine learning techniques: are we there yet? In: 25th IEEE International Conference on Software Analysis, Evolution and Reengineering, SANER 2018 - Proceedings. vol. 2018, pp. 612–621. IEEE (2018). https://doi.org/10.1109/SANER.2018.8330266

8. Fowler, M., Beck, K., Brant, J., Opdyke, W., Roberts, D.: Bad smells in code. Addison-Wesley, Boston (1999)

9. Hamilton, W., Ying, Z., Leskovec, J.: Inductive representation learning on large graphs (2017). https://doi.org/10.48550/arXiv.1706.02216

10. Huch, F.: Formal entity graphs as complex networks: assessing centrality metrics of the archive of formal proofs. In: Buzzard, K., Kutsia, T. (eds.) Intelligent Computer Mathematics, pp. 147–161. Springer, Cham (2022). https://doi.org/10.1007/978-3-031-16681-5_10

11. Kaur, A.: A systematic literature review on empirical analysis of the relationship between code smells and software quality attributes. Arch. Comput. Methods Eng. **27**(4), 1267–1296 (2019). https://doi.org/10.1007/s11831-019-09348-6

12. Khomh, F., Di Penta, M., Guéhéneuc, Y.G.: An exploratory study of the impact of code smells on software change-proneness. In: Proceedings - Working Conference on Reverse Engineering, WCRE, pp. 75–84 (2009). https://doi.org/10.1109/WCRE.2009.28

13. Khomh, F., Penta, M.D., Guéhéneuc, Y.G., Antoniol, G.: An exploratory study of the impact of antipatterns on class change- and fault-proneness. Empirical Softw. Eng. **17**(3), 243–275 (2012). https://doi.org/10.1007/s10664-011-9171-y

14. Megdiche, Y., Huch, F., Stevens, L.: A linter for isabelle: implementation and evaluation. In: Isabelle Workshop (2022). https://doi.org/10.48550/arXiv.2207.10424

15. Olbrich, S., Cruzes, D.S., Basili, V., Zazworka, N.: The evolution and impact of code smells: a case study of two open source systems. In: 2009 3rd International Symposium on Empirical Software Engineering and Measurement, ESEM 2009, pp. 390–400 (2009). https://doi.org/10.1109/ESEM.2009.5314231

16. Olbrich, S.M., Cruzes, D.S., Sjøberg, D.I.: Are all code smells harmful? A study of god classes and brain classes in the evolution of three open source systems. In: IEEE International Conference on Software Maintenance, ICSM (2010). https://doi.org/10.1109/ICSM.2010.5609564

17. Palomba, F., Bavota, G., Di Penta, M., Fasano, F., Oliveto, R., De Lucia, A.: On the diffuseness and the impact on maintainability of code smells. In: Proceedings of the 40th International Conference on Software Engineering, pp. 482–482. ACM, New York, NY, USA (2018). https://doi.org/10.1145/3180155.3182532

18. Romano, D., Raila, P., Pinzger, M., Khomh, F.: Analyzing the impact of antipatterns on change-proneness using fine-grained source code changes. In: Proceedings - Working Conference on Reverse Engineering, WCRE, pp. 437–446 (2012). https://doi.org/10.1109/WCRE.2012.53

19. Santos, J.A.M., et al.: A systematic review on the code smell effect. J. Syst. Softw. **144**, 450–477 (2018). https://doi.org/10.1016/j.jss.2018.07.035

20. Sikic, L., Kurdija, A.S., Vladimir, K., Silic, M.: Graph neural network for source code defect prediction. IEEE Access **10**, 10402–10415 (2022). https://doi.org/10.1109/ACCESS.2022.3144598

21. Sjoberg, D.I., Yamashita, A., Anda, B.C., Mockus, A., Dyba, T.: Quantifying the effect of code smells on maintenance effort. IEEE Trans. Softw. Eng. **39**(8), 1144–1156 (2013). https://doi.org/10.1109/TSE.2012.89

22. Soh, Z., Yamashita, A., Khomh, F., Guéhéneuc, Y.G.: Do code smells impact the effort of different maintenance programming activities? In: 2016 IEEE 23rd International Conference on Software Analysis, Evolution, and Reengineering, SANER 2016, vol. 1, pp. 393–402. IEEE (2016). https://doi.org/10.1109/SANER.2016.103

23. Touvron, H., et al.: Llama: open and efficient foundation language models (2023). https://doi.org/10.48550/arXiv.2302.13971

24. Veličković, P., Cucurull, G., Casanova, A., Romero, A., Liò, P., Bengio, Y.: Graph attention networks. In: International Conference on Learning Representations (2018). https://doi.org/10.48550/arXiv.1710.10903

25. Yamashita, A.: Assessing the capability of code smells to explain maintenance problems: an empirical study combining quantitative and qualitative data. Empirical Softw. Eng. **19**(4), 1111–1143 (2013). https://doi.org/10.1007/s10664-013-9250-3

26. Yamashita, A., Counsell, S.: Code smells as system-level indicators of maintainability: an empirical study. J. Syst. Softw. **86**(10), 2639–2653 (2013). https://doi.org/10.1016/j.jss.2013.05.007

27. Zazworka, N., Shaw, M.A., Shull, F., Seaman, C.: Investigating the impact of design debt on software quality. In: Proceedings - International Conference on Software Engineering, pp. 17–23. ACM, New York, NY, USA (2011). https://doi.org/10.1145/1985362.1985366

Formalizing Free Groups in Isabelle/HOL: The Nielsen-Schreier Theorem and the Conjugacy Problem

Aabid Seeyal Abdul Kharim[1], T. V. H. Prathamesh[2(✉)], Shweta Rajiv[2], and Rishi Vyas[2]

[1] Vayana Network, Pune 411016, MH, India
[2] Krea University, Sri City 517646, AP, India
prathamesh.turaga@krea.edu.in

Abstract. Free groups are central to group theory, and are ubiquitous across many branches of mathematics, including algebra, topology and geometry. An important result in the theory of free groups is the Nielsen-Schreier Theorem, which states that any subgroup of a free group is free. In this paper, we present a formalisation, in Isabelle/HOL, of a combinatorial proof of the Nielsen-Schreier theorem. In particular, our formalisation applies to arbitrary subgroups of free groups, without any restriction on the index of the subgroup or the cardinality of its generating sets. We also present a formalisation of an algorithm which determines whether two group words represent conjugate elements in a free group.

To the best of our knowledge, our work is the first formalisation of a combinatorial proof of the Nielsen-Schreier theorem in any proof assistant; the first formalisation of a proof of the Nielsen-Schreier theorem in Isabelle/HOL; and the first formalisation of the decision process for the conjugacy problem for free groups in any proof assistant.

Keywords: group theory · free groups · Isabelle/HOL

1 Introduction

Free groups arose in the late 19th century as objects associated with interesting geometries; their early theory was developed by von Dyck, Dehn, Nielsen, and Schreier, amongst others [5, 6, 13, 15]. These groups are fundamental to group theory, and continue to be an area of active research with regard to their properties and their connections with other branches of mathematics including geometry, topology, analysis, combinatorics, and logic. Given this, the need for substantial formalised libraries on free groups across proof assistants is apparent.

A foundational early result in the theory of free groups is the Nielsen-Schreier theorem, which states that any subgroup of a free group is a free group itself [13, 15]. Though the statement of this theorem seems innocuous, all known proofs are involved. Proofs of the Neilsen-Schreier theorem fall into two broad categories:

C. Dubois and M. Kerber (Eds.): CICM 2023, LNAI 14101, pp. 158–173, 2023.
https://doi.org/10.1007/978-3-031-42753-4_11

topological arguments involving ideas from algebraic topology and graph theory, and a purely algebraic approach using the combinatorics of word cancellations. A topological proof of the Nielsen-Schreier theorem stands formalised in Lean [12].

In this paper we describe a formalisation of a combinatorial approach to the Nielsen-Schreier theorem in Isabelle/HOL. In addition, we describe formalisations, in Isabelle/HOL, of decision procedures for the word and conjugacy problems in the context of free groups, as described by Dehn [5]. We expect our work here to contribute to the formal libraries of key results and algorithms in combinatorial group theory in Isabelle/HOL. It is also our hope that our work will prove useful in exploring the potential for formally verified computational tools in the domain. This work forms part of a larger project concerning formalisations in combinatorial group theory.

In Sects. 2 and 3, we discuss mathematical preliminaries and basic formal constructions. Section 4 describes our formalisation of the word and conjugacy problems for free groups, while Sect. 5 outlines our formalisation of the Nielsen-Schreier theorem. In these sections, we provide key definitions and proof sketches of the main results we are formalising followed by fragments of Isabelle code illustrating the ideas that have been formalised: these fragments resemble the formalisations in the machine proof, with some modifications to improve readability. The listed definitions and theorems are by no means exhaustive. For readability, we choose to informally describe rather than explicitly state formal definitions at certain points. We broadly follow the proofs in [10], though at times our arguments deviate slightly from those in the literature for reasons motivated by the technical challenges of constructing formal proofs. We assume the reader is familiar with some group theory. Our formalisation was carried out in Isabelle 2022 and the total length of our formalised code is approximately 8000 lines. Our code is available at:

https://github.com/aabid-tkcs/groupabelle

2   Mathematical Preliminaries

Let S be a set, and $S^{-1} := \{s^{-1} \mid s \in S\}$ a set of symbols in bijection with and disjoint from S; define $S^{\pm} := S \cup S^{-1}$. A *group word* w on S is a finite sequence $x_1, \ldots, x_n$ where $x_i \in S^{\pm}$; we describe such a word by juxtaposing its terms together. A *subword* of w is a substring of the word w. The word w is said to be *reduced* if it does not contain a subword of the form xx^{-1} or $x^{-1}x$. The set of all group words on S can be given the structure of a monoid, with the product of $x_1 \ldots x_n$ and $y_1 \ldots y_m$ defined as $x_1 \ldots x_n y_1 \ldots y_m$ and the empty word as identity. Let FG_S denote the quotient of this monoid by the smallest congruence relation $\sim$ identifying xx^{-1} and $x^{-1}x$, for $x \in S$, with the empty word: FG_S is a group, which we call the *free group on S*. Every equivalence class with respect to $\sim$ contains exactly one reduced group word. If $w = x_1 \ldots x_n$ is a reduced group word on S, define the *length* of w to be n. If $w \in FG_S$, define the *length* of w (denoted by $|w|$) to be the length of the unique reduced word equivalent to w.

There is a function $i_S : S \to FG_S$ sending $x \in S$ to the equivalence class of the word x. The group FG_S and function i_S satisfy the following *universal property*: let G be a group and let $f : S \to G$ be a function. There exists a unique group homomorphism $e_f : FG_S \to G$ such that $e_f \circ i_S = f$. A group G is said to be *free* if it is isomorphic to FG_S for some set S. Free groups admit many equivalent definitions: in [10], for example, they are defined using the universal property described above. We use e to denote the identity of a group.

Let G be a group, and let $U \subseteq G$. Define $U^{\pm} := U \cup U^{-1}$, where $U^{-1} := \{x^{-1} \mid x \in U\}$. The *subgroup generated by* U (i.e. the *span* of U) is $\langle U \rangle := \{g \in G \mid g = g_1 \ldots g_n$ for some $g_1, \ldots, g_n \in U^{\pm}\}$. This subgroup admits a characterisation as the smallest subgroup of G which contains U. We say that U *generates* G (i.e. is a *generating set for* G) if $\langle U \rangle = G$. The subset U generates G if and only if the homomorphism $FG_U \to G$ induced by the inclusion $i : U \to G$ is surjective; we say that U is a *basis* for G if this homomorphism is an isomorphism. If S is a set, $\{i_S(x) \mid x \in S\}$ is a basis for FG_S. As the map i_S is injective, we identify an element $x \in S$ with $i_S(x)$, and thus consider S a basis for FG_S.

3   Formalisation of Basic Constructions

The generating set of a group is often described with indices - e.g. $\{g_\alpha\}_{\alpha \in \Lambda}$. To mirror this, we define the type of generating elements as follows:

```
type_synonym ('a,'b) monoidgentype = "'a × 'b"
```

Here, 'a denotes the type of labels, and 'b denotes the type of indices. It is easy to see that any type can be embedded into a type of this form using Isabelle's unit datatype. In our formalization, a *generator* is an object of the type 'a × 'b. A generating set or a set of a generators denotes a set containing objects of the type 'a × 'b. We construct the type groupgentype in which every object can be construed to denote an object of the type monoidgentype (under an inclusion map) or its inverse. A *group word* can now be defined as a list of the objects of groupgentype.

```
type_synonym ('a,'b) groupgentype = "('a,'b) monoidgentype × bool"
```

```
type_synonym ('a,'b) word = "(('a,'b) groupgentype) list"
```

There exists a natural embedding of monoidgentype in groupgentype, where $x \mapsto$ (x, True); (x, False) can be interpreted as denoting x^{-1}. Thus one can represent the word $g_1 g_2^{-1} g_3$ using the list [(g_1, True), (g_2, False), (g_3, True)]. A function inverse is defined on groupgentype, which swaps True and False in the second coordinate. The invgen function maps a set S to $S^{\pm}$ (as defined in Sect. 2). Note that S is of the type monoidgentype and $S^{\pm}$ of the type groupgentype.

```
definition invgen ("_±")    where "S ± = S × {True,False}"
```

To formalise the inverse of a word, we recursively define the `wordinverse` function in terms of the `inverse` function in the following fashion. In this paper we will often use w^{-1} for `wordinverse w`, where `w` is a word.

```
fun wordinverse::"('a,'b) word ⇒ ('a, 'b) word"    where
"wordinverse [] = []"
|"wordinverse (x#xs) = (wordinverse xs)@[inverse x]"
```

For constructing a free group, only the words in the span of a generating set play a role. We construct the span as follows. First, the set of generators S is mapped to the set $S^{\pm}$, using the `invgen` function. The function `words_on` then defines an inductive set of words, where all the letters of the word belong to a given set. For the set $S^{\pm}$, this returns the list of group words generated by S.

```
inductive_set words_on ("_*") for X::"('a,'b) groupgentype set" where
empty:"[] ∈ (X*)"
|gen:"x ∈ X ⟹ xs ∈ (X*) ⟹ (x#xs) ∈ (X*)"

definition freewords_on: ("⟨_⟩") where "⟨S⟩  = words_on (invgen S)"
```

We define an equivalence relation on words such that words obtained by adding or removing adjacent pair of inverses are equivalent. The relation `reln_tuple` restricts this relation to words belonging a specified set.

```
inductive reln::"('a,'b) word⇒('a,'b) word⇒ bool" (infixr "~" 65)
   where
refl[intro!]: "x ~ x" |
sym: "x ~ y ⟹ y ~ x" |
trans: "x ~ y ⟹ y ~ z ⟹ x ~ z" |
base: "[x, inverse x] ~ []" |
mult: "xs~xs' ⟹ ys~ys' ⟹ (xs@ys)~(xs'@ys')"

definition reln_tuple where "reln_tuple X = {(x,y).x~y ∧ x∈X ∧ y∈X}"
```

It follows that `reln_tuple` is an equivalence relation on the set `X`. To define the carrier as a quotient of the span of the set of generators by this equivalence relation, we considered using `quotient_type`. This is challenging in the absence of dependent types, since the set of words generated by a set S cannot form a type. Moreover, using quotient type on the entire type rather than a set can lead to equating words which do belong to the span of generators with those which do belong to the span (e.g. $[x] \sim [x, y, y^{-1}]$, where $x \in S^{\pm}$, $y \notin S^{\pm}$). We thus chose to deploy `quotient`, as formalised in Isabelle's formalisation of equivalence relations. The product of two elements in a free group is obtained by factoring the concatenation of two words through the equivalence relation on the carrier. The function `proj_append` induces a function on the equivalence classes of the span of a set under `reln_tuple`, which corresponds to concatenation of words.

definition *ProjFun2* **where**

```
"ProjFun2 r f =  (λp q. (⋃x∈(p×q). r '' {f (fst x) (snd x)}))"
```

definition proj_append **where**
```
"proj_append A X Y =  (ProjFun2 (reln_tuple A) append) X Y"
```

ProjFun2, when applied to a relation r and a binary operation f, returns the function which maps a pair of sets X and Y to the set of those elements $r-$related to $f(x,y)$ for some $(x,y) \in X \times Y$. It follows that proj_append $\langle S \rangle$ applied to a pair of equivalence classes of words is the equivalence class of the concatenation of their representative elements; this product was shown to satisfy closure and associativity. The free group generated by a set S of the type monoidgentype is then defined as the following record:

definition freegroup **where**
```
"freegroup S ≡ (| carrier = quotient ⟨S⟩ (reln_tuple ⟨S⟩),
                 mult = proj_append ⟨S⟩,
                 one = (reln_tuple ⟨S⟩) '' {[]} |)"
```

Every group word w in the span $\langle S \rangle$ can be embedded as an element in the carrier of freegroup S by mapping w to reln_tuple $\langle S \rangle$ '' {w}. The identity element then naturally arises as the embedding of the empty list. We then prove that the free group on S satisfies the group axioms, using the closure and associativity properties of proj_append. The existence of inverses is proved by first showing that for every word w in $\langle S \rangle$, the word w^{-1} is in $\langle S \rangle$ and that w concatenated with w^{-1} is equivalent to the empty list.

theorem freegroup_is_group: "group (freegroup S)"

Finally, we define a free group as a group which is isomorphic to the free group on some set of generators.

definition is_freegroup::"_ ⇒ bool"   **where**
```
"is_freegroup G ≡ (∃ (S::(unit × 'a) set). G ≅ (freegroup S))"
```

The formalisation of the universal property posed some challenges. An important concern was that carrier set of a group is not necessarily a type in HOL-Algebra, and that the domain of homomorphisms includes all objects in the underlying type and not just the carrier set. As a consequence, two distinct homomorphisms may be extensionally equal when restricted to the carrier set, and so the lift from the generating set to the group no longer remains unique. To recover the universal property, we first prove the existence of a homomorphism and then show that any two homomorphisms which are obtained by lifting the map from S to H are extensionally equal when restricted to the generating set:

theorem (**in** group) exists_hom:
  assumes "f ∈ S → carrier G"

```
shows "∃h ∈ hom (freegroup S) G. ∀x ∈ S.
      f x = h (reln_tuple ⟨S⟩ '' {ι  x})"
```

```
theorem (in group) uniqueness_of_lift:
 assumes "f  ∈  S → carrier G"
  and "h  ∈ hom (freegroup S) G"
     "g  ∈ hom (freegroup S) G"
  and "∀x ∈ S. f x = h (reln_tuple ⟨S⟩ '' {ι  x})"
  and "∀x ∈ S. f x = g (reln_tuple ⟨S⟩ '' {ι  x})"
 shows "∀ x ∈ carrier (freegroup S).  h x  = g x"
```

We need the notion of a subgroup generated by a subset. We use the formalisation of the span of a subset of a group in [4], which is defined as follows.

```
inductive_set gen_span ("⟨_⟩₁") for G and gens where
gen_one: "1_G ∈ ⟨gens⟩_G"
    | gen_gens: "x ∈ gens ⟹ x ∈ ⟨gens⟩_G"
    | gen_inv: "x ∈ ⟨gens⟩_G ⟹ inv_G x ∈ ⟨gens⟩_G"
    | gen_mult: "⟦ x ∈ ⟨gens⟩_G; y ∈ ⟨gens⟩_G ⟧ ⟹  x ⊗_G y ∈ ⟨gens⟩_G"
```

Showing that $\langle S \rangle_G$ spans a subgroup of a group, when $S \subseteq G$, is straightforward. We then prove the following lemma, which is a mild variation (suggested by the formalisation) of the universal property of free groups.

```
lemma (in group) exist_of_hom_implies_freegroup:
    fixes S::"'a set"
 assumes "(⟨S⟩_G) = carrier G"
   and "⋀H::(unit × 'a) × bool) list set monoid).
   ⋀f. (group H) ∧ (f ∈ S → (carrier H))
        ⟶ (∃h ∈ hom G H. (∀ x ∈ S. h x = f x))"
 shows "∃S_H. G ≅ (freegroup S_H)"
```

4   The Word and Conjugacy Problems for Free Groups

Let G be a group. Elements $g, h \in G$ are said to be *conjugate* if there exists an element $k \in G$ such that $h = kgk^{-1}$. Let $S \subseteq G$ be a generating set for G. The word problem for G asks if there is an algorithm which determines whether a group word w in S is equal to e in G. The conjugacy problem for G asks if there is an algorithm which determines whether group words w, w' in S are conjugate in G. A comprehensive discussion of these problems can be found in [10].

A group word w on a set S is equivalent to a reduced word w' attained by successively cancelling subwords of the form xx^{-1} or $x^{-1}x$ in w. Two reduced group words w and w' are equal in FG_S if and only if they are identical. These observations solve the word problem for free groups: if w is a group word in S, successively cancel subwords of the form xx^{-1} or $x^{-1}x$ until we arrive at a reduced word w'. Then $w = e$ in FG_S if and only if w' is the empty word.

This decision procedure is formalised by defining an executable function `reduce` on lists and proving that group words are equivalent if and only their corresponding images after a finite number of iterations of `reduce` are equal.

```
fun reduce :: "('a,'b) word ⟹ ('a,'b) word" where
"reduce [] = []"|
"reduce [x] = [x]"|
"reduce (x#y#wrd) = (if (x = inverse y)
                     then wrd
                     else (x#(reduce (y#wrd))))"
```

```
theorem word_problem_eq:
  assumes "x ∈ ⟨S⟩" "y ∈ ⟨S⟩"
  shows "reln_tuple ⟨S⟩ '' {x} = reln_tuple ⟨S⟩ '' {y}
    ⟷ (reduce^^(length x)) x = (reduce^^(length y)) y"
```

Certain parts of the proof given above are adapted from the approach in [4]. A rewrite system on group words is defined, whose reflexive symmetric closure is the canonical equivalence relation on words; we subsequently show that this rewrite system is confluent, terminating, and admits a unique normal form. A key difference is that we also construct the normal forms in terms of `reduce`, thus rendering the normal form amenable to code generation.

We now turn to the conjugacy problem. Let $w = x_1 \ldots x_n$ be a group word on S. A word w' is said to be *cyclically equivalent* to w if $w' = x_k \ldots x_n x_1 \ldots x_{k-1}$ for some $k \in \{1, \ldots, n\}$. A reduced word $w = x_1^{\epsilon_1} \ldots x_n^{\epsilon_n}$, where $x_i \in S$, is said to be *cyclically reduced* if it is reduced and it is not the case that $x_1 = x_n$ and $\epsilon_1 \epsilon_n = -1$; then, any word cyclically equivalent to w is also reduced. An element $x \in FG_S$ is said to be cyclically reduced if the reduced word representing it is cyclically reduced.

Lemma 1. *Let w be a group word on a set S. There exists a unique reduced word z and a unique cyclically reduced word w' such that $zw'z^{-1}$ is reduced and $w = zw'z^{-1}$ in FG_S. We call w' the* cyclic reduction *of w.*

Proof. We induct on the length of w. Let $v = x_1^{\epsilon_1} \ldots x_n^{\epsilon_n}$, where $x_i \in S$, be the reduced word equivalent to w. If v is not cyclically reduced, $x_1 = x_n$ and $\epsilon_1 \epsilon_n = -1$. It follows that there exists a reduced word v' and an element $x \in S \cup S^{-1}$ such that $v = xv'x^{-1}$. The argument now follows from applying the induction hypothesis to v'. We omit the proof that z and w' are unique.

Proposition 1. *Let w and w' be two cyclically reduced words on S. Then, w and w' are conjugate in FG_S if and only if they are cyclically equivalent.*

Proof. We sketch the proof. If w and w' are conjugate, there exists a reduced group word z in S such that $zwz^{-1} = w'$ in FG_S. We can assume that $z = z_1^{\eta_1} \ldots z_k^{\eta_k}$, where $z_i \in S$, is not the empty word and does not contain w as a terminal subword (a terminal subword of z is a word of the form $z_m^{\eta_m} \ldots z_k^{\eta_k}$ for some $m \leq k$). Let $w = x_1^{\epsilon_1} \ldots x_n^{\epsilon_n}$ and $w' = y_1^{\delta_1} \ldots y_m^{\delta_m}$, where $x_i, y_i \in S$.

In FG_S, $z_1^{\eta_1} \ldots z_k^{\eta_k} x_1^{\epsilon_1} \ldots x_n^{\epsilon_n} z_k^{-\eta_k} \ldots z_1^{-\eta_1} = y_1^{\delta_i} \ldots y_m^{\delta_m}$: thus $y_1^{\delta_i} \ldots y_m^{\delta_m}$ is the unique reduced word equivalent to $z_1^{\eta_1} \ldots z_k^{\eta_k} x_1^{\epsilon_1} \ldots x_n^{\epsilon_n} z_k^{-\eta_k} \ldots z_1^{-\eta_1}$. Since $z_1^{\eta_1} \ldots z_k^{\eta_k} x_1^{\epsilon_1} \ldots x_n^{\epsilon_n} z_k^{-\eta_k} \ldots z_1^{-\eta_1}$ is not cyclically reduced, it cannot be reduced. The only cancellation in $z_1^{\eta_1} \ldots z_k^{\eta_k} x_1^{\epsilon_1} \ldots x_n^{\epsilon_n} z_k^{-\eta_k} \ldots z_1^{-\eta_1}$ is either between $z_k^{\eta_k}$ and $x_1^{\epsilon_1}$, or between $x_n^{\epsilon_n}$ and $z_k^{-\eta_k}$. Since w is cyclically reduced, there must be cancellation at exactly one of these places: we will assume that $z_k = x_1$ and $\eta_k = -\epsilon_1$. If $k = 1$, then $y_1^{\delta_i} \ldots y_m^{\delta_m} = x_2^{\epsilon_2} \ldots x_n^{\epsilon_n} x_1^{\epsilon_1}$, which is cyclically equivalent to x. If not, we continue. Iterating, we observe that $k < m$: otherwise, we would have that w is a terminal subword of z. We also observe that $z_i = x_{k-(i-1)}$ and $\delta_i = \epsilon_{k-(i-1)}$ for every $1 \leq i \leq k$, and that $y_1^{\delta_i} \ldots y_m^{\delta_m} = x_{k+1}^{\epsilon_{k+1}} \ldots x_n^{\epsilon_n} x_1^{\epsilon_1} \ldots x_k^{\epsilon_k}$. It follows that w and w' are cyclically equivalent. The converse is straightforward.

Lemma 1 and Proposition 1 solve the conjugacy problem for free groups. Given words w and w', reduce both to cyclically reduced words: the words w and w' are conjugate if and only if their cyclic reductions are cyclically equivalent. To formalise these results, we begin with two observations. First, the steps involved in the proof largely pertain to words, and the group structure is not extensively employed. In addition, many of the definitions present in the literature are existentially defined over a finite set of natural numbers. These are convenient for proofs, but not amenable to code extraction. We therefore define executable versions of cyclic reduction and cyclic equivalence.

```
definition cyclic_reduce :: "('a,'b) word ⇒ ('a,'b) word"
  where "cyclic_reduce x =  uncycle ((reduce^^(length x)) x)"
```

```
definition ccyclicp :: "('a, 'b) word ⇒ ('a, 'b) word ⇒ bool"
  where "ccyclicp x y = checkcycleeq (length x) x y"
```

The iterated **reduce** function returns the normal form of the word. The **uncycle** function recursively eliminates the first and last elements of the word if they form a pair of inverses, else it returns the original word. The function **cyclic_reduce** combines these two functions to define cyclic reduction. The **checkcycleeq** function recursively checks if two words are equal to each other, else it cyclically permutes one of the words for a fixed number of times till it equals the other, else it returns false. The function **cycylicp**, which defines cyclic equivalence, restricts the number of such cyclic permutations to the length of the first word. We then define the executable function **check_conj** on group words.

```
definition check_conj
  where "check_conj x y =(ccyclicp (cyclic_reduce x) (cyclic_reduce y))"
```

As **check_conj** is an executable function, showing that **check_conj** is equivalent to conjugacy on words amounts to formalising the decision procedure to check conjugacy in free groups.

```
definition(in group) conjugate
  where "conjugate x y ≡ (∃z ∈ (carrier G). z ⊗ x ⊗ inv z = y)"
```

```
lemma conjugacy_problem_in_freegroups:
  assumes "x ∈ ⟨S⟩" "y ∈ ⟨S⟩"
  shows "conjugate (freegroup A)
         (reln_tuple ⟨A⟩'' {x})
         (reln_tuple ⟨A⟩'' {y})
       = check_conj x y"
```

The formal proof of this lemma is along the lines of the arguments given in Lemma 1 and Proposition 1. Formally adapting the argument in the proof of Proposition 1 was particularly tedious as it involved a detailed case by case analysis depending on where cancellations in certain non-reduced words occured. Further care had to be taken while interpolating between group words and their equivalence classes in the free group. The function `conj_check` is executable, thus leading to a safe code generated from a verified formalisation.

5   The Nielsen-Schreier Theorem

The Nielsen-Schreier Theorem asserts that subgroups of free groups are free. This statement is deceptive in its simplicity: it is not immediate why this should be the case (for example, consider the subgroup of $FG_{\{a,b,c\}}$ generated by $\{abc^{-1}, cab^{-1}, b^{-1}a^{-1}\}$). The proof we present here is organised as follows: A property called N-reduced is defined on group words. It is then proved that every subgroup of a free group admits an N-reduced generating set, and that subgroups generated by N-reduced sets in free groups are free. Together, these give us the result. Our arguments follow those in [10, Chapter 1], though some ideas have been reorganised for clarity. To begin, in the following lemma we introduce a relation on group words that will play a critical role in our argument.

Lemma 2. *Let S be a set such that the $S^{\pm}$ is well-ordered via a relation $<'$, and let $<$ be the shortlex order on set of reduced group words on S. If $w = x_1^{\epsilon_1} \ldots x_n^{\epsilon_n}$ is a reduced word on S, define $L(w) := x_1^{\epsilon_1} \ldots x_m^{\epsilon_m}$, where $m = \lfloor (n+1)/2 \rfloor$. First, define a relation on the set of reduced group words on S by setting $w \prec' u$ if either $\min\{L(w), L(w^{-1})\} < \min\{L(u), L(u^{-1})\}$; or $\min\{L(w), L(w^{-1})\} = \min\{L(u), L(u^{-1})$ together with $\max\{L(w), L(w^{-1})\} < \max\{L(u), L(u^{-1})\}$. Define a second relation on the set of reduced group words on S as follows: $w \prec u$ if either $|w| < |u|$, or $|w| = |u|$ and $w \prec' u$. The relation $\prec$ is transitive and well-founded. Moreover, for reduced words w, w', neither $w \prec w'$ nor $w' \prec w$ are true precisely when either $w' = w$ or $w' = w^{-1}$.*

Lemma 2 is extracted from [10, Proposition 2.2], and is a minor modification of the construction presented there: we omit its proof. This lemma essentially states that $\prec$ is a well-order on the set of reduced group words, up to an identification of w and w^{-1} for any group word w. To formalise this relation, we begin by defining `lex_word`.

definition `lex_word`   **where** `"lex_word = lenlex (r_gen - Id)"`

The relation `r_gen` is a well founded order on the type **groupgentype**. The existence of such an order follows from the **well_ordering** theorem, which stands formalised in Isabelle/HOL. The relation `lenlex r`, which is available in Isabelle's formalisation on lists, compares two lists first by length then lexicographically using the order `r`. The formalisation of `lex_word` further allows us to formalise $\prec'$ as `lex_L2_word'`, which compares two tuples of left subwords, by first comparing the minimal elements of the tuples in the lexicographic order, and then if they are equal, by comparing the maximal elements of tuples in a similar fashion. Using `lex_L2_word'`, we formalise $\prec$ as `lex_L2_word` as follows:

definition `lex_L2_word` **where**
```
"lex_L2_word A = {(x,y).
        x ∈ (⟨A⟩ // (reln_tuple ⟨A⟩))
      ∧ y ∈ (⟨A⟩ // (reln_tuple ⟨A⟩))
      ∧ ((λt. (length (red_rep A t), t)) x,
         (λt. (length (red_rep A t), t)) y)
        ∈ (nat_less <*lex*> lex_L2_word' A)}"
```

The relation `lex_L2_word` first compares the lengths of the reduced representation of two words, and subsequently compares them using `lex_L2_word'` if the lengths are equal.

Let S be a set, and let U be a subset of FG_S. The set U is said to be N-*reduced* if it satisfies the following three conditions: (N0) U does not contain the identity; (N1) if $x, y \in U^{\pm}$ such that $xy \neq e$, then $|xy| \geq |x|, |y|$; (N2) if $x, y, z \in U^{\pm}$ such that $xy \neq e$ and $yz \neq e$, then $|xyz| > |x| + |z| - |y|$.

We formalise the properties N0, N1, and N2 as predicates on one, two, and three words, respectively. A word x satisfies N0 if it is not the empty word.

definition `N0` **where** `"N0 x = (x ≠  [])"`

Properties N1 and N2 are comparisons between the lengths of words and the length of their product. Formalising these statements directly result in definitions that are unwieldy. Therefore, we formalise these conditions in terms of cancellation between words, as described in Lemmas 3, 4, and 5 below.

Lemma 3. *Let w, w' be reduced group words on a set S. There exist unique reduced group words p, a and b such that $w = ap$, $w' = p^{-1}b$, and ab is reduced.*

Proof. Induct on the length of w. If ww' is reduced, then take p to be the empty word. If not, there exists an element $x \in S^{\pm}$ such that $w = cx$ and $w' = x^{-1}d$. Then, $ww' = cd$. By induction, there exists a reduced word q such that $c = aq$, $d = q^{-1}b$, and ab is reduced. Take $p = qx$. We omit the proof of uniqueness.

Let S be a set, and let w, w' be reduced group words on S. The reduced word p constructed in Lemma 3 is called the *cancellation* between the pair (w, w').

Lemma 4. *Let w, w' be reduced group words on a set S. Let p be the cancellation between the pair (w, w'). Then, $|ww'| \geq |w|$ and $|ww'| \geq |w'|$ if and only if $|w|/2 \geq |p|$ and $|w'|/2 \geq |p|$.*

Proof. Observe that $|ww'| = |a| + |b|$, $|w| = |a| + |p|$, and $|w'| = |b| + |p|$. Thus $|ww'| \geq |w|, |w'|$ if and only if $|p| \leq |a|, |b|$, which is equivalent to $|p| \leq |w|/2, |w'|/2$.

Lemma 5. *Let S be a set, and let w, w', w'' be reduced group words on S. Suppose $|ww'| \geq |w|, |w'|$ and $|w'w''| \geq |w'|, |w''|$. Let p be the cancellation between the pair (w, w') and q the cancellation between the pair (w', w''). There exist reduced group words a, b, and c on S such that $w = ap$, $w' = p^{-1}cq$, $w'' = q^{-1}b$. If c is not the empty word, the word acb is reduced. Moreover, $|ww'w''| > |w| + |w''| - |w'|$ if and only if c is not the empty word.*

Proof. By Lemma 3, there exist reduced words a, d, e, b, p and q such that $w = ap$, $w' = p^{-1}d$, $w' = eq$, and $w'' = q^{-1}b$. By Lemma 4, we also know that $|p|, |q| \leq |w'|/2$. Thus there exists a reduced word c such that $w' = p^{-1}cq$. Observe that $ww'w'' = acb$. If c is not the empty word, acb is reduced, and so $|ww'w''| = |a| + |b| + |c|$. A straightforward calculation proves that $|w| + |w''| - |w'| = |a| + |b| - |c|$. Since c is not empty, it follows that $|ww'w''| > |w| + |w''| - |w'|$. Conversely, suppose that c is the empty word. Then, the word $ww'w'' = ab$, while $|w| + |w''| - |w'| = |a| + |b|$. Thus $|ww'w''| \leq |w| + |w''| - |w'|$.

The predicate N1 is now formally defined as follows:

```
definition N1    where
"N1 x y = ((x ≠  wordinverse y)
  ⟶ ((length (π₂ (x⊘₂y))) ≤(length (π₁ (x⊘₂y)))
     ∧ (length (π₂ (x⊘₂y))) ≤ (length (π₃ (x⊘₂y))))))"
```

The expression x $\oslash_2$ y mentioned here returns the unique tuple w = (a,p,b) such that x = ap, y = p^{-1}b, and ab is reduced. The existence of such a tuple follows from a formalisation of Lemma 3. The functions π_i in the definition above correspond to the ith projection of the tuple. For the property N2, our formalisation is defined in the context of words already satisfying property N1:

```
definition N2    where
"N2 x y z =
((x ≠  wordinverse y  ∧ y ≠  wordinverse z)⟶(π₃ (⊘₃ x y z) ≠  [])))"
```

The expression $\oslash_3$ x y z above returns the unique tuple w = (a,p,c,q,b) with x = ap, y = p^{-1}cq, z = q^{-1}b, and acq and p^{-1}cb are reduced. The existence of such tuples follows from our formalisation of Lemma 5. These constructions allow us to formalise the property N-reduced, for a subset U of the free group, as the property which asserts that the reduced representations of all the elements in $U^{\pm}$ and their curried tuples satisfy the properties N0, N1 and N2.

Proposition 2. *Let S be a set such that the set $S^{\pm}$ is well-ordered, and let H be a subgroup of FG_S. If $g \in H$, define $T_g := \{y \in H \mid y \prec x\}$ (where $\prec$ is as in Lemma 2), and $H_g := \langle T_g \rangle$. Let $A = \{g \in H \mid g \notin H_g\}$. Then, A is an N-reduced set, and $H = \langle A \rangle$.*

Proof. Observe that $A = A^{\pm}$. The proof that $\langle A \rangle = H$ is exactly as in [10, Proposition 2.9]. To show that A is N-reduced, we extract the relevant arguments from [10, Proposition 2.2]. Observe that $e \notin A$; thus A satisfies (N0). Let $x, y \in A$ such that $xy \neq e$, and suppose that $|xy| < |x|$. This implies that $y \neq x$, and that $xy \prec x$. There are now two possibilities. If $x \prec y$, then both xy and x belong to H_y, which implies that $y \in H_y$, a contradiction. Similarly, if $y \prec x$, then both xy and y belong to H_x, and thus $x \in H_x$. Again, this is a contradiction. An identical argument rules out the possibility that $|xy| < |y|$. Thus A satisfies (N1).

To show that A satisfies (N2), we again argue exactly as in [10, Proposition 2.2]. Suppose x, y, z are elements of A such that $xy \neq 1$, $yz \neq 1$, and $|xyz| \leq |x| + |z| - |y|$. By Lemma 5, there exist reduced words a, b, and c in X such that $x = ap$, $y = p^{-1}q$, $z = q^{-1}b$, where p and q are the cancellation between (x, y) and (y, z) respectively. Since A satisfies (N1), we also observe that $|p| = |q| = |y|/2$.

If $p^{-1} \prec q^{-1}$, consider $yz = p^{-1}b$ and $z = q^{-1}b$. Suppose that $|yz| = |z|$. Then, $L((yz)^{-1}) = L(z^{-1})$ and $L(yz) < L(z)$; therefore $yz \prec z$. This gives a contradiction. On the other hand, suppose that $q^{-1} \prec p^{-1}$. Here, we can consider $x^{-1} = p^{-1}a^{-1}$ and $y^{-1}x^{-1} = q^{-1}a^{-1}$. Again, we get a contradiction.

We formalise H_g and A as `G' H S g` and `X' H S` respectively via the following definitions:

definition `G'` **where** `"G' H S g = ⟨{h∈carrier H. (h,g)∈(lex_L2_word S)}⟩`$_H$`"`
definition `X'` **where** `"X' H S = {g∈carrier H. g∉(G H S g)}"`

Proving that the set `X' H S` generates the group `H` is a simple proof by contradiction which makes use of the well-ordering theorem.

lemma `span_X'_SG_eq_SG:`
assumes `"H ≤ freegroup S"`
shows `"(let SubGp = (freegroup S)(|carrier := H|) in`
          `⟨X' SubGp S⟩`$_{SubGp}$` = carrier SubGp)"`

Note that `(freegroup S)(|carrier:=H|)` denotes the subgroup H (with its group structure) as in Isabelle's HOL-Algebra library. The following lemma formalises the remainder of Proposition 2 (i.e. showing that the set `X' H S` is N-reduced). Its proof is a tedious reproduction of the argument described in the proof of that proposition. We make use of the fact that $\prec$ relates a word to any other word, except itself and its inverse, and also that it is transitive.

lemma `N_reduced_X:` **assumes** `"H ≤ freegroup S"`
    shows `"N_reduced (X' (freegroup S)(|carrier := H|) S) S"`

We are now in a position to complete the proof of the Nielsen-Schreier theorem. We need the following proposition.

Proposition 3. *(c.f. [10, Proposition 2.3]) Let S be a set, and let U be an N-reduced set of elements in FG_S. The subgroup $H := \langle U \rangle$ is free.*

Proof. We sketch the proof. Using Zorn's lemma, we can find $V \subseteq U^{\pm}$ such that $V^{\pm} = U^{\pm}$ and $V \cap V^{-1} = \emptyset$ (we call such V a *minimal generating subset* corresponding to U). Consider the homomorphism $e_i : FG_V \to H$ induced by the inclusion of V in H. Note that $\langle U \rangle = \langle V \rangle = H$: thus e_i is surjective. To show H is free, it suffices to prove that e_i is also injective. Let $w = a_1 \ldots a_n$ be a non-empty group word in V, such that $a_i \neq a_{i+1}^{-1}$. We term such a word *non-reducible*. It suffices to prove that $e_i(w)$ is not equal to identity in H. Let p_i denote the cancellation between the pair (a_i, a_{i+1}), where we now consider the a_i as reduced words in S. Since $V^{\pm} = U^{\pm}$, V is N-reduced: therefore there exist non-empty reduced words $c_1, \ldots, c_n$ such that $a_1 = c_1 p_1$, $a_n = p_{n-1} c_n$, and $a_i = p_i^{-1} c_i p_{i+1}$ for all $i \in \{2, \ldots, n-1\}$; thus $w = a_1 \ldots a_n = c_1 \ldots c_n$ and that each word of the form $c_i c_{i+1}$ is reduced (Lemma 5). Thus w is a reduced product of non-empty words, and is therefore not equal to the identity.

Theorem 1 (The Nielsen-Schreier Theorem). *Let S be a set. Every subgroup of FG_S is free.*

Proof. Well-order $S^{\pm}$. Let H be a subgroup of FG_S. By Proposition 2, there is a set A such that A is N-reduced and $\langle A \rangle = H$. By Proposition 3, H is free.

The remainder of the formal proof of the Nielsen-Schreier theorem broadly follows the argument sketched in Proposition 3. Formally adapting this argument was quite involved, with almost every statement requiring a considerable amount of work. For example, the existence of a minimal generating subset associated to any given subset $A \subseteq \langle S \rangle$ was first proved as an application of Zorn's lemma, and then formalised in terms of a function `minimal_set` involving the choice operator; this then allowed multiple proofs to access this construction. Similarly, a sufficient condition for groups to be free in terms of homomorphisms (arising from the universal property) mapping non-reducible words to non-trivial elements was framed as a distinct lemma for arbitrary subsets of a group, and then specified to the case of minimal generating subsets. This proof involved constant navigation between the multiplicity of types involved.

The Nielsen-Schreier theorem formally appears in our work as:

```
theorem(in group) Nielsen_Schreier:
  assumes "H ≤ (freegroup S)"
  shows "is_freegroup ((freegroup S)(|carrier := H|))"
```

6   Discussion

The challenges we encountered during this work could be organised into three broad categories. The first was reorganising the mathematical ideas involved in a manner that was amenable to a formalisation project. This included expanding on tersely written arguments from our source material, and, on occasion, making small modifications to some of the mathematics involved. The second broad category of challenges concerned identifying and then resolving certain under-specifications in the manner in which certain definitions and proofs are conventionally presented. This included unraveling the distinction between objects conventionally identified by abuse of notation (e.g. the identification of an element and its image under an isomorphism, or the identification of isomorphic groups), and also in formally structuring and writing certain arguments that conventionally made use of intuition regarding the behaviour of iterative processes in the presence of a large number of cases (e.g. the decision process for the conjugacy problem). A final category of challenges emerged while adapting certain mathematical ideas to the framework of simple type theory and in the context of existent formalization of group theory (e.g. as in Sect. 3). In addition, it may be worthwhile to note that locales were not employed in the course of our formalisation beyond those already present in Isabelle's HOL-Algebra library: no major advantages were foreseen in defining additional locales for our work as the main place they may have been used (i.e. defining N-reduced words) is a definition used only in a specific proof.

7   Related Works

Definitions and basic results on free groups stand formalised in several theorem provers, including Isabelle/HOL, Coq, Lean, Agda and ACL2 [3,11,14,17]. Free group formalisations in Coq and Lean contain the word problem and the universal property of free groups [11,14]; a related implementation of the free word problem and the universal property for free abelian groups is also available in HOL Light [8]. A formalisation of free groups in ACL2 establishes an isomorphism between free groups of rank 2 and a certain group of rotation matrices [3].

A complete topological proof of the Nielsen-Schreier theorem stands formalised in Lean [12]. In addition, a homotopy type theoretic proof of a restricted case of the Nielsen-Schreier theorem for finite index subgroups, which draws from the algebraic topological proof of the Nielsen-Schreier theorem (as in [2]), was formalised in Agda [17]; while [17] also contains a proof of the general Nielsen-Schreier theorem using homotopy type theory and the axiom of choice, the proof there of the general case is not mechanised. Topological arguments for the Nielsen-Schreier theorem, as formalised in Lean and Agda, rely on a very different set of techniques (involving the theory of groupoids, fundamental groups of graphs, etc.) from those formalised in this work.

A formalisation, in Isabelle/HOL, of word combinatorics on monoids can be found in [7]; however, our work does not overlap with this.

In Isabelle/HOL, a previous formalisation of free groups can be found in the Archive of Formal Proofs [4]. This formalisation includes results on the existence of unique normal forms, a formal proof of the invariance of rank, and the ping-pong lemma. In our work, we develop a formalisation for free groups starting from the basic definitions. While we follow some of the constructions and proofs as developed in [4], our approach does diverge in certain ways. For instance, the normal form of a word in [4] is not executable since it relies on the choice operator, and the free group is defined on the set of reduced words. We choose to work with a formal definition of a free group that resembles the most frequently used definition in the mathematical literature. For this, we draw upon the definition in Sect. 2, rather than other equivalent definitions which appear in the literature. That said, the approach in [4] certainly proved useful to us, including their formalisation of the span of a subset of a group. Our work also builds on the formalised group theory content in the HOL-Algebra library of Isabelle [1]. The span of a subset of a group also stands formalised in HOL-Algebra, but we found the notation in [4] better suited for our purposes.

8   Conclusions and Future Work

In this paper, we introduce an ongoing formalisation project in the theory of free groups in Isabelle/HOL. After setting up a formalised context and foundation, we construct a formalised proof Nielsen-Schreier theorem and a decision process for the conjugacy problem. To the best of our knowledge, our work presents the first mechanised proof of the Nielsen-Schreier in complete generality in any theorem prover. In addition, our formalisation of a decision process for the conjugacy problem allows for code execution. We were able to work entirely within the framework of simple type theory for our constructions. While it might have been convenient to have access to dependent types at certain points during our formalisation, the lack thereof did not pose major challenges.

We consider this work as the start of a substantial project formalising various aspects of combinatorial and geometric group theory. We expect future work to build upon the formalised libraries that have been constructed as a part of this project. We are currently working to formalise other algorithms on free groups including Whitehead's algorithm (which determines when two elements of a free group are mapped to one another under an automorphism of the group). In the longer term, we hope to work towards formalising results in the elementary theory of free groups [9,16] and the cohomology of free groups.

Acknowledgements. This work was supported by the Krea Faculty Research Fellowship "Computational Thought in Group Theory and Geometry". In addition, we are grateful to the annonymous reviewers for their throughful comments and suggestions.

References

1. Aransay, J., et al.: The Isabelle/HOL Algebra Library (2022). https://isabelle.in.tum.de/library/HOL/HOL-Algebra/. Accessed 11 June 2023
2. Baer, R., Levi, F.: Freie Produkte und ihre Untergruppen. Compos. Math. **3**, 391–398 (1936)

3. Bapanapally, J., Gamboa, R.: A complete, mechanically-verified proof of the Banach-Tarski theorem in ACL2(R). In: Andronick, J., de Moura, L. (eds.) 13th International Conference on Interactive Theorem Proving (ITP 2022). Leibniz International Proceedings in Informatics (LIPIcs), vol. 237, pp. 5:1–5:15. Schloss Dagstuhl - Leibniz-Zentrum für Informatik, Dagstuhl, Germany (2022). https://doi.org/10.4230/LIPIcs.ITP.2022.5. https://drops.dagstuhl.de/opus/volltexte/2022/16714

4. Breitner, J.: Free groups. Archive of Formal Proofs (2010). https://isa-afp.org/entries/Free-Groups.html. Formal proof development

5. Dehn, M.: Über unendliche diskontinuierliche Gruppen. Math. Ann. **71**(1), 116–144 (1911)

6. Dyck, W.: Gruppentheoretische studien. Math. Ann. **20**(1), 1–44 (1882)

7. Holub, Š., Starosta, Š.: Formalization of basic combinatorics on words. In: Cohen, L., Kaliszyk, C. (eds.) 12th International Conference on Interactive Theorem Proving (ITP 2021). Leibniz International Proceedings in Informatics (LIPIcs), vol. 193, pp. 22:1–22:17. Schloss Dagstuhl - Leibniz-Zentrum für Informatik, Dagstuhl, Germany (2021). https://doi.org/10.4230/LIPIcs.ITP.2021.22. https://drops.dagstuhl.de/opus/volltexte/2021/13917

8. JRH13: Simple formulation of group theory with a type of "(A)group". GitHub repository. https://github.com/jrh13/hol-light/blob/master/Library/grouptheory.ml

9. Kharlampovich, O., Myasnikov, A.: Elementary theory of free non-abelian groups. J. Algebra **302**(2), 451–552 (2006)

10. Lyndon, R.C., Schupp, P.E.: Combinatorial Group Theory, vol. 188. Springer, Heidelberg (1977)

11. mathlib: Free Groups - Lean Mathematical Library. https://leanprover-community.github.io/mathlib_docs/group_theory/free_group.html. Accessed 09 Apr 2023

12. mathlib: The Nielsen-Schreier theorem - Lean Mathematical Library. https://leanprover-community.github.io/mathlib_docs/group_theory/nielsen_schreier.html. Accessed 02 June 2023

13. Nielsen, J.: Om Regning med ikke-kommutative Faktorer og dens Anvendelse i Gruppeteorien. Matematisk Tidsskrift. B 77–94 (1921)

14. Schepler, D.: Freegroups Coq contribution. GitHub repository (2011). https://github.com/coq-contribs/free-groups

15. Schreier, O.: Die untergruppen der freien gruppen. Abhandlungen aus dem Mathematischen Seminar der universität Hamburg **5**, 161–183 (1927)

16. Sela, Z.: Diophantine geometry over groups VI: the elementary theory of a free group. Geom. Funct. Anal. **16**(3), 707–730 (2006)

17. Swan, A.W.: On the Nielsen-Schreier theorem in homotopy type theory. Log. Methods Comput. Sci. **18** (2022)

Morphism Equality in Theory Graphs

Florian Rabe[(✉)] and Franziska Weber

University Erlangen-Nuremberg, Erlangen, Germany
florian.rabe@fau.de

Abstract. Theory graphs have theories as nodes and theory morphisms as edges. They can be seen as generators of categories with the nodes as the objects and the paths as the morphisms. But in contrast to generated categories, theory graphs do not allow for an equational theory on the morphisms. That blocks formalizing important aspects of theory graphs such as isomorphisms between theories.

MMT is essentially a logic-independent language for theory graphs. It previously supported theories and morphisms, and we extend it with morphism equality as a third primitive. We show the importance of this feature in several elementary formalizations that critically require stating and proving certain non-trivial morphism equalities. The key difficulty of this approach is that important properties of theory graphs now become undecidable and require heuristic methods.

1 Introduction and Related Work

Theory Graphs and Motivation. Logical **theories** are an essential meta-level concept for encapsulating a set of declarations and axioms. For example, the theory Groupof first-order logic declares a base set U, a binary operation $\circ$ on U, a unary operation $^{-1}$, a neutral element e, and the usual axioms.

Theory morphisms extend this to a category. A theory **morphism** from S to T interprets S in T or, equivalently, constructs a model of S if provided a model of T. Formally, it maps every constant declared in S to a T-expression in a way that the homomorphic extension preserves all types and theorems. For example, we can define the theory DivGroupof division groups, an alternative way to define groups, using a binary division operation $/$. Then we can define a theory morphism GtoDG : Group $\longrightarrow$ DivGroup by mapping $x \circ y$ to $x/(e/y)$, x^{-1} to e/x and e to e and proving all Groupaxioms of the thus-defined group.

The category of theories has proved extremely valuable in the large scale structuring of mathematical formalizations, especially when combined with module systems [FGT92, SW83, AHMS99]. A diagram in this category is also called a **theory graph**. Many formal systems provide support for constructing large theory graphs over various logics, including proof assistants such as IMPS [FGT93] and PVS [ORS92], specification systems such as Hets [MML07] and Specware [SJ95], and logical frameworks such as LF [RS09] and Isabelle [KWP99].[1]

---

[1] The individual theory graphs are implicit in the respective libraries and usually not the subject of specific publications.

© The Author(s), under exclusive license to Springer Nature Switzerland AG 2023
C. Dubois and M. Kerber (Eds.): CICM 2023, LNAI 14101, pp. 174–189, 2023.
https://doi.org/10.1007/978-3-031-42753-4_12

However, maybe surprisingly, none of these systems includes support for **morphism equality**. In category theory, a diagram consists of three components: a set of objects (nodes of the theory graph), a set of atomic morphisms between objects (edges), from which the set of morphisms (paths) is generated by composition, and a set of pairs of equal morphisms between the same objects (equality of two paths between the same nodes). But practical systems for theory graphs have restricted attention to the former two components even though the latter is critical for the diagram chase–style arguments that are a hallmark of category theory.

For example, we can give a second morphism $\mathtt{DGtoG} : \mathtt{DivGroup} \longrightarrow \mathtt{Group}$ that maps (among others) x/y to $x \circ y^{-1}$. We can then see that $\mathtt{DGtoG}; \mathtt{GtoDG} = id_{\mathtt{DivGroup}}$ and $\mathtt{GtoDG}; \mathtt{DGtoG} = id_{\mathtt{Group}}$, i.e., that $\mathtt{Group}$ and $\mathtt{DivGroup}$ are isomorphic. If we encode theories and morphisms in some type theory (e.g., as record types and functions or as signatures and functors), it is often possible to encode these equalities correspondingly.

But existing systems that specifically work with theory graphs and the category induced by them, do not make it possible, let alone easy, to express, prove, and use such equalities as a part of the theory graph development. Our goal is to design a theory graph language that supports defining theories and morphisms and proving equalities of morphisms.

Application to Realms. A parallel motivation of our work was provided by the goal of formalizing realms.

Working with multiple isomorphic formalizations of the same mathematical theory is often both unavoidable and cumbersome. In 2014, Carette, Farmer, and Kohlhase introduced the concept of *realms* [CFK14] as a high-level structuring feature for formal mathematics. Their basic idea is to provide an abstraction layer at which multiple isomorphic formalizations are identified. For example, users should be able to ignore the difference between $\mathtt{Group}$ and $\mathtt{DivGroup}$: when creating a group, giving either $\circ$ or/should suffice; and when using a group, both should be available.

However, while the idea of realms was well-received (best paper award), neither [CFK14] nor any follow-up work conducted a detailed investigation of how realms should be implemented in a practical system.

In a work-in-progress paper [RW22], we partially formalized several examples that were given informally in [CFK14]. A key result of these case studies was that theory graph languages with morphism equality are needed to formalize realms. This motivated the present paper, in which we introduce such a language.

Contribution and Overview. We start with the MMT language [RK13], which already allows defining theories and morphisms. MMT is independent of the base language, but some assumptions about the base language are needed to state equalities—therefore, we work with MMT's instantiation with the logical framework LF [HHP93].

Our main contribution is introducing, in Sect. 4, morphism equalities to MMT. Concretely, we add morphism equalities as a third kind of MMT toplevel declaration in addition to theories and morphisms. To our knowledge, that yields the first formal system for categories of theories in which users can state and prove the equality of arbitrary morphisms.

We apply this language, in Sect. 5, to develop a pattern for formalizing realms. Concretely, we formalize the realms of lattices and topological spaces. This shows that MMT with morphism equality can serve as a lightweight formalism for realms, and we anticipate this formalism to be more practical than the more involved definition of [CFK14].

A major technical hurdle was that many intuitively true morphism equalities do not actually hold on the nose but depend on the choice of equality. Therefore, to support practical morphism equalities, we first extend LF in Sect. 3 in a way that allows flexibly choosing what logic-specific equality to consider.

We begin by introducing MMT and LF in Sect. 2.

2   Preliminaries

2.1   LF-Expressions

We use LF [HHP93] as a logical framework for defining the logics, in which we state the theories. This is a dependently-typed λ-calculus whose expressions are the universes **type** and **kind**, typed variables x, typed or kinded constants c, dependent function types $\Pi x : A.B$, abstraction $\lambda x : A.t$, and function application $t\,t'$:

$$E, A, B, s, t ::= x \mid c \mid \lambda x : A.t \mid \Pi x : A.B \mid t\,t \mid \textbf{type} \mid \textbf{kind}$$

Theories Σ declare constants $c : A$ where A is a type or kind. Contexts Γ declare variables $x : A$ where A is a type. The type/kind of a constant and the type of a variable may refer to previously declared constants resp. variables. We usually use A, B as meta-variables for types, s, t for typed terms, E for arbitrary expressions, and we write $A \to B$ for $\Pi x : A.B$ if x does not occur in B and $E[x/t]$ for the substitution of t for x in E.

The judgments are typing $\Gamma \vdash_\Sigma t : A$ and equality $\Gamma \vdash_\Sigma E \overset{expr}{=} E'$. The rules are standard, and we give the rules for expressions in Fig. 1.

Example 1 (Typed First-Order Logic). We sketch the definition of typed first-order logic FOL as an LF-theory. This representation is routine [HHP93].

o	: **type**	tp	: **type**
pf	: $o \to$ **type**	tm	: tp $\to$ **type**
$\Leftrightarrow$	: $o \to o \to o$	$\overset{FOL}{=}$	: $\Pi A : \text{tp.tm}\,A \to \text{tm}\,A \to o$
$\forall$	: $(\Pi A : \text{tp.tm}\,A) \to o$		...

Here o is the type of propositions, pf F is the type of proofs of proposition F, tp is the LF-type of FOL-types, and tm a is the LF-type of FOL-terms of FOL-type a.

$$\frac{}{\Gamma \vdash_\Sigma \textbf{type} : \textbf{kind}} \qquad \frac{U \in \{\textbf{type}, \textbf{kind}\} \quad \Gamma, x : A \vdash_\Sigma E : U}{\Gamma \vdash_\Sigma \Pi x : A.E : U}$$

$$\frac{U \in \{\textbf{type}, \textbf{kind}\} \quad \Gamma \vdash_\Sigma E : U \quad \Gamma, x : A \vdash_\Sigma t : E}{\Gamma \vdash_\Sigma \lambda x : A.t : \Pi x : A.E} \qquad \frac{\Gamma \vdash_\Sigma f : \Pi x : A.E \quad \Gamma \vdash_\Sigma t : A}{\Gamma \vdash_\Sigma f\, t : E[x/t]}$$

$$\frac{}{\Gamma \vdash_\Sigma E \stackrel{expr}{=} E} \qquad \frac{Q \in \{\lambda, \Pi\} \quad \Gamma \vdash_\Sigma A \stackrel{expr}{=} A' \quad \Gamma, x : A \vdash_\Sigma E \stackrel{expr}{=} E'}{\Gamma \vdash_\Sigma Qx : A.E \stackrel{expr}{=} Qx : A'.E'}$$

$$\frac{\Gamma \vdash_\Sigma E \stackrel{expr}{=} E' \quad \Gamma \vdash_\Sigma F \stackrel{expr}{=} F'}{\Gamma \vdash_\Sigma E\,F \stackrel{expr}{=} E'\,F'}$$

$$\frac{}{\Gamma \vdash_\Sigma (\lambda x : A.E)F \stackrel{expr}{=} E[x/F]} \qquad \frac{\Gamma \vdash_\Sigma f : \Pi x : A.B}{\Gamma \vdash_\Sigma \lambda x : A.(f\,x) \stackrel{expr}{=} f}$$

Fig. 1. Typing and Equality Rules of LF

Note that FOL provides its own equality *connective* $\stackrel{FOL}{=}$, which is different from the LF-*judgment* $\stackrel{expr}{=}$. We use higher-order abstract syntax for binders (e.g., $\forall A\,(\lambda x : i.F)$ represents the proposition $\forall x : A.F$) and curried functions for the connectives (e.g., $\Leftrightarrow F\,G$ represents $F \Leftrightarrow G$), and we will use the common notations in the sequel for those expressions.

2.2   Theory Graphs in MMT

The grammar of the instantiation of MMT with LF is given in Fig. 2, where A, E, t are LF-expressions as above and $\emptyset$ denotes the empty theory graph.

$$
\begin{aligned}
G &::= \emptyset \mid G, \textbf{theory } s = \{\sigma\} \mid G, \textbf{theory } s = S \\
&\quad \mid G, \textbf{morph } m : S \longrightarrow T = \{\mu\} \mid G, \textbf{morph } m : S \longrightarrow T = M \\
\sigma &::= D^* \qquad D ::= c : A \mid \textbf{include } S\,[= M] \\
\mu &::= d^* \qquad d ::= c[: A] = E \mid \textbf{include } S = M \\
S &::= s \mid S \cup S \\
M &::= m \mid id_S \mid M; M \mid M \cup M
\end{aligned}
$$

Fig. 2. MMT Grammar

A theory graph G consists of theory and morphism declarations. A **primitive theory declaration theory** $s = \{\sigma\}$ introduces the theory named s given by the list of declarations σ. The declarations in the body of a theory are of the form $c : A$ where c is a name and A is the type/kind of c. Alternatively, we can introduce a **defined theory** by **theory** $s = S$, which defines s as an abbreviation for a theory expression S. **Theory expressions** S are either references s to theory names or unions $S \cup T$ of theories.

The syntax of morphisms is analogous to that of theories. The names we use for meta-variables are summarized on the right. A **primitive morphism declaration morph** $m : S \longrightarrow T = \{\mu\}$ introduces the morphism named m from S to T given by the list of declarations μ. The declaration is well-formed if μ con-

meta-vars	thy	morph
name	s	m
expression	S	M
body	σ	μ

tains exactly one declaration $c[: A'] = E$ for every constant $c : A$ of S such that $E : m(A)$ holds over T. (The type A' is redundant and must be equal to $m(A)$ if given.) m induces a compositional type-preserving mapping $m(-)$ of S-expressions to T-expressions by homomorphic extension, i.e., by replacing every constant with the image provided by μ.

Alternatively, we can introduce **defined morphisms** by **morph** $m : S \longrightarrow T = M$ for a morphism expression M. **Morphism expressions** M are references m to morphism names, identity morphisms $id_S : S \longrightarrow S$, compositions $M;N : R \longrightarrow T$ of $M : R \longrightarrow S$ and $N : S \longrightarrow T$, or unions $M_1 \cup M_2 : S_1 \cup S_2 \longrightarrow T$ of $M_1 : S_1 \longrightarrow T$ and $M_2 : S_2 \longrightarrow T$. Every morphism expression M defines a compositional homomorphic mapping $M(-)$ given by, respectively, $m(-)$, the identity map, the composition of $M(-)$ and $N(-)$, and the union of $M_1(-)$ and $M_2(-)$. In particular, we have $(M_1 \cup M_2)(E) = M_i(E)$ if E is an S_i-expression.

In addition to the above, a primitive theory or morphism may contain **include declarations**. In a theory with name t, the declaration **include** $S[= M]$ reuses all constants of S for t. A recent and previously unpublished feature of MMT that will prove critical for our formalizations is that such includes may carry a definiens $M : S \longrightarrow t$. Defined includes can be seen as analogous to defined constants: from the perspective of t, (i) a morphism $M : S \longrightarrow t$ can be seen as an object of "type" S, (ii) an include of S specifies that t is a subtype of S, and (iii) a definiens M specifies that t can be viewed as an instance of S via M. In terms of object-oriented programming an undefined include is inheritance of S into t, and a defined include is delegation from t to M for interface S. Similarly, in a primitive morphism $m : S \longrightarrow T$, the declaration **include** $R = N$ for a morphism $N : R \longrightarrow T$ reuses all mappings of N, i.e., we have $m(c) = N(c)$ for every R-constant c.

Example 2. We spell out our running example in MMT syntax in Fig. 3. We omit the axioms for brevity and only remark that axioms are treated in the same way as constants: they are declared as constants (of type pf F for some F) and mapped by morphisms to appropriate FOL-proof terms. Note how the morphisms include $id_{\texttt{Carrier}}$. This makes explicit that, e.g., GtoDG is equal to the identity when restricted to the smaller domain Carrier.

Relative to a theory graph G, the type system uses **judgments** given in Fig. 4. Due to include declarations, the semantics of a theory now depends on the entire theory graph. Therefore, we have to index the LF-judgments for expressions with G as well.

Figure 5 gives the most important rules, which we explain in the remainder. But before doing so, we state the **main theorem** about MMT to solidify the

```
theory Carrier = include FOL, U : tp
theory Group =                          theory DivGroup =
   include Carrier                          include Carrier
   e   : tm U                               e : tm U
   ∘   : tm U → tm U → tm U                 / : tm U → tm U → tm U
   ⁻¹  : tm U → tm U

morph GtoDG : Group ⟶ DivGroup =         morph DGtoG : DivGroup ⟶ Group =
   include id_Carrier                       include id_Carrier
   e   =  e                                 e  =  e
   ∘   =  λx, y : x/(e/y)                    /  =  λx, y : x ∘ y⁻¹
   ⁻¹  =  λx : e/x
```

Fig. 3. Example Theory Graph in MMT

Judgment	Intuition
$\Gamma \vdash^G_T E : E'$	typing of LF-expression over theory T
$\Gamma \vdash^G_T E \overset{expr}{=} E'$	equality of LF-expressions over theory T
$\vdash^G T$ THY	well-formed theory expression
$\vdash^G S \overset{M}{\hookrightarrow} T$	S included into T ($M = id_S$ if omitted)
$\vdash^G M : S \longrightarrow T$	well-formed morphism expression
$\vdash^G M \overset{mor}{=} N : S \longrightarrow T$	morphism equality

Fig. 4. MMT Judgments

intuition of morphisms: they preserve all judgments, i.e., the following rules are admissible.

$$\frac{\Gamma \vdash^G_T t : A \qquad \vdash^G M : S \longrightarrow T}{M(\Gamma) \vdash^G_S M(t) : M(A)} \qquad \frac{\Gamma \vdash^G_T t \overset{expr}{=} t' \qquad \vdash^G M : S \longrightarrow T}{M(\Gamma) \vdash^G_S M(t) \overset{expr}{=} M(t')}$$

The rules for **well-formed theories** are straightforward. Technically, we need an equality judgment for theory expressions here with rules for definition expansion and idempotence, commutativity, associativity of union, but we omit that for brevity.

The rules for the **inclusion judgment** $\vdash^G S \overset{M}{\hookrightarrow} T$ build the category generated by the **include** declarations in theories. The morphism M is optional, and if it is omitted, we assume $M = id_S$. Its intuition is formalized in the rule *Lookup*, which makes all constants from an included theory available to the including theory. Consider a declaration **include** S in a primitive theory t. Then we have $\vdash^G S \overset{id_S}{\hookrightarrow} t$, and *Lookup* makes any declaration $c : A$ of S available to T unchanged. The second conclusion of *Lookup* vacuously establishes $c \overset{expr}{=} c$. Alternatively, consider a declaration **include** $S = M$ for $\vdash^G M : S \longrightarrow t$. Now $\vdash^G S \overset{M}{\hookrightarrow} t$, and *Lookup* makes the declaration $c : M(A)$ available to T, and its second conclusion makes c an abbreviation for $M(c)$. Thus, defined includes are always conservative and just add defined constants.

$$\frac{\textbf{theory } t = \{\sigma\} \text{ in } G \quad c : A \text{ in } \sigma \quad \vdash^G t \overset{M}{\hookrightarrow} T}{\vdash^G_T c : M(A) \quad \text{and} \quad \vdash^G_T c \overset{expr}{=} M(c)} Lookup$$

$$\frac{\textbf{theory } t = \_ \text{ in } G}{\vdash^G t \text{ THY}} \qquad \frac{\vdash^G S \text{ THY} \quad \vdash^G T \text{ THY}}{\vdash^G S \cup T \text{ THY}}$$

$$\frac{\textbf{theory } t = \{\sigma\} \text{ in } G \quad \textbf{include } S[= M] \text{ in } \sigma}{\vdash^G S \overset{[M]}{\hookrightarrow} t} \qquad \frac{}{\vdash^G T \hookrightarrow T} \qquad \frac{\vdash^G R \overset{M}{\hookrightarrow} S \quad \vdash^G S \overset{N}{\hookrightarrow} T}{\vdash^G R \overset{M;N}{\hookrightarrow} T}$$

$$\frac{\textbf{morph } m : S \longrightarrow T = \_ \text{ in } G}{\vdash^G m : S \longrightarrow T} \qquad \frac{\vdash^G M : S \longrightarrow T \quad \vdash^G R \hookrightarrow S}{\vdash^G M : R \longrightarrow U} \qquad \frac{\vdash^G T \hookrightarrow U}{} complIncl$$

$$\frac{\vdash^G M : R \longrightarrow S \quad \vdash^G N : S \longrightarrow T}{\vdash^G M;N : R \longrightarrow T} \qquad \frac{}{\vdash^G S_1 \hookrightarrow S_1 \cup S_2} \qquad \frac{}{\vdash^G S_2 \hookrightarrow S_1 \cup S_2}$$

$$\frac{\vdash^G S_1 \overset{M_1}{\hookrightarrow} T \quad \vdash^G S_2 \overset{M_2}{\hookrightarrow} T \quad \vdash^G M_1 \overset{mor}{=} M_2 : S_1 \cap S_2 \longrightarrow T}{\vdash^G S_1 \cup S_2 \overset{M_1 \cup M_2}{\hookrightarrow} T}$$

$$\frac{\vdash^G M_1 : S_1 \longrightarrow T \quad \vdash^G M_2 : S_2 \longrightarrow T \quad \vdash^G M_1 \overset{mor}{=} M_2 : S_1 \cap S_2 \longrightarrow T}{\vdash^G M_1 \cup M_2 : S_1 \cup S_2 \longrightarrow T}$$

Fig. 5. Typing Rules for Theory Graphs

The rules for **well-formed morphisms** build the category generated by the named morphisms. If $\vdash^G S \hookrightarrow T$, we do not introduce a name for the induced embedding of S-expressions into T-expressions; instead, rule *complIncl* allows composing morphisms with inclusions. In particular, if $\vdash^G S \hookrightarrow T$, we have $\vdash^G id_S : S \longrightarrow T$.

The judgment for **morphism equality** comes in critically in the two rules in Fig. 5 that involve morphisms out of a union theory. For example, the rule for the morphism union $M_1 \cup M_2 : S_1 \cup S_2 \longrightarrow T$ requires that the M_i agree on the intersection of their domains. Formally, we define $S_1 \cap S_2$ as the union of all named theories t that are included without definition into both S_i, i.e., all t for which $\vdash^G t \hookrightarrow S_1$ and $\vdash^G t \hookrightarrow S_2$. Then to say that the M_i agree on $S_1 \cap S_2$ means that $\vdash^G M_1 \overset{mor}{=} M_2 : t \longrightarrow T$ for every such t.

Morphism equality is also critical in the well-formedness of include declarations. Include declarations in theories are only well-formed if for any S, T, there is at most one M such that $\vdash^G S \overset{M}{\hookrightarrow} T$, i.e., theories must not be included via two different morphisms. Similarly, in a morphism m, include declarations are only well-formed if no two different morphisms are included for the same theory. In both cases, the formal condition checked by MMT is that the declarations **include** $S_1 = M_1$ and **include** $S_2 = M_2$ may only occur together in the same primitive theory/morphism if $\vdash^G M_1 \overset{mor}{=} M_2 : S_1 \cap S_2 \longrightarrow T$, where T is the containing theory or, respectively, the codomain of the containing morphism.

Figure 5 omits the rules for establishing morphism equality. Generally, two morphisms are equal if they induce the same homomorphic mapping, which is equivalent to mapping every constant of the domain to equal expressions. But even if the equality of expressions is decidable (as for LF), this is a far too expensive criterion in practice—morphism equality must be checked very frequently, and each time an expression equality check would be needed for every domain constant. Therefore, MMT uses an incomplete sufficient criterion that implements diagram chase–reasoning without ever inspecting the bodies of primitive morphisms. We defer the presentation to Sect. 4, where we change the rules anyway.

3   Propositional Equality of LF-Expressions

Example 3 (Failure of Morphism Equality). To prove

$$\vdash^G \texttt{DGtoG}; \texttt{GtoDG} \overset{\text{mor}}{=} id_{\texttt{DivGroup}} : \texttt{DivGroup} \longrightarrow \texttt{DivGroup}$$

we must show that both morphisms map each constant to equal expressions, e.g., we need the equality of $\texttt{GtoDG}(\texttt{DGtoG}(/)) = \texttt{GtoDG}(\lambda x, y.x \circ y^{-1}) = \lambda x, y.x/y^{-1-1}$ and $id_{\texttt{DivGroup}}(/) = /$ (where we have silently applied the necessary β-reductions). But these terms are only *provably equal* in the FOL-theory $\texttt{DivGroup}$. LF, which only uses $\alpha\beta\eta$-equality, does *not* consider them equal.

Example 3 shows that morphism equality cannot easily be defined generically at the MMT- or LF-level because it may depend on logic-specific equalities. For example, FOL-constants can be type, function, predicate symbols, or axioms, and FOL does not support equality for any of them out of the box. Consider functions f, g of type $\texttt{tm } U \to \texttt{tm } U$. The natural choice for equality is the formula $\forall x : \texttt{tm } U.f\, x \overset{FOL}{=} g\, x$. For predicates $p, q : \texttt{tm } U \to o$, it would be $\forall x : \texttt{tm } U.p\, x \Leftrightarrow q\, x$. For types, FOL does not provide any equality, and we have to fall back to LF-equality. For axioms, the simplest choice is a proof irrelevance rule, where any expressions $P, Q : \texttt{pf } F$ are considered equal.

Our key idea is to define LFQ by adding a propositional equality predicate to LF that logic developers can use to spell out these equalities, so that MMT can consider them when checking the equality of two morphisms.

The idea of adding propositional equality to LF is not new. One approach is to add rewriting as in Dedukti [CD07]. Another option is to add identity types as in Martin-Löf type theory [ML74]. Our formulation below is essentially the same as the one worked out in [Har21].

We add a kind $E \overset{LF}{=}_A E'$ for the equality of terms E and E' of type A. We could make this a type, but that would amount to using identity types and be much more expressive than needed for our purposes. Because LF can quantify over types but not over kinds, $E \overset{LF}{=}_A E'$ can only occur as the output of LF-constants but not as input. Thus, users can declare new propositional equalities but can never do anything with them—it remains the discretion of the system how to use them. That is important because user-declared propositional equalities make typing in LFQ undecidable, and implementations will only be able to handle them to a limited degree.

The LFQ grammar extends the one of LF with

$$E ::= E \stackrel{LF}{=}_A E \mid \texttt{refl} \mid \texttt{funExt}\, E$$

Note that we now distinguish the *kind* $E \stackrel{LF}{=}_A E$ for equality of typed terms and the *judgment* $\vdash E \stackrel{expr}{=} E'$ for the equality of expressions. LFQ adds the following rules to LF

$$\frac{\Gamma \vdash^G_T A : \texttt{type} \quad \Gamma \vdash^G_T E : A \quad \Gamma \vdash^G_T E' : A}{\Gamma \vdash^G_T (E \stackrel{LF}{=}_A E') : \texttt{kind}}$$

$$\frac{\Gamma \vdash^G_T P : \Pi x_1 : A_1, \ldots, x_n : A_n.(E\, x_1\, \ldots\, x_n \stackrel{LF}{=}_B E'\, x_1\, \ldots\, x_n)}{\Gamma \vdash^G_T \texttt{funExt}\, P : (E \stackrel{LF}{=}_{\Pi x_1:A_1,\ldots,x_n:A_n.B} E')}$$

$$\frac{\Gamma \vdash^G_T P : (E \stackrel{LF}{=}_A E')}{\Gamma \vdash^G_T E \stackrel{expr}{=} E'} \qquad \frac{\Gamma \vdash^G_T A : \texttt{type} \quad \Gamma \vdash^G_T E : A}{\Gamma \vdash^G_T \texttt{refl} : (E \stackrel{LF}{=}_A E)}$$

The first rule enables users to declare new propositional equalities. The second allows using funExt to show the equality of two functions by functional extensionality. The other two rules map back and forth between the judgment $\stackrel{expr}{=}$ and the kind $\stackrel{LF}{=}$.

From now on, we work in the instantiation of MMT with LFQ. Because MMT allows the modular definition of logical frameworks, and LFQ only adds constructors and rules to LF, any LF-theory graph is also an LFQ theory graph.

Example 4. (FOL-Specific Equality). We extend FOL from Example 1 to the logic FOLQ in LFQ by adding propositional equalities that quotient FOL-expressions:

> **theory** FOLQ =
>> **include** FOL
>>
>> eqT : $\Pi A : \texttt{tp}.\, \Pi x, y : \texttt{tm}\, A.(\texttt{pf}\, x \stackrel{FOL}{=} y) \to x \stackrel{LF}{=}_{\texttt{tm}\, A} y$
>>
>> eqF : $\Pi f, g : o.(\texttt{pf}\, f \Leftrightarrow g) \to f \stackrel{LF}{=}_o g$
>>
>> eqP : $\Pi f : o.\, \Pi p, q : \texttt{pf}\, f.\, p \stackrel{LF}{=}_{\texttt{pf}\, f} q$

eqTmakes terms LF-equal if they are provably equal in FOL. Using functional extensionality, this implies, e.g., for two unary functions $f, g : \texttt{tm}\, U \to \texttt{tm}\, U$

$$\vdash f \stackrel{LF}{=}_{\texttt{tm}\, U \to \texttt{tm}\, U} g \qquad \text{iff} \qquad x : \texttt{tm}\, U \vdash P : \texttt{pf}(f\, x \stackrel{FOL}{=} g\, x)$$

The constant eqFdoes the same for formulas and, e.g., for unary predicates $p, q : \texttt{tm}\, A \to o$. The constant eqP adds proof irrelevance.

FOLQ injects its undecidable equality into LFQ, thus rendering $\vdash E \overset{expr}{=} E'$ undecidable. But the deep research problems associated with that go way beyond the purpose of this paper. Instead, our plan is to use FOLQ only as the codomain of morphism equality judgments, in which case the undecidability is manageable:

Example 5 (Morphism Equality via a Stronger Codomain). Consider the theory graph below that summarizes our running example

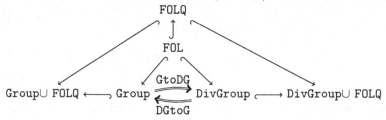

The judgment $\vdash^G$ DGtoG; GtoDG $\overset{mor}{=} id_{\text{DivGroup}}$: DivGroup $\longrightarrow$ DivGroup $\cup$ FOLQ holds. Here the same morphisms as in Example 3 are compared relative to a bigger codomain in which additional propositional equalities are declared. Thus, the resulting proof obligations (which are equalities of expressions over the codomain) are checked relative to a stronger theory.

Indeed, we have a FOL-proof

$$x : \text{tm}\,U,\ y : \text{tm}\,U \vdash_{\text{DivGroup}\cup\text{FOLQ}} I : \text{pf}\big(x/(y^{-1}{}^{-1})\overset{FOL}{=} x/y\big)$$

which we can use to show $\vdash_{\text{DivGroup}\cup\text{FOLQ}} \lambda x, y.x/y^{-1}{}^{-1} \overset{expr}{=} /$. The corresponding cases for the other constants of DivGroup as well as for the dual equality of GtoDG; DGtoG and id_{Group} can be shown accordingly.

Thus, Group and DivGroup are not isomorphic in the category of theories that include FOL, but Group $\cup$ FOLQ and DivGroup $\cup$ FOLQ are isomorphic in the category of theories that include FOLQ.

Example 5 shows that we can model different equality relations on morphisms by using different codomains. This is extremely valuable because it keeps the formalism simple by retaining a single equality judgment and uses the modularity of the theory graph to capture different levels of equality.

4   Propositional Equality of MMT-Morphisms

It remains to extend the MMT language in a way that can utilize the propositional *expression* equality introduced in Sect. 3 to prove *morphism* equalities. We extend the grammar as below and explain all new productions in the remainder:

$$G ::= \ldots \mid G, \textbf{morpheq}\ k : M \overset{mor}{=} N : S \longrightarrow T = \{\kappa\}$$
$$\mid G, \textbf{morpheq}\ k : M \overset{mor}{=} N : S \longrightarrow T = K$$
$$\kappa ::= d^* \qquad d ::= c[: A] = E \mid \textbf{include}\ S = K$$
$$K ::= k \mid \textbf{refl}\ M \mid (\text{other proof terms})$$

A **morphism equality declaration** is a theorem named k stating the equality of two morphisms M and N, both from S to T. In the **primitive** case, k is proved by giving a body κ. Just like the body σ of a primitive theory t gives the constructors of t-expressions, and the body μ of a primitive morphism m with domain t gives the cases of a compositional mapping of t-expressions, the body κ of a primitive morphism equality gives the cases of the inductive equality proof for two such morphisms.

A primitive morphism equality **morpheq** $k : M \overset{\text{mor}}{=} N : s \longrightarrow T = \{\kappa\}$, where s is a primitive theory with body σ, is well-formed if:

- For every constant $c : A$ in σ, κ contains exactly one $c[: A'] = E$ where $\vdash^G_T E : (M(c) \overset{LF}{=}_{M(A)} N(c))$. (The expression A' is redundant. If given, it must be equal to the type of E.)
- For every **include** R in σ, κ contains exactly one **include** $R = K$ where K is a proof term for $\vdash^G R \overset{\text{mor}}{=} T : M \longrightarrow N$.

If the domain of k is a union theory $S_1 \cup S_2$, κ must provide cases for the declarations of each S_i. If it is a *defined* named theory, we expand the definiens first and apply the definition above.

Example 6. We show one of the two isomorphism properties of our example:

> **morpheq** $k :$ DGtoG; GtoDG $\overset{\text{mor}}{=} id_{\text{DivGroup}} :$ DivGroup $\longrightarrow$ DivGroup $\cup$ FOLQ $=$
>   **include** Carrier $=$ refl id_{Carrier}
> $e :$ $e \overset{LF}{=}_{\text{tm } U} e$ $=$ refl
> $/ :$ $\lambda x, y. x/(y^{-1^{-1}}) \overset{LF}{=}_{\text{tm } U \to \text{tm } U \to \text{tm } U} / $ $=$
>   funExt $\lambda x, y.$ eqT U $(x/(y^{-1^{-1}}))$ (x/y) I

Both morphisms restrict to id_{Carrier} on the theory Carrier. Consequently, we use a reflexivity proof for $\vdash^G id_{\text{Carrier}} \overset{\text{mor}}{=} id_{\text{Carrier}} :$ Carrier $\longrightarrow$ DivGroup $\cup$ FOLQ. In the declaration for e, we have $(\text{DGtoG; GtoDG})(e) = e = id_{\text{DivGroup}}(e)$ so that the reflexivity proof for LF expressions suffices. In practical implementations, those two cases could be omitted and filled in by the system as defaults. Finally, the declaration for $/$ discharges the proof obligation that failed in Example 3 using the proof I from Example 5.

If we had not omitted the axiom declarations from DivGroup, we would also have to show the equality of the proofs assigned to the axioms. That would be trivial due to the use of proof irrelevance in FOLQ.

In the **defined** case **morpheq** $k : M \overset{\text{mor}}{=} N : s \longrightarrow T = K$, we require that K is a proof term for the morphism equality judgment $\vdash^G M \overset{\text{mor}}{=} N : S \longrightarrow T$. Originally, we wanted to support only the primitive case. However, our case studies showed that, apart from making the syntax of theories, morphisms, and equalities analogous, the defined case is critically important in practice. Because propositional equality is undecidable but must be called frequently, practical implementations must employ cheap incomplete heuristics instead of running a theorem prover to discharge a morphism equality. But incompleteness threatens scalability—it is imperative that users are able to workaround situations where the system runs into a proof obligation $\vdash^G M \stackrel{\mathrm{mor}}{=} N : S \longrightarrow T$ that it cannot prove. We found defined morphism equalities to be the right compromise here: if a morphism equality is implied by the given primitive morphism equalities but the system cannot find the proof, the user can give a defined morphism equality to show the proof to the system. Because K is a diagram chase-style proof term, that is orders of magnitude easier than proving a new primitive morphism equality. We give an example in Sect. 5.

For brevity, our grammar omits the productions for **morphism equality proof terms** K. They arise as the straightforward proof term assignment to the inference system for the judgment $\vdash^G M \stackrel{\mathrm{mor}}{=} N : S \longrightarrow T$, whose rules we give now. The key rules are

$$\frac{\textbf{morpheq } k : M \stackrel{\mathrm{mor}}{=} N : S \longrightarrow T = \_ \text{ in } G}{\vdash^G M \stackrel{\mathrm{mor}}{=} N : S \longrightarrow T}\ base$$

$$\frac{\textbf{morph } m : S \longrightarrow T = M \text{ in } G}{\vdash^G m \stackrel{\mathrm{mor}}{=} M : S \longrightarrow T}\ def$$

$$\frac{\textbf{morph } m : S \longrightarrow T = \{\mu\} \text{ in } G \quad \textbf{include } R = L \text{ in } \mu}{\vdash^G m \stackrel{\mathrm{mor}}{=} L : R \longrightarrow T}\ morphIncl$$

$$\frac{\vdash^G M : S \longrightarrow T \quad \vdash^G R \hookrightarrow S \quad \vdash^G M \stackrel{\mathrm{mor}}{=} N : R \longrightarrow T}{\vdash^G M \stackrel{\mathrm{mor}}{=} M \cup N : S \longrightarrow T}\ unionIncl$$

The first two rules are straightforward: *base* gives the base case of equalities explicitly proved by the user, and *def* expands the definition of defined morphisms. *morphIncl* gives the semantics of **include** $R = L$ in a primitive morphism m: L is the restriction of m to R. *unionIncl* is a subsumption rule that allows removing redundant parts in a union of morphisms.

The remaining rules are routine, and we only sketch them for brevity:

- equivalence (reflexivity, symmetry, transitivity) and congruence (substitution of equals by equals) of morphism equality
- category axioms (associativity of composition, neutrality of identity)
- semilattice properties of union (idempotence, commutativity, associativity)

Finally, we can obtain the **main theorem** that captures the soundness of the morphism equality calculus: equal morphism induce equal expression mappings, i.e., the following rule is admissible

$$\frac{\vdash^G M \stackrel{\mathrm{mor}}{=} N : S \longrightarrow T \quad \Gamma \vdash^G_S t : A}{M(\Gamma) \vdash^G_T M(t) \stackrel{expr}{=} N(t)}$$

It is proved by induction on the derivations of $\vdash^G M \stackrel{\mathrm{mor}}{=} N : S \longrightarrow T$.

5 Case Studies

With morphism equality in place, we can now finish the two case studies that we had to leave incomplete in [RW22].[2] Both are essentially the same as in [RW22]. But we are now able to state and prove the various morphism equalities.

Topological Spaces. There are many isomorphic definitions of topological space. Even more interestingly, many of them extend closure systems, for which there are also multiple isomorphic definitions. Concretely, our formalization consists of three isomorphic theories for closure systems and six isomorphic theories for topological spaces as shown in the theory graph below. Here the inner triangle and the outer rectangle are isomorphism cycles.

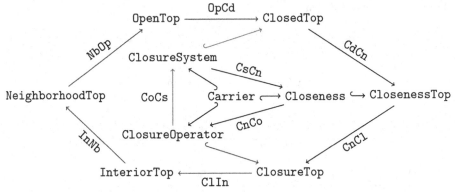

The bodies of these theories and morphisms are inessential for our purposes here. For example, `ClosureSystem` uses an intersection-closed set of subsets of the carrier set whereas `ClosureOperator` uses an idempotent mapping on subsets.

Crucially, the whole theory graph commutes. In particular, to show the isomorphisms, we have proved three primitive morphism equalities to show that the inner triangle commutes and six to show that the outer hexagon commutes. For example, we prove **morpheq isoClosureSystem** : CsCn;CnCo;CoCs $\overset{\text{mor}}{=}$ $id_{\texttt{ClosureSystem}}$: ClosureSystem $\longrightarrow$ ClosureSystem = {...}. While we have not fully implemented morphism equality in MMT yet, all proofs in the bodies of these morphism equalities were done in and checked by MMT.

The commutativity of the rectangles connecting the inner with the outer ring hold definitionally: for example, **include ClosureSystem = CsCn** is contained in the body of `CdCn`, at which point the rule *morphIncl* yields $\vdash^G$ CdCn $\overset{\text{mor}}{=}$ CsCn : ClosureSystem $\longrightarrow$ ClosenessTop. Similarly, all edges of the inner triangle include $id_{\texttt{Carrier}}$, which makes the triangles involving `Carrier` commute.

The only rectangle whose commutativity requires a non-trivial proof term is $\vdash^G$ ClIn;InNb;NbOp;OpCd $\overset{\text{mor}}{=}$ CoCs : ClosureOperator $\longrightarrow$ ClosedTop (*). This equality follows from the other morphism equalities mentioned above by diagram chase, i.e., by applying the rules given in Sect. 4, mostly tedious uses

---

[2] Both (as well as our running example) are available at https://gl.mathhub.info/ MMT/LATIN2/-/tree/devel/source/casestudies/2023-morpheq.

of associativity and substitution. A concrete implementation of this undecidable property may or may not manage to discharge ($*$) automatically and swiftly. If it fails, users can state a defined morphism equality to work around this incompleteness.

To integrate all the isomorphic theories into a single realm in the sense of [CFK14], we use MMT's defined includes as follows:

```
theory   Closure =
    include ClosureSystem
    include ClosureOperator = CoCs
    include Closeness = CnCo
```

```
theory   Topology =
    include Closure
    include ClosedTop
    include OpenTop = OpCd
    include NeighborhoodTop = NbOp
    include InteriorTop = InNb
    include ClosureTop = ClIn
    include ClosenessTop = CnCl
```

Here `Topology` can use all operations from any one of the six isomorphic theories because they are all included. Critically, the definitions of the includes ensure that all six includes refer to the same underlying topology. For example, **include** `ClosureTop = ClIn` also includes the theory `ClosureOperator`, which has already been included via `Closure`. Thus, checking the well-formedness of `Topology` generates the proof obligation ($*$). Previously, MMT could not discharge ($*$), and users had no way to help it along.

Lattices. We give two isomorphic formalizations of lattices in the theory graph below: Firstly, `LatticeAlgebra` is based on two copies of `Semilattice` (with operation $\circ$) given by the two morphisms `meet` (mapping $\circ$ to $\sqcap$) and `join` (mapping $\circ$ to $\sqcup$). Secondly, `LatticeOrder` is based on an order $\leq$ and arises as the union of `Infimum` and `Supremum`. Even just giving the morphism `OrdAlg` (without even trying to prove it to be an isomorphism) was previously impossible in MMT.

The issue is subtle. The isomorphism `absorb` defines an infimum relation for every semilattice by mapping $\leq\ =\ \lambda x, y.x \circ y \overset{FOL}{=} x$. By composing it with `meet`, we obtain the infimum operation in algebraic lattices. Correspondingly, we obtain the supremum by composing it with `join` and `OpSup` (which maps $\leq\ =\ \lambda x, y.y \leq x$).

Thus, `OrdAlg` can be defined elegantly using **include** `Infimum = absorb;meet` and **include** `Supremum = OpSup;absorb;join`. These two morphisms now have to agree on `Infimum`$\cap$`Supremum = Order`, i.e., we have the morphism equality proof obligation $\vdash^G$ (absorb;meet) $\overset{mor}{=}$ (OpSup;absorb;join) : `Order` $\longrightarrow$ `LatticeAlgebra`. That in turn generates the expression equality proof obligation $\vdash_{\text{LatticeAlgebra}} (x \sqcap y \overset{FOL}{=} x) \overset{expr}{=} (y \sqcup x \overset{FOL}{=} y)$ ($*$). But this holds in `LatticeAlgebra` only up to $\Leftrightarrow$.

We can remedy this by proving a morphism equality **morpheq ordersAgree :** (absorb;meet) $\overset{mor}{=}$ (OpSup;absorb;join) : `Order` $\longrightarrow$ `LatticeAlgebra` $\cup$ `FOLQ` $= \{\leq\ =\ $ funExt $\lambda x, y.$ eqF(...)$\}$, where we use `eqF` to discharge

(∗). With this equality in place, OrdAlg becomes well-formed as a morphism
LatticeOrder ⟶ LatticeAlgebra ∪ FOLQ.

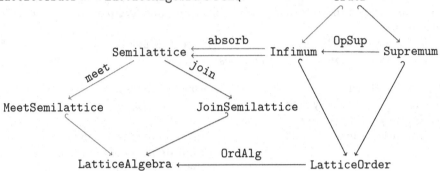

6   Conclusion and Future Work

We showed how to extend theory graph formalisms with proofs of equality of
morphisms. Besides theories and morphisms, morphism equality is the third con-
stitutive component of categorical diagrams, but it had received little attention
in prior work on theory graphs. We showed that even elementary examples of
theory graphs, such as the definitions of lattices and topological spaces, require
a systematic treatment of morphism equality that had not been done before,
and we have shown how our design enables this treatment. We used the MMT
language for theory graphs instantiated with the logical framework LF to present
our design in a concrete and logic-independent setting, and our ideas carry over
easily to other theory graph formalisms. Moreover, by combining our design
with defined includes, we have demonstrated a promising formalization pattern
for realms, a theory graph formalism feature that had previously been called for
[CFK14] but not realized by any practical system.

We are currently implementing our design by extending the MMT tool for
theory graphs. To ensure the feasibility of this, we have taken care to evaluate our
approach in multiple case studies. These are already available in the anticipated
MMT syntax, and all proofs in them have already been developed in and verified
by MMT.

References

[AHMS99] Autexier, S., Hutter, D., Mantel, H., Schairer, A.: Towards an evolutionary
formal software-development using CASL. In: Bert, D., Choppy, C., Mosses,
P.D. (eds.) WADT 1999. LNCS, vol. 1827, pp. 73–88. Springer, Heidelberg
(2000). https://doi.org/10.1007/978-3-540-44616-3_5

[CD07]   Cousineau, D., Dowek, G.: Embedding pure type systems in the lambda-pi-
calculus modulo. In: Della Rocca, S.R. (ed.) TLCA 2007. LNCS, vol. 4583,
pp. 102–117. Springer, Heidelberg (2007). https://doi.org/10.1007/978-3-
540-73228-0_9

[CFK14] Carette, J., Farmer, W.M., Kohlhase, M.: Realms: a structure for consolidating knowledge about mathematical theories. In: Watt, S.M., Davenport, J.H., Sexton, A.P., Sojka, P., Urban, J. (eds.) CICM 2014. LNCS (LNAI), vol. 8543, pp. 252–266. Springer, Cham (2014). https://doi.org/10.1007/978-3-319-08434-3_19

[FGT92] Farmer, W.M., Guttman, J.D., Javier Thayer, F.: Little theories. In: Kapur, D. (ed.) CADE 1992. LNCS, vol. 607, pp. 567–581. Springer, Heidelberg (1992). https://doi.org/10.1007/3-540-55602-8_192

[FGT93] Farmer, W., Guttman, J., Thayer, F.: IMPS: an interactive mathematical proof system. J. Autom. Reason. 11(2), 213–248 (1993)

[Har21] Harper, R.: An equational logical framework for type theories (2021). https://arxiv.org/abs/2106.01484

[HHP93] Harper, R., Honsell, F., Plotkin, G.: A framework for defining logics. J. ACM 40(1), 143–184 (1993)

[KWP99] Kammüller, F., Wenzel, M., Paulson, L.C.: Locales a sectioning concept for Isabelle. In: Bertot, Y., Dowek, G., Théry, L., Hirschowitz, A., Paulin, C. (eds.) TPHOLs 1999. LNCS, vol. 1690, pp. 149–165. Springer, Heidelberg (1999). https://doi.org/10.1007/3-540-48256-3_11

[ML74] Martin-Löf, P.: An intuitionistic theory of types: predicative part. In: Proceedings of the '73 Logic Colloquium, pp. 73–118. North-Holland (1974)

[MML07] Mossakowski, T., Maeder, C., Lüttich, K.: The heterogeneous tool set, HETS. In: Grumberg, O., Huth, M. (eds.) TACAS 2007. LNCS, vol. 4424, pp. 519–522. Springer, Heidelberg (2007). https://doi.org/10.1007/978-3-540-71209-1_40

[ORS92] Owre, S., Rushby, J.M., Shankar, N.: PVS: a prototype verification system. In: Kapur, D. (ed.) CADE 1992. LNCS, vol. 607, pp. 748–752. Springer, Heidelberg (1992). https://doi.org/10.1007/3-540-55602-8_217

[RK13] Rabe, F., Kohlhase, M.: A scalable module system. Inf. Comput. 230(1), 1–54 (2013)

[RS09] Rabe, F., Schürmann, C.: A practical module system for LF. In: Cheney, J., Felty, A. (eds.) Proceedings of the Workshop on Logical Frameworks: Meta-Theory and Practice (LFMTP), pp. 40–48. ACM Press (2009)

[RW22] Rabe, F., Weber, F.: Three case studies on realms. In: Buzzard, K., Kutsia, T. (eds.) Intelligent Computer Mathematics, Informal Proceedings, pp. 46–51. Research Institute for Symbolic Computation (2022)

[SJ95] Srinivas, Y.V., Jüllig, R.: Specware: formal support for composing software. In: Möller, B. (ed.) MPC 1995. LNCS, vol. 947, pp. 399–422. Springer, Heidelberg (1995). https://doi.org/10.1007/3-540-60117-1_22

[SW83] Sannella, D., Wirsing, M.: A kernel language for algebraic specification and implementation extended abstract. In: Karpinski, M. (ed.) FCT 1983. LNCS, vol. 158, pp. 413–427. Springer, Heidelberg (1983). https://doi.org/10.1007/3-540-12689-9_122

Towards an Annotation Standard for STEM Documents
Datasets, Benchmarks, and Spotters

Jan Frederik Schaefer$^{(\boxtimes)}$ and Michael Kohlhase

Friedrich-Alexander-Universität Erlangen-Nürnberg, Erlangen, Germany
`jan.frederik.schaefer@fau.de`

Abstract. When publishing papers, researchers in mathematics and related disciplines typically focus on the presentation, i.e. type-setting, of their ideas and provide little semantic information. This impedes the development of services that benefit from semantic information, such as semantic search and screen readers for vision-impaired researchers. As a remedy, there have been attempts to infer semantic data from already published papers using small programs that we call *spotters*. Unfortunately, there is no standardized format for semantic annotations and spotter authors typically invent their own format. This leads to two problems: *i*) there is no ecosystem of tools for common tasks like the visualization of results or the manual annotation of a gold standard, and *ii*) re-using, evaluating and combining results becomes very difficult.

In this paper, we address these issues by describing a standardized, flexible way to represent semantic annotations, using semantic web technologies and, in particular, the Web Annotation standard. Furthermore, we describe **SpotterBase**, a set of tools to help with processing the annotations and creating new ones.

1 Introduction

With the number of publications in STEM (Science, Technology, Engineering and Mathematics) rising rapidly, the challenge of managing and efficiently accessing the knowledge they carry becomes ever more relevant. A variety of services could help, for example

- *Specialized formula search engines* can help discover formulae, which traditional search engines are notoriously bad at. For example, we might be looking for a closed-form expression of $\sum_{n=0}^{\infty} n \frac{2^n}{n!}$. A unification-based search engine could unify that expression with the left-hand-side of the equation $\sum_{k=0}^{\infty} k \frac{z^k}{k!} = z e^z$.
- *Active documents* provide functionality for interacting with a document. They could, for example, convert units on demand, show where a variable was declared, or allow inserting concrete values into formulae for computation.
- *Screen readers* can read out documents for vision-impaired researchers.

C. Dubois and M. Kerber (Eds.): CICM 2023, LNAI 14101, pp. 190–205, 2023.
https://doi.org/10.1007/978-3-031-42753-4_13

– *A semantic document checker* can help authors find certain types of errors, e.g. by pointing out that in *"a density of 12 g/m"* the unit does not match the expected SI dimension of mass per volume.

Such services are easy to realize if the semantic information implied in the text is made explicit: a formula search engine delivers better results if it knows what identifiers stand for and how they are quantified, an active document can only convert units if it knows what the units are, screen readers can read formulae better if they understand them (e.g. "$|x|$" could be *"the magnitude of x"*), etc. In practice, such information is rarely available because publications are typically type-set for human consumption with little regard for explicit semantic annotations, and if such information is present in the source, e.g. by using LaTeX packages like siunitx.sty, it gets lost in the compilation to PDF.

A well-known remedy is to add semantic annotations to existing publications with **spotters**: programs that search a corpus for occurrences of a particular semantic phenomenon. A diverse collection of spotters can build up a large set of semantic annotations, which can then be used to create or improve semantic services. Over the years, a number of spotters has been implemented, but a shared collection of semantic annotations that would allow to synergize remains elusive. The main reason seems to be the lack of an agreed-upon standard for annotations, which has led spotter authors to either share their annotations in a custom format incompatible with other annotation sets, or to abandon the idea of publishing a re-usable dataset altogether.

The lack of a standard leads to another problem: based on our experience of supervising bachelor's and master's theses, a large part of their effort goes into building tools for visualizing results, manually annotating a test dataset, automatically evaluating their results against the test dataset, etc. A shared standard for annotations would allow for the development of re-usable tools for such tasks.

The natural language processing (NLP) community benefits from a long tradition of annotation tasks and benchmarks, but very few of them exist for mathematical language specifically. A note-worthy exception are the math information retrieval tasks at NTCIR [AK20] and more recently at CLEF [Man+22]. An annotation standard could facilitate the development of tasks and benchmarks for processing STEM documents. Effectively, anything that we might want to have a spotter for could be turned into a task. We hope that an ecosystem of datasets, tools and benchmarks facilitated by a common representation will incentivize others to adopt it.

Contribution. We present a flexible representation for semantic annotations based on the Web Annotation Standard [Webb]. We have successfully used it for different types of annotations on the arXMLiv corpus [Gin20]. Furthermore, we present SpotterBase[1], a collection of tools to create and work with annotations in that format.

---

[1] Open source; code at https://github.com/jfschaefer/spotterbase.

Overview. In Sect. 2, we discuss related work. Afterwards, we discuss our approach of accumulating semantic information with spotters in Sect. 3, followed by a discussion of what documents we are interested in (Sect. 4). In Sect. 5 we will discuss the annotation format and in Sect. 6 SpotterBase, a set of tools to create and work with such annotations. Section 7 discusses our experience with this setup so far and Sect. 8 concludes the paper.

2   Related Work

Text Annotations for Natural Language Processing. When processing texts without formulae, there is a more-or-less generally accepted plaintext representation. This simplifies the processing and allows for either stand-off annotations via string offsets or in-document annotations via simple markup. Furthermore, such texts can be conveniently represented as a sequence of tokens (words), which can then be annotated with tags. The family of CoNLL formats, which is often used for NLP tasks (see e.g. [Con]), is based on this idea. Formulae complicate this as there is no generally accepted way to represent complex formulae in plain text or as a token sequence, and replacing entire formulae with a single token loses relevant information.

Manual Annotation Tools. Even though our goal is to create annotations automatically, it is also necessary to manually create annotations for evaluation and training of machine learning models. We can distinguish between general-purpose annotation tools and more specialized ones. General-purpose tools would, e.g., be PDF viewers that support annotating documents or the hypothes.is tool [HYP], which allows users to annotate web pages. More specialized tools were developed for NLP tasks, such as part-of-speech tagging or named entity recognition. Examples of this are WebAnno [Cas+16] (not to be confused with the Web Annotation recommendations) and brat [BR]. There are also tools that are specialized in the annotation of mathematical language and can handle formulae: KAT [Gin+15] uses semantic web technologies for annotating HTML documents and can be customized for different annotation tasks. MioGatto [Asa+21] is a much more recent system, specifically designed for annotating the grounding of identifiers. KAT and MioGatto each have their own, custom format for representing and storing annotations.

Semantic Authoring. Our work is based on the assumption that authors do not put effort into providing semantic annotations. However, there are attempts to enable authors to supply semantic markup, e.g. by using the sTeX package [CICM22], which can be used to annotate LaTeX sources via semantic macros.

In-document Annotations. Annotations can be stored either in-document or in a separate database that references the documents, which is the approach we follow (Sect. 3). RDFa [Her+13] is a common approach to store metadata in HTML documents. When it comes to formulae, another option is to use some of the features provided by MathML, the Mathematical Markup Language. MathML is used to represent formulae in HTML5 and it provides Content MathML to annotate formulae with a semantic representation. There is ongoing work to extend MathML with "intents" as a way to describe the intended meaning of a (sub-) formula to improve accessibility (e.g. to help screen readers read out formulae properly). While we are primarily interested in stand-off annotations, adding intent attributes to the documents from the semantic annotations would be an interesting application once MathML intents have stabilized.

Full Formalization. Our goal is to accumulate annotations of different semantic phenomena. A much more ambitious goal is the full formalization of publications, i.e. translating them into a logic. A well-known example of this is the proof of the Kepler conjecture, which has been fully formalized to the extent that its correctness could be automatically verified [Hal+17]. A less ambitious variant is to only formalize the key results of the paper, as e.g. envisioned by the formal abstracts project [FA]. There have also been attempts to use deep learning approaches for formalizing mathematics (e.g. [Wan+20]), but the automated formalizing of STEM publications with reasonable accuracy appears to be beyond the state of the art. While it is conceivable that semantic annotations could aid automated formalization endeavours in the future, this is not our goal in this paper. Indeed, we consider the semantic annotation approach largely independent of full formalization efforts. We observe that a full formalization does not immediately satisfy all information needs for semantic services, unless it is tightly linked to the original document for human consumption.

3   Accumulating Semantic Information

Our approach is centered around a shared collection of semantic annotations. Figure 1 illustrates the setup. Using stand-off annotations—as opposed to in-document annotations—has the advantage that there can be many independent contributors of annotations.

When a corpus is imported, there is typically a lot of metadata resulting in document-level annotations. Examples are: titles, authors, classifications, publication years, etc. The main contributor of annotations, though, are **spotters**, of which we distinguish three different types:

- *Simple spotters* process documents and create annotations without using the results of other spotters. An example of this would be a spotter that detects references to mathematical objects in the text (e.g. that the string *"Abelian group"* in a document refers to Abelian groups). Another example would be a part-of-speech tagger.
- *Hybrid spotters* additionally consider annotations made by other spotters. For example, a spotter for identifier declarations (*"let G be an Abelian group"*) might benefit from the annotation that *"Abelian group"* refers to a mathematical object.

– *Meta spotters* only act on annotations. Such spotters can combine the results of different spotters into a new set of annotations, resolving conflicts in the process. Let us take the example of a text containing the identifier "C". A spotter for units might annotate it as referring to the unit Coulomb, while a different spotter might link it to a previously declared variable C. A meta spotter could resolve this, e.g., by always prioritizing the interpretation that it references a declared variable. In this case it could also be reasonable to take further annotations into consideration, such as the topic of the publication.

Hybrid and meta spotters tend to find more complex semantic information than simple spotters. In the past, the lack of an agreed-upon annotation format made it difficult to create anything other than simple spotters and prevented the build-up of a dataset of diverse semantic annotations that could be harvested for semantic services.

While spotters provide the bulk of annotations, we also need a small amount of human-created annotations—to evaluate spotters and, if machine learning is used, as training sets. As we can have different sources of the same kind of annotation (a human, a spotter, a different spotter, etc.), we also need to track where the annotations come from.

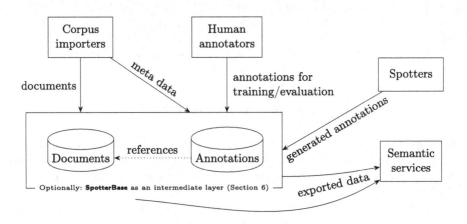

Fig. 1. Overview of the setup.

4 The Document Corpus

The setup sketched in Fig. 1 does not impose any restrictions on the types of documents that are annotated and could, in principle, work for documents in any format. Our focus, however, is on STEM publications in the HTML format. HTML might seem like an unintuitive choice—after all, STEM publications are mostly written in LATEX or Office and distributed as PDF documents. However, neither format is particularly well suited for semantics extraction. Depending on the author, macro expansion (or rather a full TEX engine) is required to reasonably process a LATEX document. PDF and Office documents, on the other hand, are too focused on presentation, i.e. placing symbols on a page, which makes text processing very difficult, especially, if formulae are involved. Another advantage of HTML over LATEX and PDF is that it can be used much more easily for the development of semantic services.

We have mostly worked with the **arXMLiv** corpus [Gin20], but none of the presented ideas are specific to it. ArXMLiv has been created by processing the LATEX sources of arxiv.org with the LaTeXML [Mil] tool to obtain HTML5 documents with MathML for the formulae. LaTeXML tries to carry any semantic information from the TEX sources into the resulting HTML5 document, e.g. if "semantic" macros like \sin are used. With about 1.6 million documents in the last release, the corpus is large enough that scalability becomes a major concern.

5 Annotations as RDF Triples

The Resource Description Framework, short RDF, uses triples of URIs to represent data [RDF]. A triple (s, p, o) can be thought of as an edge from s to o with label p. A collection of triples therefore encodes a directed graph. Triples can be stored in specialized triple stores and queried with SPARQL queries. We use this well-established framework to encode, store and retrieve annotations. In particular, our encoding is based on the recommendations by the W3C Web Annotation Working Group [Webb].

To illustrate the encoding of an annotation, let us assume that a document doc00.html contains the text *"it has a density of 1292.1 gm^{-3}"* and we want to annotate that *"1292.1 gm^{-3}"* is a quantity consisting of the scalar 1292.1 and the unit grams per cubic meter. In the Web Annotation recommendations, the main components of an annotation are the **target**, which describes what is annotated (in this case a particular text fragment), and the **body**, which contains some information about the target (in this case what the quantity is). Additionally, the annotation may be associated with metadata indicating, for example, who has created the annotation. Figure 2 sketches the RDF graph for the example annotation. We use the oa: prefix for the Web Annotation vocabulary [Weba], which is based on the Open Annotation vocabulary. The prefix sb: (SpotterBase) is used for URIs from our extension.

In the following subsections, we will take a closer look at how the target and the body of the annotation are represented and how a triple store of such annotations can be queried using SPARQL (Sect. 5.4).

5.1 Annotation Targets

The annotation target describes what we want to annotate. That could be an entire document, e.g. if we want to annotate its language, but often we only want to annotate part of a document, like in the example shown in Fig. 2. The Web

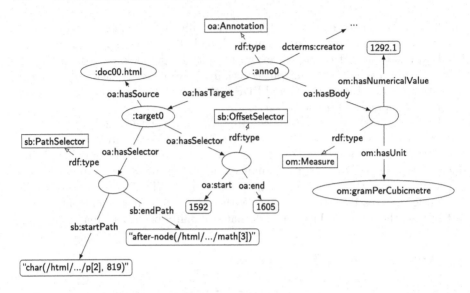

Fig. 2. An example annotation.

Annotation specification provides **selectors** to specify what part of the document we are interested in. However, the provided selectors did not work well in our setting as we need to select both text offsets and XML nodes with high precision. Instead, we specify three new selectors: sb:PathSelector, sb:OffsetSelector and sb:ListSelector. It is imaginable that in the future yet another type of selector should be supported, for example, to annotate figure contents.

The **sb:PathSelector** selects a continuous document fragment. The start and end of the selection are specified as strings:

1. "char(p, n)" points to the n-th character in the node referenced by the XPath p (an XPath [XPa10] is a standardized way to select an XML node in a document).
2. "node(p)" points to the node that is referenced by the XPath p.
3. "after-node(p)" points to whatever comes right after the node that is referenced by the XPath p.

after-node was introduced because the end is not included in the selected fragment (to be compatible with similar selectors in the Web Annotation recommendations). Note that it is necessary to be able to select HTML nodes, not just text characters. For example, the formula "$\sqrt{x}$" has the MathML representation <msqrt><mi>x</mi></msqrt> and it makes a big difference whether the <msqrt> or the <mi> ("math identifier") node are selected.

The **sb:OffsetSelector** can select fragments with the same granularity as the sb:PathSelector, but it specifies the beginning and end of the fragment with integer offsets. Providing multiple, equivalent selectors improves the chances that a consumer can process them. The sb:PathSelector is designed to be easy to use by a wide range of tools, while the sb:OffsetSelector makes it possible to compare the order of annotations easily (and without the need to load the document). For example, we can use it in SPARQL queries to check if an annotated range lies inside another annotated range (see also Sect. 5.4).

Before discussing the sb:ListSelector, which can select discontinuous fragments, we will take a look at the annotation body.

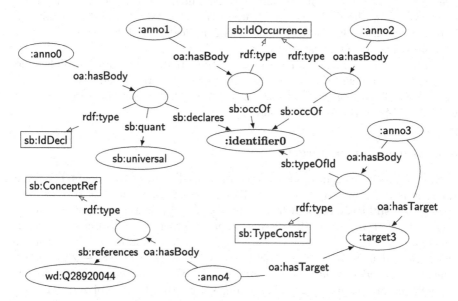

Fig. 3. Multiple annotations referencing the same identifier. For brevity, most targets are omitted and the sb:* URIs are simplified.

5.2   Annotation Bodies

The body of an annotation describes what information is attached to the annotation target. For some annotation tasks, we can develop a standardized representation of the body. For example, many annotation tasks simply require a tag as a body, such as the theorem tag to annotate a paragraph as a theorem. The advantage of annotations with a standardized body is that we can develop tools to process them without the need for customization. More complex annotations, however, will require a custom representation. For the example shown in Fig. 2, we use the Ontology of units of Measure (OM) [RVAT13] and associate a numerical value and a unit with the body. The Ontology of units of Measure contains further information about om:gramPerCubicmetre like its dimension (a density) or how it can be converted to other units. In general, loading ontologies like the Ontology of units of Measure into the triple store along with our annotations allows us to perform more complex queries.

Sometimes, the body of an annotation should reference another annotation. As an example, we will annotate the occurrences of k in the following theorem:

"*Let* $k \leq n$ *be positive integers. Then* $\binom{n}{k} = \binom{n}{n-k}$". Figure 3 visualizes the resulting annotations. The first annotation, :anno0, targets the k in the first sentence. It records that k is universally quantified (i.e. the theorem holds for *all* values of k) and links it to a node :identifier0 that represents the newly introduced identifier. That allows us to link the occurrences of k in the second sentence to :identifier0 (annotations :anno1 and :anno2), which indirectly links them to the declaration of k. Similarly, we can create further annotations to attach additional information about k. For example, :anno3 indicates that "*positive integer*" is something like a type constraint on k.

So far, we have linked annotations via their bodies. We can also link annotations by referencing the same target. For example, we can additionally annotate "*positive integer*" with the semantic concept it refers to (here the entry wd:Q28920044 of the WikiData ontology).

5.3   Discontinuous Targets

In Sect. 5.1 we described selectors for continuous document fragments, but sometimes it is desirable to annotate a discontinuous fragment. For this we have created the **sb:ListSelector**, which combines (lists) selectors for the continuous fragments that make up the discontinuous fragment. For example, in "*every submonoid H of* $(\mathbb{Z}, +)$ *is* ...", we might want to annotate the discontinuous fragment "*submonoid of* $(\mathbb{Z}, +)$", which means that the sb:ListSelector combines selectors for "*submonoid*" and for "*of* $(\mathbb{Z}, +)$". We do not expect every tool to support discontinuous ranges. Therefore, we attach this list of selectors as a refinement to a selector for the surrounding continuous fragment ("*submonoid H of* $(\mathbb{Z}, +)$") as shown in Fig. 4. A consumer of the annotation can then choose to ignore the refinement and treat the selection as a continuous fragment.

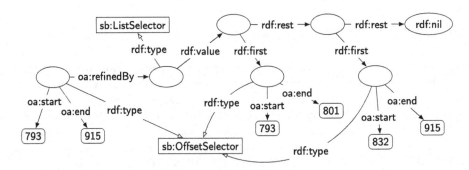

Fig. 4. Example of an sb:OffsetSelector being refined with an sb:ListSelector to select a discontinuous fragment. Using an RDF collection (rdf:rest, rdf:nil, ...) allows us to represent a closed collection despite the open world assumption of RDF.

5.4   Querying Annotations with SPARQL

If annotations are stored in a triple store, we can query them with SPARQL queries [HS13]. Usually, we use SPARQL queries to retrieve annotations in a fairly straight-forward way. For example, a hybrid spotter (Sect. 3) could retrieve all annotations for a particular document.

However, we can also use more interesting and complex queries to look for particular phenomena in our corpus. An example of this would be a query to find papers on group theory that have a theorem which mentions rational numbers:

```
# prefix declarations ommitted for conciseness
SELECT DISTINCT ?paper WHERE {
  # make sure that ?paper is about group theory
  ?paper sb:isBasedOn/^oa:hasTarget/oa:hasBody/rdf:value arxivcat:math\.GR .
  # find theorems in ?paper and look up their offsets
  ?theorem_anno oa:hasBody/rdf:value sbp:Theorem .
  ?theorem_anno oa:hasTarget [
    oa:hasSource ?paper ;
    oa:hasSelector [ a sb:OffsetSelector ; oa:start ?t_start ; oa:end ?t_end ; ]
  ] .
  # Same with mentions of rational numbers (offsets ?q_start, ?q_end)
  ?q_anno oa:hasBody/rdf:value <http://www.wikidata.org/entity/Q1244890> .
  ?q_anno oa:hasTarget [
    oa:hasSource ?paper ;
    oa:hasSelector [ a sb:OffsetSelector ; oa:start ?q_start ; oa:end ?q_end ; ]
  ] .
  # make sure that mention is inside theorem
  FILTER (?t_start < ?q_start && ?t_end > ?q_end)
}
```

Meta spotters (Sect. 3) could be realized via complex SPARQL queries similar to the one above. For very complex queries, performance can be a concern, given the large amounts of data involved.

6   SpotterBase

The success of our efforts hinges on how easily people of different backgrounds can work with our annotations and create new ones. To support that, we have created a collection of tools and libraries that we call **SpotterBase**. This section discusses some of its features.

6.1   JSON Serialization of Annotations

Sometimes, working with RDF triples is rather inconvenient: a typical annotation consists of 10–20 triples and RDF parsing or a SPARQL endpoint might not be readily available for every task. Furthermore, not everyone is familiar with RDF, which poses a substantial barrier of entry to potential users. To improve accessibility, we provide a simple JSON format that can be used to import and export annotations. It is a subset of JSON-LD (JSON Linked Data) [Jso], which is a format for representing RDF triples and is recommended by the Web Annotation standard. Many triple stores support JSON-LD and require no additional processing for importing data. ·

JSON-LD contexts make the JSON content more compact; in addition to the context suggested by the Web Annotation recommendation, we created a SpotterBase JSON-LD context. This context states e.g. that "val" is an abbreviation for http://www.w3.org/1999/02/22-rdf-syntax-ns#value and that the value should be interpreted as a URI (and not e.g. a string literal). For example, the annotation of a word as a noun would be exported as:

```
{
  "type": "Annotation",
  "id": ".../arxmliv/2020/1910.06709#spostag.anno.1089",
  "target": ".../arxmliv/2020/1910.06709#spostag.target.1089",
  "body": {
    "type": "SimpleTagBody",
    "val": "http://sigmathling.kwarc.info/spotterbase/universal-pos-tags#NOUN"
  }
},
```

SpotterBase can create additional JSON objects to provide more information about the target and the NOUN part-of-speech tag.

So far, we have mostly used the JSON serialization to export all annotations for a single document, so that they can be visualized and edited in a separate tool. Despite its convenience, the JSON format does not replace the need for a triple store because we need the triple store's querying capabilities.

6.2   Document Narrative Model

Non-STEM NLP tools typically act on plain text and not on HTML documents with large amounts of markup. While converting HTML documents to plain text is fairly straight forward, linking the discovered annotations back to the original document tends to be somewhat tricky. To help with this, SpotterBase provides the **Document Narrative Model (DNM)**: a plain text representation that is linked to the DOM (Document Object Model) of the original HTML document. DNM generation is customizable: depending on the use case, we may ignore certain nodes or process them in a different way. For example, if we want to find identifier declarations with a simple, rule-based approach and have a sentence *"let $F : C \to D$ be an exact functor"*, then we might want to get the plain text representation *"let MATH be an exact functor"* to make the processing easier. Now we can use simple regular expressions to find potential declarations. Since the DNM links *"MATH"* back to the DOM, we can still retrieve the MathML node for further processing such as to extract the identifier F.

If we develop a hybrid spotter, we could even mark existing annotations in the DNM. For example, if we have already annotated *"exact functor"* as referring to a mathematical object, we can replace it with a token in the example above, so that we get *"let MATH be an MATH_OBJ"*.

6.3 Document Pre-processing

The document narrative model described in the previous section requires spotter authors to directly use SpotterBase as a library. Alternatively, SpotterBase can also pre-process documents into different formats that are easier to work with. Some of the previous annotation efforts (e.g. [Rab17, Asa+21]) pre-processed the HTML documents by wrapping all words in a <span> node with an identifier to make referencing easier. With SpotterBase, we can do the same thing, except that we attach to every node offset information that allows the spotter to easily create annotations for the original document (using the sb:OffsetSelector described in Sect. 5.1, from which SpotterBase can then create the corresponding sb:PathSelector).

SpotterBase also allows spotter authors to avoid the trouble of HTML processing altogether with a converter to a JSON format. Essentially, each word in the original document is represented as JSON object of the form

{"word": [THE WORD], "from": [OFFSET], "to": [OFFSET]}

As with the HTML pre-processing, the offsets allow to annotate the original document. Formulae are represented the same way with a replacement token for [THE WORD], but they have an additional field for the MathML representation. In the future, it might be interesting to explore alternative ways to represent formulae as token sequences.

7   Datasets, Spotters and Experiences

We have tested the annotation format and SpotterBase by creating several datasets. Concretely, we have imported the following datasets:

1. A *quantity expressions dataset* [Rab17], which was created with a rule-based spotter for finding physical quantities, i.e. pairs of a scalar and a unit.
2. A *formula grounding dataset* [AMA22], which annotates identifier occurrences with a description of what the identifier stands for and, optionally, a source of grounding in the document.
3. A *paragraph classification dataset* [GM20], which contains paragraph classifications (theorem, definition, proof, ...) inferred from markup based on the amsthm LATEX package. Technically, we re-generated the annotations because the original dataset does not link back into the corpus.

Furthermore, we have implemented a number of prototype spotters. Concretely, we have the following spotters:

1. A spotter for *part-of-speech tags*. As it annotates every word in a document, it produces many annotations (and thus RDF triples), which may stress-test some triple stores.
2. A spotter for *math concepts* that references concepts in the WikiData ontology.

3. A spotter for *variable declarations* that delivers results similar to the one shown in Fig. 3. It is a hybrid spotter as it uses the results of the spotter for math concepts to find type constraints.

We have run the last two spotters over 100 000 documents, resulting in roughly 50 million annotations and 800 million triples. After loading them into a triple store, which took a few hours, we can now run SPARQL queries like the one described in Sect. 5.4 (looking for theorems in papers about group theory that mention rational numbers). The example query takes roughly 350 ms. By changing the query to cover more papers/more common concepts, we determined that the engine can produce roughly 200 results per second for such queries. It should be noted that simpler queries without range comparisons run much more efficiently (e.g. finding all papers that mention rational numbers at all).

As all the datasets are ultimately derived from arxiv.org, they inherit licensing issues. The SIGMathLing project [SML] tries to work around these issues with a data sharing cooperative based on mutual non-disclosure agreements. As some of the created datasets are affected by the same licensing issues, they are only accessible for SIGMathLing members. However, brief excerpts of the annotations are available in a public repository[2]. As the spotters are merely prototypes, the data sets are of limited practical use anyways.

Nevertheless, the prototype spotters allowed us to evaluate and adjust our design decisions. For example, we abandoned an original plan to specify annotation targets using the RangeSelector and FragmentSelector from the Web Annotation specification as it resulted in substantially more triples. The development of the example spotters has also informed and validated the design of Spotter-Base features like the document narrative model (Sect. 6.2), which significantly simplified the spotter implementation.

The ongoing development of a tool for manual annotation by a master's student allowed us to test how well the annotation format works in the context of a web browser. The annotation tool uses the JSON serialization (Sect. 6.1) to import existing annotations and export the results. While there were some challenges (such as the browser inserting additional nodes into the DOM while loading a document), it was fairly easy to work around them and the sb:PathSelector seems to work quite well. The annotation tool does not generate sb:OffsetSelectors – instead, SpotterBase generates them afterwards from the sb:PathSelectors. In the future, this could be taken further with SpotterBase supporting a variety of selectors, optimized for different applications, and converting between them.

8   Conclusion, Ongoing and Future Work

We have presented a spotter-based approach for accumulating a large collection of diverse semantic annotations to support or enable various semantic services for STEM publications. We use various semantic web technologies to represent, store, and query the annotations. Furthermore, we presented SpotterBase, a set

[2] https://gl.kwarc.info/SIGMathLing/cicm23-spotterbase.

of tools to create and process annotations. We have tested the setup by importing several existing datasets and creating a few new ones with simple spotters.

The most obvious next step is implementing many different spotters and, afterwards, semantic services like the ones mentioned in the introduction. As spotters are intended to be relatively simple, they can also be an attractive topic for a bachelor's or master's thesis. We tried this in the past with mixed results. A key problem was that a substantial effort of every thesis project was to develop infrastructure for pre-processing, testing, etc. SpotterBase alleviates all of that.

We also plan to grow an ecosystem of tools for working with annotations. Currently, a student is developing a tool for manually creating and editing annotations. While annotations have a standardized target representation, some tasks may require a custom body representation (see also Sect. 5.2). While a manual annotation tool may therefore support a set of standard representations, it also has to be easily extensible for future annotation tasks. A related tool would be an annotation visualizer that allows us to query the database for interesting annotations and visualize them. For example, we might want to visualize annotations where a spotter disagrees with a test dataset. We are also planning to explore in-document annotations (e.g. via RDFa) as an alternative representation that may be more suitable for certain applications.

In order to have more hybrid spotters and meta spotters, annotations must be available to the community. The easiest way is to share RDF files with the annotations, e.g. as part of the SIGMathLing [SML] effort. We also recently created a SPARQL endpoint which can be used to query some of the annotations. While this is still at a prototype stage, it could become a valuable resource in the future that makes the annotations more accessible. Unfortunately, the prototype SPARQL endpoint is only available to SIGMathLing members for the licensing reasons discussed above.

References

[AK20]   Aizawa, A., Kohlhase, M.: Mathematical information retrieval. In: Sakai, T., Oard, D.W., Kando, N. (eds.) Evaluating Information Retrieval and Access Tasks. TIRS, vol. 43, pp. 169–185. Springer, Singapore (2021). https://doi.org/10.1007/978-981-15-5554-1_12

[AMA22] Asakura, T., Miyao, Y., Aizawa, A.: Building dataset for grounding of formulae - annotating coreference relations among math identifiers. In: Proceedings of the Language Resources and Evaluation Conference. Marseille, France: European Language Resources Association, pp. 4851–4858 (2022). https://aclanthology.org/2022.lrec-1.519

[Asa+21] Asakura, T., et al.: Miogatto: a math identifier-oriented grounding annotation tool. In: 13th MathUI Workshop at 14th Conference on Intelligent Computer Mathematics (MathUI 2021) (2021)

[BR]   Brat rapid annotation tool. http://brat.nlplab.org. Accessed 06 Apr 2023

204   J. F. Schaefer and M. Kohlhase

[Cas+16] de Castilho, R.E., et al.: A web-based tool for the integrated annotation of semantic and syntactic structures. In: Proceedings of the Workshop on Language Technology Resources and Tools for Digital Humanities (LT4DH), Osaka, Japan: The COLING 2016 Organizing Committee, pp. 76–84 (2016). https://www.aclweb.org/anthology/W16-4011

[CICM22] Kohlhase, M., Müller, D.: System description: sTeX3 - a LATEX-based ecosystem for semantic/active mathematical documents. In: Buzzard, K., Kutsia, T. (eds.) CICM 2022. LNCS, vol. 13467, pp. 184–188. Springer, Cham (2022). https://doi.org/10.1007/978-3-031-16681-5_13

[Con] CoNLL-U Format. https://universaldependencies.org/format.html

[FA] Formal Abstracts. https://formalabstracts.github.io/. Accessed 15 Feb 2020

[Gin+15] Ginev, D., et al.: KAT: an annotation tool for STEM documents. In: Kohlhase, A., Libbrecht, P. (eds.) Mathematical User Interfaces Workshop (2015). http://www.cermat.org/events/MathUI/15/proceedings/Lal-Kohlhase-Ginev_KAT_annotations_MathUI_15.pdf

[Gin20] Ginev, D.: arXMLiv:2020 dataset, an HTML5 conversion of arXiv.org. SIG-MathLing - Special Interest Group on Math Linguistics (2020). https://sigmathling.kwarc.info/resources/arxmliv-dataset-2020/

[GM20] Ginev, D., Miller, B.R.: Scientific Statement Classification over arXiv org. English. In: Proceedings of the Twelfth Language Resources and Evaluation Conference. European Language Resources Association, Marseille, France, pp. 1219–1226 (2020). https://aclanthology.org/2020.lrec-1.153

[Hal+17] Hales, T., et al.: A formal proof of the Kepler conjecture. In: Forum of Mathematics, Pi, vol. 5 (2017). https://doi.org/10.1017/fmp.2017.1

[Her+13] Herman, I., et al.: RDF 1.1 Primer (Second Edition). Rich Structured Data Markup for Web Documents. W3CWorking Group Note. World Wide Web Consortium (W3C) (2013). http://www.w3.org/TR/rdfa-primer

[HS13] Harris, S., Seaborne, A.: SPARQL 1.1 Query Language. W3C Recommendation. World Wide Web Consortium (W3C) (2013). https://www.w3.org/TR/sparql11-query/

[HYP] Hypothes.is. http://hypothes.is. Accessed 06 Apr 2023

[Jso] JSON for Linking Data. https://json-ld.org/

[Man+22] Mansouri, B., et al.: Overview of ARQMath-3 (2022): third CLEF Lab on answer retrieval for questions on math. In: Barrón-Cedeño, A., et al. (eds.) CLEF 2022. LNCS, vol. 13390, pp. 286–310. Springer, Cham (2022). https://doi.org/10.1007/978-3-031-13643-6_20

[Mil] Bruce Miller. LaTeXML: A LATEX to XML Converter. http://dlmf.nist.gov/LaTeXML/. Accessed 22 Mar 2023

[Rab17] Rabenstein, U.: Meaning Extraction and Semantic Services in STEM-Documents - A case study on Quantity Expressions and Units. Master's Thesis. Informatik, FAU Erlangen-Nürnberg (2017). https://gl.kwarc.info/supervision/MSc-archive/blob/master/2017/urabenstein/Rabenstein.pdf

[RDF] World Wide Web Consortium (W3C), ed. Resource Description Framework (RDF). http://www.w3.org/RDF/. Accessed 05 Apr 2023

[RVAT13] Rijgersberg, H., Van Assem, M., Top, J.: Ontology of units of measure and related concepts. Semant. Web 4(1), 3–13 (2013)

[SML] SIGMathLing - Special Interest Group on Maths Linguistics. http://sigmathling.kwarc.info. Accessed 07 Dec 2018

[Wan+20] Wang, Q., et al.: Exploration of neural machine translation in autoformalization of mathematics in Mizar. In: Proceedings of the 9th ACM SIG-
PLAN International Conference on Certified Programs and Proofs, pp. 85–
98 (2020)

[Weba] Web Annotation Ontology. https://www.w3.org/ns/oa

[Webb] Web Annotation Working Group. https://www.w3.org/annotation/

[XPa10] XPath Reference (2010). http://www.w3.org/TR/xpath/. Accessed 05 Apr
2023

Verified Correctness, Accuracy, and Convergence of a Stationary Iterative Linear Solver: Jacobi Method

Mohit Tekriwal[1]([✉]), Andrew W. Appel[2], Ariel E. Kellison[3], David Bindel[3], and Jean-Baptiste Jeannin[1]

[1] University of Michigan, Ann Arbor, USA
{tmohit,jeannin}@umich.edu
[2] Princeton University, Princeton, USA
appel@princeton.edu
[3] Cornell University, Ithaca, USA
{ak2485,bindel}@cornell.edu

Abstract. Solving a sparse linear system of the form $Ax = b$ is a common engineering task, e.g., as a step in approximating solutions of differential equations. Inverting a large matrix A is often too expensive, and instead engineers rely on iterative methods, which progressively approximate the solution x of the linear system in several iterations, where each iteration is a much less expensive (sparse) matrix-vector multiplication.

We present a formal proof in the Coq proof assistant of the correctness, accuracy and convergence of one prominent iterative method, the Jacobi iteration. The accuracy and convergence properties of Jacobi iteration are well-studied, but most past analyses were performed in real arithmetic; instead, we study those properties, and prove our results, in floating-point arithmetic. We then show that our results are properly reflected in a concrete implementation in the C language. Finally, we show that the iteration will not overflow, under assumptions that we make explicit. Notably, our proofs are faithful to the details of the implementation, including C program semantics and floating-point arithmetic.

Keywords: Formal Verification · Numerical Methods · Jacobi Method

1 Introduction

Many scientific and engineering computations require the solution x of large sparse linear systems $Ax = b$ given an $n \times n$ matrix A and a vector b. There are many algorithms for doing this; Gaussian elimination is rare when n is large, since it takes $\mathcal{O}(n^3)$ time. The widely used *stationary iterative methods* have an average time complexity of $\mathcal{O}(nsk)$, where sparseness s is the number of nonzeros per row (often $s \ll n$) and k is the number of iterations (often small). Even where iterative methods are not the principal algorithms for solving $Ax = b$, they are often used in transformations of the problem (preconditioning) before using other workhorses such as Krylov subspace methods [27].

When using a stationary iterative method, one starts with an initial vector x_0 and uses A and b to derive successive vectors $x_1, x_2, \ldots$ that—one hopes—will

© The Author(s), under exclusive license to Springer Nature Switzerland AG 2023
C. Dubois and M. Kerber (Eds.): CICM 2023, LNAI 14101, pp. 206–221, 2023.
https://doi.org/10.1007/978-3-031-42753-4_14

converge to a value x_k such that the *residual* $Ax_k - b$ is small and x_k is close to the true solution. Because these methods are often used as subroutines deep within larger computational libraries and solvers, it is quite inconvenient to the end user if some such subroutine reports that it failed to converge—often, the user has no idea what is the subproblem A, b that has failed. Thus it is useful to be able to prove theorems of the following form: "Given inputs A and b with certain properties, the algorithm will converge to tolerance τ within k iterations."

Since these methods are so important, analyses of their convergence properties have been studied in detail. However, most of these analyses assume real number arithmetic operations [27], whereas their implementations use floating-point; or the analysis uses a simplified floating-point model that omits subnormal numbers [14]; or the analysis is for a *model* of an algorithm [19] but not the actual software. And when one reaches correctness and accuracy proofs of actual software, it's useful to have machine-checked proofs that connect in a machine-checkable way to the actual program that is executed, for programs can be complex and as programs evolve one must ensure that their correctness theorems evolve with them.

We focus on Jacobi iteration applied to *strictly diagonally dominant matrices*, i.e., in which in each row the magnitude of the diagonal element exceeds the sum of the magnitudes of the off-diagonals. Strict diagonal dominance is a simple test for invertibility and guarantees convergence of Jacobi iteration in exact arithmetic [27]. Strictly diagonally dominant matrices arise in cubic spline interpolation [1], analysis of Katz centrality in social networks [18], Markov chains associated with PageRank and related network analysis methods [12], and market equilibria in economic theory [24], among other domains.

We present both a Coq *functional model* of floating-point Jacobi iteration (at any desired floating-point precision) and a C program (in double-precision floating-point), with Coq proofs that:

- the C program (which uses efficient sparse-matrix algorithms) correctly implements the functional model (which uses a simpler matrix representation);
- for any inputs A, b and desired accuracy τ that satisfy the *Jacobi preconditions* for a given natural number k, the functional model (and the C program) will converge within k iterations to a vector x_k such that $||Ax_k - b||_2 < \tau$;
- this computation will not overflow into floating-point "infinity" values;
- and the *Jacobi preconditions* are natural properties of A, b, τ, k that (1) are easily tested and (2) for many natural engineering problems of interest (mentioned above), are guaranteed to be satisfied.

Software packages not written in C can still be related to our functional model and make use of our floating-point convergence and accuracy theorems. And even for inputs that do not satisfy the Jacobi preconditions, we have proved that our C program correctly and robustly detects overflow.

Together, these theorems guarantee that a Jacobi solver deep within some larger library will not be the cause of a mysterious "failed to converge" message; and that when it does believe it has converged, it will have a correct answer.

Contributions. First convergence proof of Jacobi that takes into account floating-point underflow or overflow; first machine-checked proof of a stationary iterative method; first machine-checked connection to a real program. Our Coq formalization is available at:

https://github.com/VeriNum/iterative_methods/tree/v0.1.0

2   Overview of Iterative Methods and Our Proof Structure

Stationary iterative methods [27] are among the oldest and simplest methods for solving linear systems of the form $Ax = b$, for $A \in \mathbb{R}^{n \times n}$, $b \in \mathbb{R}^n$. The nonsingular matrix A and vector b in such systems typically appear, for example, in the solution of a partial differential equation. In stationary methods, matrix A is decomposed into $A = M + N$ where M is chosen such that it is easily invertible; for Jacobi it is simply the diagonal of A and we will often call it D. Rather than solving the system $Ax = b$ exactly, one can approximate the solution vector x using stationary iterations of the form

$$Mx_m + Nx_{m-1} = b, \tag{1}$$

where the vector x_m is an approximation to the solution vector x obtained after m iterations; we typically start with $x_0 = \mathbf{0}$. The unknown x_m is therefore

$$x_m = M^{-1}(b - Nx_{m-1}) \qquad \text{that is for Jacobi,} \qquad x_m = D^{-1}(b - Nx_{m-1}) \tag{2}$$

This iterates until x_k satisfies $\|Ax_k - b\|_2 < \tau$, or until the program detects *failure:* overflow in computing x_k, or maximum number of iterations exceeded. Throughout this paper, we let $\|\cdot\|$ denote the infinity vector norm and its induced matrix norm, and we let $\| \cdot \|_2$ denote the ℓ^2 norm on vectors.

For our model problem, the steps are as follows.

1. Write a C program that implements (2) by Jacobi iterations (and also implements an appropriate stopping condition).
2. Write a *floating-point functional model* in Coq (a recursive functional program that operates on floating-point values) that models Jacobi iterations of the form (2). This model must perform almost exactly (see Sect. 7.1) the same floating-point operations as the C program. (As we will explain, we have two statements of this model and we prove the two *models equivalent.*)
3. Prove that the program written in Step 1 implements the floating-point functional model of Step 2, using a program logic for C.
4. Write a *real functional model* in Coq that performs Jacobi iteration $x_m = D^{-1}(b - Nx_{m-1})$ in the exact reals. Of course, it is impractical to compute with this model, but it is useful for proofs.
5. Prove a relation between x_k (the k-th iteration of the floating-point model) and the real solution x of the real functional model: the *Jacobi forward error bound.* If one could run the Jacobi method purely in the reals, this is obviously contractive: $\|x_{k+1} - x\| < \rho \|x_k - x\|$, where $\rho < 1$ is the spectral radius of $D^{-1}N$. But in the floats, there is an extra term caused by roundoff error.

6. Prove *floating-point convergence:* under certain conditions (*Jacobi preconditions*), this extra term does not blow up, and within a specified k iterations the residual $\|Ax_k - b\|_2$ is less than tolerance τ.
7. Compose these to prove the main theorem: the C program converges to an accurate result.

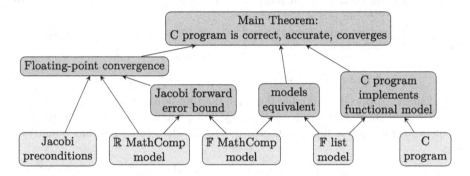

Fig. 1. Theorem dependency. Bottom row: models and definitions; middle row: theorems relating models.

Figure 1 shows our correctness and accuracy theorem as a modular composition of reusable models and lemmas. We have two float-valued models: for proving the relation of the float-valued model to the real solution we use the MathComp library (in Coq). For proving the C program implements the float-valued model, we use the Verified Software Toolchain (in Coq). But MathComp [22] and VST [10] prefer different notations and constructions for specifying data structures such as matrices and vectors; so we write the same functional model in each of the two styles, and prove their equivalence. We used Coq for our formalization because of Coq's expressive general-purpose logic, with powerful libraries such as MathComp, Flocq [8], VCFloat [3], LAProof [21], Coquelicot [7], VST, support both high-level mathematical reasoning and low-level program verification.

The float-valued model will experience round-off errors compared to the real-valued model; we prove bounds on these errors in a *forward error bound* lemma (Sect. 4). Under certain "Jacobi preconditions" the float-valued model is guaranteed to converge to a result of specified accuracy without ever overflowing; this is the *Jacobi iteration bound* lemma (Sect. 5).

3   Parametric Models and Proofs; Important Constants

We have proved accuracy bounds for any floating-point precision. That is, our floating-point functional models, and the proofs about them, are parameterized by a *floating-point type*, expressed in Coq as type:Type, with operations: [3]

fprec: type $\rightarrow \mathbb{Z}$ (* number of mantissa bits *)
femax: type $\rightarrow \mathbb{Z}$ (* maximum binary exponent *)
ftype: type $\rightarrow$ Type   (* floating–point numbers *)

So for t:type, we have x:ftype(t) meaning that x is a floating-point number in format t. We will write p for fprec(t) and $e_{\max}$ for femax(t). The maximum representable finite value is $F_{\max} = 2^{e_{\max}}(1 - 2^{-p})$. If $|r| \leq F_{\max}$ then rounding r to the nearest float yields a number f such that $f = r(1 + \delta_f) + \epsilon_f$, where $|\delta_f| \leq \delta = \frac{1}{2}2^{1-p}$ and $|\epsilon_f| \leq \epsilon = \frac{1}{2}2^{3-e_{\max}-p}$.

Given a floating-point format t and matrix-dimension n, the following functions will be useful in reasoning:

$$g_\delta(n) = (1 + \delta)^n - 1 \qquad g_\epsilon(n) = n\epsilon(1 + g_\delta(n - 1)) \qquad (3)$$

For example, suppose t is double-precision floating-point ($p = 53$, $e_{\max} = 1024$), $n = 10^6$ (Jacobi iteration on a million-by-million matrix), $s = 5$ (the million-element *sparse* matrix has 5 nonzeros per row). Then some relevant quantities are,

$$\delta = 2^{-54} = 5.6 \cdot 10^{-17} \qquad g_\delta(n) = 5.6 \cdot 10^{-11} \qquad g_\epsilon(n) = 2.5 \cdot 10^{-318}$$
$$\epsilon = 2^{-1075} = 2.5 \cdot 10^{-324} \qquad g_\delta(5) = 2.8 \cdot 10^{-16} \qquad g_\epsilon(5) = 1.2 \cdot 10^{-323}.$$

Our error analyses will often feature formulas with $\delta, \epsilon, g_\delta, g_\epsilon$; remember that in double-precision these are *small* quantities (in single- or half-precision, not so small). Henceforth we will write g_δ, g_ϵ for $g_\delta(n), g_\epsilon(n)$.

4   Forward Error Bound for Dot Product

In separate work, Kellison *et al.* [21] prove (in Coq) the correctness and accuracy of floating-point dot-product and sparse matrix-vector multiply, as Coq functional models and as C programs.

Define dot-product $\langle u, v \rangle$ between two real vectors u and v as $\sum_{0 \leq i < n} u_i v_i$. A matrix-vector multiplication Av can be seen as the dot-product of each row of A with vector v. Forward error bounds for a matrix-vector multiplication are therefore based on forward error bounds for dot-product.

Our implementation and functional model of the dot-product use *fused multiply-add* (FMA), which computes a floating-point multiplication and addition (i.e., $a \otimes b \oplus c$) with a single rounding error rather than two.

Definition dotprod {t: type} (u v: list (ftype t)) : ftype t :=
    fold_left (fun z a $\Rightarrow$ FMA (fst a) (snd a) z) (List.combine u v) (Zconst t 0).

The parameters to the dotprod functional model are the floating-point format t and two lists of floating-point numbers. The algorithm zips the two lists into a list of pairs (using List.combine) and then adds them from left to right, starting with a floating-point 0 in format t.

We denote floating-point summation by $\oplus$, so the floating-point dot product is $\bigoplus_{0 \leq i < n} u_i v_i$; real-valued summation is denoted as $\sum_{0 \leq i < n} u_i v_i$. The notation finite($z$) signifies that the floating-point number z is within the range of the floating-point format (not an infinity or NaN).

Theorem 1 (forward error + no overflow). *Let u, v be lists of length n of floats in format $t = (p, e_{\max})$, in which every element is $\leq v_{\max}$, and no more than s elements of u are nonzero. The absolute forward error of the resulting dot product is*

$$\left| \bigoplus_{0 \leq i < n} u_i v_i - \sum_{0 \leq i < n} u_i v_i \right| \leq g_\delta(s) \sum_{0 \leq i < n} |u_i v_i| + g_\epsilon(s). \tag{4}$$

Proof. See Kellison *et al.* [21].

Subnormal Numbers. When some of the vector elements are order-of-magnitude 1, the term $g_\epsilon(s)$ is negligible. But if the u and v vectors are composed of subnormal numbers, then neglecting the underflow-error term would be unsound. Most previous proofs about dot-product error (and about Jacobi iteration), and all previous machine-checked proofs to our knowledge, omit reasoning about underflow.

5   Jacobi Forward Error

We prove an explicit bound on the distance between the approximate solution x_k at step k and the exact solution x of the problem. Such bounds are commonly studied in computational science, but rarely take into account the details of floating-point arithmetic (including underflow and overflow). They also usually have paper proofs while we provide a machine-checked proof.

Theorem 2 (jacobi_forward_error_bound). *After k Jacobi iterations, if no iteration resulted in an overflow, then the distance between the approximate (floating-point) solution x_k and the exact (real) solution x is bounded:*

$$\|x - x_k\| \leq \rho^k \|x - x_0\| + \frac{1 - \rho^k}{1 - \rho} d_{\mathrm{mag}}$$

where ρ is a bound on the spectral radius (largest eigenvalue) of $D^{-1}N$, adjusted for floating-point roundoff errors that arise in one iteration of the Jacobi method. The (small) value d_{mag} is the floating-point roundoff error in computing the residual $\|Ax_k - b\|$. In Coq,

```
Theorem jacobi_forward_error_bound {ty} {n:nat}
 (A: 'M[ftype ty]_n.+1) (b: 'cV[ftype ty]_n.+1): ∀x0: 'cV[ftype ty]_n.+1,
  forward_error_cond A x0 b →
  ∀k i, finite (x_{k, i})) ∧
  (f_error k ≤ rho^k * (f_error 0) + ((1 − rho^k) / (1−rho)) * d_mag.
```

where f_error(k) is $\|x - x_k\|$, and the conditions on $A \in \mathbb{F}^{(n+1) \times (n+1)}, x_0 \in \mathbb{F}^{(n+1) \times 1}, b \in \mathbb{F}^{(n+1) \times 1}$ for $n \geq 0$, are characterized as follows:

Definition forward_error_cond {ty} {n:nat}
(A: 'M[ftype ty]_n.+1) (x0 b: 'cV[ftype ty]_n.+1) :=
($\forall$ i, finite (A _{i,i}) $\wedge$ (rho < 1) $\wedge$ invertible A $\wedge$ ($\forall$ i, finite (1 / A_{i,i})) $\wedge$
($\forall$ i, finite (x_{o,i}) $\wedge$ ($\forall$ i j, finite(N_{i,j})) $\wedge$ ($\forall$ i, finite (b_i) $\wedge$
size_constraint n $\wedge$ input_bound A x0 b.

`size_constraint n` is a constraint on the dimension n of the matrix A (in double-precision, about $6 \cdot 10^9$). The predicate `input_bound` provides conditions on the bounds for the inputs A, b, x_0; it is implied by the *Jacobi preconditions* (Definition 1) defined in the next section.

Proof. Assuming no overflow, the floating-point iteration satisfies

$$x_{k+1} = \tilde{D}^{-1} \otimes (b \ominus (N \otimes x_k))$$

where the operators $\otimes$, $\ominus$ represent the floating-point multiplication and subtraction operations respectively. $\tilde{D}^{-1}$ is the floating-point (not exact) inverse of the diagonal elements. The forward error at step $k + 1$ is defined as

$$f_{k+1} = \|x_{k+1} - x\| = \|(\tilde{D}^{-1} \otimes (b \ominus (N \otimes x_k))) - (D^{-1}(b - Nx))\|$$

Here, we write the true solution as $x = D^{-1}(b - Nx)$ which can be derived from $Ax = b$. To move forward, we will be using the following auxiliary error bounds on matrix-vector operations.

- Matrix-vector multiplication: $\|N \otimes x - Nx\| \leq \|N\|\|x\|g_\delta + g_\epsilon$. This bound is derived from the dot product error bound that we stated in Sect. 4. In the $\|\cdot\|$ norm, the dot product errors directly give the error bound for matrix-vector multiplication.
- Vector subtraction: $\|(b \ominus (N \otimes x_k)) - b(N \otimes x_k)\| \leq (\|b\| + \|N \otimes x_k\|)\delta$. Here, we use the fact that $|x \ominus y - (x - y)| \leq (|x| + |y|)\delta$.
- Vector inverse: $\|\tilde{D}^{-1} - D^{-1}\| \leq \|D^{-1}\|\delta + \epsilon$. Here, we make use of the fact that inverting each element of the vector D satisfies, $|(1 \oslash D_i) - (1/D_i)| \leq |(1/D_i)|\delta + \epsilon$.

We use these norm-wise errors to expand the error definition f_{k+1}:

$$f_{k+1} \leq (((\|\tilde{D}^{-1}\| (\|b\| + \|N\| \|x_k\|(1 + g_\delta + g_\epsilon))(1 + \delta)g_\delta + g_\epsilon) +$$
$$\|\tilde{D}^{-1}\| (\|b\| + \|N\| \|x_k\|(1 + g_\delta) + g_\epsilon)\delta +$$
$$\|\tilde{D}^{-1}\| (\|N\| \|x_k\|g_\delta + g_\epsilon) +$$
$$(\|D^{-1}\|\delta + \epsilon) (\|b\| + \|N\| \|x_k\|) + \|D^{-1}\| \|N\|f_k$$

We then collect the coefficients of $\|x_k\|$ and expand using the error relation for f_k as $\|x_k\| \leq f_k + \|x\|$ to get the error recurrence relation:

$$f_{k+1} \leq \rho f_k + d_{\mathrm{mag}}$$

where d_{mag} is a constant independent of k depending only on $\|x\|$, δ, ϵ, g_δ, g_ϵ. We can then expand the above error recurrence relation to get

$$f_{k+1} \le \rho^{k+1} f_o + (1 + \rho + \rho^2 + \dots + \rho^k) d_{\text{mag}}$$

This geometric series converges if $\rho < 1$ with closed form

$$f_{k+1} \le \rho^{k+1} f_o + \frac{1 - \rho^{k+1}}{1 - \rho} d_{\text{mag}}$$

Note that if the above iterative process were done in reals, then we would only require $\rho_r := \|D^{-1}N\|$ to be less than 1. Thus, the presence of rounding errors forces us to choose a more conservative convergence radius ρ.

6   Convergence Guarantee: Absence of Overflow

Theorem 2 had the premise, "if no iteration resulted in an overflow." Most previous convergence theorems for Jacobi iteration [27] have been in the real numbers, where overflow is not an issue: multiplying two finite numbers cannot "overflow." Higham and Knight [14] proved convergence (but not absence of overflow), on paper, in a simplified model of floating-point (without underflows). Let us now state a theorem, for an accurate model of floating-point, *not* conditioned on absence of overflow.

Theorem 3 (jacobi_iteration_bound_lowlevel). *If the inputs A, b, desired tolerance τ, and projected number of iterations k satisfy the (efficiently testable) Jacobi preconditions, then the floating-point functional model of Jacobi iteration converges, within $j \le k$ iterations, to a solution x_j such that $\|Ax_j - b\|_2 < \tau$, without overflowing.*

Proof. The proof for this theorem follows by the following cases:

- If A is diagonal then N is a zero matrix. Therefore, the solution vector at each iteration is given by the constant vector $x_k = \tilde{D}^{-1} \otimes b$. Hence, the solution of Jacobi iteration has already converged after the first step, assuming certain bounds on b and A implied by the *Jacobi preconditions*.
- If A is not diagonal but the vector b is small enough, Jacobi iteration has already converged, without even running the iteration.
- Suppose A is not diagonal and the vector b is not too small. Then
  (a) The residual does not overflow for every iteration $\le j$. This follows from the *Jacobi preconditions* and Theorem 2.
  (b) We can calculate $k_{\min}$ such that the residual $< \tau$ within $k_{\min}$ iterations.

The *Jacobi preconditions* (Definition 1) are efficiently computable: a straightforward arithmetic computation with computational complexity linear in the number of nonzero matrix elements.

Definition 1 (jacobi_preconditions_Rcompute). *A, b, τ, k satisfy the* Jacobi preconditions *when:*

- *All elements of A, b, and $\tilde{D}^{-1}$ are finite (representable in floating-point);*
- *A is strictly diagonally row-dominant, that is, $\forall i.\ D_{ii} > \sum_j |N_{ij}|$;*
- *$\tilde{\tau}^2$ is finite;*
- $\tilde{\tau}^2 > g_\epsilon + n(1 + g_\delta)(g_\epsilon) + 2(1 + g_\delta)(1 + \delta)\|D\|(\hat{d}_{\mathrm{mag}}/(1 - \hat{\rho}))^2;$
- $\tilde{\tau}^2 > n(1 + g_\delta)(\|D\|(\|\tilde{D}^{-1}\|(\|A\|\hat{d}_{\mathrm{mag}}/(1 - \hat{\rho}) + g_\epsilon)(1 + \delta)(1 + g_\delta) + g_\epsilon)(1 +$
  $\delta)(1 + g_\delta) + g_\epsilon)^2 + g_\epsilon;$
- $k_{\min} \leq k;$
- $n < ((F_{\max} - \epsilon)/(1 + \delta) - g_\epsilon - 1)/(g(n - 1) + 1);\ n < F_{\max}/((1 + g(n + 1))\delta) - 1$
- $\forall i.\ |A_{ii}|(1 + \hat{\rho})x_{\mathrm{bound}} + 2\hat{d}_{\mathrm{mag}}/(1 - \hat{\rho}) + 2x_{\mathrm{bound}} < v_{\max} - \epsilon)/(1 + \delta)^2;$
- $\forall i, j.\ |N_{ij}| < v_{\max};$
- $\forall i.\ |b_i| + (1 + g_\delta)((2x_{\mathrm{bound}} + \hat{d}_{\mathrm{mag}}/(1 - \hat{\rho}))\sum_j |N_{ij}|) + g_\epsilon < F_{\max}/(1 + \delta);$
- $\forall i.\ |\tilde{D}_{ii}^{-1}|(|b_i| + (1 + g_\delta)(2x_{\mathrm{bound}} + \hat{d}_{\mathrm{mag}}/(1 - \hat{\rho}))\sum_j |N_{ij}|) + g_\epsilon < F_{\max}/(1 + \delta);$
- $(1 + \hat{\rho})x_{\mathrm{bound}} + 2\hat{d}_{\mathrm{mag}}/(1 - \hat{\rho}) + 2x_{\mathrm{bound}} < F_{\max}/(1 + \delta);$
- $\forall i.\ |b_i| < (F_{\max} - \epsilon)/(1 + \delta);$
- $\forall i.\ |\tilde{D}_{ii}^{-1}|\|b_i\| < (F_{\max} - \epsilon)/(1 + \delta);$
- $\forall i.\ |\tilde{D}_{ii}^{-1}|\|b_i\|(1 + \delta) + \epsilon < (F_{\max} - \epsilon)/(1 + \delta);$
- $\forall i.\ |A_{ii}|(|\tilde{D}_{ii}^{-1}|\|b_i\|(1 + \delta) + \epsilon) < (v_{\max} - \epsilon)/(1 + \delta).$

where $\hat{d} = (\|\tilde{D}^{-1}\| + \epsilon)/(1 - \delta)$ is a bound on $\|D^{-1}\|$. Defining $R = \hat{d}\,\|N\|$, we define an upper bound on the norm of the solution x to $Ax = b$ as $x_{\mathrm{bound}} = \hat{d}\|b\|/(1 - R)$. $\hat{\rho}$ is the adjusted spectral radius ($\rho_r = \|D^{-1}N\|$) of the iteration matrix, obtained by accounting for the floating-point errors in its computation. For the iteration process to converge in presence of rounding, we want $\hat{\rho} < 1$. $\hat{d}_{\mathrm{mag}}$ is a bound on the additive error in computing the residual $\|Ax_k - b\|$, the difference between computing the residual in the reals versus in floating-point. $\tilde{\tau}^2 = \tau \otimes \tau$ is the floating-point square of τ. The minimum k for which we guarantee convergence is calculated as

$$k_{\min} = 1 + \left\lceil \frac{\ln\left(\dfrac{x_{\mathrm{bound}}(1 + \delta)}{((\sqrt{(\tilde{\tau}^2 - g_\epsilon)/(n(1 + g_\delta))} - g_\epsilon)/((1 + g_\delta) + \|D\|(1 + \delta))) - 2\hat{d}_{\mathrm{mag}}/(1 - \hat{\rho})} \right)}{\ln(1/\hat{\rho})} \right\rceil$$

Indeed these conditions are quite tedious – one might have difficulty trusting them without a machine-checked proof. But they are all easy to compute in linear time. And, although we state them here (mostly) in terms of operations on the reals, they are all straightforwardly boundable by floating-point operations.

Remark 1 (not proved in Coq). The Jacobi preconditions can be computed in time linear in the number of nonzero entries of A.

Proof. Let S be the number of nonzeros. Then $n < S$ since the diagonal elements are nonzero. The inverse diagonal $\tilde{D}^{-1}$ is computed in linear time. The infinity norm ($\|N\|$, $\|D\|$, $\hat{d}$, $\|b\|$) is simply the largest absolute value of any row-sum (for matrix) or element (for vector), which can be found in $O(S)$ time. Then the values $x_{\mathrm{bound}}, \hat{\rho}, \hat{d}_{\mathrm{mag}}, v_{\max}, k_{\min}$ can all be computed in constant time. Then each of the tests in Definition 1 can be done in $O(S)$ time.

7   An Efficient and Correct C Program

Our C program uses standard numerical methods to achieve high performance and accuracy: sparse matrix methods, fused multiply-add, efficient testing for overflow, and so on. What's not so standard is that we have proved it correct, with a foundational machine-checked proof that composes in Coq with the numerical accuracy (and convergence) proof of our functional model.

7.1   Sparse Matrix-Vector Multiply

Many implementations of stationary iterative methods, including Jacobi, are on large sparse matrices. A naive dense matrix-vector multiply would take $O(n^2)$ time per iteration, while sparse representations permit $O(sn)$ time per iteration, there are s nonzeros per row. Our program uses Compressed Row Storage (CRS), a standard sparse representation [4, §4.3.1].

Kellison *et al.* [21] describe the Coq floating-point functional model, an implementation in C, and the Coq/VST proof that the C dot-product program correctly implements the model. VST (Verified Software Toolchain) [10] is a tool embedded in Coq for proving C programs correct. From that, here we prove that the Jacobi program implements *its* model.

For sweep-form Jacobi iteration it is useful to have a function that computes *just one row* of a sparse matrix-vector multiply, which in CRS form is implemented as,

```
double crs_row_vector_multiply(struct crs_matrix *m, double *v, unsigned i);
/* compute dot−product of row i of matrix m with vector v */
```

Separation of Concerns. The floating-point *accuracy* proof should be kept completely separate from the sparse-matrix data-structure-and-algorithm proof. This function is proved to calculate (almost) exactly the same *floating-point* computation as the naive dense matrix multiply algorithm.

Almost exactly – because where $A_{ij} = 0$, the dense algorithm computes $A_{ij} \cdot x_i + s$ where the sparse algorithm just uses s. In floating-point it is not the case that $\forall y.\ 0 \cdot y + s = s$, for example when y is ∞ or NaN. Even when y and s are finite, it is not always true that $y \cdot 0 + s$ is the same floating-point value as s: it could be that one is +0 and the other is −0. And finally, even when matrix A and vector x are all finite, we cannot assume that intermediate results s are finite—there may be overflow.

So we reason modulo equivalence relations (using Coq's Parametric Morphism system for rewriting with partial equivalence relations). We define feq x y to mean that either both x and y are finite and equal (with +0 = −0), or neither is finite. Our function will have a precondition that A and x are all finite, and postcondition that the computed result is feq to the result that a dense matrix multiply algorithm would compute.

7.2   Jacobi Iteration

Listing 1.1. C program for a single iteration of Jacobi iteration

```
double jacobi2_oneiter(double *A1, struct crs_matrix *A2, double *b, double *x,
                                                              double *y) {
   unsigned i, n=crs_matrix_rows(A2); double s = 0.0;
   for (i=0; i<n; i++) {
      double u = b[i] − crs_row_vector_multiply(A2,x,i);
      double a1 = A1[i], new = (1/a1)*u, r = a1*(new − x[i]);
      s = fma(r,r,s);
      y[i] = new;
      }
   return s;
}
```

The C program in the Lisiting 1.1 loops over rows i of the matrix, which is also elements i of the vectors b and x. For each i it computes a new element y_i of the result vector, as well as an element r_i of residual vector. It returns s, the sum of the squares of the r_i. By carefully computing r_i from y_i, and not vice versa, we can prove (in Coq, of course) that all overflows are detected: if s is finite, then all the y_i must be finite.

The program in the Listing 1.2 runs until convergence ($s < \tau^2$), giving up early if there's overflow (tested by s*0=0.0, since if s overflows then s*0 is NaN) or if maxiter iterations is reached.

Listing 1.2. C program for Jacobi iteration until convergence

```
double jacobi2(double *A1, struct crs_matrix *A2, double *b, double *x, double τ²,
                                                             unsigned maxiter) {
   unsigned i, n=crs_matrix_rows(A2);
   double s, *t, *z=x, *y = (double *)surely_malloc(n*sizeof(double));
   do { s = jacobi2_oneiter(A1,A2,b,z,y);
        t=z; z=y; y=t;
        maxiter−−;
   } while (s*0==0.0 && s ≥ τ² && maxiter);
   if (y==x) y=z; else { for (i=0; i<n; i++) x[i]=y[i]; }
   free(y);
   return s;
}
```

This program starts with $x^{(0)}$ in x, computes $x^{(1)}$ into y, then $x^{(2)}$ back into x, and so on. It mallocs y for that purpose and frees it at the end. Depending on whether the number of iterations is odd or even, it may need to copy from y to x at the end.

This program is conventional and straightforward. Our proof tools allow the numerical analyst to use standard methods and idioms—and nontrivial data structures—and still get an end-to-end correctness proof. For each of these functions we prove in VST that the function exactly implements the functional model, modulo equivalence relations on floating-point numbers. At this level there are no accuracy proofs, the programs *exactly* implement the functional models, except that one might have -0 where the other has $+0$, and one might have different NaNs than the other, if any arise.

Correctness Theorem. The jacobi2 function is specified and proved with a VST function-spec that we will not show here, but in English it says,

Theorem 4 (body_jacobi2). *Let A be a matrix, let b and $x^{(0)}$ be vectors, let Alp be the address of a 1-dimensional array holding the diagonal of A, let A2p be the address of a CRS sparse matrix representation of A without its diagonal, let bp and xp be the addresses of arrays holding b and $x^{(0)}$, let τ be desired residual accuracy, and let maxiter be an integer. Suppose these **preconditions** hold: the dimension of A is $n \times n$, b and $x^{(0)}$ have length n, $0 < n < 2^{32}$, $0 < $ maxiter $< 2^{32}$, all the elements of A, b, x, acc^2 (as well as the inverses of A's diagonal) are finite double-precision floating-point numbers; the data structures Alp,A2p,bp have read permission and xp has read/write permission. Suppose one calls jacobi2(Alp,A2p,bp,xp,acc,maxiter); then afterward it will satisfy this **postcondition:** the function will return some s and the array at xp will contain some $x^{(k)}$, such that $(s, x^{(k)}) \simeq$ jacobi $A\,b\,x\,\tau^2$, maxiter, where $\simeq$ is the floating-point equivalence relation and jacobi is our functional model in Coq of Jacobi iteration; and the data structures at Alp,A2p,bp will still contain their original values.*

8 The Main Theorems, Residuals, and Stopping Conditions

The C program jacobi2() (and its functional model jacobi) satisfies either of two different specifications:

Theorem 4 (above): if A, b, x satisfy the *basic preconditions*[1] then perhaps Jacobi iteration will return after maxiter iterations—having failed to converge—or might overflow to floating-point infinities and stop early. But even so, the result (s, y) will be such that the (squared) residual $s = |Ay - b|_2^2$ accurately characterizes the result-vector y: if y contains an ∞ then $s = \infty$, but if $\sqrt{s} < \tau$ then y is indeed a "correct" answer. That's because the *functional model* preserves infinities in this way, and the C program correctly implements the model.

Theorem 5: if A, b, x, maxiter satisfy the *Jacobi preconditions* then the result (s, y) will be such that $s = |Ay - b|_2^2$, and $\sqrt{s} < \tau$ and indeed y is a "correct" finite answer. In fact this is our main result:

Theorem 5 (main_jacobi). *If the inputs satisfy the Jacobi preconditions, then the C program will converge within k iterations to an accurate result.*

Proof. Using Theorems 3 and 4, with some additional reasoning about the stopping condition in the functional model of the C program.

---

[1] A an $n \times n$ matrix; b and x dimension n; $0 < n < 2^{32}$; A, b, x all finite; A, b, x stored in memory in the right places—but nothing else about the *values* of A, b, x.

Jacobi Iteration on Inputs Not Known to Satisfy the Jacobi Preconditions. Theorem 4 is useful on its own, since there are many useful applications of stationary iterative methods where one has not proved in advance the convergence conditions (e.g., Jacobi preconditions)—one just runs the program and tests the residual. For such inputs we must take care to correctly stop on overflow.

The induction hypothesis, for $0 < k \leq$ maxiter iterations, requires that x_k has not yet overflowed, otherwise our sparse-matrix reasoning cannot be proved (see Sect. 7.1). Therefore the program must check for floating-point overflow in x_k after each iteration. In order to do that efficiently, the program tests $s \otimes 0 = 0$ (which is a portable and efficient way of testing that s is finite); and if so, then x_{k+1} is all finite.

9   Related Work

Convergence of Jacobi Iteration. The standard error analysis for Jacobi iteration in exact arithmetic is well-described in standard books on iterative solvers [27]. A floating-point error analysis of Jacobi and related iterations was carried out by Higham and Knight in the early 90s [14], and is summarized along with references to related work in [13, Ch. 17]. The style of analysis is similar to what we present in this paper. However, earlier analyses implicitly assumed that all intermediates remain in the normalized floating-point range, and did not consider the possibility of underflow or overflow.

Formalization of numerical analysis has been facilitated by advancements in automatic and interactive theorem proving [7,11,23,25]. Some notable works in the formalization of numerical analysis are the formalization of Kantorovich theorem [26], matrix canonical forms by Cano et al. [9], Perron-Frobenius theorem in Isabelle/HOL [30], Lax–equivalence theorem for finite difference schemes [28], consistency, stability and convergence of a second-order centered scheme for the wave equation [5,6], formalized flows, Poincaré map of dynamical systems, and verified rigorous bounds on numerical algorithms in Isabelle/HOL [15–17]. However, these works do not study the problem of iterative convergence formally. Even though the iterative convergence has been formalized in exact arithmetic [29], the effect of rounding error on iterative convergence has not been formalized before.

End-to-End Machine-Checked Proofs. There are few truly end-to-end (C code to high-level accuracy) machine-checked formal proofs in the literature of numerical programs. Our approach has been to prove that a C program exactly implements a functional model (using VST), prove how accurately the functional model approximates a real-valued model, prove the accuracy of the real-valued model; and compose these results together. Something similar has been done for scalar Newton's method [2] and for ordinary differential equations [20], but those works did not leverage the power of the Mathematical Components and MathComp Analysis libraries for the upper-level proofs.

Other previous work [6] verified a C program implementing a second-order finite difference scheme for solving the one-dimensional acoustic wave equation, with a total error theorem in Coq that composes global round-off and discretization error bounds; this was connected (outside of Coq) to a Frama-C correctness proof of the C program. The inexpressiveness of Frama-C's assertion language was a challenge in that verification effort.

10   Conclusion and Future Work

In this paper, we have presented a formal proof in Coq of the correctness, accuracy, and convergence of Jacobi iteration in floating-point arithmetic. The same type of analysis should generalize to many other iterative methods, for both linear and nonlinear problems. Even within the scope of stationary iterations for linear problems, there are several avenues for future work.

We have not fully taken advantage of **sparseness** in our error bound; many of our $g_\delta(n)$ and $g_\epsilon(n)$ could be $g_\delta(s), g_\epsilon(s)$—functions of the number of nonzero elements per row. It would be useful to tighten the bound.

Jacobi iteration is one of the simplest stationary iterative methods. More complicated stationary methods involve splittings $A = M + N$, where M is **not a diagonal matrix**. Solving linear systems with such M is more complicated than diagonal scaling, and requires algorithms like forward and backward substitution that may require their own error analysis. Formalizing the floating-point error analysis of these solvers is an important next step.

Strict diagonal dominance is not a necessary condition for the convergence of Jacobi. We would like to formalize **other sufficient conditions for convergence** of Jacobi and related iterations. For example, irreducible diagonal dominance is sufficient for convergence of Jacobi in general, while positive definiteness is sufficient for convergence of Gauss-Seidel. However, while these conditions guarantee convergence, they do not guarantee an easy-to-compute *rate* of convergence in the same way that strict diagonal dominance does, and hence we expect the analysis to be more subtle.

Finally, we would like to extend our analysis to **mixed precision** methods, in which computations with M are done in one precision, while the residual is computed in a higher precision. These methods are often used to get errors associated with a higher floating-point precision while paying costs associated with a lower precision. However, the use of multiple precisions opens the door for a host of potential problems related to overflow and underflow, and we see formal verification as a particularly useful tool in this setting.

Efforts and Challenges: The formalization effort in this work includes about 1,826 lines of Coq proof script for C program verification and about 14,000 lines of Coq proof script for the convergence and accuracy proofs. A total of about 60 lines of C code were verified, which includes 12 lines for header files, 5 lines for surely_malloc, 14 lines of crs_row_vector_multiply, and about 31 lines for jacobi2 and jacobi2_oneiter. It took us about 5 person-months for the formalization of accuracy and convergence of the functional model. The most time-consuming part was the proof of absence of overflow, which involved deriving and formalizing bounds on the input conditions. The proof of correctness of C programs with respect to the functional model, including developing an understanding of what the termination condition should be, determining best ways to compute residuals such that the program properly detects overflow, developing functional models and proving properties about termination of the functional model took us about a couple of weeks.

The main challenge, in an end-to-end verification, is that each layer's theorem must be sufficiently strong to compose with the next layer. The published theorems about Jacobi convergence were insufficient (no treatment of underflow, error bounds relating the wrong quantities, no handling of -0, inadequate treatment of overflow), and new methods were required, which we address in this work.

Acknowledgement. We thank Yves Bertot for feedback on earlier drafts of this paper. This research was supported in part by NSF Grants CCF-2219997 and CCF-2219757, by a US Department of Energy Computational Science Fellowship DE-SC0021110, and by the Chateaubriand fellowship program.

References

1. Ahlberg, J.H., Nilson, E.N.: Convergence properties of the spline fit. J. Soc. Indust. Appl. Math. **11**, 95–104 (1963)
2. Appel, A.W., Bertot, Y.: C-language floating-point proofs layered with VST and Flocq. J. Formalized Reason. **13**(1), 1–16 (2020)
3. Appel, A.W., Kellison, A.E.: VCFloat2: floating-point error analysis in Coq (2022). https://github.com/VeriNum/vcfloat/blob/master/doc/vcfloat2.pdf
4. Barrett, R., et al.: Templates for the Solution of Linear Systems: Building Blocks for Iterative Methods. SIAM (1994)
5. Boldo, S., Clément, F., Filliâtre, J.C., Mayero, M., Melquiond, G., Weis, P.: Wave equation numerical resolution: a comprehensive mechanized proof of a C program. J. Autom. Reason. **50**(4), 423–456 (2013)
6. Boldo, S., Clément, F., Filliâtre, J.C., Mayero, M., Melquiond, G., Weis, P.: Trusting computations: a mechanized proof from partial differential equations to actual program. Comput. Math. Appl. **68**(3), 325–352 (2014)
7. Boldo, S., Lelay, C., Melquiond, G.: Coquelicot: a user-friendly library of real analysis for Coq. Math. Comput. Sci. **9**(1), 41–62 (2015)
8. Boldo, S., Melquiond, G.: Flocq: a unified library for proving floating-point algorithms in Coq. In: 2011 IEEE 20th Symposium on Computer Arithmetic, pp. 243–252. IEEE (2011)
9. Cano, G., Dénès, M.: Matrices à blocs et en forme canonique. In: Pous, D., Tasson, C. (eds.) JFLA - Journées francophones des langages applicatifs. Aussois, France (2013). https://hal.inria.fr/hal-00779376
10. Cao, Q., Beringer, L., Gruetter, S., Dodds, J., Appel, A.W.: VST-Floyd: a separation logic tool to verify correctness of C programs. J. Autom. Reason. **61**(1–4), 367–422 (2018)
11. Garillot, F., Gonthier, G., Mahboubi, A., Rideau, L.: Packaging mathematical structures. In: Berghofer, S., Nipkow, T., Urban, C., Wenzel, M. (eds.) TPHOLs

2009. LNCS, vol. 5674, pp. 327–342. Springer, Heidelberg (2009). https://doi.org/10.1007/978-3-642-03359-9_23

12. Gleich, D.F.: Pagerank beyond the web. SIAM Rev. **57**(3), 321–363 (2015)
13. Higham, N.J.: Accuracy and Stability of Numerical Algorithms. SIAM (2002)
14. Higham, N.J., Knight, P.A.: Componentwise error analysis for stationary iterative methods. In: Meyer, C.D., Plemmons, R.J. (eds.) Linear Algebra, Markov Chains, and Queueing Models, pp. 29–46. Springer, New York (1993). https://doi.org/10.1007/978-1-4613-8351-2_3
15. Immler, F.: A Verified ODE Solver and Smale's 14th Problem. Dissertation, Technische Universität München, München (2018)
16. Immler, F., Hölzl, J.: Numerical analysis of ordinary differential equations in Isabelle/HOL. In: Beringer, L., Felty, A. (eds.) ITP 2012. LNCS, vol. 7406, pp. 377–392. Springer, Heidelberg (2012). https://doi.org/10.1007/978-3-642-32347-8_26
17. Immler, F., Traut, C.: The flow of ODEs: formalization of variational equation and Poincaré map. J. Autom. Reason. **62**(2), 215–236 (2019)
18. Katz, L.: A new status index derived from sociometric analysis. Psychometrika **18**(1), 39–43 (1953)
19. Kellison, A., Tekriwal, M., Jeannin, J.B., Hulette, G.: Towards verified rounding error analysis for stationary iterative methods. In: 2022 IEEE/ACM Sixth International Workshop on Software Correctness for HPC Applications (Correctness), pp. 10–17 (2022). https://doi.org/10.1109/Correctness56720.2022.00007
20. Kellison, A.E., Appel, A.W.: Verified numerical methods for ordinary differential equations. In: 15th International Workshop on Numerical Software Verification (2022)
21. Kellison, A.E., Appel, A.W., Tekriwal, M., Bindel, D.: LAProof: a library of formal accuracy and correctness proofs for sparse linear algebra programs (2023). https://www.cs.princeton.edu/~appel/papers/LAProof.pdf
22. Mahboubi, A., Tassi, E.: Mathematical components. Online book (2021)
23. Martin-Dorel, É., Rideau, L., Théry, L., Mayero, M., Pasca, I.: Certified, efficient and sharp univariate Taylor models in Coq. In: 15th International Symposium on Symbolic and Numeric Algorithms for Scientific Computing, pp. 193–200. IEEE (2013)
24. McKenzie, L.: Matrices with dominant diagonals and economic theory. In: Arroa, K., Karlin, S., Puppes, S. (eds.) Mathematical Methods in the Social Sciences, pp. 47–60. Stanford University Press (1960)
25. O'Connor, R.: Certified exact transcendental real number computation in Coq. In: Mohamed, O.A., Muñoz, C., Tahar, S. (eds.) TPHOLs 2008. LNCS, vol. 5170, pp. 246–261. Springer, Heidelberg (2008). https://doi.org/10.1007/978-3-540-71067-7_21
26. Pasca, I.: Formal verification for numerical methods. Ph.D. thesis, Université Nice Sophia Antipolis (2010)
27. Saad, Y.: Iterative Methods for Sparse Linear Systems. SIAM (2003)
28. Tekriwal, M., Duraisamy, K., Jeannin, J.-B.: A formal proof of the lax equivalence theorem for finite difference schemes. In: Dutle, A., Moscato, M.M., Titolo, L., Muñoz, C.A., Perez, I. (eds.) NFM 2021. LNCS, vol. 12673, pp. 322–339. Springer, Cham (2021). https://doi.org/10.1007/978-3-030-76384-8_20
29. Tekriwal, M., Miller, J., Jeannin, J.B.: Formal verification of iterative convergence of numerical algorithms (2022). https://doi.org/10.48550/arXiv.2202.05587
30. Thiemann, R.: A Perron-Frobenius theorem for deciding matrix growth. J. Log. Algebraic Methods Program. 100699 (2021)

Multiple-Inheritance Hazards in Dependently-Typed Algebraic Hierarchies

Eric Wieser[⊠][iD]

Department of Engineering, University of Cambridge, Cambridge, UK
efw27@cam.ac.uk

Abstract. Abstract algebra provides a large hierarchy of properties that a collection of objects can satisfy, such as forming an abelian group or a semiring. These classifications can arranged into a broad and typically acyclic directed graph. This graph perspective encodes naturally in the typeclass system of theorem provers such as Lean, where nodes can be represented as structures (or records) containing the requisite axioms. This design inevitably needs some form of multiple inheritance; a ring is both a semiring and an abelian group.

In the presence of dependently-typed typeclasses that themselves consume typeclasses as type-parameters, such as a vector space typeclass which assumes the presence of an existing additive structure, the implementation details of structure multiple inheritance matter. The type of the outer typeclass is influenced by the path taken to resolve the typeclasses it consumes. Unless all possible paths are considered judgmentally equal, this is a recipe for disaster.

This paper provides a concrete explanation of how these situations arise (reduced from real examples in mathlib), compares implementation approaches for multiple inheritance by whether judgmental equality is preserved, and outlines solutions (notably: kernel support for η-reduction of structures) to the problems discovered.

Keywords: Dependent types · Multiple inheritance · Typeclasses · Formalization · mathlib

1 Introduction

It becomes clear very early in the development of mathematical libraries that a generalization over algebraic properties is essential; as soon as we are able to speak about $\mathbb{N}$ and $\mathbb{Z}$, we will want to have available that $a + b = b + a$ whether $a, b : \mathbb{N}$ or $a, b : \mathbb{Z}$, and it would be strongly preferable that we can refer to this property by a single name.

The generalization we seek is of course well-studied as the field of abstract algebra, and the commutativity property above can be phrased as "$\mathbb{N}$ and $\mathbb{Z}$ are both semirings", or using language more precise to the specific property we care about "$\mathbb{N}$ and $\mathbb{Z}$ are both abelian monoids". At least when considering only those

C. Dubois and M. Kerber (Eds.): CICM 2023, LNAI 14101, pp. 222–236, 2023.
https://doi.org/10.1007/978-3-031-42753-4_15

which operate on a single carrier type, algebraic structures can be connected into a directed graph; all rings are semirings and abelian groups, so we can draw a pair of edges from "ring" to "semiring" and "abelian group". An illustration of the depth and breadth of such a graph can be seen in [19, fig. 1], while a reduced example that we will use in this paper can be seen in Fig. 1.

Encoding this directed graph into the machinery of a particular theorem prover can be done in multiple ways, which are outlined in [3, §1] and presented with example code across a variety of languages in [6, fig. 1]. This paper focuses on the typeclass approach used by mathlib [19] in the Lean 3 theorem prover [14]; though the observations generalize to other implementations in dependent type theory built upon "structure" types.

In this approach, the graph is pruned to be acyclic, and then a typeclass is created for each node carrying its operators (data fields) and the properties they satisfy (proof fields). The edges correspond to functions converting from stronger structures to weaker structures, each registered as a typeclass instance. This encodes naturally in "record" or "structure" types with multiple inheritance, where we can write down the desired edges declaratively in the form of a list of base structures, and have the language generate the necessary "forgetful" instances automatically. A simple example of this can be found in [3, §4].

Unfortunately, the devil is in the details; in Lean, Coq, Agda, and Isabelle, support for multiple inheritance is not part of the underlying type theory, so types that use multiple inheritance have to be translated by the elaborator into inductive types that do not. There are multiple ways to perform such a translation, and the choice is not inconsequential.

In Sect. 2 we outline two such approaches, and show how they can each be used to construct a much-reduced version of mathlib's abstract algebra library. Section 3 introduces a more complex use of a typeclass from mathlib, and demonstrates how in the absence of special kernel support for η-reduction on structure types, its design is incompatible with "nested" approach to structures. Section 4 outlines some workarounds that permit the "nested" approach to be used even in the absence of this support. Section 5 explains how the problem is not unique to typeclass-based approaches.

The problems explored here are far from hypothetical; the migration of mathlib from Lean 3 to Lean 4 [15] forces a switch from the approach in Sect. 2.1 to that in Sect. 2.2, which has presented a significant stumbling block [5].

2   Types of Structure Inheritance

Lean 3 supports two types of structure inheritance: the default "new style", which we will refer to as "nested", and does not support multiple inheritance; and the legacy "old style" (enabled with **set_option** old_structure_cmd true) which we will refer to as "flat", and *does* support multiple inheritance. Lean 4 (as a language) does away with the "flat" mode, but extends the "nested" mode to support multiple inheritance.

To compare these approaches, this section demonstrates how to build the miniature algebraic hierarchy shown in Fig. 1. If we permit ourselves to use the

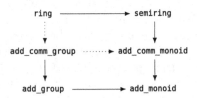

Fig. 1. A hierarchy of algebraic typeclasses, where arrows indicate a stronger typeclass implying a weaker typeclass. Dotted arrows correspond to the "non-preferred" typeclass paths which are relevant to Sect. 2.2.

```
class add_monoid (α : Type) :=
(zero : α) (add : α → α → α)
```

```
class add_comm_monoid (α : Type) extends add_monoid α
```

```
class semiring (α : Type) extends add_comm_monoid α :=
(one : α) (mul : α → α → α)
```

```
class add_group (α : Type) extends add_monoid α :=
(neg : α → α)
```

```
class add_comm_group (α : Type) extends add_group α, add_comm_monoid α
```

```
class ring (α : Type) extends semiring α, add_comm_group α
```

Listing 1: The hierarchy in Fig. 1 described using **extends** clauses.

builtin language support for multiple inheritance, we could write this as in listing 1. As they are not going to be relevant to the discussion in this paper, the proof fields such as one_mul : ∀ a : α, mul one a = a have all been omitted.

To avoid this paper being about a specific implementation of inheritance in a specific version of Lean, we will avoid the **extends** keyword, instead emulating it via different possible encodings of inheritance into regular structures. For simplicity this paper is largely presented as about Lean, but the supplemental repository referenced in Sect. 7 demonstrates how the Lean 3 samples presented here can be replicated in Coq[1] and in Lean 4[2].

2.1 Flat Structures

The "flat" approach to structure inheritance is to copy all of the fields from the base classes into the derived class. If multiple base classes share a field of the same name, then these fields are merged[3]. The forgetful instances are then implemented by unpacking all the relevant fields of the derived class and passing them to each base class constructor (which in Lean can be written as { ..derived }).

---

[1] Albeit somewhat non-idiomatically.

[2] At least, in old versions without pertinent fixes!.

[3] Unless they are of different types, which raises an error.

This can be seen for the toy example from listing 1 in listing 2a; `ring` extends both `semiring` and `add_comm_group`, so inherits the union of the four fields of `semiring` (`zero`, `add`, `one`, `mul`) and the three fields of `add_comm_group` (`zero`, `add`, `neg`). The `ring.to_semiring` and `ring.to_add_comm_group` instances generate constructor applications that reassemble the corresponding fields.

This approach is straightforward to implement in a theorem prover, and is the one used (via **set_option** old_structure_cmd true) in the majority of mathlib's algebraic hierarchy in Lean 3. A downside to this approach is that it can produce more work for unification (leading to poor performance) in long inheritance chains [3, §10].

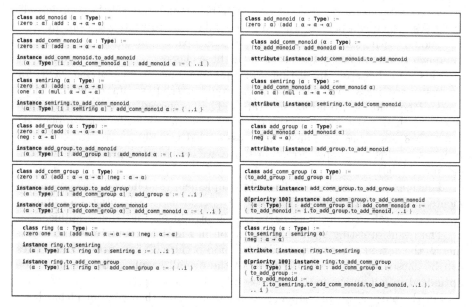

(a) The flat approach (Sect. 2.1), copying base fields to derived classes.

(b) The nested approach (Sect. 2.2), inserting the first parent as a field and copying the remaining fields.

Listing 2: Two approaches to implementing inheritance, by elaborating the **extends** clauses in listing 1 as the highlighted lines.

2.2   Nested Structures

A naïve approach to multiple inheritance for `ring` would be simply to create a structure containing a `to_semiring` field and a `to_add_comm_group` field. The problem with this approach is that the resulting structure contains two separate `add` fields. Compatibility of these fields could in principle be enforced with a proof field along the lines of `add_ok : to_semiring.add = to_add_comm_group.add`, but this makes the API very unpleasant to use as the user now has to rewrite between all the different copies of `add`.

The way to modify this approach to avoid this pitfall is to add a field for each base class that doesn't overlap with any previous base classes, otherwise fall back to the "flat" approach and add the non-overlapping fields directly. We call these non-overlapping base-classes "preferred" instances, as the projections for these fields can be registered directly with the typeclass system using **attribute** [**instance**] `derived.to_base`. What remains are the "non-preferred" instances, which can be constructed in a similar way to what was done in Sect. 2.1, though with somewhat messier expressions. Note that unlike Sect. 2.1, this approach is influenced by the order of the base classes.

This can be seen in listing 2b; `ring` contains a `to_semiring` field for its first base class, but `add_comm_group` would overlap so its remaining non-overlapping field (`neg`) is added separately. The "preferred" `ring.to_semiring` projection is then registered with the typeclass system, while the "non-preferred" `ring.to_add_comm_group` is painstakingly assembled piece-by-piece. To encourage Lean to avoid the "non-preferred" instance, we give it a low priority of 100 (the default is 1000).

This approach is more complicated to implement (and indeed, was not implemented in Lean until Lean 4), but can have performance advantages for unification as the "preferred" instance paths do not introduce a constructor application.

The result of listing 2b is that the graph in Fig. 1 is imbued with an asymmetry; the dotted edges are provided by "non-preferred" instances. These edges can be chosen on any spanning tree[4] of the overall graph, and indeed can be optimized to fall on the paths most used by the library [11].

For the purpose of this paper, the opposite is true; their placement has been pessimized to deliberately cause a failure, which we shall see in Sect. 3.2!

3   Typeclasses Depending on Typeclasses

In Sect. 2, we concerned ourselves with the typical examples of typeclasses which depend on a single type. In Lean, it is possible for typeclasses to depend not only on multiple types, but on typeclasses that constrain those types. A simple typeclass of this form is `module R M`, which is used to declare that given a semiring R and an abelian monoid M, there is an R-module structure on M. A more complete explanation of this typeclass can be found in [20] and [3, §5]. For the purpose of this paper, we can imagine the simpler definition as follows:

---

[4] In general this is a spanning diamond-free directed acyclic graph, but for this paper it suffices to consider a tree.

```
class module (R M : Type) [semiring R] [add_comm_monoid M] :=
(smul : R → M → M)
-- (one_smul : ∀ (x : M), smul 1 x = x)
-- (mul_smul : ∀ (r s : R) (x : M), smul (r * s) x = smul r (smul s x))
-- (add_smul : ∀ (r s : R) (x : M), smul (r + s) x = smul r x + smul s x)
-- (zero_smul : ∀ (x : M), smul 0 x = 0)
```

Here, the proof fields within the typeclass depend on the operators imbued upon the types R and M. Just as in Sect. 2, we shall ignore these proof fields as they are not relevant to the discussion other than providing motivation for the `[semiring R] [add_comm_monoid M]` parameters.

3.1 Equality of Typeclass Arguments

A natural use of this typeclass is to record the fact that any semiring is a module over itself, where the scalar action `smul` is just multiplication [20, §2.1]. This can be written in Lean as

```
instance semiring.to_module (R) [iS : semiring R] : module R R :=
{ smul := semiring.mul }
```

The type of this instance is misleading; while a human reader could be forgiven for assuming that the type is just `module R R`, to Lean the type is

```
@module R R iS (@semiring.to_add_comm_monoid R iS)
```

where `@` is syntax to tell Lean that even the automatically-populated typeclass arguments should be spelled out explicitly[5]. The expressions for these implicit arguments are visualized graphically in Fig. 2a.

Lean can now tell us that a *ring* is a module over itself, as after all every ring is also a semiring. We can ask this question with:

```
example (R) [iR : ring R] : module R R := by apply_instance
```

Once again, the type is misleading; the true type can be seen in Fig. 2b. Comparing the types for Fig. 2a and Fig. 2b, we see that the former unifies with the latter by setting `iS = @ring.to_semiring R iR`; for this reason, Lean finds our instance as `@semiring.to_module R (@ring.to_semiring R iR)`.

3.2 Inequality of Typeclass Arguments

Let's imagine now that we want to write a lemma that applies to a module over a ring (as opposed to a semi-module over a semiring), and states that $(-r)m = -(rm)$. We write this as[6]

---

[5] This style of display can be enabled with **set_option** pp.implicit true in Lean 3 and **set_option** pp.explicit true in Lean 4.

[6] Omitting the usual - and • notation to keep listing 2 short.

```
lemma neg_smul {R M} [ring R] [add_comm_group M] [module R M] (r : R) (m : M) :
  module.smul (add_group.neg r) m = add_group.neg (module.smul r m) := sorry
```

To complete our setup, let's check that this lemma applies to the R-module structure on R:

```
example {R} [iR : ring R] (r : R) (r' : R) :
  module.smul (add_group.neg r) r' = add_group.neg (module.smul r r') :=
neg_smul r r'
```

If we use the "flat" design in listing 2a, then this continues to work as expected. The same is not true of the "nested" design in listing 2b, which fails to synthesize type class instance for

```
@module R R (@ring.to_semiring R iR)
  (@add_comm_group.to_add_comm_monoid R (@ring.to_add_comm_group R iR))
```

which is shown graphically in Fig. 2c. The neg_smul lemma is an example of how typeclass resolution can be steered through a specific node of the graph in Fig. 1.

In Lean 3, the reason this fails is nothing to do with typeclass search; the problem is that the type in Fig. 2c is not equal to type in Fig. 2b, due to the implicit add_comm_monoid M arguments (shown in red) not being considered equal. Considerations of equality between the red paths in Fig. 2 and 2c are often referred to as a "typeclass diamonds" due to the shape they form when overlaid; though this is a rather more subtle diamond problems than the ones described in [20, §5] and [2, §3.1] as it is caused by code that would normally be invisible to the user.

To mathematicians, this diagram obviously commutes; weakening a ring to an abelian monoid via a semiring is the same as doing so via an abelian group. But Lean doesn't care about "obviously": when determining equality of types, it's not enough for them to just be *provably* the same; they need to be *definitionally* (sometimes called judgmentally) so. A proof of rfl can be used to determine if two terms are judgmentally equal; under listing 2b, we get an error confirming they are not:

```
example (R) [iR : ring R] :
  (@semiring.to_add_comm_monoid R (@ring.to_semiring R iR)) =
  (@add_comm_group.to_add_comm_monoid R (@ring.to_add_comm_group R iR)) :=
rfl -- fails in Lean 3 with listing 2b
```

3.3   Impact of the Inheritance Strategy

The rfl in Sect. 3.2 that fails under listing 2b but not listing 2a tells us that the nested inheritance is certainly to blame here. The underlying cause is the difference between the "preferred" and "non-preferred" paths.

The "non-preferred" edges in listing 2b are implemented directly as a constructor application via the { } syntax; so by virtue of following "non-preferred" edges, the red path in Fig. 2c unfolds to an application of the add_comm_monoid

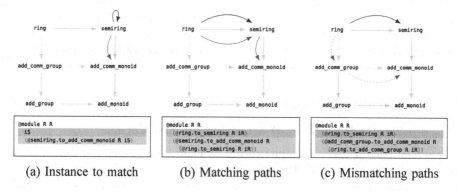

Fig. 2. Paths taken through the graph in Fig. 1 when filling the two implicit arguments of the type of module R R. Dotted lines again refer to "non-preferred" edges. (Color figure online)

constructor. The "preferred" edges correspond to a projection; unless applied to something that unifies against a constructor, these operations themselves do not unify against a constructor. As the red path in Fig. 2b consists of only "preferred" edges, it only unifies with this add_comm_monoid constructor if iR unifies with a ring constructor.

If iR is a concrete instance such as **instance** int.ring : ring $\mathbb{Z}$, then it will almost certainly unify with a ring constructor, and the overall unification problem is solvable. However if iR is a free variable, it will only unify with a constructor in systems which support "η-reduction for structures". Lean 3 is not such a system, which makes unification impossible.

3.4 Other Examples in mathlib

The module typeclass is far from the only typeclass in mathlib that follows the pattern introduced in Sect. 3; some others typeclasses (all of which fall afoul of the issue in Sect. 3.2) include

- algebra (R A : **Type**) [comm_semiring R] [semiring A], indicating that A is an R-algebras.
- star_ring (R : **Type**) [non_unital_semiring R], indicating that there is a ⋆ operator compatible with the existing ring structure on R.
- cstar_ring (R : **Type**) [non_unital_normed_ring R] [star_ring R], indicating that the existing norm, ⋆, and ring structure are suitable to declare R a C*-ring.

Like the module example, the design of the first of these is brought on by a need to work with two separate carrier types, and the need to avoid "dangerous instances" [3, §5.1].

The other two can be described as "mixin" typeclasses, and are motivated by a desire to avoid a combinatorial explosion of typeclass variations: an attempt at star_ring without mixins could easily end up needing all 16 variations of unital/non-unital commutative/non-commutative normed? star rings/fields. This motivation is largely a pragmatic one; the introduction of a tool like Coq's Hierarchy Builder [7] to mathlib would eliminate the cost of manually authoring such an explosion of typeclasses.

4   Mitigation Strategies

4.1   Perform η-Reduction of Structures in the Kernel

A key difference between the type theory of Lean 3 and Lean 4 is that Lean 4 adds a kernel reduction rule that η-reduces structures[7], which is precisely what we concluded we needed in Sect. 3.3. The following example demonstrates what this means:

```
structure point := (x y : ℤ)

-- fails in Lean 3, succeeds in Lean 4
example (p : point) : p = { x := p.x, y := p.y } := rfl
```

In essence, any value from a **structure** type is considered judgmentally equal to its constructor applied to its projections.

This feature was motivated by various "convenience" definitional equalities (as requested by [8]), such as wanting e.symm.symm = e for an equivalence e : α $\simeq$ β ; but in a thankful coincidence happens to be precisely the tool needed to resolve the trap in Sect. 3.2 that Lean 4 dropping support for "flat" structures would otherwise have ensnared us in. In particular, the Lean 4 version of the failing **example** ... := rfl above succeeds.

Until 2023-02-22, the structure η-reduction rule was disabled in Lean 4 during typeclass search; both due to performance concerns, and an absence of any evidence that it was necessary in the first place. As evidence mounted [5], a compromise was reached to unblock the Lean 4 version of mathlib that allowed it to be temporary enabled[8] in places where there was no other choice but taking the performance hit. After some unification performance improvements which are out of scope for this paper, this behavior was turned on globally on 2023-05-16 [9].

Lean 4 is not the only language to have taken an experimental approach to structural η; Coq supports it too, under the disabled-by-default Primitive Projections option. In contrast, Agda enables it by default for inductive types[9], but allows it to be disabled via no-eta-equality.

4.2   Use "Flat" Inheritance

The obvious approach to avoiding problems with "nested" inheritance is to simply not use it. Unfortunately, in the absence of elaborator support for translating

---

[7] Strictly speaking, it η-reduces **inductive** types with one constructor; **structures** are not native to the type theory of Lean, and instead just syntax for generating a suitable inductive type.

[8] Via **set_option** synthInstance.etaExperiment true.

[9] Some motivating discussion can be found in [1].

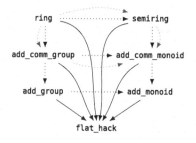
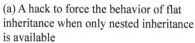
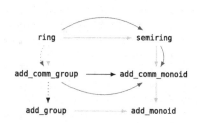

(a) A hack to force the behavior of flat inheritance when only nested inheritance is available

(b) A variant of fig. 1 formed by swapping the two black arrows, that prevents the problem in fig. 2c.

Fig. 3. Alternate placements of the "preferred" spanning tree, with the diamond discussed in Fig. 2 overlaid in red (Color figure online).

a variation of listing 1 into listing 2a (such as in Lean 4) this would have to be done by hand, which can be rather tedious and error-prone.

There is however a trick; since the elaborator can translate listing 1 into listing 2b, we can construct a pathological graph such that all the edges we care about are forced to be "non-preferred". We do this by adding an empty flat_hack structure as the first base class of every structure, which ensures that the base classes always overlap (due to the to_flat_hack field), and so the only "preferred" base class is the unused to_flat_hack projection. The spanning tree of "preferred" base classes across all such typeclasses is a star with flat_hack at its center, as shown in Fig. 3a.

This forces all the typeclass resolution to go through the "non-preferred" paths, which behave identically to their "flat" counterparts by unfolding to a constructor application.

4.3 Carefully Select "Preferred" Paths

In Sect. 2.2, we mention that the choice of where to place the spanning tree of "preferred" paths could be optimized for performance. In light of Sect. 3.2, we could instead attempt to optimize to ensure that the problematic diamonds never arise. Indeed, there are many arrangements of the "preferred" paths in Fig. 1 that do not run into the *specific example* in Fig. 2c, such as Fig. 3b.

For our purposes, an adequate rule for why the red arrows of Fig. 3 commute but the ones of Fig. 2 do not is that the paths commute only if their last segments are either both "preferred" (as in Fig. 3b) or both "non-preferred" (as in Fig. 3a).

As discussed in [12] and visualized in Fig. 4, it is not in general possible to choose a spanning tree for a set of 8 typeclasses arranged in a cube, while simultaneously making the pairs of paths around each face commute. This can be adapted into a working solution by inserting extra nodes in the style of Sect. 4.2's flat_hack to force some additional paths to be "non-preferred", but this is far from an elegant solution.

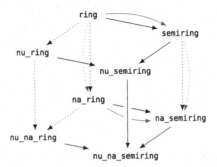

Fig. 4. An algebraic hierarchy where no spanning tree placement can ensure all squares commute, shown with one such inadequate spanning tree. The red paths highight the one square that does not commute. na and nu are abbreviated from mathlib's non_unital and non_assoc(iative). (Color figure online)

4.4 Ban Non-root Structures in Dependent Arguments

The problem in Sect. 3.2 is caused by a typeclass argument to a typeclass being inferable both via "preferred" and "non-preferred" routes. In Sect. 4.2, this can be worked around by ensuring every path is maximally "non-preferred". An alternative is to ensure that every path is "preferred", by only accepting typeclass arguments that appear as roots of the spanning subgraph. This could look like

```
class module (R M : Type)
  [has_zero R] [has_add R] [has_one R] [has_mul R]
  [has_zero M] [has_add M] :=
(smul : R → M → M)
-- (one_smul : ∀ (x : M), smul 1 x = x)
-- (mul_smul : ∀ (r s : R) (x : M), smul (r * s) x = smul r (smul s x))
-- (add_smul : ∀ (r s : R) (x : M), smul (r + s) x = smul r x + smul s x)
-- (zero_smul : ∀ (x : M), smul 0 x = 0)
```

where each of the operators for *R* and *M* is taken as a separate typeclass argument.

This approach has two main downsides: it results in larger proof terms, because now it has 6 typeclass arguments instead of four, which have to be resolved all the way down to the smallest typeclass instead of stopping part-way along the graph; and it doesn't extend to cases where not just the data fields carrying the operators on the type arguments, but also the proof fields carrying their properties, are needed to define the fields of the dependent typeclass.

5 Implications for Packed Structures

Up until this point we have focused only on typeclasses, as these are (at the time of this paper) the idiomatic way to represent algebraic structure in Lean. While Coq also supports typeclasses, and the previous examples can be faithfully reproduced in it, this is not the idiomatic way to do things in MathComp.

Instead, Coq's "Hierarchy builder" [7, §4] generates "packed" structures [10] with a field for the type itself, rather than consuming the type as a parameter. These structures are then ineligible for typeclass search, but can be located automatically via "canonical structures" (or as they are known in Lean, "unification hints") instead. These can in fact be built on top of the typeclasses from Sect. 2.1 or Sect. 2.2:

```
structure packed_semiring := (carrier : Type) [semiring carrier]
structure packed_add_comm_monoid := (carrier : Type) [add_comm_monoid carrier]
```

A naïve encoding of a module in this packed view would be:

```
structure packed_module :=
(R : packed_semiring) (M : packed_add_comm_monoid) [module R.carrier M.carrier]
```

As `packed_module` has no parameters and is therefore not dependently-typed, it cannot fall afoul of the problem in Sect. 3.2.

Unfortunately, this encoding is effectively useless mathematically [18, §3]; we have no way to talk about two modules over the same ring without something involving equality of types and operators[10] like (V W : packed_module) (hVW : V.R = W.R); a much worse version of the duplicate `add` fields described at the start of Sect. 2.2.

A more reasonable representation that avoids this problem is to only partially pack the structure, as

```
structure packed_module (R : packed_semiring) :=
(M : packed_add_comm_monoid M) [module R.carrier M.carrier]
```

which allows (V W : packed_module R). This is roughly analogous to the approach taken in Coq's MathComp [13] and in mathlib's category theory library.

While this representation avoids the *specific* problem in Sect. 3.2 due to its type not depending on the `add_comm_monoid` path (the red arrows in Fig. 2), it is nonetheless dependently-typed. This make it vulnerable to an analogous problem where the diamond is instead formed by the `semiring` path (the blue arrows in Fig. 2) after adding two new `comm_semiring` and `comm_ring` nodes.

Fortunately for MathComp, the "Hierarchy builder" uses *flat* packed structures[11], and so avoids these issues for the same reason that flat typeclasses do in Sect. 3.1.

---

[10] Or alternatively, by packing the ring and both modules into a single structure, as (VW : packed_module$_2$) (v : VW.1) (w : VW.2). This is a viable approach for a module over two rings (as rarely are many rings needed), but doesn't scale for n modules over the same ring.

[11] Presumably due to simplicity of implementation; there is no mention in [7] that using nested inheritance instead would have run into the issues described here.

6   Related Work

While this work is of course directly related to the work of porting Lean 3's mathlib to Lean 4, the lessons here are transferable to Coq (where [7] seemingly correctly chose to use flat structures by coincidence) and Agda (which has adopted structure η-reduction globally due to other motivations [1]); even if only to provide further understanding of why the respective choices that have already been made in those systems are the correct ones. To the author's awareness, no previously demonstrated *algebraic* motivations have been given for η-reduction in the kernel. Some in-depth analysis of "coherence" in algebraic typeclass paths is provided by [17, definition 3.3] (another name for our comparison in Fig. 2), but it does not provide an example to show *why* η-reduction specifically should be assumed.

The analysis in Sects. 3 and 4 is only relevant to systems that use dependent type theory, as concerns of equalities between the values of type parameters cannot arise in a language that does not permit those parameters in the first place. The Isabelle proof assistant which uses simple type theory is therefore immune to this class of problem; and at any rate [4, §5.4] advocates avoiding its record types entirely for algebraic structure, in favor of using locales.

Algebraic hierarchies certainly do not only exist in proof assistants; they are an essential part of computer algebra systems too. However, most computer algebra systems do not make use of dependent types [16, §1], with a notable exception being the Axiom Library Compiler, Aldor. Despite supporting dependent types, the type system of Aldor is too restrictive for Sects. 3 and 4 to be relevant. Aldor does not implement definitional equality of types (referred to as "value-equality" by [16, §2.4]), and so falls at a much earlier hurdle than the one in Sect. 3; it does not consider Vector(2+3) and Vector(5) to be the same type [16, §2.3], meaning that even Fig. 2b would be considered a mismatch, and *every* square in Fig. 4 would not commute.

This work focuses on how a seemingly innocuous implementation detail can be crucial to ensuring the success of *existing* approaches to algebraic hierarchies in dependently-typed proof assistants. The broader analysis of these hierarchies, and possible alternative designs (for which computer algebra systems can provide inspiration), is left to [3, 6, 7, 18].

7   Conclusion

In this paper we have shown that for the "nested" approach to multiple inheritance to be viable in the context of dependently-typed typeclasses or packed structures, either we have to severely restrict how such inheritance is used (Sects. 4.2 to 4.4), or the kernel of the theorem prover must implement η-reduction for structures (Sect. 4.1).

This scenario was a major stumbling block for mathlib's transition from Lean 3 to Lean 4, as typeclasses of this form are used extensively in linear algebra. This paper provides a clear explanation of exactly what was going wrong, and a selection of various solutions that were considered before ultimately settling on the kernel change.

The code examples throughout this paper, along with translations into Lean 4 and Coq, and the version information needed to run them, can be found at https://github.com/eric-wieser/lean-multiple-inheritance.

Acknowledgments. The author is grateful to: Gabriel Ebner, for campaigning for η-reduction support in Lean 4; Kazuhiko Sakaguchi, for providing insight into analogous situations in Coq; the anonymous referees, as well as Yaël Dillies and Filippo A. E. Nuccio, for valuable feedback on the manuscript; and the wider Lean community for collaboratively diagnosing [5] that the diamond problems discussed in Sect. 3.2 existed. The author is funded by a scholarship from the Cambridge Trust.

References

1. Abel, A.: On Extensions to Definitional Equality in Agda (2009). https://www.cse.chalmers.se/~abela/talkAIM09.pdf
2. Affeldt, R., Cohen, C., Kerjean, M., Mahboubi, A., Rouhling, D., Sakaguchi, K.: Competing inheritance paths in dependent type theory: a case study in functional analysis. In: Peltier, N., Sofronie-Stokkermans, V. (eds.) IJCAR 2020. LNCS (LNAI), vol. 12167, pp. 3–20. Springer, Cham (2020). https://doi.org/10.1007/978-3-030-51054-1_1
3. Baanen, A.: Use and abuse of instance parameters in the Lean mathematical library. In: ITP 2022, Haifa, Israel (2022). https://arxiv.org/abs/2202.01629
4. Ballarin, C.: Exploring the structure of an algebra text with locales. J. Autom. Reason. **64**(6), 1093–1121 (2019). https://doi.org/10.1007/s10817-019-09537-9
5. Buzzard, K.: leanprover/lean4#2074: typeclass inference failure (2023). https://github.com/leanprover/lean4/issues/2074
6. Carette, J., Farmer, W.M., Sharoda, Y.: Leveraging the information contained in theory presentations. In: Benzmüller, C., Miller, B. (eds.) CICM 2020. LNCS (LNAI), vol. 12236, pp. 55–70. Springer, Cham (2020). https://doi.org/10.1007/978-3-030-53518-6_4
7. Cohen, C., Sakaguchi, K., Tassi, E.: Hierarchy builder: algebraic hierarchies made easy in Coq with Elpi (system description). In: Ariola, Z.M. (ed.) 5th International Conference on Formal Structures for Computation and Deduction (FSCD 2020). Leibniz International Proceedings in Informatics (LIPIcs), vol. 167, pp. 34:1–34:21. Schloss Dagstuhl-Leibniz-Zentrum für Informatik, Dagstuhl, Germany (2020). https://doi.org/10.4230/LIPIcs.FSCD.2020.34. ISSN 1868-8969
8. Ebner, G.: leanprover/lean4#777: Definitional eta for structures (2021). https://github.com/leanprover/lean4/issues/777
9. Ebner, G.: leanprover/lean4#2210: Skip proof arguments during unification, and try structure eta last (2023). https://github.com/leanprover/lean4/pull/2210
10. Garillot, F., Gonthier, G., Mahboubi, A., Rideau, L.: Packaging mathematical structures. In: Berghofer, S., Nipkow, T., Urban, C., Wenzel, M. (eds.) TPHOLs 2009. LNCS, vol. 5674, pp. 327–342. Springer, Heidelberg (2009). https://doi.org/10.1007/978-3-642-03359-9_23
11. Gouëzel, S.: leanprover-community/mathlib4#3840: tweak priorities for linear algebra (2023). https://github.com/leanprover-community/mathlib4/pull/3840

12. Gouëzel, S.: #mathlib4 Some observations on eta experiment (2023). https://leanprover.zulipchat.com/#narrow/stream/287929-mathlib4/topic/Some.20observations.20on.20eta.20experiment/near/355336941

13. Mahboubi, A., Tassi, E.: Mathematical Components (2022). https://zenodo.org/record/7118596. Zenodo Version Number: 1.0.2

14. de Moura, L., Kong, S., Avigad, J., van Doorn, F., von Raumer, J.: The lean theorem prover (system description). In: Felty, A.P., Middeldorp, A. (eds.) CADE 2015. LNCS (LNAI), vol. 9195, pp. 378–388. Springer, Cham (2015). https://doi.org/10.1007/978-3-319-21401-6_26

15. Moura, L., Ullrich, S.: The lean 4 theorem prover and programming language. In: Platzer, A., Sutcliffe, G. (eds.) CADE 2021. LNCS (LNAI), vol. 12699, pp. 625–635. Springer, Cham (2021). https://doi.org/10.1007/978-3-030-79876-5_37

16. Poll, E., Thompson, S.: Integrating computer algebra and reasoning through the type system of Aldor. In: Kirchner, H., Ringeissen, C. (eds.) FroCoS 2000. LNCS (LNAI), vol. 1794, pp. 136–150. Springer, Heidelberg (2000). https://doi.org/10.1007/10720084_10

17. Sakaguchi, K.: Validating mathematical structures. In: Peltier, N., Sofronie-Stokkermans, V. (eds.) IJCAR 2020. LNCS (LNAI), vol. 12167, pp. 138–157. Springer, Cham (2020). https://doi.org/10.1007/978-3-030-51054-1_8

18. Spitters, B., Van Der Weegen, E.: Type classes for mathematics in type theory. Math. Struct. Comput. Sci. **21**(4), 795–825 (2011). https://doi.org/10.1017/S0960129511000119

19. The mathlib Community: The lean mathematical library. In: Proceedings of the 9th ACM SIGPLAN International Conference on Certified Programs and Proofs, New Orleans, LA, USA, pp. 367–381. ACM (2020). https://doi.org/10.1145/3372885.3373824

20. Wieser, E.: Scalar actions in Lean's mathlib. In: CICM 2021, Timisoara, Romania (2021). https://arxiv.org/abs/2108.10700

CoProver: A Recommender System for Proof Construction

Eric Yeh[(⊠)], Briland Hitaj, Sam Owre, Maena Quemener,
and Natarajan Shankar

SRI International, Menlo Park, CA 94025, USA
{eric.yeh,briland.hitaj,sam.owre,maena.quemener,
natarajan.shankar}@sri.com

Abstract. Interactive Theorem Provers (ITPs) are an indispensable tool in the arsenal of formal method experts as a platform for construction and (formal) verification of proofs. The complexity of the proofs in conjunction with the level of expertise typically required for the process to succeed can often hinder the adoption of ITPs. A recent strain of work has investigated methods to incorporate machine learning models trained on ITP user activity traces as a viable path towards full automation. While a valuable line of investigation, many problems still require human supervision to be completed fully, thus applying learning methods to assist the user with useful recommendations can prove more fruitful. Following the vein of user assistance, we introduce CoProver, a proof recommender system based on transformers, capable of learning from past actions during proof construction, all while exploring knowledge stored in the ITP concerning previous proofs. CoProver employs a neurally learnt sequence-based encoding of sequents, capturing long distance relationships between terms and hidden cues therein. We couple CoProver with the Prototype Verification System (PVS) and evaluate its performance on two key areas, namely: (1) Next Proof Action Recommendation, and (2) Relevant Lemma Retrieval given a library of theories. We evaluate CoProver on a series of well-established metrics originating from the recommender system and information retrieval communities, respectively. We show that CoProver successfully outperforms prior state of the art applied to recommendation in the domain. We conclude by discussing future directions viable for CoProver (and similar approaches) such as argument prediction, proof summarization, and more.

1 Introduction

Interactive theorem proving (ITP) is a well-entrenched technology for formalizing proofs in mathematics, computing, and several other domains. While ITP tools provide powerful automation and customization, the task of manually guiding the theorem prover toward QED is still an onerous one. For inexperienced users, this challenge translates to crafting mathematically elegant formalizations, identifying suitable proof commands, and diagnosing the root cause of failed proof attempts. Whereas for the expert users, the challenge consists in navigating a large body of formalized content to ferret out the useful definitions and the right

© The Author(s), under exclusive license to Springer Nature Switzerland AG 2023
C. Dubois and M. Kerber (Eds.): CICM 2023, LNAI 14101, pp. 237–251, 2023.
https://doi.org/10.1007/978-3-031-42753-4_16

lemmas. Both novice and expert users can benefit from recommendations in the form of proof commands and lemma retrieval that can guide proof construction.

The goal of the present project is to scale up proof technology by introducing CoProver as a proof recommender system that discerns suitable cues from the libraries, the proof context, and the proof goal to offer recommendations for ITP users. Building on the proof technology and proof corpora of the Prototype Verification System (PVS) a state-of-the-art proof assistant [37], we focus on recommendations for two key tasks in ITP: Suggesting PVS commands and lemmas. The first is to recommend the likely command an expert user would take given the current proof state. As the number of possible commands can number over 100, recommending steps an expert may take would be beneficial, particularly for novices. The second is to identify lemmas for inclusion from a library of lemmas that may help with forward progress on a proof. Currently, only lemmas from user-imported theories are considered and selection of a lemma relies on user familiarity with candidate theories and their lemmas. For the problems PVS is commonly employed on, there are usually several hundred theories with thousands of possible lemmas combined to consider. At this scale, even expert users with decades of experience may not be aware of all possible lemmas (or even their names) that may be relevant for their proof. A mechanism that can automatically identify relevant lemmas at scale would be desirable.

To develop these capabilities, we leverage the expert proof traces for NASA's PVS Library[1] (PVSLib), a large collection of highly polished formal developments centered on safety-critical applications, and the PVS Prelude, a collection of theories built into PVS. We aim to capture the expertise and intuition of the developers by training systems to emulate user decisions on these completed proofs. Key to our approach is the use of recent machine learning techniques that can capture sequential information across a greater window than previously possible. We show how these methods using a simple sequence-based encoding of formulas better capture relationships between proof states with commands and libraries than prior sequence encoding techniques such as bag-of-words or graph-based representations [47].

We start with an overview in Sect. 2 of the CoProver system, describing the core recommendation tasks. Section 3 contains implementation details of how sequents and states are featurized into a common representation used to provide inputs for the command prediction and lemma retrieval capabilities. Sections 4 and 5 provide specific details of how these are implemented, along with experiments detailing their effectiveness described in Sect. 6. Section 7 examines and contrasts against prior work, and Sect. 8 concludes with a discussion of future directions.

2   CoProver Overview

Figure 1 illustrates the CoProver system. Featurization converts the sequent and previous commands into a token sequence for the transformer model.

---

[1] https://shemesh.larc.nasa.gov/fm/pvs/PVS-library/.

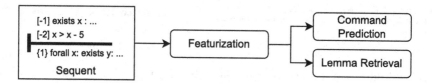

Fig. 1. The CoProver system employs a common sequent featurization, which is used to recommend commands and retrieve relevant lemmas.

This is provided to the Command Prediction and Lemma Retrieval modules. Command Prediction identifies the next likely command an expert user would take in successful proofs, given similar states. When a lemma is to be imported, Lemma Retrieval examines the state and suggests the most relevant ones from a given library, based off a history of human-selected lemmas that have progressed their proofs.

Both of these use RoBERTa [30], a transformers-based neural language model [46] capable of learning long-range sequences, to encode the proof state sequence tokens. Unlike n-grams or other Markov window methods, transformers employ a self-attention mechanism that allows features to derived from a significantly wider window of tokens. Tokens are represented as real-valued vectors tailored as inputs for a variety of tasks, and have been used to give state-of-the-art performance across multiple tasks such as large language modeling, text classification, and visual understanding. For command prediction, the RoBERTa-based encoding of the proof state is used as input to a multinomial classifier for predicting the next command an expert user would take. Backpropagated error from the classifier is used to adjust, or to *fine-tune* these representations make them more suitable for the classification task.

Lemma retrieval aims to make forward progress in a proof by identifying relevant lemmas from a library of theories for inclusion. A major challenge is the fact these lemmas may exist in theories that the user is not aware of, nor remember. This is similar to the core problem of information retrieval (IR) [33], where the goal is to retrieve documents from a collection most relevant to a query. IR models rely on heuristics motivated by natural language, such as overlap and term rarity to assess relevance. These assumptions may not hold in theorem-proving, so CoProver is trained on user-made lemma import decisions to fine-tune the proof state representations to learn combinations of sequent and lemma symbols useful for identifying lemma relevance. This focus on human-driven selection also differs from other work in premise selection, where the primary aim is to identify lemmas that allow a hammer to automatically complete the proof.

3   Data Generation

For both command prediction and lemma retrieval, we used proof sequences from the PVSLib library, a large set of formal developments containing theorems

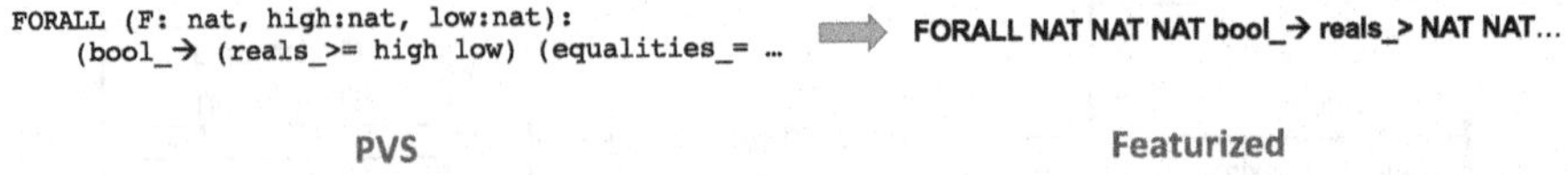

```
FORALL (F: nat, high:nat, low:nat):          FORALL NAT NAT NAT bool_→ reals_> NAT NAT...
   (bool_→ (reals_>= high low) (equalities_= ...
```

PVS   Featurized

Fig. 2. Featurization converts formulas in PVS (left) into a more machine learning friendly token stream (right).

proofs for a variety of mathematical and engineering areas. In total PVSLib contains $184,335$ proof steps. We note that these are completed and polished proofs so that backtracked sequences of steps are pared and only the successful sequence of proof commands and imported lemmas are retained.

To make the logical formulas amenable to machine learning, we first tokenize them and then use Byte Pair Encoding (BPE) [11,43] from the Huggingface Library [49] to train a token vocabulary customized for PVS. BPE encodes words as a sequences of byte pairs instead of singular tokens, reducing the size of the vocabulary: Rare or unknown words can be encoded as constituent byte pairs, while common words are encoded in their entirety to improve efficiency. Transformer models have fixed width inputs, so a more parsimonious encoding that strips away boilerplate while retaining the original semantics will allow longer formulas to work without truncating them. For this work, we used a window of $1,000$ tokens, which was sufficient to capture the majority of the sequents and lemmas in our experiments. Given this, all symbol names for functions and operators are copied over as-is. Constant and variable names are replaced by a placeholder, to generalize the model, while integer values are retained. Syntactic constructs such as parentheses are excluded as the ordering of the above can roughly capture the syntactic arrangement of the original form. Figure 2 provides an example: Symbols such as the FORALL quantifier and implication operator are preserved, while the variables F, HIGH, and LOW are replaced with their type, NAT representing the natural numbers.

Following common practice in transformer-based encodings, we use special tokens <ANT>, <CONS>, and <HID> to delimit the antecedent, consequent, and hidden formulas (formulas reserved from being operated on by PVS commands). The lefthand side of Fig. 3 gives an example of a featurized sequent with no antecedents and one consequent.

Our current setup makes the Markov assumption, that only the current state is sufficient for making our predictions. At least anecdotally knowing which commands were performed can inform what steps are taken next, so incorporating previous commands can capture some non-Markovian information. This is done by prefixing the state representation with the previous three commands issued by the user.

For the lemma retrieval experiments, we modified the above procedure to allow constant and variables to be replaced with their type name. This was done to allow matching by type, as arguments for imported lemmas also need to match by type. Higher-order and custom types are currently represented by placeholders. Accounting for matches on higher-order types and on advanced type operations such as predicate-based approaches is reserved for future work.

As with other transformers-based works, the model is first trained using a series of self-supervised tasks, where supervised targets are generated from unabeled data. Masked language modeling is one such task, where random tokens are masked and the model is trained to predict its identity [8]. By conducting this type of self-supervised training on a large corpus, the resulting representations can capture distributional information about the domain that makes training downstream components easier. For our experiments, the language model was trained for $1,100,000$ steps[2] over our dataset, using the default set of self-supervised language tasks used by RoBERTa.

We note that some works start from a model trained on natural language, in order to capture correspondences based on human naming. In our experience this applies for tasks where wider distributional knowledge of natural language is required to perform the main task. At least for PVS and our tasks, the structure of the formulas tends to be more important. Examination of the effect of human language understanding is also reserved for future investigation.

4   Command Prediction

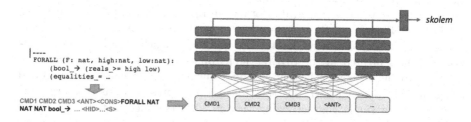

Fig. 3. The process for featurizing a sequent and then using repeated self-attention to create representations capturing information for predicting the next command.

Command prediction's task is to predict the command an expert would take given the current step in the proof. We use the T5 sequence to sequence training framework [39] implemented in Huggingface [49], with the RoBERTa encoding of the proof state used as input to predict the user selected command (Fig. 3. The sequent and command history are tokenized and converted into classification-suitable vector representations via repeated applications of self-attention. These are then integrated by the classifier to emit predicted command. The top-N most confident hypotheses can be emitted, allowing for a window of predictions to be

---

[2] A step is a single forward-predict pass over a training instance, and multiple steps can be performed over the same data during the training phase.

generated. We note that as with other ITPs, PVS allows users to program their own commands. For this work, we focus on the closed set of existing commands, leaving the program synthesis aspect for future work.

5   Lemma Retrieval

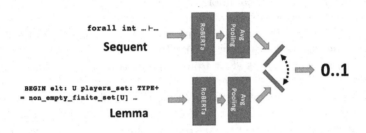

Fig. 4. Siamese architecture used to determine whether a lemma is relevant to a given sequent.

Following the information retrieval approach, the proof state acts as a query against a library of available lemmas. We use user imported lemmas in PVS-lib proof traces to train a neural information retrieval model [35], which learns the best combination of features between sequents and lemmas to assess lemma relevance. Figure 4 our lemma retrieval approach, which uses a Siamese Network [6] implemented in the SBERT [40] framework to score the relevance of a lemma to the sequent. The lemma and sequent token sequences are encoded using RoBERTa encoder to construct token-level representations that are averaged to give a single characterizing vector. The relevance of the lemma and sequent vectors is scored using cosine similarity, with 0 indicating no relevance and 1 indicating maximal relevance. The representation is tuned for the similarity task with supervised training over known relevant and irrelevant pairs. These approach scales well as the bulk of the representations can be pre-computed, and has been used to learn ranking functions for tasks with a large amount of data, such as using clickthrough data [18].

6   Experiments and Results

6.1   Command Prediction

From the full PVSLib library of proofs, we subsampled 20,000 proof steps to create a tractable command prediction training set[3]. From these we randomly sampled 90% of these for the training data, and used the remaining 10% as a

---

[3] Initial experiments with larger samples showed no difference in performance with a system trained with the smaller set.

held out test-set. We trained for 10 epochs on four NVIDIA GeForce RTX 3090 cards using distributed data parallel training (DDP) [28] implemented using PyTorch Lightning[4], selecting the model with the best validation error. We follow prior literature on tactic prediction [13] and used classifiers trained over term-frequency inverse document frequency (TF-IDF) [23,32] weighted feature counts of the CoProver featurized tokenization observed in the sequent for our baseline. TF-IDF incorporates frequency of occurrence of a term and its distinguishability against the backdrop of the entire collection. We experimented with multiple classifiers to strengthen this baseline: Linear support vector classifier (Linear SVC), support vector machines using a radial basis kernel (RBF) and one using a polynomial kernel (Poly), and a k-nearest neighbor classifier (k-NN). We used the Scikit-Learn[5] implementations with default parameters. For the k-nearest neighbor classifier, we used a distance weighted variant with $n = 5$ following prior literature [13].

Table 1. Command prediction test accuracies by method and combinations of sequent and command history information.

Method	Acc. cmdhist + sequent	Acc., sequent only	Acc., cmdhist only
Linear SVC	$0.30 \pm 1.1 \times 10^{-2}$	$0.20 \pm 9.1 \times 10^{-3}$	$0.30 \pm 1.1 \times 10-2$
SVM (RBF)	$0.29 \pm 1.0 \times 10^{-2}$	$0.22 \pm 9.5 \times 10^{-3}$	$0.30 \pm 1.0 \times 10^{-2}$
SVM (Poly)	$0.20 \pm 8.9 \times 10^{-3}$	$0.20 \pm 8.9 \times 10^{-3}$	$0.22 \pm 1.0 \times 10^{-2}$
k-NN	$0.28 \pm 1.0 \times 10^{-2}$	$0.19 \pm 8.6 \times 10^{-3}$	$0.27 \pm 9.6 \times 10^{-3}$
CoProver	$\mathbf{0.48 \pm 7.3 \times 10^{-3}}$	$0.28 \pm 9.8 \times 10^{-3}$	$0.21 \pm 9.3 \times 10^{-3}$

Table 1 shows the test command predication accuracy for each of the methods on different combinations of the sequent and the command history. We find that CoProver predictions are more significantly more accurate when the full sequent and command histories are used. Most of baseline performance is from the command history, whereas CoProver is able to integrate the sequent and command history together to score significantly better than the next-best baseline, k-NN. Variances for each method were estimated using bootstrap resampling [9] and significance was determined using a two-sample t-test with $\alpha = 0.001$.

To assess the significance of structural information, we tested with TF-IDF sequent featurizations of increasing maximum n-gram degree, where a n-gram featurization consists of all symbol sequences of length n. Table 2 shows the accuracies for each classification method by the maximum n-gram degree. With the exception of the SVM using the polynomial kernel (SVM Poly), every method benefits from increasing structural information. We suspect that model's poorer performance may be due to the greater number of hyperparameters given the polynomial kernel, which greatly increases the risk of overfitting on sparse data [16].

---

[4] https://www.pytorchlightning.ai/.
[5] https://scikit-learn.org/.

Table 2. Command prediction accuracy for baseline methods using features that incorporate more structural information (left to right).

Method	n=1	n=2	n=3
Linear SVC	0.30	0.37	0.30
SVM (RBF)	0.29	0.32	0.33
SVM (Poly)	0.20	0.18	0.19
k-NN	0.28	0.30	0.32

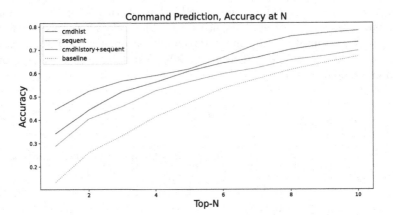

Fig. 5. Command prediction test accuracies by method, with and without command history information.

Recommender systems often present the top N-most relevant predictions, as users can usually scan a set of candidates. To assess performance in this regime, we score the top-N test set accuracy, where matches are made if the correct prediction is within the top N predictions. Figure 5 shows CoProver accuracy at different sizes of N using just the command history (cmdhist), sequent (sequent) and both (cmdhist+sequent) for N ranging from 1 to 10. As baseline we use the top-N most frequent commands in the training set as the candidate window. We find combining the sequent and command history information gives consistently higher accuracy than using either alone, while all methods outperform the baseline.

6.2   Lemma Retrieval

For lemma retrieval, we examined PVSLib traces where users imported lemmas using the lemma command. While other commands also import lemmas, this is done implicitly and not a user-driven decision. From these $20,221$ imports, $12,132$ were randomly selected for training, with $8,089$ for testing. These reference both PVSLib and PVS Prelude, giving $9,468$ candidate lemmas.

This model is trained on `lemma` commands in the training set of proof sequences in the PVSLib. For each `lemma` invocation, we record the sequent at that point in the proof and the name of the referenced lemma. PVSLib has 20,221 such pairs in its proof traces, consisting of the sequent state when the `lemma` command was entered by the user and the name of the lemma. We randomly split them into 12,132 train and 8,089 test pairs. This is against a combined library of PVS and PVSLib theories, with a total of 747 theories and 9,468 available lemmas. For training the Siamese network, observed sequents and lemmas in the training invocations have a score of 1. An equal number of negative sequent and lemma pairs were sampled, with their score set to 0, as a randomly selected lemma is very unlikely to be relevant.

We evaluated the resulting network on the test pairs and measured performance using mean reciprocal rank (MRR), an IR metric that assesses relevacne-ranking ability [33]. MRR is computed from the rank position of the ground truth lemma in the relevance-ordered scores given the sequent (Formula 1), with higher values indicating better ranking ability.

$$MRR = \frac{1}{N} \sum_i^N \frac{1}{r_i} \tag{1}$$

For a given test pair consisting of a sequent s, selected lemma l_{gt} and library of lemmas L with $l_{gt} \in L$, we score $f_{rel}(s, l)$, the relevance of lemma $l \in L$ to the sequent. We derive a rank ordering over all lemmas L, where r_i is the rank of the ground truth lemma for the ith lemma pair.

Method	MRR
Baseline	0.0015
Count	0.0030
TF-IDF	0.043
CoProver	**0.51**

We find that the CoProver approach to outperform the other methods including representation used by previous work [5,12]. A MRR of 0.51 corresponds to an average mean rank of 1.98, which corresponds to the relevant lemma appearing around position 2 in a score-based rank ordering of all lemmas.

7   Related Work

In the last decade, there has been a significant amount of activity in applying machine learning to automated deduction, and can be classified in terms of the predictive goal of machine learning [38]:

1. Learning search heuristics (E-prover [41], SAT/SMT solvers [4]): The systems ENIGMA [20], MaLeCoP [45] and FEMaLeCoP [24] augment a tableau-based prover LeanCoP [36] with a naïve Bayes classifier for clause selection. Graph neural nets have been used to predict the clauses that are in the unsatisfiable core set of clauses from a clause set [42] and to guide SMT solvers [2].

2. Premise selection from a library of facts (DeepMath [19], CoqHammer, HOLy-Hammer, HOList [3], Thor [21]): Several proof assistants invoke hammers (theorem provers and SAT/SMT solvers) on each subgoal together with a set of background lemmas (the premises). These hammers can fail if there are too many premises. Machine learning has been used to identify the most promising premises to pick from the background library [26]. As with tactic selection below, a range of learning techniques have been employed for premise selection, including sequence, tree, and graph representations [47].

3. Step or tactic selection (GPT-f, Holophrasm [48], CoqGym [51], HOL4RL [50], HOList [31], GamePad [17], Tactic-Toe [13], proof synthesis [10,22,27]): Interactive proof assistants build proof trees by applying tactics to goals to generate zero or more subgoals. The SEPIA system [15] predicts tactics for the Coq proof assistant based purely on analyzing proofs. GPT-f uses the GPT-3 transformer model to train on Goal/Proof pairs from the Metamath corpus (augmented with synthesized proofs) to predict the proof given the goal. This is used to construct a proof tree by applying the proof steps suggested by the model to the open subgoals in the tree. The system was able to find shorter proofs for 23 theorems in the Metamath corpus. CoqGym [51] uses a much larger training corpus spanning 71,000 proofs from various Coq libraries. TacticToe [14] is trained on proofs from HOL4 libraries and combines tactic prediction using k-nearest neighbors with A* search, and in some cases yields better (more perspicuous and maintainable) proofs than the alternatives using Hammers. IsarStep [29] uses a transformer encoding to identify intermediate formulas in a declarative Isar proof. ML4PG [25] extracts useful statistical patterns from higher-order logic proofs using unsupervised learning techniques like K-Means clustering.

Prior work in step selection focused on the ability of the system to fully automate the proof, with performance was measured in number of proofs that can be automatically completed. CoProver's focus is on the ability of the system to capture human-selected proof steps. Prior work in this area featurized sequents as histograms of tokens. As we have shown, structural information matters, and using neural language modeling technology captures this over wider portions of the formulas. Premise selection has been a topic of investigation, albeit focused on selection of useful premises for application of hammers and evaluating based on automatic completion [1,34,47]. In contrast, we focus on a broader use case, retrieving useful recommendations that can progress the proof via additional user interactions as well as application of hammers. Treating lemma retrieval as an information retrieval problem has been done in prior work [5,13], which used term-weighted histograms of the sequent (query) and lemma (document) for comparison. While this "bag-of-words" approach removes sequentiality and thus structural information, vocabulary overlap between query and candidate document is a good approximator for relevance. However, bag-of-words modeling and the TF-IDF weighting scheme are assumptions targeting how relevance appears for natural language queries and documents. Logical formula observed in lemmas and sequents may not exhibit the same behavior, particularly for determining if a lemma is relevant to moving proof progress in a sequent. Indeed, neural information retrieval has focused on using supervised queries and document pairs to learn relevance functions that may not be captured by assumptions taken in standard IR modeling. Here, the Magnushammer approach is similar to ours [34], leveraging a Transformer-based architecture to encode the string representation of the proof-state and the lemma. However, we include variable type information into the encodings and conduct an evaluation focusing on retrieval quality.

8   Conclusions

In this work, we have demonstrated how a simple featurization of proof state can be used to perform two recommendation tasks, predicting next commands and retrieving relevant lemmas. For command prediction, CoProver's approach has been shown to outperform prior methods, giving significantly higher accuracies. In the context of recommendation systems, showing the top 3−5 commands is a reasonable amount, with these windows capturing 50%−70% of the original prediction correctly on the validation set. As with systems trained on user interaction traces, there are often cases where the system can learn a solution that the user did not consider. As one internal user commented, the application of an automated hammer (the `grind` command) in a convergence proof was unexpected, but lead to completion of the proof. Similarly, using a neural learning approach with CoProver's featurization can give significantly better performance on lemma retrieval, in comparison with retrieval using IR-derived baselines.

In spite of these results, we note that the neural learning mechanism are not necessarily learning deep reasoning structures, and may more likely be learning complex structural cues. Indeed, an analysis of large language models found them to be impressive memorization machines that are incapable of performing arithmetic [7]. A cursory examination of the attention heads in the command prediction task revealed the model's attention weightings did not consistently align with experienced users' intuitions about what should govern the direction of the proof.

Future directions of proof command recommendation include identification of arguments used for these commands. These primarily consist of the formula to use, but in some cases more complex arguments are needed. Of particular interest is pairing this capability with explanation mechanisms. Perhaps the simplest explanation capability is to run the top-N commands in the background and displaying the results provides a look ahead capability that allows users to see the envelope of outcomes. When paired with heuristics that measure proof completion, this may be beneficial for developing an intuitive understanding.

To the best of our knowledge, we are the first work to treat lemma retrieval as an information retrieval problem. Previous work focused on if a selected lemma can progress a proof towards completion in an automated solver. For the type of problems addressed by interactive theorem provers, automatic completion may not be feasible in all cases. Importing a lemma to progress the proof becomes useful, similar to how retrieving the right document can help a querying user perform a task. To that end, we have demonstrated how a neurally trained architecture can determine which lemma an expert user would have selected. This approach can provide a better relevance ranking for lemmas, as opposed to the representation and scoring methods discussed in previous work. We note that setup only considers lemmas selected by the user as relevant for a given sequent. This disregards the possibility that another lemma may be just as useful for the proof as well. This is a well known issue in natural language information retrieval corpora, and thus measures like MRR are used more to compare system performance as opposed to acting as a standalone performance measure.

Possible future work in this area can focus on analyzing relevant structural elements that trigger a match between a sequent and a lemma. While the final comparison is performed using a cosine similarity computation, the nature of the highest scoring feature matches can be hard to discern. In particular, it is possible that the formula for the lemma and sequent may not have much apparent overlap, but relevant token sequences may map to the same feature.

For future work, we are examining the application of CoProver's transformer based sequent representation towards tasks such as nominating witnesses, proof repair, and developing a measure for proof progress. The code and the data used for this work are open-sourced and will be available at https://github.com/SRI-CSL/coproof.

Acknowledgement. This material is based upon work supported by the Defense Advanced Research Projects Agency (DARPA) under Contract No. HR00112290064 and by the National Institute of Aeronautics. Any opinions, findings, and conclusions or recommendations expressed in this material are those of the author(s) and do not necessarily reflect the views of the United States Government or DARPA.

References

1. Alama, J., Kühlwein, D., Tsivtsivadze, E., Urban, J., Heskes, T.: Premise selection for mathematics by corpus analysis and kernel methods. CoRR abs/1108.3446 (2011). arXiv:1108.3446
2. Balunovic, M., Bielik, P., Vechev, M.T.: Learning to solve SMT formulas. In: NeurIPS, pp. 10338–10349 (2018)
3. Bansal, K., Loos, S., Rabe, M., Szegedy, C., Wilcox, S.: Holist: An environment for machine learning of higher order logic theorem proving. In: International Conference on Machine Learning, pp. 454–463. PMLR (2019)
4. Biere, A., Heule, M., van Maaren, H., Walsh, T. (eds.): Handbook of Satisfiability. IOS Press (2009)
5. Blanchette, J.C., Greenaway, D., Kaliszyk, C., Kühlwein, D., Urban, J.: A learning-based fact selector for Isabelle/HOL. J. Autom. Reason. **57**(3), 219–244 (2016)
6. Bromley, J., Guyon, I., LeCun, Y., Säckinger, E., Shah, R.: Signature verification using a "siamese" time delay neural network. In: Advances in Neural Information Processing Systems, vol. 6 (1993)

7. Brown, T.B., et al.: Language models are few-shot learners. CoRR abs/2005.14165 (2020). arXiv:2005.14165

8. Devlin, J., Chang, M.W., Lee, K., Toutanova, K.: BERT: Pre-training of deep bidirectional transformers for language understanding. In: Proceedings of the 2019 Conference of the North American Chapter of the Association for Computational Linguistics: Human Language Technologies, Volume 1 (Long and Short Papers), pp. 4171–4186. Association for Computational Linguistics, Minneapolis, Minnesota (Jun 2019). 10.18653/v1/N19-1423, http://aclanthology.org/N19-1423

9. Efron, B., Tibshirani, R.J.: An Introduction to the Bootstrap. No. 57 in Monographs on Statistics and Applied Probability, Chapman & Hall/CRC, Boca Raton, Florida, USA (1993)

10. First, E., Brun, Y., Guha, A.: Tactok: semantics-aware proof synthesis. In: Proceedings of the ACM on Programming Languages 4(OOPSLA), pp. 1–31 (2020)

11. Gage, P.: A new algorithm for data compression. C Users J. $D(2)$, 23–38 (1994)

12. Gauthier, T., Kaliszyk, C., Urban, J.: Learning to reason with hol4 tactics. arXiv preprint arXiv:1804.00595 (2018)

13. Gauthier, T., Kaliszyk, C., Urban, J., Kumar, R., Norrish, M.: Learning to prove with tactics. CoRR abs/1804.00596 (2018), arXiv:1804.00596

14. Gauthier, T., Kaliszyk, C., Urban, J., Kumar, R., Norrish, M.: Tactictoe: learning to prove with tactics. J. Autom. Reason. **65**(2), 257–286 (2021)

15. Gransden, T., Walkinshaw, N., Raman, R.: SEPIA: search for proofs using inferred automata. In: Felty, A.P., Middeldorp, A. (eds.) CADE 2015. LNCS (LNAI), vol. 9195, pp. 246–255. Springer, Cham (2015). https://doi.org/10.1007/978-3-319-21401-6_16

16. Hsu, C.W., Chang, C.C., Lin, C.J.: A practical guide to support vector classification. Tech. rep., Department of Computer Science, National Taiwan University (2003). http://www.csie.ntu.edu.tw/~cjlin/papers.html

17. Huang, D., Dhariwal, P., Song, D., Sutskever, I.: Gamepad: A learning environment for theorem proving. arXiv preprint arXiv:1806.00608 (2018)

18. Huang, P.S., He, X., Gao, J., Deng, L., Acero, A., Heck, L.: Learning deep structured semantic models for web search using clickthrough data. In: Proceedings of the 22nd ACM International Conference on Information and Knowledge Management, pp. 2333–2338. CIKM '13, Association for Computing Machinery, New York, NY, USA (2013). https://doi.org/10.1145/2505515.2505665

19. Irving, G., Szegedy, C., Alemi, A.A., Eén, N., Chollet, F., Urban, J.: Deepmath-deep sequence models for premise selection. Adv. Neural. Inf. Process. Syst. **29**, 2235–2243 (2016)

20. Jakubův, J., Urban, J.: ENIGMA: efficient learning-based inference guiding machine. In: Geuvers, H., England, M., Hasan, O., Rabe, F., Teschke, O. (eds.) CICM 2017. LNCS (LNAI), vol. 10383, pp. 292–302. Springer, Cham (2017). https://doi.org/10.1007/978-3-319-62075-6_20

21. Jiang, A.Q., et al.: Thor: Wielding hammers to integrate language models and automated theorem provers (2022). https://doi.org/10.48550/ARXIV.2205.10893, arXiv:2205.10893

22. Jiang, A.Q., et al.: Draft, sketch, and prove: Guiding formal theorem provers with informal proofs (2022). https://doi.org/10.48550/ARXIV.2210.12283, arXiv:2210.12283

23. Jones, K.S.: A statistical interpretation of term specificity and its application in retrieval. J. Document. **28**, 11–21 (1972)

24. Kaliszyk, C., Urban, J.: Femalecop: Fairly efficient machine learning connection prover. In: Logic for Programming, Artificial Intelligence, and Reasoning. pp. 88–96. Springer (2015)

25. Komendantskaya, E., Heras, J., Grov, G.: Machine learning in proof general: Interfacing interfaces. arXiv preprint arXiv:1212.3618 (2012)

26. Kühlwein, D., Blanchette, J.C., Kaliszyk, C., Urban, J.: MaSh: machine learning for sledgehammer. In: Blazy, S., Paulin-Mohring, C., Pichardie, D. (eds.) ITP 2013. LNCS, vol. 7998, pp. 35–50. Springer, Heidelberg (2013). https://doi.org/10.1007/978-3-642-39634-2_6

27. Lample, Get al.: Hypertree proof search for neural theorem proving (2022). https://doi.org/10.48550/ARXIV.2205.11491, arXiv:2205.11491

28. Li, S., et al.: PyTorch Distributed: Experiences on accelerating data parallel training. CoRR abs/2006.15704 (2020), arXiv:2006.15704

29. Li, W., Yu, L., Wu, Y., Paulson, L.C.: Isarstep: a benchmark for high-level mathematical reasoning. arXiv preprint arXiv:2006.09265 (2020)

30. Liu, Y., et al.: RoBERTa: A robustly optimized BERT pretraining approach (2019). https://doi.org/10.48550/ARXIV.1907.11692, arXiv:1907.11692

31. Loos, S., Irving, G., Szegedy, C., Kaliszyk, C.: Deep network guided proof search. arXiv preprint arXiv:1701.06972 (2017)

32. Luhn, H.P.: A statistical approach to mechanized encoding and searching of literary information. IBM J. Res. Dev. **1**(4), 309–317 (1957). https://doi.org/10.1147/rd.14.0309

33. Manning, C.D., Raghavan, P., Schatze, H.: Introduction to Information Retrieval. Cambridge University Press, Cambridge, UK (2008). http://nlp.stanford.edu/IR-book/information-retrieval-book.html

34. Mikuła, M., et al.: Magnushammer: A transformer-based approach to premise selection (2023)

35. Mitra, B., Craswell, N.: (2018)

36. Otten, J., Bibel, W.: leancop: lean connection-based theorem proving. J. Symb. Comput. **36**(1–2), 139–161 (2003)

37. Owre, S., Rushby, J.M., Shankar, N.: PVS: a prototype verification system. In: Kapur, D. (ed.) CADE 1992. LNCS, vol. 607, pp. 748–752. Springer, Heidelberg (1992). https://doi.org/10.1007/3-540-55602-8_217

38. Rabe, M.N., Szegedy, C.: Towards the automatic mathematician. In: Platzer, A., Sutcliffe, G. (eds.) CADE 2021. LNCS (LNAI), vol. 12699, pp. 25–37. Springer, Cham (2021). https://doi.org/10.1007/978-3-030-79876-5_2

39. Raffel, C., et al.: Exploring the limits of transfer learning with a unified text-to-text transformer. CoRR abs/1910.10683 (2019), arXiv:1910.10683

40. Reimers, N., Gurevych, I.: Sentence-BERT: Sentence embeddings using Siamese BERT-Networks. CoRR abs/1908.10084 (2019). arXiv:1908.10084

41. Schulz, S.: E - a brainiac theorem prover. J. AI Commun. **15**(2/3), 111–126 (2002)

42. Selsam, D., Bjørner, N.: Guiding high-performance SAT solvers with Unsat-core predictions. In: Janota, M., Lynce, I. (eds.) SAT 2019. LNCS, vol. 11628, pp. 336–353. Springer, Cham (2019). https://doi.org/10.1007/978-3-030-24258-9_24

43. Sennrich, R., Haddow, B., Birch, A.: Neural machine translation of rare words with subword units. In: Proceedings of the 54th Annual Meeting of the Association for Computational Linguistics (Volume 1: Long Papers), pp. 1715–1725. Association for Computational Linguistics, Berlin, Germany (Aug 2016). https://doi.org/10.18653/v1/P16-1162, http://aclanthology.org/P16-1162

44. Shankar, N.: Automated reasoning, fast and slow. In: Proceedings of the 24th international conference on Automated Deduction, pp. 145–161. CADE'13, Springer-Verlag, Berlin, Heidelberg (2013). https://doi.org/10.1007/978-3-642-38574-2_10, http://dx.doi.org/10.1007/978-3-642-38574-2_10

45. Urban, J., Vyskočil, J., Štěpánek, P.: MaLeCoP machine learning connection prover. In: Brünnler, K., Metcalfe, G. (eds.) TABLEAUX 2011. LNCS (LNAI), vol. 6793, pp. 263–277. Springer, Heidelberg (2011). https://doi.org/10.1007/978-3-642-22119-4_21

46. Vaswani, A.,et al.: Attention is all you need. In: Advances in Neural Information Processing Systems, vol. 30 (2017)

47. Wang, M., Tang, Y., Wang, J., Deng, J.: Premise selection for theorem proving by deep graph embedding. arXiv preprint arXiv:1709.09994 (2017)

48. Whalen, D.: Holophrasm: a neural automated theorem prover for higher-order logic. arXiv preprint arXiv:1608.02644 (2016)

49. Wolf, T., et al.: Transformers: State-of-the-art natural language processing. In: Proceedings of the 2020 Conference on Empirical Methods in Natural Language Processing: System Demonstrations, pp. 38–45. Association for Computational Linguistics, Online (Oct 2020), www.aclweb.org/anthology/2020.emnlp-demos.6

50. Wu, M., Norrish, M., Walder, C., Dezfouli, A.: Tacticzero: Learning to prove theorems from scratch with deep reinforcement learning. arXiv preprint arXiv:2102.09756 (2021)

51. Yang, K., Deng, J.: Learning to prove theorems via interacting with proof assistants. In: International Conference on Machine Learning, pp. 6984–6994. PMLR (2019)

Project and Survey Papers

Proving an Execution of an Algorithm Correct?

James Harold Davenport[✉]

University of Bath, Bath BA2 7AY, UK
masjhd@bath.ac.uk

Abstract. Many algorithms in computer algebra and beyond produce answers. For some of these, we have formal proofs of the correctness of the algorithm, and for others it is easy to verify that the answer is correct. Other algorithms produce either an answer or a proof that no such answer exists. It may still be easy to verify that the answer is correct, but what about the "no such answer" case. The claim of this paper is that, at least in some cases, it is possible for the algorithm to produce "hints" such that a theorem prover can prove that, in this case, there is no such answer. This leads to the paradigm of "*ad hoc* UNSAT verification".

1   Introduction

We consider algorithms that solve problems of the following form:

Problem 1 (Generic). Given a question Q, produce

either an answer A of an appropriate form
or $\perp$ indicating that no such answer A exists.

We assume that verifying that A answers Q is (comparatively) easy, and are concerned rather with verifying $\perp$. Of course, if the algorithm is proved correct, then this isn't a challenge, but if we don't have a proof of complete correctness (i.e. the correctness of $\perp$ as well as A), then there is an issue, i.e. the following.

Research Question 1. *Given an algorithm P solving a particular problem of the format of Problem 1, can we modify P such that, as well as outputting $\perp$ when given Q, it outputs a proof, verifiable by tools such as Coq/Isabelle/Lean, that $\perp$ is correct, i.e. no such answer A to question Q exists.*

2   SAT Solving

SAT solving is the quintessential NP-complete problem [Coo66].

Problem 2 (SAT). Given a Boolean statement $\Phi(x_1, \ldots, x_n)$, produce

© The Author(s), under exclusive license to Springer Nature Switzerland AG 2023
C. Dubois and M. Kerber (Eds.): CICM 2023, LNAI 14101, pp. 255–269, 2023.
https://doi.org/10.1007/978-3-031-42753-4_17

either $f : \{x_i\} \mapsto \{T, F\}$ such that $\Phi(f(x_1), \ldots, f(x_n)) = T$ (a satisfying assignment)

or $\perp$ indicating that no satisfying assignment exists.

The first can be verified easily enough: what about the second?

Since at least 2016, contestants in the annual SAT contests have been required to produce proofs (occasionally 2PB!) of UNSAT in DRAT format [Heu18], which can be checked, though [Heu23] states there are subtleties to "easy" checking, and not all DRAT proofs are equally easy. This gives rise to a second question, which we mention but won't explicitly address here. [Heu18] states that their computation took over 14 CPU-years to produce, and just over 36 CPU-years to verify.

Research Question 2. *Can we produce an "efficient" proof of $\perp$?*

This would require a definition of "efficient" (one might say that verification took at most a constant multiple (depending on P) of the time taken to produce the proof, *and* that the time taken to produce the proof was at most a constant multiple (depending on P) of the time taken to produce the naked assertion of $\perp$. But we might also want to understand issues such as the minimal length of a proof of $\perp$ in a particular case. See some remarks in Sect. 3.2.

3   Polynomial Factorisation

For simplicity we will consider factorisation over the integers of polynomials with integer coefficients. Algebraic number fields add complications, but not, we believe, fundamental ones. The problem of factorisation is normally stated as follows.

Problem 3 (Factorisation). Given $f \in \mathbf{Z}[x_1, \ldots, x_n]$, write $f = \prod f_i$ where the f_i are *irreducible* elements of $\mathbf{Z}[x_1, \ldots, x_n]$.

Verifying that $f = \prod f_i$ is, at least relatively, easy. The hard part is verifying that the f_i are *irreducible*. The author knows of no implementation of polynomial factorisation that produces any evidence, let alone a proof, of this. In the framework of Problem 1, we could phrase this as

Problem 4 (Factorisation after Problem 1). Given $f \in \mathbf{Z}[x_1, \ldots, x_n]$, produce

either a proper factor g of f,

or $\perp$ indicating that no such g exists.

3.1   Univariate Polynomials

We may as well assume f is square-free (else factor each square-free factor separately). Then the basic algorithm goes back to [Zas69]: step M is a later addition [Mus75], and the H' variants are also later.

1. Choose a prime p (not dividing the leading coefficient of f) such that f (mod p) is also square-free.

2. Factor f modulo p as $\prod f_i^{(1)}$ (mod p).

M Take five p and compare the factorisations.

3. If f can be shown to be irreducible from modulo p factorisations, return f.

4. Let B be such that any factor of f has coefficients less than B in magnitude, and n such that $p^n \geq 2B$.

5. Use Hensel's Lemma to lift the factorisation to $f = \prod f_i^{(n)}$ (mod p^n)

H Starting with singletons and working up, take subsets of the $f_i^{(n)}$, multiply them together and check whether, regarded as polynomials over $\mathbf{Z}$ with coefficients in $[-B, B]$, they divide f — if they do, declare that they are irreducible factors of f.

H' Use some alternative technique, originally [LLL82], but now e.g. [ASZ00] to find the true factor corresponding to $f_1^{(n)}$, remove $f_1^{(n)}$ and the other $f_i^{(n)}$ corresponding to this factor, and repeat.

In practice, there are a lot of optimisations, which would greatly complicate a proof of correctness of an implementation of this algorithm.

We found that, although the Hensel construction is basically neat and simple in theory, the fully optimised version we finally used was as nasty a piece of code to write and debug as any we have come across [MN81].

Since if f is irreducible modulo p, it is irreducible over the integers, the factors produced from singletons in step 5 are easily proved to be irreducible. Unfortunately, the chance that an irreducible polynomial of degree n is irreducible modulo p is $1/n$. Hence the factorisation in step 2 is very likely to be an overestimate, in that we have more factors modulo p than over the integers.

Musser introduced step M, saying we should take five[1] primes p_i and compare the factorisations. This is more than just taking the best (where the chance of irreducibility would then be roughly $5/n$). For example, if f factors as 3×1 (i.e. a factor of degree 3 times a linear factor) modulo p_1 and 2×2 modulo p_2, then it must in fact be irreducible. For a generic polynomial (Galois group S_n) this is very likely to prove f irreducible.

However, [SD69] showed that there are irreducible polynomials which factor *compatibly* modulo every prime. The easiest example is $x^4 + 1$, which factors as 2×2 (or 2×1^2 or 1^4) modulo every prime, which is also compatible with a 2×2 factorisation over the integers, and the recombination part of step 5 may be required.

Hence we can see that a factorisation algorithm could, even though no known implementation does, relatively easily produce the required information for a proof of irreducibility unless the recombination step is required. Note that *verifying* the Hensel lifting, the "nasty piece" from [MN81] is easy: the factors just

---

[1] Subsequently [LP97] showed that asymptotically the correct number is seven, not Musser's experimentally-derived five.

have to have the right degrees from the factorisation of f (mod p) and multiply to give f (mod p^n).

3.2 Comments on Research Question 2

We have seen that the time required to produce the factorisation (and $\perp$ that each factor is irreducible) can vary widely, depending on whether or not recombination after Hensel lifting is required. In fact there are several possibilities, as in Table 1.

Table 1. Possible factorisation routes

Case	description	Times for		
		result	result + proof	verify
1:	irreducible by Musser	t_1	$t_1 + \epsilon$	$O(t_1)$
2:	factors, each irreducible as above	t_2	$t_2 + \epsilon$	$O(t_2)$
3:	factors, but not trivially Musser	t_2	$t_2 + \epsilon$	$O(t_2)$ with work
4:	factors, needs recombining	t_4	$t_4 + \epsilon$	$O(t_4)$, hard?

2. A typical example would be where, modulo some p, f factors into three irreducible factors, of degrees 3,5,7, and the other primes are consistent with this. Then we have to lift the factors to be modulo a suitable $N = p^n$ (time $O(N^3)$ with classical arithmetic), when we will discover that these are indeed factors. They are then irreducible by the Musser test. Verifying that this is a factorisation takes time $O(N^2)$ with classical arithmetic), so in this case the verification is asymptotically cheaper.

3. A typical example would be where, modulo some p, f factors into three irreducible factors, of degrees 3,5,8, and the other primes are consistent with this. Then we lift as above, and verify these are factors. The Musser test on the original polynomial does not directly prove that the 8 is irreducible (because a 3,5 split is feasible), but repeating the Musser test on that factor will actually prove it irreducible. With this change, the timings are the same as case 2.

4. Swinnerton-Dyer polynomials are the classic case. If we use classic recombination [Zas69] then the verification is essentially equivalent to the initial computation. More advanced methods [LLL82, ASZ00] would require proving their results in the prover, but this would only need to be done once. This might be hard, but is currently unknown.

There are many other possibilities, which depend essentially on the Galois groups of the factors of the polynomial. To the best of the author's knowledge, no work has been done on extending the theory of factoring ([DS00, LP97, etc.]) to retrospective verification.

3.3 Multivariate Polynomials

The algorithm is basically similar, replacing primes by evaluations $x_i \to v_i$. The difference is that, if $f(x_1, \ldots, x_n)$ is irreducible, then with probability 1, $f(x_1, v_2, \ldots, v_n) \in \mathbf{Z}[x_1]$ is also irreducible. Hence this is probably not significantly easier than the univariate case in terms of proving, unlike implementation [MN81].

4 Integration "in Closed Form"

4.1 What Exactly Do We Mean?

In this dialogue, **P** is an algebra professor, and **S** is a questioning student.

P e^{-x^2} has no integral.
S But in analysis the professor proved that every continuous function has an integral.
P I meant that there was no formula for the integral.
S But in statistics the professor used erf(x) and everything seemed OK.
P I meant that there was no *elementary* formula, in terms of exp, log and the solution of polynomial equations.
S How do you prove that?
P Differential Algebra!
S What's that?
P The study of a field K equipped with a unary (postfix) operator $' : K \to K$ such that $(a + b)' = a' + b'$ and $(ab)' = a'b + ab'$.

Those two axioms are what calculus calls the "Sum Rule" and "Product Rule": the "Quotient Rule" is in fact an algebraic consequence of the product rule.

  The study of such fields (generally assumed to be of characteristic 0: the characteristic p case has peculiarities since $(x^p)' = 0$) is *Differential Algebra* [Kol73]. In such a field, if $f' = 0$, we say that f is *constant*. The set of all constants of F is denoted by const F, and is a subfield of F.

  We need to define "elementary".

Definition 1. *Let K be a differential field (of characteristic 0) and $\theta \in L$, where L is a differential extension of K. θ is said to be* elementary *over K if it satisfies (at least) one of the following cases:*

algebraic *θ satisfies a polynomial equation with coefficients in K.*
logarithmic $\theta' = \frac{u'}{u}$, $u \in K$;
exponential $\theta' = u'\theta$, $u \in K$;

Note that if $\theta' = i\theta$, then θ corresponds to our intuitive e^{ix}, and then $\frac{1}{2}(\theta + 1/\theta)$ corresponds to our intuitive $\cos(x)$. Similarly, if $\theta' = \frac{i - \frac{x}{\sqrt{-x^2+1}}}{ix + \sqrt{-x^2+1}}$, then θ corresponds to $\log\left(ix + \sqrt{-x^2 + 1}\right)$ and $-i\theta$ corresponds to $\arcsin(x)$, differentiating to $\frac{1}{\sqrt{1-x^2}}$. Hence the above definition of "elementary" corresponds to the general usage.

Observation 2. *The cases in Definition 1 are not mutually exclusive, in particular the fact that case logarithmic (or exponential) applies doesn't mean that θ is transcendental, or that we haven't introduced a new constant rather than a genuinely new non-constant.*

Example 1. Suppose $K = \mathbf{Q}(\phi)$ where $\phi' = \phi$ (intuitively $\phi = e^x$). Consider $\theta' = \frac{1}{2}\theta$. Then this certainly satisfies the **exponential** clause. But $\sqrt{\phi}$ has $\left(\sqrt{\phi}\right)' = \phi'\left(\frac{1}{2\sqrt{\phi}}\right) = \frac{1}{2}\sqrt{\phi}$, so $\sqrt{\phi}$ is one solution, which is also **algebraic** over $\mathbf{Q}(\phi)$. However, another possible solution would be $\theta = e\sqrt{\phi}$, which is not algebraic over $\mathbf{Q}(\phi)$.

Example 2. Suppose $K = \mathbf{Q}(\phi_1, \phi_2)$ where $\phi_1' = \frac{1}{x-1}$ and $\phi_2' = \frac{1}{x-2}$. Consider $\theta' = \frac{2x-3}{(x-1)(x-2)}$. Then this certainly satisfies the **logarithmic** clause. But $(\phi_1 + \phi_2)' = \frac{1}{x-1} + \frac{1}{x-2} = \frac{2x-3}{(x-1)(x-2)}$, so $\phi_1 + \phi_2$ is one solution. However, another possible solution would be $\theta = \phi_1 + \phi_2 + e$, which is not algebraic over $\mathbf{Q}(\phi_1, \phi_2)$.

Observation 3. *The usual solution to the difficulties raised in Observation 2 is two-fold:*

1. *to insert "and where clause **algebraic** does not apply" in the other clauses;*
2. *to insert a check that $K(\theta)$ has the same field of constants as K, relying on the Risch Structure Theorem [Ris79].*

The key point for us is that a proof of $\perp$ would have to include a proof of these statements. Hence we probably need a formal proof of the Risch Structure Theorem.

4.2   The Algebraic Theory of Integration [Rit48, Rit50]

Problem 5. (Integration). Given $f \in K = C(x, \theta_1, \ldots, \theta_n)$ where C is an algebraic extension of $\mathbf{Q}$, $x' = 1$ and each θ_i is elementary[2] over $C(x, \theta_1, \ldots, \theta_{i-1})$ produce

either F in some elementary extension L of K such that $F' = f$ (an elementary integral)
or $\perp$ indicating that no such elementary integral exists.

The first can be verified: what about the second? Before we look at this, there are a few observations we should make.

1. This verification isn't necessarily trivial: there are issues of simplification of elementary functions.
2. Although the student's memory of analysis will say that an integral has to be continuous, because of branch cuts, the formula F might not denote a continuous function $\mathbf{R} \to \mathbf{R}$ [CDJW00].
3. As example, the Heaviside function differentiates to 0, so it's a "constant" in terms of differentiable algebra.

---

[2] In fact we also need these fields C, K to be *decidable* [Ric68].

4.3   Liouville's Principle [Lio35, Rit50]

Looking for "an elementary extension L of K" might seem like "looking for a needle in a haystack", but there is substantial help.

Theorem 1 (Liouville's Principle). *Let f be a expression from some expression field K. If f has an elementary integral over K, it has an integral of the following form:*

$$\int f = v_0 + \sum_{i=1}^{n} c_i \log v_i, \tag{1}$$

where v_0 belongs to K, the v_i belong to $\hat{K}$, an extension of K by a finite number of constants algebraic over const(K), and the c_i belong to $\hat{K}$ and are constant.

Alternatively

$$f = v_0' + \sum_{i=1}^{n} c_i \frac{v_i'}{v_i}. \tag{2}$$

Hence we only need to search a single bale of hay! The proof of this is by equating coefficients in $f = F'$, which is turn relies on knowing whether expressions are transcendental or not (see Observation 3).

4.4   Risch's Idea [Ris69]

Let C be a fixed algebraic extension of $\mathbf{Q}$. Suppose that $f, g \in K := C(x, \theta_1, \dots, \theta_n)$ where each θ_i is either

logarithmic $\theta_i' = \frac{u_i'}{u_i}$, $u_i \in C(x, \theta_1, \dots, \theta_{i-1})$.
exponential $\theta_i' = u_i'\theta_i$, $u_i \in C(x, \theta_1, \dots, \theta_{i-1})$.

Suppose also that K has transcendence degree $n + 1$ over C, and that K has C as field of constants (see Observation 3).
Induct on n, that we can:

Integration Given f, solve (or $\perp$): write f in the form $v_0' + \sum_{i=1}^{m} c_i \frac{v_i'}{v_i}$;
Risch ordinary differential equation Given f, g, solve (or $\perp$) $y' + fy = g$ for $y \in K$.

This essentially converts Problem 5 into two mutually recursive problems.

In both cases, the algorithm is a fairly messy "comparison of terms" argument, and the Risch ordinary differential equation case for exponential θ_n was a "similarly", which wasn't quite as similar as I thought: see [Dav86].

The "mess" comes in showing that every case is covered, and that the "bug fix" in [Dav86] is complete: each individual case is fairly straightforward.

4.5 Producing a Proof of ⊥

So how might we produce a proof of ⊥?

1. Have a formal proof of Liouville's Principle.

⚡ I haven't done this formally, but it doesn't look outrageous: it's all algebra in [Rit48]. The main issue will probably be formalising Observation 3.

2. At each comparison of terms, spit this out in a form that a theorem-prover can digest.

⚡ Again, I haven't done this, but I did have an implementation in Axiom which produced a (very stylised) informal proof, hence I believe this is feasible, subject again to formalising Observation 3.

Note that I am *not* considering the case of θ_i algebraic. θ_1 algebraic is in [Dav81] for integration (and [Dav84] for the Risch ordinary differential equation case), but there is *much* more mathematics involved in finding the c_i, v_i or proving they don't exist. The more general cases are in [Bro90,Bro91], again requiring more mathematics. "Mathematics" *may* reduce to "is a divisor on an algebraic curve a torsion divisor", and ⊥ here is hard. In the special case where $C = \mathbf{Q}$ and the algebraic curve is elliptic, [Dav81] relied on the following theorem.

Theorem 2 ([Maz77]). *The torsion subgroup of the Mordell–Weil groups of an elliptic curve E over the rationals is isomorphic to one of the following:*

$$\begin{cases} \mathbf{Z}/m\mathbf{Z}, & m \le 10 \\ \mathbf{Z}/12\mathbf{Z}, \\ (\mathbf{Z}/2\mathbf{Z}) \times (\mathbf{Z}/2\nu\mathbf{Z})\ \nu \le 4 \end{cases}.$$

Hence the torsion of an element is one of $1, \ldots, 10, 12$.

This is a fairly deep theorem, but one that *might* be formally provable by a specialist [Baa23]: see [BBCD23].

5 Real Geometry and Quantifier Elimination

The following problem is known as "Quantifier-Free Nonlinear Real Arithmetic" or QF_NRA in SMTLIB terminology [BFT21].

Problem 6 (QF_NRA). Given a statement $\exists x_1, \ldots, x_n \Phi$, where Φ is a Boolean combination of polynomial equalities and inequalities in $x_1, \ldots, x_n$, find a satisfying assignment of values $\in \mathbf{R}$ to $x_1, \ldots, x_n$ or prove that there is no such (i.e. ⊥).

This can be regarded as a special case of Real Quantifier Elimination (QE), since eliminating these quantifiers would lead to "true" (in practice with a witness) of ⊥. Though Real Quantifier Elimination is a common approach, we will see in the rest of this section that it doesn't answer the problem of *proving* ⊥, which we will consider in the following section.

5.1   Real Quantifier Elimination

Let each Q_i be one of the quantifiers $\forall, \exists$ (possibly applied to several variables). Then the Real Quantifier Elimination problem is the following: given a statement

$$\Phi_0 := Q_1 x_{1,1}, \ldots, x_{1,k_1} \cdots Q_{a+1} x_{a+1,1}, \ldots, x_{a+1,k_{a+1}} \Phi(y_i, x_{i,j}), \qquad (3)$$

where Φ is a Boolean combination of equalities and inequalities between real polynomials $P_\alpha(y_i, x_{i,j})$, produce Ψ, a Boolean combination of equalities and inequalities between polynomials $\overline{P}_\beta(y_i)$, which is equisatisfiable, i.e. Ψ is true if and only Φ_0 is true.

If all the polynomials $\overline{P}_\beta(y_i)$ in $\Psi(y_i)$ have integer coefficients, we call $\Psi(y_i)$ a Tarski formula. One might think that we needed to express constructs such as "the third real root of $\overline{P}(x)$", but in fact Thom's Lemma [CR88] means that this can be expressed in terms of the signs of $\overline{P}$ and its derivatives.

Real Quantifier Elimination was first proved decidable in the 1950s s [Tar51, Sei54]. However, the complexity was infeasible, and the first feasible solution was by Collins [Col75] through his Cylindrical Algebraic Decomposition (CAD) algorithm, but we should note that [Wüt76] is essentially simultaneous.

5.2   The [Sampled] Cylindrical Algebraic Decomposition Algorithm

[Col75] talks about Cylindrical Algebraic Decomposition, but in fact a key component to the decision procedure is that each cell has a sample point, hence we add "Sampled" to the title. We need to fix coordinates in $\mathbf{R}^n$ consistent with quantifier order. Let $\mathrm{Proj}_{\mathbf{R}^k}$ denote the projection onto the *first* k coordinates.

Given a set of polynomials $\{p_\alpha\}$ in $\overline{\mathbf{Q}}[x_1, \ldots, x_n]$, CAD produces a finite set of cells $C_i \subset \mathbf{R}^n$ which is:

Cylindrical $\forall i, j, k \, \mathrm{Proj}_{\mathbf{R}^k}(C_i), \mathrm{Proj}_{\mathbf{R}^k}(C_i)$ are equal or disjoint;
Algebraic Each cell is defined by polynomials in $\overline{Q}[x_1, \ldots, x_n]$;
Decomposition The cells are disjoint and cover $\mathbf{R}^n$;
Sampled each cell C_i has a sample point s_i (and these are cylindrical, in the sense that if $\mathrm{Proj}_{\mathbf{R}^k}(C_i) = \mathrm{Proj}_{\mathbf{R}^k}(C_i)$, the first k coordinates of s_i and s_j are equal);

such that on each cell every p_α is sign-invariant (everywhere $+, -, 0$).

Then the truth of Φ is invariant on a cell, and if coordinate k is quantified with $\exists$, a cell with sample point $(s_1, \ldots, s_{k-1})$ is true for Φ if one of the sample points $(s_1, \ldots, s_{k-1}, s_k^{(i)})$ is true for Φ, whereas if coordinate k is quantified with $\forall$, a cell with sample point $(s_1, \ldots, s_{k-1})$ is true for Φ if all of the sample points $(s_1, \ldots, s_{k-1}, s_k^{(i)})$ is true for Φ. Then we can write down Ψ as the union of those cells where Φ_0 is true at the sample point.

Unfortunately QE is doubly exponential in n [DH88], so CAD's worst case must be, and in practice CAD nearly always is.

5.3 Challenges with Cylindrical Algebraic Decomposition

Note that, once we have a Cylindrical Algebraic Decomposition for a set of polynomials, we can write down the solution to *any* Real Quantifier Elimination problem with the variables in the same order. In particular $\exists x_1, \ldots, x_n \Phi$ (the SAT problem) isn't treated as a special case. Similarly, as initially formulated, or as improved by [McC84] or [MPP19], CAD doesn't care about the Boolean structure of Φ.

However, when $\Phi \equiv (p_1 = 0) \wedge \Phi'$ we can do better [McC99b], and essentially produce a decomposition of the variety $p_1 = 0$ rather than the whole of $\mathbf{R}^n$, and this can be extended to several equational constraints [McC01]. Even if $(p_1 = 0) \wedge \Phi'$ is only part of Φ, we can use the equality to reduce the cost of the decomposition [EBD15].

It is well known that nested resultants (and discriminants) tend to factor [McC99a]. If f, g, h have degree d, $R(x) := \mathrm{res}_y(\mathrm{res}_z(f, g), \mathrm{res}_z(f, h))$ has degree $O(d^4)$, even though there are only $O(d^3)$ common solutions $f(x, y, z) = g(x, y, z) = h(x, y, z)$, whose x-coordinates are roots of R. But those x values such that $\exists y, z_1, z_2 : f(x, y, z_1) = g(x, y, z_1); f(x, y, z_2) = h(x, y, z_2)$ with $z_1 \neq z_2$ are also roots of R. Note that these points *are* relevant for cylindricity in the worst case, and are used in [DH88].

5.4 Proving Cylindrical Algebraic Decomposition Correct

Despite attempts (e.g. [CM10]), there is no formal proof of correctness of even basic Cylindrical Algebraic Decomposition [Col75]. Major improvements to CAD import more mathematics, via [McC84]'s use of Zariski's work [Zar65], up to "Puiseux with parameters" used in [MPP19], and hence would require still harder proofs.

5.5 Solving Problem 6 via CAD

If we have a sampled CAD, then we have a *finite* set of sample points, such that the truth of Φ at any point $\mathbf{x}$ is the same as the truth of $\Phi(\mathbf{s})$, where $\mathbf{s}$ is the sample point of the cell to which $\mathbf{x}$ belongs. So a solution to Problem 6 is to check $\Phi(\mathbf{s}_i)$ at all the sample points $\mathbf{s}_i$. If any of these $\Phi(\mathbf{s}_i)$ are true, then we have a witness of truth, and if none are true, then, *subject to the correctness of the CAD*, we have a proof of $\bot$. However, we don't have such a proof, either for the CAD algorithm as a whole, or, as far as is known, for a specific CAD. So if we want such a proof, we need a different approach, given in the next section.

6 Cylindrical Algebraic Coverings (CAC)

This algorithm is given in [ADEK21a], and applies to the purely existential case of quantifier elimination, in particular Problem 6. Since $\exists z(\Phi_1 \vee \Phi_2) \equiv (\exists z \Phi_1) \vee (\exists z \Phi_2)$, we can assume that Φ is a pure conjunction. This does not change the asymptotic complexity (Φ might already have been a pure conjunction), but may well be useful in practice.

[ADEK21a] allows for $\sigma_{i,j} \in \{=, <, \leq, >, \geq\}$, but for simplicity of exposition in this paper, we assume all $\sigma_{i,j} \in \{<, >\}$.

6.1 The Algorithm

1. Choose a sample point $(s_1, \ldots, s_n^{(1)})$.
2. If this satisfies Φ_i return SAT (and witness)
3. Otherwise $\exists j : p_{i,j}(s_1, \ldots, s_n^{(1)}) \not\sigma_{i,j} 0$. Remember j with $(s_1, \ldots, s_n^{(1)})$.
4. Compute largest interval $I_{n,1} = (l, u)$ such that $\forall x_n \in (l, u) p_{i,j}(s_1, \ldots, x_n) \not\sigma_{i,j} 0$.
5. If $I_{n,1} \neq \mathbf{R}$ choose $s_n^{(2)} \notin I_1$. If $(s_1, \ldots, s_n^{(2)})$ satisfies Φ_i return SAT (and witness).
6. Repeat steps 3–5 until $(s_1, \ldots, s_{n-1}, \mathbf{R})$ is covered.
* Some intervals might be redundant, so prune.
7. Each of $I_{n,i}$ defines an oval in $(s_1, \ldots, s_{n-2}, x, y)$ space which cover $(s_1, \ldots, s_{n-1}, \mathbf{R})$.
8. Compute largest interval $I_{n-1,1} = (l, u)$ such that $\forall x_{n-1} \in (l, u)$ the $I_{n,i}$ cover $(s_1, \ldots, s_{n-2}, x_{n-1}, \mathbf{R})$.
9. If $I_{n-1,1} \neq \mathbf{R}$ choose a different value of $s_{n-1}, \notin I_{n-1,1}$.
10. Repeat steps 2–9 until $(s_1, \ldots, s_{n-2}, \mathbf{R})$ is covered.
11. Repeat, decreasing the dimension, until we're covered the whole of the x_1-axis (or we get SAT).

Termination isn't entirely obvious, but each cell we compute contains at least one cell (the cell its sample point is in) from a CAD for the same polynomials, and the CAD itself is finite.

6.2 How Might a CAC Be Verifiable?

This section is based on [ADE+20, ADEK21b]. More accurately, the question being considered is "How might a CAC be verifiable in the SAT/UNSAT context?", i.e. Problem 6. This question falls squarely in the context of this paper, since verifying SAT, i.e. checking that a point satisfies the conditions is easy, whereas verifying UNSAT isn't obvious. The more general question, how one might verify a Cylindrical Algebraic Covering when there are unquantified variables left, seems more like the general Cylindrical Algebraic Decomposition verification question, and is probably currently out of reach.

This is still work in progress, and there are at least two options.

A. Verifying each (non-redundant) calculation in reverse
   1. For each $I^{(1)} = (l_1, r_1)$ as an interval of $\mathbf{R}^1$ prove that it's covered because
   2. For each $I^{(2)} = (l_2, r_2)$ covering the cylinder above $I^{(1)}$ prove that $I^{(1)} \times I^{(2)}$ is covered because
   3. ...

4. For each $I^{(n)} = (l_n, r_n)$ covering the cylinder above $I^{(1)} \times I^{(2)} \times \cdots$ prove that $I^{(1)} \times I^{(2)} \times \cdots \times I^{(n)}$ is covered by the p_j we remembered for that sample point.

B Reverse-engineering a rough "CAD".

1. For each sample point $(s_1, \ldots, s_n)$ check that the corresponding cuboid $I^{(1)} \times I^{(2)} \times \cdots I^{(n)}$ is contained within the $p_j \not\lessgtr_j 0$ region.
2. Verify that these cuboids are arranged cylindrically, and are complete.

It is not clear how this method will adapt to the case where we *do* have equalities as well as strict inequalities, but the method may still be useful for the strict inequality case.

For both options, we need resultants, discriminants and inequalities, but no topology (beyond arranging cuboids).

7 Conclusions

These thoughts are at an early stage, and readers can probably think of other examples to which this paradigm of *"ad hoc* UNSAT verification" can apply.

1. Completeness proofs of algorithms can be challenging, and UNSAT, or its equivalent, often relies on completeness, so can be a bigger challenge to prove than positive answers.
2. But *in some contexts*, we may not need the general completeness proof: it is sufficient *in this case* to know that the UNSAT is verified. This can be true for integration, and the special QF_NRA case.
3. This may require more book-keeping in the algorithm, to keep the "hints" that drove us this way.
4. Possibly (e.g. algebraic integration) we may not be able to prove UNSAT in all circumstances: is it still valuable to have a more nuanced return, e.g.

$$\begin{cases} F \text{ with proof} \\ \bot \text{ with proof} \\ \bot \text{ with proof but with assumptions} \\ \bot \text{ without proof} \end{cases} ?$$

Acknowledgements. The author is supported by EPSRC grant EP/T015713. This paper was motivated by an invitation to speak at *Machine-Assisted Proof*, held at the Institute for Pure and Applied Mathematics at UCLA, and the author is very grateful to the Institute, the organisers, those who discussed the talk, and to Anne Baanen for some discussions. The author is grateful to Ali Uncu for his comments on several drafts.

References

[ADE+20] Ábrahám, E., Davenport, J.H., England, M., Kremer, G., Tonks, Z.P.: New opportunities for the formal proof of computational real geometry?

In: SC^2 '20: Fifth International Workshop on Satisfiability Checking and Symbolic Computation CEUR Workshop Proceedings, vol. 2752, pp. 178–188 (2020)

[ADEK21a] Ábrahám, E., Davenport, J.H., England, M., Kremer, G.: Deciding the consistency of non-linear real arithmetic constraints with a conflict driven search using cylindrical algebraic coverings. J. Logical Algebr. Methods Program. Article **100633**, 119 (2021)

[ADEK21b] Ábrahám, E., Davenport, J.H., England, M., Kremer, G.: Proving UNSAT in SMT: the case of quantifier free non-linear real arithmetic (2021). http://arxiv.org/abs/2101.05320

[ASZ00] Abbott, J.A., Shoup, V., Zimmermann, P.: Factorization in $Z[x]$: the searching phase. In: Traverso, C. (ed.) Proceedings ISSAC 2000, pp. 1–7 (2000)

[Baa23] Baanen, A.: Provability of Ogg's Conjecture. Personal Communication at "Machine Assisted Proofs 2023" (2023)

[BBCD23] Baanen, A., Best, A.J., Coppola, N., Dahmen, S.R.: Formalized class group computations and integral points on Mordell Elliptic curves. In: CPP 2023: Proceedings of the 12th ACM SIGPLAN International Conference on Certified Programs and Proofs, pp. 47–62 (2023)

[Ber70] Berlekamp, E.R.: Factoring polynomials over large finite fields. Math. Comput. **24**, 713–735 (1970)

[BFT21] Barrett, C., Fontaine, P., Tinelli, C.: The SMT-LIB Standard: Version 2.6 (2021). http://smtlib.cs.uiowa.edu/papers/smt-lib-reference-v2.6-r2021-05-12.pdf

[Bro90] Bronstein, M.: Integration of elementary function. J. Symbol. Comput. **9**, 117–173 (1990)

[Bro91] Bronstein, M.: The algebraic Risch differential equation. In: Proceedings ISSAC 91, pp. 241–246 (1991)

[CDJW00] Corless, R.M., Davenport, J.H., Jeffrey, D.J., Watt, S.M.: According to Abramowitz and Stegun, or arccoth needn't be uncouth. SIGSAM Bull. **2**(34), 58–65 (2000)

[CM10] Cohen, C., Mahboubi, A.: A formal quantifier elimination for algebraically closed fields. In: Autexier, S., et al. (eds.) Proceedings CICM 2010, pp. 189–203 (2010)

[Col75] Collins, G.E.: Quantifier elimination for real closed fields by cylindrical algebraic decompostion. In: Brakhage, H. (ed.) Automata Theory and Formal Languages. LNCS, vol. 33, pp. 134–183. Springer, Berlin, Heidelberg (1975). https://doi.org/10.1007/3-540-07407-4_17

[Coo66] Cook, S.A.: On the minimum computation time of functions. PhD thesis, Department of Mathematics Harvard University (1966)

[CR88] Coste, M., Roy, M.-F.: Thom's lemma, the coding of real algebraic numbers and the computation of the topology of semi-algebraic sets. J. Symbol. Comput. **5**, 121–129 (1988)

[Dav81] Davenport, J.H.: On the Integration of Algebraic Functions. LNCS, vol. 102. Springer, Heidelberg (1981). (Russian ed. MIR Moscow 1985). https://doi.org/10.1007/3-540-10290-6

[Dav84] Davenport, J.H.: Intégration Algorithmique des fonctions élémentairement transcendantes sur une courbe algébrique. Annales de l'Institut Fourier **34**, 271–276 (1984)

[Dav86] Davenport, J.H.: On the Risch differential equation problem. SIAM J. Comput. **15**, 903–918 (1986)

[DH88]   Davenport, J.H., Heintz, J.: Real quantifier elimination is doubly exponential. J. Symbol. Comput. **5**, 29–35 (1988)

[DS00]   Davenport, J.H., Smith, G.C.: Fast recognition of alternating and symmetric groups. J. Pure Appl. Algebra **153**, 17–25 (2000)

[EBD15]   England, M., Bradford, R., Davenport, J.H.: Improving the use of equational constraints in cylindrical algebraic decomposition. In: Robertz, D. (ed.) Proceedings ISSAC 2015, pp. 165–172 (2015)

[Heu18]   Heule, M.J.H.: Schur number five. In: AAAI'18/IAAI'18/EAAI'18: Proceedings of the Thirty-Second AAAI Conference on Artificial Intelligence and Thirtieth Innovative Applications of Artificial Intelligence Conference and Eighth AAAI Symposium on Educational Advances in Artificial Intelligence Article No.: 808, pp. 6598–6606 (2018)

[Heu23]   Heule, M.J.: Organising SAT contests and DRAT proofs. Personal Commun. **15**, 2023 (2023)

[Kol73]   Kolchin, E.R.: Differential Algebra and Algebraic Groups. Academic Press, Cambridge (1973)

[Lio35]   Liouville, J.: Mémoire sur l'intégration d'une classe de fonctions transcendantes. Crelle's J. **13**, 93–118 (1835)

[LLL82]   Lenstra, A.K., Lenstra Jun, H.W., Lovász, L.: Factoring polynomials with rational coefficients. Math. Ann. **261**, 515–534 (1982)

[LP97]   Łuczak, T., Pyber, L.: On random generation of the symmetric group. In: Proceedings Combinatorics Geometry and Probability, pp. 463–470 (1997)

[Maz77]   Mazur, B.: Rational points on modular curves. In: Modular Functions of One Variable V, pp. 107–148 (1977)

[McC84]   McCallum, S.: An improved projection operation for cylindrical algebraic decomposition. Ph.D. thesis, University of Wisconsin-Madison Computer Science (1984)

[McC99a] McCallum, S.: Factors of iterated resultants and discriminants. J. Symbol. Comput. **27**, 367–385 (1999)

[McC99b] McCallum, S.: On projection in CAD-based quantifier elimination with equational constraints. In: Dooley, S. (ed.) Proceedings ISSAC '99, pp. 145–149 (1999)

[McC01]   McCallum, S.: On propagation of equational constraints in CAD-based quantifier elimination. In: Mourrain, B. (ed.) Proceedings ISSAC 2001, pp. 223–230 (2001)

[MN81]   Moore, P.M.A., Norman, A.C.: Implementing a polynomial factorization and GCD package. In: Proceedings SYMSAC 81, pp. 109–116 (1981)

[MPP19]   McCallum, S., Parusiński, A., Paunescu, L.: Validity proof of Lazard's method for CAD construction. J. Symbol. Comput. **92**, 52–69 (2019)

[Mus75]   Musser, D.R.: Multivariate polynomial factorization. J. ACM **22**, 291–308 (1975)

[Ric68]   Richardson, D.: Some unsolvable problems involving elementary functions of a real variable. J. Symbol. Log. **33**, 514–520 (1968)

[Ris69]   Risch, R.H.: The problem of integration in finite terms. Trans. A.M.S. **139**, 167–189 (1969)

[Ris79]   Risch, R.H.: Algebraic properties of the elementary functions of analysis. Am. J. Math. **101**, 743–759 (1979)

[Rit48]   Ritt, J.F.: Integration in Finite Terms: Liouville's Theory of Elementary Methods. Columbia University Press, New York (1948)

[Rit50]   Ritt, J.F.: Differential Algebra. Colloquium Proceedings, vol. XXXIII. American Mathematical Society (1950)

[SD69] Swinnerton-Dyer, H.P.F.: Letter to E.R. Berlekamp. Mentioned in [Ber70] (1969)

[Sei54] Seidenberg, A.: A new decision method for elementary algebra. Ann. Math. **60**, 365–374 (1954)

[Tar51] Tarski, A.: A Decision Method for Elementary Algebra and Geometry. 2nd edn. Univ. Cal. Press. Reprinted in Quantifier Elimination and Cylindrical Algebraic Decomposition (Ed. by, B.F. Caviness, J.R. Johnson), Springer, Wein-New York, 1998, pp. 24–84 (1951). https://doi.org/10.1007/978-3-7091-9459-1_3

[Wüt76] Wüthrich, H.R.: IX. Ein Entscheidungsverfahren für die Theorie der reellabgeschlossenen Kürper. In: Strassen, V. (ed.) Komplexität von Entscheidungsproblemen Ein Seminar. LNCS, vol. 43, pp. 138–162. Springer, Berlin, Heidelberg (1976). https://doi.org/10.1007/3-540-07805-3_10

[Zar65] Zariski, O.: Studies in equisingularity II. Am. J. Math. **87**, 972–1006 (1965)

[Zas69] Zassenhaus, H.: On Hensel factorization I. J. Number Theory **1**, 291–311 (1969)

Proving Results About OEIS Sequences
with Walnut

Jeffrey Shallit[✉][iD]

School of Computer Science, University of Waterloo, 200 University Ave. W.,
Waterloo, ON N2L 3G1, Canada
shallit@uwaterloo.ca

Abstract. We show how to "automatically" prove results about
sequences in the *On-Line Encyclopedia of Integer Sequences* (OEIS) using
a free software tool called Walnut, and illustrate it with a number of
examples chosen from the OEIS.

1 Introduction

The *On-Line Encyclopedia of Integer Sequences* (OEIS), originally created by
Neil Sloane [26], is an enormous database of mathematical information, containing over 361,000 integer sequences and theorems, conjectures, and citations to
papers about them. We owe Neil Sloane a huge debt of gratitude for his work
on this, and also to all the volunteers who edit the database.

In this paper I will discuss a theorem prover called Walnut that can "automatically" prove results about many sequences in the OEIS, illustrate its use in
proving some theorems, explain how you can use it in your own work, and talk
about its limitations.

2 What is Walnut?

Walnut is free software, written in Java, originally designed by Hamoon Mousavi
[17], with additions and changes by Aseem Raj Baranwal, Laindon C. Burnett,
Kai Hsiang Yang, and Anatoly Zavyalov.

It is available at

https://cs.uwaterloo.ca/~shallit/walnut.html.

Walnut can *rigorously prove* theorems about the natural numbers and some
sequences. It has already been used in over 60 papers in the literature, to prove
dozens of theorems (and even correct some incorrect ones in the literature!) For
a list, see the URL above.

Walnut is based on extensions of Presburger arithmetic; more precisely, on
systems such as $FO(\mathbb{N}, +, <, V_k)$, where $V_k(n)$ is the highest power of k dividing

Research supported by NSERC Grant number 2018-04118.

n. It also can handle variations on this logic where V_k is replaced by a suitable analogue in other numeration systems, such as Zeckendorf representation. `Walnut` implements a decision procedure first explained by Büchi [8], and later corrected and extended by Bruyère et al. [7]. It is powerful enough to handle statements about finite automata.

However, `Walnut` is *not* a general-purpose tool. It can prove results about sequences, but not *all* of them—just a special class called the (generalized) *automatic sequences*. Examples of sequences in this class include the Thue-Morse sequence [1], the Rudin-Shapiro sequence [20,24], the infinite Fibonacci word [4], the infinite Tribonacci word [18], Sturmian words [15, Chap. 2], paperfolding words [9], etc.

`Walnut` can prove theorems about automatic sequences, but not all of them. The theorem must be stated in first-order logic, and you can only do things like add, subtract, and compare integers, and index into the sequence. You can also use the existential ($\exists$) and universal ($\forall$) quantifiers. However, you *cannot* do multiplication by variables, or division, square root, arbitrary real numbers, primes, etc. You can multiply or divide by a constant, however. These restrictions are unavoidable, because allowing operations like multiplication of variables leads to undecidability.

The running time and space requirements of `Walnut` *in the worst-case* are extraordinarily high, so sometimes `Walnut` proof attempts fail because it runs out of space or would take years to complete the proof. Even so, you can do a lot with it, because the worst case seems to occur rather rarely in practice.

For a fairly complete introduction to `Walnut` and its capabilities, see my book [22].

3   An Example

Let us begin by using `Walnut` to prove the following extremely simple theorem:

Theorem 1. *The sum of two odd natural numbers is even.*

Proof. The first step is to translate the theorem into a more precise formulation in the language of first-order logic. So we will need to define what it means to be "odd" and "even". Here are the definitions:

$$\text{odd}(n) := \exists k \; n = 2k + 1$$
$$\text{even}(n) := \exists k \; n = 2k.$$

Here $\exists$ is the symbol for "there exists". So to say a number n is even just means it is a multiple of 2, and to say it is odd just means that when divided by 2, it leaves a remainder of one.

Next, we restate the desired theorem in first-order logic:

$$\forall m, n \; (\text{odd}(m) \wedge \text{odd}(n)) \implies \text{even}(m + n).$$

Here $\forall$ is the symbol for "for all", $\wedge$ is the symbol for "and", and $\implies$ is the symbol for logical implication.

Now we simply translate these statements into a form `Walnut` can understand. `Walnut` uses the capital letter E for ∃ and the capital letter A for ∀. It uses the ampersand & for ∧ and the symbols => for ⟹ . The `def` command is used to define logical formulas that can be reused in later commands by prefixing them with a dollar-sign. The `eval` command evaluates the truth of a formula with no free variables. (A variable is "free" if it is not bound by a quantifier.) Here is the output from `Walnut`:

```
[Walnut]$ def odd "Ek n=2*k+1";

[Walnut]$ def even "Ek n=2*k";

[Walnut]$ eval thm "Am,n ($odd(m) & $odd(n)) => $even(m+n)":
(odd(m))&odd(n))):2 states - 3ms
 ((odd(m))&odd(n)))=>even((m+n)))):1 states - 2ms
  (A m , n ((odd(m))&odd(n)))=>even((m+n))))):1 states - 1ms
Total computation time: 33ms.

----
TRUE
```

`Walnut` returns `TRUE`, so the theorem is now proved.   □

But the *real* power of `Walnut` is only apparent when you use it to deal with infinite sequences.

4   A More Serious Example

We turn to a more serious example. I searched the OEIS with search terms "Fibonacci conjecture" and I quickly found one that `Walnut` can handle.

A260311	Difference sequence of A260317.	2

1, 1, 1, 1, 1, 2, 2, 1, 2, 1, 2, 3, 2, 3, 2, 3, 3, 2, 3, 3, 2, 3, 5, 3, 2, 3, 5, 3, 2, 3,
5, 3, 5, 3, 2, 3, 5, 3, 5, 3, 2, 3, 5, 3, 5, 5, 3, 5, 3, 2, 3, 5, 3, 5, 5, 3, 5, 3, 2, 3,
5, 3, 5, 5, 3, 5, 5, 3, 5, 3, 2, 3, 5, 3, 5, 5, 3, 5, 3, 5, 5, 3, 5, 3 (list; graph; refs;
listen; history; text; internal format)

OFFSET   1,6

COMMENTS   Conjecture: a(n) is a Fibonacci number (A000045) for every n.

This conjecture, previously unsolved, asserts that the first difference of sequence A260317 is always a Fibonacci number. When we look this up sequence A260317 in the OEIS, we find the following:

A260317	Numbers not of the form v(m) + v(n), where v = A001950 (upper Wythoff numbers) and 1 <= m <= n - 1, for n >= 2.	2

1, 2, 3, 4, 5, 6, 8, 10, 11, 13, 14, 16, 19, 21, 24, 26, 29, 32, 34, 37, 40, 42, 45, 50,
53, 55, 58, 63, 66, 68, 71, 76, 79, 84, 87, 89, 92, 97, 100, 105, 108, 110, 113, 118, 121,
126, 131, 134, 139, 142, 144, 147, 152, 155, 160, 165, 168, 173, 176, 178, 181 (list; graph; refs;
listen; history; text; internal format)

OFFSET   1,2

COMMENTS   It appears that the difference sequence consists entirely of Fibonacci
              numbers (A000045); see A260311.

(Recall that the Fibonacci numbers, mentioned in the conjecture, are defined by $F_0 = 0$, $F_1 = 1$, and $F_n = F_{n-1} + F_{n-2}$ for $n \geq 2$.)

The sequence [A260317](A260317) is itself defined in terms of the upper Wythoff numbers, sequence [A001950](A001950), which is described as follows in the OEIS:

A001950	Upper Wythoff sequence (a Beatty sequence): a(n) = floor(n*phi^2), where phi = (1+sqrt(5))/2.	243
	(Formerly M1332 N0509)	

2, 5, 7, 10, 13, 15, 18, 20, 23, 26, 28, 31, 34, 36, 39, 41, 44, 47, 49, 52, 54, 57, 60, 62, 65, 68, 70, 73, 75, 78, 81, 83, 86, 89, 91, 94, 96, 99, 102, 104, 107, 109, 112, 115, 117, 120, 123, 125, 128, 130, 133, 136, 138, 141, 143, 146, 149, 151, 154, 157 (list; graph; refs;

listen; history; text; internal format)

OFFSET   1,1

Let us solve this conjecture with `Walnut`. First, we need a way to express the *upper Wythoff sequence:* this is the defined by the map

$$n \to \lfloor \varphi^2 n \rfloor,$$

where $\varphi = (1 + \sqrt{5})/2$ is the golden ratio. Luckily, there is already some `Walnut` code for this in the book [22]. (I'll explain how this was derived later.)

In `Walnut`, though, the only functions that we can handle *directly* must have finite range. So instead we use a small amount of subterfuge to define a function indirectly: we create a `Walnut` formula phi2n of *two* arguments, n and x, such that the result is TRUE if and only if $x = \lfloor \varphi^2 n \rfloor$. Such a function is called *synchronized* [21]. In `Walnut` the assertion that $x = \lfloor \varphi^2 n \rfloor$ is then expressed as follows:

$$\text{phi2n}(n, x).$$

Next, we need code for the OEIS sequence [A260317](A260317). Its description in the OEIS says "Numbers not of the form $v(m) + v(n)$, where $v = $ [A001950](A001950) (upper Wythoff numbers) and $1 \le m \le n-1$ for $n \ge 2$". Let us create a formula s2uw(z) that evaluates to TRUE iff z belongs to [A260317](A260317). In other words, s2uw(z) is true iff there do *not* exist m, n, x, y such that $z = x + y$ where phi2n(m,x) and phi2n(n,y) both hold, and m, n satisfy the constraints $1 \le m$, $m \le n - 1$, and $n \ge 2$.

This can be written as a first-order logical statement in `Walnut` as follows:

```
def s2uw "?msd_fib ~Em,n,x,y z=x+y & $phi2n(m,x) & $phi2n(n,y) &
    1<=m & m<=n-1 & n>=2":
```

Here ~ represents logical negation.

Now we need to define the gaps g between successive values of [A260317](A260317). To do that we say we create a logical formula gap(g) that evaluates to TRUE iff g belongs to [A260317](A260317). In other words, gap(g) is true iff there exist t, v such that $t < v$ and s2uw(t) and s2uw(v) both hold, but for all u between t and v, the assertion s2uw(u) does not hold, and $g = v - t$.

```
def gap "?msd_fib Et,v t<v & $s2uw(t) & $s2uw(v) &
    (Au (u>t & u<v) => ~$s2uw(u)) & g=v-t":
```

Finally, we assert that every gap is a Fibonacci number:

```
reg isfib msd_fib "0*10*":
eval thm "?msd_fib Ax $gap(x) => $isfib(x)":
```

and here is what we get:

```
[Walnut]$ eval thm "?msd_fib Ax $gap(x) => $isfib(x)":
(gap(x))=>isfib(x))):2 states - 44ms
 (A x (gap(x))=>isfib(x)))):1 states - 11ms
Total computation time: 96ms.

----
TRUE
```

This proves the conjecture!

In fact, we get even more. How is `gap` stored? It is a *finite automaton* that accepts the Fibonacci representation of those g that are elements of A260311, as given in Fig. 1.

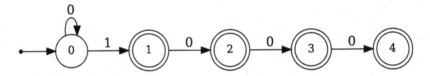

Fig. 1. Automaton recognizing the Fibonacci representations of elements of A260311.

In the Fibonacci numeration system [14, 27], the natural numbers are represented (uniquely) as sums of distinct Fibonacci numbers, subject to the criterion that no two consecutive Fibonacci numbers appear. We write such a representation as a binary string, $(n)_F := a_1 \cdots a_t$, where $n = \sum_{1 \le i \le t} a_i F_{t+2-i}$ for $a_i \in \{0, 1\}$ obeying the condition $a_i a_{i+1} \ne 1$. For example, $(43)_F = 10010001$.

By examining Fig. 1, we actually obtain something more:

Theorem 2. *The only possible gaps are* $1, 2, 3, 5$.

Finally, how did we get `phi2n`? We obtained the automaton for `phi2n` using a theorem in a paper of Don Reble in the OEIS [19]!

Theorem 3. *We have* $\lfloor n\varphi^2 \rfloor = x + 2$, *where* x *is the number obtained by taking the Fibonacci representation of* $n - 1$ *and concatenating two zeros on the end.*

This example also illustrates another feature (or perhaps limitation) of `Walnut`: the *particular representation chosen for numbers must be geared in some way to the particular problem*. Here we chose to use the Fibonacci numeration system because of the problem's obvious relationship to the golden ratio φ. If we had chosen an unrelated numeration system, such as base 2, we could not have found an automaton that computes $\lfloor \varphi^2 n \rfloor$. This is a consequence of a deep generalization of Cobham's theorem due to Durand [12].

5   How Does `Walnut` Work?

Internally, assertions such as `gap` and `s2uw` are stored as *finite automata*.

A finite automaton is a simple model of a computer. There are two variations that we use: an automaton with output (DFAO), that can compute a function of its input, and an automaton (DFA) as accepter/rejecter of its input.

With each logical formula f, we associate a DFA. The DFA has one or more inputs; these are the variables of the formula. The DFA accepts exactly those natural number values of the variables that make the formula f true.

In automaton diagrams, states are represented by circles or ovals. A DFA starts in a start state (denoted by a headless arrow coming into the state). It processes the symbols of the input one-by-one, following the arrow labeled with the symbol. If, after processing the whole input, it is in a final state (denoted by double circle), the input is accepted. Otherwise it is rejected.

By contrast, a DFAO returns an output specified in the state last reached when processing the input.

Here is the DFA for phi2n.

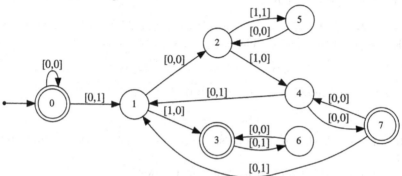

For example, phi2n(10,26) is true. The reader can check with the input

$$[0,1][0,0][1,0][0,1][0,0][1,0][0,0].$$

Here $[0010010]_F = 10$ and $[1001000]_F = 26$.

Walnut compiles a logical formula into the appropriate automaton. Each logical and arithmetic operation corresponds to some well-studied automaton transformation that can be carried out; see, for example, [13].

Some of these operations only increase the automaton size by a small amount. For example, AND and OR only multiply the sizes of the two automata. Other operations, like $\forall$, can blow up the size of the automata exponentially. This means that if there are t quantifier alternations, then the resulting automaton could be, in the worst case, of size something like

$$2^{2^{2^{\cdots 2^n}}},$$

where the height of the tower of exponents is t. Luckily, this sort of extraordinary space and time requirement seems to occur rarely in practice.

Numbers in Walnut have to be represented in some *numeration system*. Walnut can handle

- base-k representation for any fixed $k \geq 2$

- Fibonacci representation (aka Zeckendorf representation), where numbers are represented as sums of Fibonacci numbers
- Tribonacci representation
- Pell representation
- Ostrowski representation
- base-$(-k)$ representation

as well as user-defined numeration systems.

Walnut can prove first-order logical statements about (generalized) automatic sequences. These are sequences that are expressible as the outputs of DFAO's where the input is one of the 6 types of numeration system listed above. In particular, Walnut can handle words that are images (under a coding) of a fixed-point of a k-uniform morphism.

6 Another Example

Let us use Walnut to solve a previously-unsolved problem of Vladimir Shevelev [25]. He observed that for the Thue-Morse sequence

$$\mathbf{t} = t_0 t_1 t_2 \cdots = 0110100110010110 \cdots$$

there do not exist integers $0 < i < j$ such that

$$t_n \in \{t_{n+i}, t_{n+j}\}$$

for all n. Here t_n is the number of 1's, computed modulo 2, in the binary representation of n.

We can prove this claim with Walnut as follows:

```
eval shev1 "Ei,j 0<i & i<j & An (T[n]=T[n+i]|T[n]=T[n+j])":
```

and Walnut returns FALSE.

However, there *do* exist integers $0 < i < j < k$ such that

$$t_n \in \{t_{n+i}, t_{n+j}, t_{n+k}\}$$

for all n. Shevelev asked for a characterization of these valid triples (i, j, k). We can solve this problem by finding an automaton that accepts all valid triples, as follows:

```
def shev2 "0<i & i<j & j<k &
    An (T[n]=T[n+i]|T[n]=T[n+j]|T[n]=T[n+k])":
```

This was a big computation in Walnut! It used 6432 s of CPU time and 18 Gigs of RAM. The largest intermediate automaton had 2952594 states.

The resulting automaton shev2 has 53 states, and encodes all the valid triples (i, j, k). With it we can easily determine if a given triple has the desired property. We can also use it to prove various results of Shevelev, such as the following.

Theorem 4. *All triples of the form* $(a, a + 2^j, a + 2^k)$ *for* $a \geq 1$, $0 \leq j < k$, *are valid.*

For more details about these results, see [16].

7   Proving Conjectures by Guessing the Automaton

`Walnut` can sometimes *prove* conjectures obtained by *guessing!* The idea is to "guess" an automaton for a sequence using heuristics. Once the automaton is guessed, we then *rigorously verify* that it is correct using `Walnut`.

Let us work through an example. Consider OEIS sequence A140100:

A140100	Start with Y(0)=0, X(1)=1, Y(1)=2. For n > 1, choose least positive integers Y(n) > X(n) such that [25] neither Y(n) nor X(n) appear in {Y(k), 1 <= k < n} or {X(k), 1 <= k < n} and such that Y(n) - X(n) does not appear in {Y(k) - X(k), 1 <= k < n} or {Y(k) + X(k), 1 <= k < n}; sequence gives X(n) (for Y(n) see A140101).

1, 3, 4, 6, 7, 9, 10, 12, 14, 15, 17, 18, 20, 21, 23, 24, 26, 27, 29, 30, 32, 34, 35, 37, 38, 40, 41, 43, 44, 46, 47, 49, 51, 52, 54, 55, 57, 58, 60, 61, 63, 64, 66, 67, 69, 71, 72, 74, 75, 77, 78, 80, 82, 83, 85, 86, 88, 89, 91, 92, 94, 95, 97, 98, 100, 102, 103, 105, 106

Julien Cassaigne conjectured that for all k the sum $X(k) + Y(k)$ equals either $X(Y(k))$ or $Y(X(k))$. Our goal is to prove this conjecture.

The definition of the sequences $X(k)$ and $Y(k)$ are as follows: Start with $X(0) = 0$, $Y(0) = 0$, $X(1) = 1$, $Y(1) = 2$. For $n > 1$, choose the least positive integers $Y(n) > X(n)$ such that

neither $Y(n)$ nor $X(n)$ appear in $\{Y(k) : 1 \leq k < n\}$ or $\{X(k) : 1 \leq k < n\}$

and such that

$Y(n) - X(n)$ does not appear in $\{Y(k) - X(k) : 1 \leq k < n\}$

$$\text{or } \{Y(k) + X(k) : 1 \leq k < n\}.$$

There is no known foolproof way to take a definition like this and directly turn it into an automaton computing the sequence. However, in this case, we can "guess" an automaton for it as follows.

First, we decide on an appropriate numeration system. In this case, it is already known that this sequence is related to the Tribonacci numbers (see the OEIS description), so it is reasonable that we should use the Tribonacci numeration system. This system, analogous to the Fibonacci numeration system discussed earlier, is based on the sequence (T_n), where $T_0 = 0$, $T_1 = 1$, $T_2 = 1$, and $T_n = T_{n-1} + T_{n-2} + T_{n-3}$ for $n \geq 3$. Once again numbers are represented as sums of Tribonacci numbers, this time subject to the condition that no three consecutive Tribonacci numbers appear. We then represent pairs (n, x) in the Tribonacci numeration system, padding the shorter sequence with leading zeros, if needed.

Let us say that a pair is *valid* if $x = X(n)$. Say two strings y and z are equivalent if (yw is valid iff zw is valid), for all w of length $\leq i$, for some fixed i. We used $i = 6$.

Do a breadth-first search on the set of all possible strings, identifying the (finitely many) equivalence classes. One can then construct a candidate automaton out of these equivalence classes. When we do this, we find a Tribonacci automaton of 27 states for $X(n)$ and 30 states for $Y(n)$. This is our guess.

Now comes the important part: we use `Walnut` to verify that our guess is correct, using mathematical induction. Recall that to prove some proposition

$P(n)$ about all natural numbers n by induction, one needs to prove (a) $P(0)$ holds (or some other suitable base case) and (b) $P(n) \implies P(n+1)$. We can use `Walnut` to carry out both (a) and (b).

For our particular candidate automaton, this works as follows. We say that a triple (n, x, y) is *good* if all of the following conditions hold:

1. $y > x$;
2. $x \notin \{X(k) : 1 \le k < n\}$
3. $y \notin \{X(k) : 1 \le k < n\}$
4. $x \notin \{Y(k) : 1 \le k < n\}$
5. $y \notin \{Y(k) : 1 \le k < n\}$
6. $y - x \notin \{Y(k) - X(k) : 1 \le k < n\}$
7. $y - x \notin \{Y(k) + X(k) : 1 \le k < n\}$

To carry out the induction proof we must show three things:

1. The triple $(n, X(n), Y(n))$ is good for all $n \ge 1$;
2. If (n, x, y) is good then $x \ge X(n)$;
3. If $(n, X(n), y)$ is good then $y \ge Y(n)$.

The latter two conditions ensure that each value of $X(n)$ and $Y(n)$ chosen iteratively is indeed the minimal possible value among good candidates.

The verification of (1)–(3) can then be carried out by the following `Walnut` code.

```
def good "?msd_trib y>x & (~Ek k<n & $xaut(k,x)) &
    (~Ek k<n & $xaut(k,y)) & (~Ek k<n & $yaut(k,x)) &
    (~Ek k<n & $yaut(k,y)) & (~Ek,a,b k<n & $xaut(k,a) &
    $yaut(k,b) & y+a=b+x) & (~Ek,a,b k<n & $xaut(k,a) &
    $yaut(k,b) & y+a=b+x)":
eval check1 "?msd_trib An,x,y (n>=1 & $xaut(n,x) & $yaut(n,y)) =>
    $good(n,x,y)":
eval check2 "?msd_trib An,x,y (n>=1 & $good(n,x,y)) =>
    (Ez $xaut(n,z) & x>=z)":
eval check3 "?msd_trib An,x,y (n>=1 & $xaut(n,x) & $good(n,x,y)) =>
    (Ez $yaut(n,z) & y>=z)":
```

and the last three commands all return `TRUE`. After the (trivial) verification of the base cases $X(0) = 0$, $Y(0) = 0$, $X(1) = 1$, $Y(1) = 2$, the induction proof is complete, and we know our candidate automaton is correct.

Now that we have verified the automaton, we are ready to prove Cassaigne's conjecture.

Theorem 5. *For all k the sum $X(k)+Y(k)$ equals either $X(Y(k))$ or $Y(X(k))$.*

```
eval julien1 "?msd_trib An,x,y,xy,yx ($xaut(n,x) & $yaut(n,y) &
    $xaut(y,xy) & $yaut(x,yx)) => (xy=x+y|yx=x+y)":
```

And `Walnut` returns `TRUE`. The conjecture is proved.

For more details about this conjecture, see [23].

8   Other Capabilities of Walnut

Walnut can also count things. In some cases it can find what is known as a *linear representation* for a function.

A linear representation for a function $f : \mathbb{N} \to \mathbb{N}$ is a triple of the form (v, γ, w), where

- v is a $1 \times r$ matrix,
- $\gamma(a)$ is an $r \times r$ matrix for all a
- w is an $r \times 1$ matrix

and $f(n) = v\gamma(x)w$ for all representations x of n. If $x = a_1 a_2 \cdots a_i$, then $\gamma(x) = \gamma(a_1)\gamma(a_2) \cdots \gamma(a_i)$. Here the representations can be base k, Fibonacci, Tribonacci, etc.

Linear representations can often be used to prove theorems about $f(n)$ and its growth rate.

For example, let us evaluate $\rho(n)$, the number of distinct length-n blocks appearing in the Thue-Morse sequence **t**. This sequence is <u>A005942</u> in the OEIS. This was computed independently by Brlek [6], de Luca and Varricchio [10], and Avgustinovich [2].

```
def equalblock "At (t<n) => T[i+t]=T[j+t]":
def novelblock "Ak (k<i) => ~$equalblock(i,k,n)":
def countblock n "$novelblock(i,n)":
```

Walnut outputs a linear representation in a form that Maple can understand:

$$v = \begin{bmatrix} 1 \\ 1 \\ 0 \\ 0 \\ 1 \\ 0 \\ 0 \\ 0 \end{bmatrix}^T \quad \gamma(0) = \begin{bmatrix} 1 & 1 & 0 & 0 & 0 & 0 & 0 & 0 \\ 0 & 0 & 0 & 1 & 0 & 0 & 0 & 0 \\ 0 & 0 & 2 & 0 & 0 & 0 & 0 & 0 \\ 0 & 0 & 1 & 0 & 0 & 1 & 0 & 0 \\ 0 & 0 & 0 & 0 & 0 & 0 & 0 & 0 \\ 0 & 0 & 1 & 0 & 0 & 1 & 0 & 0 \\ 0 & 0 & 0 & 0 & 0 & 0 & 1 & 0 \\ 0 & 0 & 0 & 0 & 0 & 0 & 2 & 0 \end{bmatrix} \quad \gamma(1) = \begin{bmatrix} 0 & 0 & 1 & 1 & 0 & 0 & 0 & 0 \\ 0 & 0 & 0 & 0 & 0 & 1 & 1 & 0 \\ 0 & 0 & 2 & 0 & 0 & 0 & 0 & 0 \\ 0 & 0 & 2 & 0 & 0 & 0 & 0 & 0 \\ 0 & 0 & 0 & 0 & 0 & 0 & 1 & 1 \\ 0 & 0 & 2 & 0 & 0 & 0 & 0 & 0 \\ 0 & 0 & 0 & 0 & 0 & 1 & 1 & 0 \\ 0 & 0 & 0 & 0 & 0 & 2 & 0 & 0 \end{bmatrix} \quad w = \begin{bmatrix} 1 \\ 0 \\ 1 \\ 1 \\ 1 \\ 0 \\ 0 \\ 0 \end{bmatrix}$$

With this representation we can quickly compute $\rho(n)$, the number of distinct length-n blocks in **t**, very efficiently.

Furthermore, we can compute the exact value of $\rho(2^k)$ as follows: we have

$$\rho(2^k) = v \cdot \gamma(1) \cdot \gamma(0)^k \cdot w,$$

and the minimal polynomial of $\gamma(0)$ is $X^2(X-1)(X-2)$. This means that $\rho(2^k) = a + b \cdot 2^k$ for some constants a, b and $k \geq 2$. We can now use the linear representation to compute $\rho(2^k)$ for $k = 2, 3$ and solve for a, b. We have $\rho(4) = 10$ and $\rho(8) = 22$. Hence $a = -2$, $b = 3$. So $\rho(2^k) = 3 \cdot 2^k - 2$ for $k \geq 2$.

In the OEIS, several different characterizations of $\rho(n)$ are given:

(a) $\rho(n) = 3(n-1) + d(n-1)$ for $n > 2$, where $d(n)$ is the distance from n to the closest power of 2.
(b) $\rho(2n) = \rho(n) + \rho(n+1)$ for $n \geq 2$.
(c) $\rho(2n+1) = 2\rho(n+1)$ for $n \geq 2$.

Let us prove each of these. We start with (a): define a synchronized function $\rho'(n)$ by $\rho'(n) = \rho(n)$ for $n \leq 2$, and otherwise $\rho'(n) = 3(n-1) + d(n-1)$. Our goal is to show $\rho'(n) = \rho(n)$. To do so, first we trap n between two powers of 2: $2^i \leq n < 2^{i+1}$. Then the distance is either $n - 2^i$ or $2^{i+1} - n$, depending on which is smallest. This works for all $n \geq 1$. Now we can use `Walnut` to compute a linear representation for $\rho'(n)$, as follows:

```
reg power2 msd_2 "0*10*":
def dist2 "(n=0&y=1) | Ex $power2(x) & x<=n & n<2*x &
   ((2*n<=3*x & y+x=n)|(2*n>3*x & y+n=2*x))":
def rhop "(n=0&z=1) | (n=1&z=2) | (n=2&z=4) |
   (n>=3 & Ey $dist2(n-1,y) & z+3=3*n+y)":
def lrc n "Ez i<z & $rhop(n,z)":
```

The last command gives a linear representation of rank 14 for $\rho'(n)$; we just need to see it is the same as $\rho(n)$. To do so, from the two linear representations we compute one for the difference $\rho(n) - \rho'(n)$ and then minimize it using an algorithm of Schützenberger [5]. It minimizes to the 0 function, so the two are identical.

With the synchronized representation for $\rho'(n)$ in hand, we can very easily verify (b) and (c) now:

```
eval testb "An,x,y,z (n>=2 & $rhop(2*n,x) & $rhop(n,y) &
   $rhop(n+1,z)) => x=y+z":
eval testc "An,x,y (n>=2 & $rhop(2*n+1,x) & $rhop(n+1,y)) => x=2*y":
```

and both return `TRUE`.

Linear representations can be extremely useful for proving properties of sequences. As an example, let's consider the recent refutation of a conjecture of Dombi [11]. He conjectured that there is no set $A \subset \mathbb{N}$ such that (a) the complement $\mathbb{N} \setminus A$ is infinite and (b) the sequence $r(n)$ counting the number of (ordered) triples $(x, y, z) \in A^3$ that sum to n is strictly increasing. However, in a recent paper [3], Bell and I found a counterexample: let $F = \{2^{n+2} - 1 : n \geq 0\}$ and define $A = \mathbb{N} \setminus F$.

To prove that it works, we first use `Walnut` to find linear representations for the two sequences $(r(n))_{n \geq 0}$ and $(r(n-1))_{n \geq 0}$; then we use a simple block matrix construction to find a linear representation for their difference $d(n) := r(n) - r(n-1)$. Graphing this sequence $d(n)$ suggests that $d(n)$ is approximately $n - 3\lfloor \log_2 n \rfloor$. If $e(n) = d(n) - n + 3\lfloor \log_2 n \rfloor$, then we can easily compute a linear representation for $e(n)$, too. Then a simple idea called the "semigroup trick" [22, §4.11] proves that $e(n)$ takes only finitely many values, and hence is automatic in base 2. The resulting bounds on $e(n)$ are enough to prove that $d(n) > 0$ for all n.

9   Common Mistakes When Using `Walnut`

- Watch out for edge cases. Sometimes a theorem is true for all $n \geq 1$ but fails for $n = 0$.

- Don't use logical assertions with variables in the wrong order. The order of arguments in a multi-variable assertion is alphabetical order of the variable names used to define it.
- Since the domain of variables is understood to be $\mathbb{N}$, the natural numbers, subexpressions that give negative numbers can cause incorrect results. All subexpressions must be non-negative.

10   Tips for Using Walnut

- There are often different ways to translate the same logical statement into Walnut. Some can take much longer to translate than others.
- There are often multiple characterizations of the same property. Some may be first-order expressible, some may not.
- Sometimes being more general takes much more time and space than being specific.

11   A Final Word

Walnut is free and downloadable from https://cs.uwaterloo.ca/~shallit/walnut.html.

If you use it to solve a problem, please let me know about it!

References

1. Allouche, J.P., Shallit, J.O.: The ubiquitous Prouhet-Thue-Morse sequence. In: Ding, C., Helleseth, T., Niederreiter, H. (eds.) Sequences and Their Applications, pp. 1–16. Springer, London (1999). https://doi.org/10.1007/978-1-4471-0551-0_1
2. Avgustinovich, S.V.: The number of different subwords of given length in the Morse-Hedlund sequence. Sibirsk. Zh. Issled. Oper. 1, 3–7, 103 (1994, in Russian). English translation in A. D. Korshunov (ed.) Discrete Analysis and Operations Research, pp. 1–5. Kluwer (1996)
3. Bell, J.P., Shallit, J.: Counterexamples to a conjecture of Dombi in additive number theory. Acta Math. Hung. (2023, to appear)
4. Berstel, J.: Fibonacci words-a survey. In: Rozenberg, G., Salomaa, A. (eds.) The Book of L, pp. 13–27. Springer, Heidelberg (1986). https://doi.org/10.1007/978-3-642-95486-3_2
5. Berstel, J., Reutenauer, C.: Noncommutative Rational Series with Applications. Encyclopedia of Mathematics and Its Applications, vol. 137. Cambridge University Press, Cambridge (2011)
6. Brlek, S.: Enumeration of factors in the Thue-Morse word. Disc. Appl. Math. 24, 83–96 (1989)
7. Bruyère, V., Hansel, G., Michaux, C., Villemaire, R.: Logic and p-recognizable sets of integers. Bull. Belgian Math. Soc. 1, 191–238 (1994). Corrigendum, Bull. Belg. Math. Soc. 1, 577 (1994)

8. Büchi, J.R.: Weak secord-order arithmetic and finite automata. Zeitschrift für mathematische Logik und Grundlagen der Mathematik **6**, 66–92 (1960). Reprinted in S. Mac Lane and D. Siefkes (eds.) The Collected Works of J. Richard Büchi, pp. 398–424. Springer (1990)

9. Davis, C., Knuth, D.E.: Number representations and dragon curves-I, II. J. Recreational Math. **3**(66–81), 133–149 (1970)

10. de Luca, A., Varricchio, S.: Some combinatorial properties of the Thue-Morse sequence and a problem in semigroups. Theoret. Comput. Sci. **63**, 333–348 (1989)

11. Dombi, G.: Additive properties of certain sets. Acta Arith **103**, 137–146 (2002)

12. Durand, F.: Cobham's theorem for substitutions. J. Eur. Math. Soc. **13**, 1799–1814 (2011)

13. Hopcroft, J.E., Ullman, J.D.: Introduction to Automata Theory, Languages, and Computation. Addison-Wesley, Boston (1979)

14. Lekkerkerker, C.G.: Voorstelling van natuurlijke getallen door een som van getallen van Fibonacci. Simon Stevin **29**, 190–195 (1952)

15. Lothaire, M.: Algebraic Combinatorics on Words. Encyclopedia of Mathematics and Its Applications, vol. 90. Cambridge University Press, Cambridge (2002)

16. Meleshko, J., Ochem, P., Shallit, J., Shan, S.L.: Pseudoperiodic words and a question of Shevelev (2022). arxiv preprint arXiv:2207.10171. https://arxiv.org/abs/2207.10171

17. Mousavi, H.: Automatic theorem proving in Walnut (2016). arxiv preprint arXiv:1603.06017. http://arxiv.org/abs/1603.06017

18. Rauzy, G.: Nombres algébriques et substitutions. Bull. Soc. Math. France **110**, 147–178 (1982)

19. Reble, D.: Zeckendorf vs. Wythoff representations: comments on A007895 (2008). https://oeis.org/A007895/a007895.pdf

20. Rudin, W.: Some theorems on Fourier coefficients. Proc. Amer. Math. Soc. **10**, 855–859 (1959)

21. Shallit, J.: Synchronized sequences. In: Lecroq, T., Puzynina, S. (eds.) WORDS 2021. LNCS, vol. 12847, pp. 1–19. Springer, Cham (2021). https://doi.org/10.1007/978-3-030-85088-3_1

22. Shallit, J.: The Logical Approach To Automatic Sequences: Exploring Combinatorics on Words with Walnut, London Math. Society Lecture Note Series, vol. 482. Cambridge University Press, Cambridge (2022)

23. Shallit, J.: Some Tribonacci conjectures (2023). arXiv preprint arXiv:2210.03996. https://arxiv.org/abs/2210.03996. To appear, Fibonacci Quart

24. Shapiro, H.S.: Extremal problems for polynomials and power series. Master's thesis, MIT (1952)

25. Shevelev, V.: Equations of the form $t(x + a) = t(x)$ and $t(x + a) = 1 - t(x)$ for Thue-Morse sequence (2012). arxiv preprint arXiv:0907.0880. https://arxiv.org/abs/0907.0880

26. Sloane, N.J.A., et al.: The on-line encyclopedia of integer sequences (2023). https://oeis.org

27. Zeckendorf, E.: Représentation des nombres naturels par une somme de nombres de Fibonacci ou de nombres de Lucas. Bull. Soc. Roy. Liège **41**, 179–182 (1972)

System and Dataset Descriptions

ProofLang: The Language of arXiv Proofs

Henry Hammer⬥, Nanako Noda⬥, and Christopher A. Stone(✉)⬥

Harvey Mudd College, Claremont, CA 91711, USA
{stone,hhammer,nnoda}@cs.hmc.edu

Abstract. The ProofLang Corpus includes 3.7M proofs (558 million words) mechanically extracted from papers that were posted on arXiv.org between 1992 and 2020. The focus of this corpus is proofs, rather than the explanatory text that surrounds them, and more specifically on the *language* used in such proofs. Specific mathematical content is filtered out, resulting in sentences such as Let MATH be the restriction of MATH to MATH. This dataset reflects how people prefer to write (informal) proofs, and is also amenable to statistical analyses and experiments with Natural Language Processing (NLP) techniques.

Keywords: Dataset · Informal proofs · Natural Language Processing

1 Introduction

How do people use language in proofs written for other humans? Is "Assume..." more or less common than "Suppose..."? How closely do the English-language subsets accepted by tools like Mizar [1], Naproche-SAD [2], or Isar [3] correspond to the way proofs are written in the literature? How well do off-the-shelf NLP tools like NLTK [4] work on the stylized language of English-language proofs? Is Ganesalingam [5] correct that "Mathematical language is exceptionally well-suited" to analysis "in the way that generative syntacticians and semanticists analyze natural languages"?

The ProofLang Corpus[1] is a resource for addressing such questions. It consists of the text of English-language proofs mechanically extracted from the LaTeX sources of papers posted on arXiv.org from 1992 through April 2020. In order to focus on the language used in proofs (and make repeated word patterns more apparent), LaTeX mathematical content is replaced by the token MATH. Further cleanup steps include replacing references like \ref{...} or Theorem 2(a) by REF; replacing citations like \cite{...} or Smith [42] with CITE; and replacing proper names with NAME.

---

[1] https://huggingface.co/datasets/proofcheck/prooflang.

This research was supported in part by the Jean Perkins Foundation and by the NSF under Grant No. 1950885. Any opinions, findings, or conclusions are those of the authors alone, and do not necessarily reflect the views of the NSF or JPF.

C. Dubois and M. Kerber (Eds.): CICM 2023, LNAI 14101, pp. 285–290, 2023.
https://doi.org/10.1007/978-3-031-42753-4_19

The resulting dataset (a few examples appear in Fig. 1) is freely available for download or can be directly accessed from Python scripts.

1   Existence is a special case of CITE. Uniqueness follows from the proof of CITE.
2   This is exactly REF. (Actually, that reference works with the abelian variety MATH ...
3   We have MATH if and only if MATH, which is equivalent to MATH.
4   REF stays valid when considered locally at a prime number MATH, that is, replacing ...
5   What we need to prove is equivalent to the statement that the subgroup MATH acts ...
6   This follows by taking MATH in the following lemma.
7   Interpret MATH as a MATH real matrix by identifying MATH with MATH. Let MATH be ...
8   Let us recall the situation of REF : we have a symplectic basis MATH of MATH with ...
9   We already know MATH by REF , which is the first statement in REF . Next, we have ...
10 REF is a special case of REF as follows. Pick MATH. Then MATH since multiplication by ...
11 Note that REF already implies that MATH acts trivially on MATH, so that it remains to ...
12 Assume that MATH is an extension of degree MATH, so MATH, MATH and MATH as in ...
13 This follows with some algebraic manipulation from REF (see also CITE). Indeed, ...
14 Let MATH be a quotient of theta constants as in REF . We start by proving MATH. Note ...
15 The NAME coefficients are finite sums of factors MATH from the definition of MATH. ...
16 We have already proven the result for MATH. Any element MATH can be written as MATH ...
17 Given MATH, let MATH be a generator of MATH as in the definition of MATH. Let MATH ...
18 This is an elementary calculation built on the observation that each element MATH in ...
19 Substituting MATH into REF gives the result.
20 See REF.

Fig. 1. The Beginnings of 20 Extracted Proofs

2   Constructing the ProofLang Corpus

We started with LaTeX sources for 1.6M papers submitted to arXiv.org between 1992 and mid-2020, retrieved using arXiv's Bulk Data Access. We identified 352K candidate papers where some source file contained the line \begin{proof}. After skipping papers where no proof could be extracted and running language detection on extracted proofs (to remove non-English output), we ended up with 328K papers with at least one extracted proof. These papers hail from a variety of different fields but the bulk of relevant papers are in mathematics or computer science: looking at arXiv subject tags, 281K papers have a math tag, 68K CS, 20K physics, 5.1K systems, 3.4K economics, and 2.4K biology.

The proofs were extracted using a Python script simulating parts of LaTeX (including defining/expanding macros). It does no real typesetting, throws away text not in \begin{proof}... \end{proof}, and compresses math content to MATH. Surprisingly, trying to implement LaTeX more faithfully gave worse results; the more the extractor knew about idiosyncrasies of TeX, the more it ran into other imperfectly simulated constructs, with unrecoverable errors in complex macros. It worked better to hard-code common cases (e.g., common environments to skip because they represent figures or diagrams; common macros to ignore because they only affect spacing or color) and to ignore unrecognized macros.

During extraction, math-mode formulas (signalled by $, \[, \begin{equation}, etc.) become MATH; \ref{...} and its variants (\autoref, \subref, etc.) become \REF; \cite{...} and its variants (\Citet, \shortciteNP, etc.) become CITE; words that appear to be proper names become NAME; and \item becomes CASE:.

We then run a cleanup pass on the extracted proofs that includes fixing common extraction errors (e.g., due to uninterpreted macros); replacing textual references by REF (e.g., Theorem A.2 or Postulate (*)); replacing textual citations with CITE (e.g., Page 47 of [3]); and replacing more proof-case markers with CASE: (e.g., Case 3)).

The resulting dataset (3.7M proofs containing 558M words in 38.9M sentences) is publicly available under a Creative Commons Attribution 4.0 license.[2] Data can be downloaded as TSV files; accessing the data programmatically from Python is also possible using the Hugging Face `Datasets` library [6], e.g.,

```
from datasets import load_dataset
dataset = load_dataset('proofcheck/prooflang', 'proofs', split='train')
for d in dataset:
    print(d['paper'], d['proof'])
```

To loop over individual sentences from the proofs, replace `'proofs'` and `d['proof']` by `'sentences'` and `d['sentence']`.

Also available is a mapping from paper IDs to a comma-separated list of arXiv subject tags (which allows filtering proofs by subject area), and a "raw" version of the proofs that shows the extracted proofs before the cleanup pass. Further metadata for proofs can be found on arXiv, since each sentence or proof tagged with paper `<id>` is from the paper at `https://arxiv.org/abs/<id>`.

3 Experimenting with the Corpus

So far, we have focused on collecting the data, and have only run relatively simple experiments. For example, it's easy to count occurrences of words. In this corpus, the word assume appears more often than suppose (1119 K vs. 784 K case-insensitive occurrences), but at the start of a sentence Suppose... occurs much more often than Assume... (436 K vs. 263 K occurrences).

3.1 Identifying Collocations

We can also count occurrences of repeated sentences. Of course short ones like Let MATH. or Then MATH. are most likely to repeat exactly (315 K and 185 K times), but we can also compare counts for variants of longer sentences, e.g.,

---

[2] Papers on arXiv.org are not in the public domain, but all relevant legal factors (the purpose and character of the use, the nature of the original works, the amount and substantiality of the copied text, and the effect upon the potential market for the original) favor a conclusion of Fair Use under US copyright law.

Without loss of generality we may assume that MATH. 4.0 K
Without loss of generality assume that MATH.   2.3 K
Without loss of generality we assume that MATH.   2.2 K
Without loss of generality we can assume that MATH. 2.2 K
We may assume without loss of generality that MATH. 0.8 K

Longer sentences rarely have a large number of exact repeats, so one can also look for collocations (idiomatic phrases) occurring inside sentences.

ad absurdum	equally likely	regularly varying
almost surely	finitely many	roughly speaking
arithmetic progressions	greater than	slowly varying
barycentric subdivision	MATH-differentially private	social welfare
blow ups	maximally entangled	spherical harmonics
brownian motion	mutatis mutandis	sufficently large
brute force	one-point compactification	supplementary material
compactly supported	pigeon hole	tamely ramified
complementary slackness	principally polarized	train track
dominated convergence	purely inseparable	vice versa
dynamic programming	references therein	without loss

Fig. 2. Selected 2-Word Collocations from the Corpus

We started from bigrams (2-word sequences) in our corpus. For example, the sentence Let MATH be even contains the three bigrams (let, MATH), (MATH, be), and (be, even). For bigrams occurring more than 500 times we calculated statistics such as Pointwise Mutual Information and χ^2 to identify pairs of words that appeared together more often than could be explained by chance. This automatically finds a large number of conventional phrases; a few are shown in Fig. 2. By treating the discovered collocations as single-word units and iterating the bigram process, we can find longer collocations like induces an isomorphism between and it suffices to check that.

3.2   Testing the NLTK Part-of-Speech Tagger

NLTK, the Natural Language Toolkit [4], is a Python package for traditional NLP statistical algorithms. We were curious how well it would do at POS (Part-of-Speech) tagging on our corpus, i.e., identifying a part of speech for each word in a sentence. As a simple example, the three words in We like proofs should be tagged as personal-pronoun, third-person-present-verb, and plural-noun.

NLTK's default POS tagger (a perceptron trained on text from the Wall Street Journal) is reasonably accurate for many purposes, but experiments with the corpus showed it performs more poorly on mathematical language.

The first aspect is the vocabulary, not only because mathematical jargon is rare in the training corpus, but also because the usage of more common words differs. For example, integral is generally used as an adjective in newspapers, so the default tagger always tags integral as an adjective even though within proofs integral is often a noun. Worse, integral is in the top 300 most-frequent words (occurring 187K times), and whenever the tagger mis-tags integral, it is likely to mis-tag neighboring words as well. Other problems include literal, metric, and variable (where the default tagger confuses noun vs. adjective) and partition, factor, and embedding (where the default tagger confuses verb vs. noun).

The most consistent problem is the mis-tagging of verbs in imperative sentences. Trained on news text, the default tagger seems unaware that sentences can start with verbs and tags these unexpected verbs as proper nouns, apparently because the start of a sentence is always capitalized. For example, given the sentence Suppose MATH is even, NLTK mis-tags Suppose MATH as proper nouns as if this were a declarative sentence like "John Smith is tall" (except that it further mis-tags even as an adverb instead of an adjective).

Similarly, Consider for all MATH the subtree MATH of MATH spanned by the root and the first MATH leaves MATH with MATH is mis-tagged with Consider as a proper noun, subtree as an adjective, and leaves as a verb.

Preliminary experiments with re-training the NLTK POS tagger showed that adding manually tagged sentences from our corpus to the training set—5 imperative sentences for each of 50 common verbs—significantly improved its performance on imperative sentences with these and other verbs. Interestingly, adding more sentences for each verb made performance worse overall; we hypothesize it was over-fitting and memorizing just the specific imperative verbs we provided.

4 Conclusion and Future Work

The ProofLang Corpus is a new dataset showing how people naturally phrase their claims, structure mathematical arguments, and use language in proofs written for humans. We hope it can aid the development of language-based proof assistants and proof checkers for professional and educational purposes.

As the corpus is heuristically extracted from LaTeX files, it does contain errors; one can probably spend arbitrary amounts of time polishing the corpus by handling more corner cases. More general cleanup strategies might be helpful, e.g., training *Named Entity Recognition* to recognize references to mathematical facts (e.g., Theorem 2a.) replacing our ad hoc regular expressions.

It would also be interesting to distinguish MATH-as-noun (e.g., Then $n > 1$ is prime) from MATH-as-clause (e.g., If $n > 1$ then the theorem holds). We conjecture that generalized POS tagging might be helpful here.

While we plan further analyses ourselves (e.g., identifying more general collocations and applying language-model techniques), we also hope that others can find interesting applications for this dataset.

References

1. Grabowski, A., Kornilowicz, A., Naumowicz, A.: Mizar in a Nutshell. J. Formal. Reasoning **3**(2), 153–245 (2010). https://doi.org/10.6092/issn.1972-5787/1980

2. De Lon, Adrian, Koepke, Peter, Lorenzen, Anton: Interpreting mathematical texts in Naproche-SAD. In: Benzmüller, Christoph, Miller, Bruce (eds.) CICM 2020. LNCS (LNAI), vol. 12236, pp. 284–289. Springer, Cham (2020). https://doi.org/10.1007/978-3-030-53518-6_19

3. Wenzel, Markus: Isar — a generic interpretative approach to readable formal proof documents. In: Bertot, Yves, Dowek, Gilles, Théry, Laurent, Hirschowitz, André, Paulin, Christine (eds.) TPHOLs 1999. LNCS, vol. 1690, pp. 167–183. Springer, Heidelberg (1999). https://doi.org/10.1007/3-540-48256-3_12

4. Bird, S., Loper, E., Klein, E.: Natural Language Processing with Python. O'Reilly Media Inc. (2009)

5. Ganesalingam, Mohan: The Language of Mathematics. LNCS, vol. 7805. Springer, Heidelberg (2013). https://doi.org/10.1007/978-3-642-37012-0

6. Hugging Face: Datasets. https://huggingface.co/docs/datasets

True Crafted Formula Families for Benchmarking Quantified Satisfiability Solvers

Simone Heisinger$^{(\boxtimes)}$ and Martina Seidl

Institute for Symbolic Artificial Intelligence, Johannes Kepler University,
Linz, Austria
simone.heisinger@jku.at

Abstract. As the application of quantified Boolean formulas (QBF) continues to expand in various scientific and industrial domains, the development of efficient QBF solvers and their underlying proving strategies is of growing importance. To understand and to compare different solving approaches, techniques of proof complexity are applied. To this end, formula families have been crafted that exhibit certain properties of proof systems. These formulas are valuable to test and compare specific solver implementations. Traditionally, the focus is on false formulas, in this work we extend the formula generator QBFFam to produce true formulas based on two popular formula families from proof complexity.

Keywords: QBF · Solver · Benchmarking · KBKF · QParity

1 Introduction

Quantified Boolean Formulas (QBFs) extend the language of propositional logic by existential and universal quantifiers over the Boolean variables [3]. For example $(x \leftrightarrow y)$ is propositional formula while $\forall x \exists y.(x \leftrightarrow y)$ and $\exists y \forall x.(x \leftrightarrow y)$ are QBFs. The decision problem of QBF is PSPACE-complete. In contrast to SAT, which has the asymmetry that the solution of a true formula is easy to validate (by propagating the satisfying assignment returned by the solver), but unsatisfiability most likely not, the situation in QBF is different. Because of universal quantification, there is a duality between true and false formulas. Inspired by the progress in SAT in the field of proof complexity, many techniques and ideas have been transferred to QBF, but the focus is mainly on false formulas, while true formulas need to be considered as well [5,9]. The intention is to understand the behavior of solving paradigms based on their underlying proof systems. In QBF, much progress has been made in this regard, establishing relationships between proof systems like Q-resolution, the formal basis of conflict/solution-driven clause/cube learning (QCDCL), ∀Exp+Res proofs which characterize expansion-based systems and others [3]. Here, a core technique is to craft formula families of certain structure that enforce a certain behavior of the proof

Supported by the LIT AI Lab funded by the State of Upper Austria.

systems and therefore also of the implementing solvers. These formulas are not only of theoretical interest, but also provide valuable benchmarks for testing and evaluating solvers. Many of such formula families are implemented in the tool QBFFam [4]. So far, all of these formulas are false. In this paper, we present two families of crafted formulas that are true. Inspired by popular families of false crafted formulas they are constructed in a such a way that they reveal weaknesses of proof systems, i.e., even their shortest proofs are exponential in the formula size. A small experimental evaluation shows that the behavior of the solvers can indeed be characterized by crafted formulas.

We include the generator for the two new formula families with options *PARITYTrue* and *KBKFTrue* in the QBFFam tool which is available at:

$$\text{https://github.com/marseidl/qbffam}$$

2 Preliminaries

We consider quantified Boolean formulas in prenex normal form, i.e., formulas of the structure $Q_1 X_1 \ldots Q_n X_n.\phi$ where X_i are disjoint sets of Boolean variables, $Q_i \in \{\forall, \exists\}$, and ϕ is a propositional formula with connectives negation ($\neg$), conjunction ($\wedge$), disjunction ($\vee$), implication ($\rightarrow$), equivalence ($\leftrightarrow$), and xor ($\oplus$) over variables in X_i. A QBF $\Pi.\phi$ is in prenex conjunctive normal form (PCNF) if ϕ is a conjunction of clauses. As usual a clause is a disjunction of literals and a literal is a variable or a negated variable. By $x \rightarrow (l_1 \wedge \ldots \wedge l_n)$ we denote the clauses $(\bar{x} \vee l_1), \ldots, (\bar{x} \vee l_n)$. A QBF $\forall x \Pi.\phi$ is true iff both $\Pi.\phi[x/\top]$ and $\Pi.\phi[x/\bot]$ are true where $\phi[x/t]$ denotes the formula obtained when setting variable x to term t, which can be true ($\top$) or false ($\bot$). A QBF $\exists x \Pi.\phi$ is true iff $\Pi.\phi[x/\top]$ or $\Pi.\phi[x/\bot]$ is true. From the semantics it directly follows that $\neg(Q_1 X_1 \ldots Q_n X_n.\phi)$, i.e., the negation of a formula that is obviously not in prenex form, has the same truth value as $(\bar{Q}_1 X_1 \ldots \bar{Q}_n X_n.\neg\phi)$ where $\bar{Q}_i = \exists$ if $Q_i = \forall$ and $\bar{Q}_i = \forall$ otherwise.

3 Two Families of True Formulas

In this section, we present two families of crafted formulas that are true. The formulas are based on the KBKF formula family which was originally introduced in [10] for showing that there are formula families which do not have a short proof in the basic Q-resolution proof system. Since then, several variants have been introduced which are also hard for stronger calculi like QU-resolution [6] or LD-Q-resolution [1] which extend Q-resolution. The other formula family which we consider are the so-called Parity formulas. These formulas also play an important role for proof theoretical investigations [2].

True Formulas Based on the KBKF-Family. To obtain interesting true formulas from the KBKF family, we consider their negations, hence swapping the quantifiers, Boolean connectives, and the polarities of the literals. As the resulting formulas are not in prenex conjunctive normal form, but in prenex *disjunctive* normal form, which is not processable by most state-of-the-art QBF solvers, we additionally apply the Plaisted-Greenbaum transformation [13] to obtain a PCNF formula again. The following definition describes the true QBFs that are members of the $TKBKF_t$ family where $t > 2$ parameterizes the formula size.

Definition 1. *A formula φ_t of the family $TKBKF_t$ has the quantifier prefix*

$$\forall d_1 e_1 \exists x_1 \forall d_2 e_2 \exists x_2 \ldots \forall d_t e_t \exists x_t \forall f_1 \ldots f_t \exists y_1 \ldots y_{2t+1} z_1 \ldots z_{2t}$$

and a propositional matrix consisting of the following clauses

$$
\begin{aligned}
& & y_1 &\to (d_1 \wedge e_1) & \\
y_{2j} &\to (\bar{d}_j \wedge \bar{x}_j \wedge d_{j+1} \wedge e_{j+1}) & y_{2j+1} &\to (\bar{e}_j \wedge x_j \wedge d_{j+1} \wedge e_{j+1}) & 1 \le j \le t-1 \\
y_{2t} &\to (\bar{d}_t \wedge \bar{x}_t \wedge f_1 \wedge \ldots \wedge f_t) & y_{2t+1} &\to (\bar{e}_t \wedge x_t \wedge f_1 \wedge \ldots \wedge f_t) & \\
z_{2j} &\to (x_j \wedge \bar{f}_j) & z_{2j-1} &\to (\bar{x}_j \wedge \bar{f}_j) & 1 \le j \le t \\
(y_1 &\vee \cdots \vee y_{2t+1} \vee z_1 \vee \ldots \vee z_{2t}) & &
\end{aligned}
$$

Following the argumentation that the false KBKF formulas are hard for Q-resolution to refute, i.e., the proof size is exponential in t, it is straight-forward to show that there are no short satisfaction Q-resolution proofs for the $TKBKF_t$ formulas since the proof size is also exponential. Note that this also holds for a slightly different version of $TKBKF_t$ where the y_i variables are positioned as left as possible in the prefix, which has then the structure

$$\forall d_1 e_1 \exists y_1 x_1 \forall d_2 e_2 \exists y_2 y_3 x_2 \ldots \forall d_t e_t \exists x_t \forall f_1 \ldots f_t \exists y_{2t} y_{2t+1} z_1 \ldots z_{2t}$$

True Formulas Based on the Parity-Family. The false Parity formula family contains formulas that encode the constraint $((x_1 \oplus \ldots \oplus x_t) \oplus y)$. The prefix is $\exists x_1 \ldots \exists x_n \forall y$. In addition, the variables z_j are appended in the innermost existential quantifier block, needed for an efficient transformation to PCNF. Here Tseitin transformation [17] is applied, i.e., not only implication as above is used for the definition of the labels, but bi-implication. To obtain true formulas, we change the quantifiers of the x_i variables to universal and the quantifier of y to existential. The quantifiers of the z_j variables remain existential and the matrix unchanged. Hence, the formula family $Parity_t$ is defined as follows.

Definition 2. *A formula φ_t of the family $Parity_t$ has the quantifier prefix*

$$\forall x_1 \cdots x_t \exists y \exists z_2 \cdots z_t$$

and a propositional matrix consisting of the following clauses where $2 < i \le t$:

$$
\begin{aligned}
(\bar{z}_2 \vee x_1 \vee x_2) \quad & (\bar{z}_2 \vee \bar{x}_1 \vee \bar{x}_2) \quad & (z_2 \vee \bar{x}_1 \vee x_2) \quad & (z_2 \vee x_1 \vee \bar{x}_2) \\
(\bar{z}_i \vee z_{i-1} \vee x_i) \quad & (\bar{z}_i \vee \bar{z}_{i-1} \vee \bar{x}_i) \quad & (z_i \vee \bar{z}_{i-1} \vee x_i) \quad & (z_i \vee z_{i-1} \vee \bar{x}_i) \\
(y \vee z_t) \quad & (\bar{y} \vee \bar{z}_t) & &
\end{aligned}
$$

Already from the structure of the formula it is visible that there cannot be short Q-resolution satisfaction proofs following the argumentation of [2] for false formulas: Strategy extraction is easy from a Q-resolution proof: in terms of circuit complexity it falls in the class of AC^0. It is well known that Parity formulas have no efficient representation in AC^0, hence also the Q-resolution proofs have to be exponential, since the unique solution for y depends on $(x_1 \oplus \ldots \oplus x_n)$.

Fig. 1. Runtimes of $TKBKF_t$ and $Parity_t$ formulas for $2 \le t \le 30$.

4   Evaluation

We selected three different solvers based on different solving paradigms representing the state of the art in QBF solving to evaluate how they perform on the generated formulas as described above. The solver RAReQS [8] is an expansion-based QBF solver that has its theoretical foundations on the ∀Exp+Res calculus [2]. In contrast, the solver DEPQBF [11] implements conflict/solution-driven clause/cube learning (QCDCL), a generalization of the CDCL approach that can be found in most SAT solvers. Hence, DEPQBF's search is theoretically founded on Q-resolution. We run DEPQBF in two versions: the older 3.04 supporting full proof generation for true and false formulas and the most recent 6.03, additionally implementing advanced inprocessing and pruning techniques like generalized axioms [12]. Such techniques have been observed to considerably improve solving time, but full certification is not possible at the moment. As a third solver we ran CAQE [14] which relies on CEGAR-based clausal abstraction [16] and which has been extremely successful in recent QBF competitions.

Our experiments were executed on a cluster of dual-socket AMD EPYC 7313 @ 3.7 GHz machines with 8 GB memory per task and a timeout of 900 s. For both families we generated 29 instances, ranging parameter t from 2 to 30.

Figure 1 shows the result of our experiments. The plot on the left compares the runtimes of the solvers for the $TKBKF_t$ family. The definition variables introduced for the normal form transformation are introduced as early as possible. We also tested appending the definition variables at the end of the prefix, but observed similar runtimes. As a recent paper shows, in general this is not always the case and strongly depends on the benchmarks [15]. The formulas are hard for all solvers and the runtime seems to grow exponentially in the parameter t. When analyzing the proofs produced by DEPQBF 3.04, the number of axioms from which the satisfaction proof is generated is linear in t, but the proofs are exponential indicating that the proofs are constructed as to be expected (see also the discussion above). Also in the plot on the right for the $Parity_t$ formulas we can observe a similar behavior except for DEPQBF 6.03. In this configuration, the formulas become easy, i.e., they can immediately be solved. This is not surprising, because for simplification techniques like blocked clause elimination [7] reasoning on Parity formulas is simple. The Q-resolution proofs generated by DEPQBF 3.04 have an exponential number of axioms that are all needed to show the truth of the formulas. In consequence, the function that is extracted for variable y is also exponential. Currently, there is no solver that supports the generation of $\forall$Exp+Res proofs for true formulas.

5   Conclusion

We presented two families of crafted true formulas, based on their false counterparts widely used for evaluating proofs of unsatisfiability. We argued and empirically showed that the true formulas are also hard for Q-resolution. The hardness could also be observed for expansion-based proof systems, however, the theoretical reasoning is less obvious. While there is always a dual variant based on a representation in PCNF, it is not clear how to construct them during search for a solution. This is in contrast to QCDCL solvers which directly build Q-resolution satisfaction proofs during the search. It remains as future work to practically investigate satisfaction proofs for expansion-based solvers in more detail.

References

1. Balabanov, V., Jiang, J.R.: Unified QBF certification and its applications. Formal Methods Syst. Des. **41**(1), 45–65 (2012)
2. Beyersdorff, O., Chew, L., Janota, M.: New resolution-based QBF calculi and their proof complexity. ACM Trans. Comput. Theory **11**(4), 26:1–26:42 (2019)
3. Beyersdorff, O., Janota, M., Lonsing, F., Seidl, M.: Quantified Boolean formulas. In: Handbook of Satisfiability - Second Edition, pp. 1177–1221. IOS Press (2021)
4. Beyersdorff, O., Pulina, L., Seidl, M., Shukla, A.: QBFFam: a tool for generating QBF families from proof complexity. In: Li, C.-M., Manyà, F. (eds.) SAT 2021. LNCS, vol. 12831, pp. 21–29. Springer, Cham (2021). https://doi.org/10.1007/978-3-030-80223-3_3
5. Böhm, B., Peitl, T., Beyersdorff, O.: Should decisions in QCDCL follow prefix order? In: SAT. LIPIcs, vol. 236, pp. 11:1–11:19. Schloss Dagstuhl - Leibniz-Zentrum für Informatik (2022)
6. Gelder, A.: Contributions to the theory of practical quantified Boolean formula solving. In: Milano, M. (ed.) CP 2012. LNCS, pp. 647–663. Springer, Heidelberg (2012). https://doi.org/10.1007/978-3-642-33558-7_47
7. Heule, M., Järvisalo, M., Lonsing, F., Seidl, M., Biere, A.: Clause elimination for SAT and QSAT. J. Artif. Intell. Res. **53**, 127–168 (2015)
8. Janota, M., Klieber, W., Marques-Silva, J., Clarke, E.: Solving QBF with counterexample guided refinement. In: Cimatti, A., Sebastiani, R. (eds.) SAT 2012. LNCS, vol. 7317, pp. 114–128. Springer, Heidelberg (2012). https://doi.org/10.1007/978-3-642-31612-8_10

9. Janota, M., Marques-Silva, J.: An Achilles' heel of term-resolution. In: Oliveira, E., Gama, J., Vale, Z., Lopes Cardoso, H. (eds.) EPIA 2017. LNCS (LNAI), vol. 10423, pp. 670–680. Springer, Cham (2017). https://doi.org/10.1007/978-3-319-65340-2_55

10. Kleine Büning, H., Lettmann, T.: Aussagenlogik: Deduktion und Algorithmen. Teubner (1994)

11. Lonsing, F., Egly, U.: DepQBF 6.0: a search-based QBF solver beyond traditional QCDCL. In: de Moura, L. (ed.) CADE 2017. LNCS (LNAI), vol. 10395, pp. 371–384. Springer, Cham (2017). https://doi.org/10.1007/978-3-319-63046-5_23

12. Lonsing, F., Egly, U., Seidl, M.: Q-resolution with generalized axioms. In: Creignou, N., Le Berre, D. (eds.) SAT 2016. LNCS, vol. 9710, pp. 435–452. Springer, Cham (2016). https://doi.org/10.1007/978-3-319-40970-2_27

13. Plaisted, D.A., Greenbaum, S.: A structure-preserving clause form translation. J. Symb. Comput. **2**(3), 293–304 (1986)

14. Rabe, M.N., Tentrup, L.: CAQE: a certifying QBF solver. In: FMCAD, pp. 136–143. IEEE (2015)

15. Reeves, J.E., Heule, M.J.H., Bryant, R.E.: Moving definition variables in quantified Boolean formulas. In: TACAS 2022. LNCS, vol. 13243, pp. 462–479. Springer, Cham (2022). https://doi.org/10.1007/978-3-030-99524-9_26

16. Tentrup, L.: On expansion and resolution in CEGAR based QBF solving. In: Majumdar, R., Kunčak, V. (eds.) CAV 2017. LNCS, vol. 10427, pp. 475–494. Springer, Cham (2017). https://doi.org/10.1007/978-3-319-63390-9_25

17. Tseitin, G.S.: On the complexity of derivation in propositional calculus. In: Siekmann, J.H., Wrightson, G. (eds.) Automation of Reasoning. Symbolic Computation, pp. 466–483. Springer, Heidelberg (1983). https://doi.org/10.1007/978-3-642-81955-1_28

An Augmented MetiTarski Dataset for Real Quantifier Elimination Using Machine Learning

John Hester[1], Briland Hitaj[2], Grant Passmore[1]([✉]), Sam Owre[2], Natarajan Shankar[2], and Eric Yeh[2]

[1] Imandra Inc., Austin, TX 78704, USA
{john,grant}@imandra.ai
[2] SRI International, Menlo Park, CA 94025, USA
{briland.hitaj,natarajan.shankar,sam.owre,eric.yeh}@sri.com

Abstract. We contribute a new dataset composed of more than 41K MetiTarski challenges that can be used to investigate applications of machine learning (ML) in determining efficient variable orderings in Cylindrical Algebraic Decomposition. The proposed dataset aims to address inadvertent bias issues present in prior benchmarks, paving the way to development of robust, easy-to-generalize ML models.

Keywords: MetiTarski Variable Ordering · Machine Learning Datasets · Generalizability · Bias

1 Introduction

Cylindrical Algebraic Decomposition (CAD) is a key proof technique for the formal verification of cyber-physical systems such as aircraft collision avoidance systems, autonomous vehicles and medical robotics. While CAD is a complete decision procedure, it is computationally expensive with worst-case exponential complexity. Prior work has demonstrated that machine learning (ML) may be successfully applied to determining efficient variable orderings [2,5]. Much of this work has been driven by CAD problems extracted from applications of the MetiTarski theorem prover [1,7].

However, the original MetiTarski benchmark data is highly imbalanced, inadvertently introducing preferences towards certain variable orders, thus hindering the ability of resulting ML models to generalize to new data [4,6]. Data augmentation can address bias issues while substantially improving the robustness of trained models [3]. In this vein, we make use of inherent symmetries present

This material is based upon work supported by the Defense Advanced Research Projects Agency (DARPA) under Contract No. HR00112290064. Any opinions, findings, and conclusions or recommendations expressed in this material are those of the author(s) and do not necessarily reflect the views of the United States Government or DARPA.

C. Dubois and M. Kerber (Eds.): CICM 2023, LNAI 14101, pp. 297–302, 2023.
https://doi.org/10.1007/978-3-031-42753-4_21

in the data to create a new *balanced* MetiTarski dataset composed of more than 41K additional challenges. We make the new dataset together with our models publicly available.[1]

2   The Proposed MetiTarski Dataset Setup

In this section, we provide details about the datasets that we have used in our experiments, and we introduce a new *augmented* dataset designed to remove bias. In addition to the datasets, we provide details on the features considered based on England et al. [2] and Huang et al. [5] respective works, followed by a discussion of our labeling strategy. We conclude the section with a discussion of the machine learning models considered together with their respective hyperparameter setup.

2.1   MetiTarski Datasets

Dataset 1 (Original): The first dataset is predominantly gathered from MetiTarski, by logging MetiTarski's RCF subproblem queries during its proof search [2,7]. The dataset contains 6,895 polynomial systems, together with data on the performance of a CAD-based decision procedure on different orderings of their variables. Every problem in this data set has 3 variables (x_1, x_2, x_3) and thus 6 possible variable orderings.

Dataset 2 (Augmented): We noted that the original MetiTarski dataset was highly imbalanced. While class 0, corresponding to the (x_1, x_2, x_3) variable order contained 580 records, class 5, corresponding to (x_3, x_2, x_1) contained 2,657 records, nearly 4-times more, Fig. 1a. We note that this may *bias* ML models towards certain label/s, thus preventing the models from learning relevant information and hindering their generalizability to new, previously unseen data.

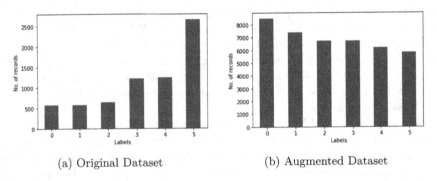

(a) Original Dataset   (b) Augmented Dataset

Fig. 1. Data distribution per label on both the original MetiTarski dataset and the second, balanced one.

We recognize that variables in the formula and ordering can be swapped without changing the time and cost needed to perform the computation. For

---

instance, swapping variables x_1 with x_2 in the formulas and in the ordering leads to a CAD with the same time and cell cost. While this may seem apparent to a human or a machine reasoner that already has the ability to recognize this symmetry, for current machine learning systems it needs to be made explicit in the training data. This procedure resulted in a new augmented composed of 41,370 polynomial systems (cf. Figure 1b).

2.2 Feature Engineering and Labeling

We process each set of polynomials extracting features enlisted in [2,5], including the number of polynomials, maximum total degree of polynomials, maximum degree of each x_i, and proportion of each x_i appearing in polynomials and monomials. In addition to the feature set, we assign to each polynomial problem a label ranging from 0...5, where each label translates to one of the 6-possible variable orderings. At present, the label for each polynomial problem corresponds to the variable ordering that takes the least amount of time.

2.3 Models

To evaluate our approach, we used 5-ML classifiers: 1) Support Vector Machines (SVM), 2) k-Nearest Neighbours (k-NN), 3) Decision Trees (DT), 4) Random Forests (RF), and 5) Multi-Layer Perceptrons (MLP). England et al. [2] relies on SVMs, k-NNs, DTs, and MLPs. By following a similar approach, we ensure that our strategy is comparable to the state-of-the-art and thus can be used as a foundation for future adoption of more complex ML strategies, such as Transformers [9] or Graph Neural Networks (GNNs) [8]. We used the `scikit-learn`[2]-based implementations of the ML algorithms. Similar to the works of England et al. [2] and Huang et al. [5], we employed a grid-search strategy with 5-fold cross-validation to identify the right parameter setup for each of the models.

3 Evaluation

In this section, we proceed with the evaluation of the performance of the selected machine learning models (cf. Section 2.3) on identifying the preferred (best) variable order for a given input problem. We transform the problem of determining the best variable order into a multi-class classification problem. In these kind of problems the training set is composed of (x, y) tuples of data, where x is an input sample and y is the corresponding label for that sample. The goal of the learning process translates into the task of finding a function f, such that $f(x) = y$.

In our setting, the input data corresponds to the series of 11-features (cf. Sect. 2.2) whereas y is one of the 6-labels from $[0, \ldots, 5]$ belonging to a preferred variable order from $[(x_1, x_2, x_3), \ldots, (x_3, x_2, x_1)]$. The features were scaled by subtracting the mean and then scaling to unit variance[3].

---

[2] https://scikit-learn.org/stable/.

[3] https://scikit-learn.org/stable/modules/generated/sklearn.preprocessing.Standard Scaler.html.

Training: For each of the datasets, we used 80% of the data for training and kept the remaining 20% as part of the testing set. For Dataset 1 (original), this corresponded to 5,516 samples for training and 1,379 for testing, whereas for Dataset 2 (augmented), 33,095 samples were used during training and the remaining 8,274 samples for testing. Tables 1 and 2 provide accuracy of each model obtained on the respective training set.

Table 1. Performance of models trained on Dataset 1 when evaluated on Testing set 1 and entire Dataset 2.

Model Trained on Dataset 1	Performance on Training Set 1	Performance on Testing Set 1	Performance on Dataset 2 (all)
SVM	69.38%	58.88%	28.9%
k-NN	75.27%	57.36%	32.21%
DT	75%	55.69%	31.44%
RF	76.39%	58.23%	34.15%
MLP	58.81%	53%	33.64%

Testing: We test each model on 20% of the respective datasets: 1,379 samples for Dataset 1, and 8,274 samples for Dataset 2.

Table 2. Performance of models trained on Dataset 2 evaluated on Testing set 2 and Dataset 1. **Perf. on Dataset 1 (all)** also shows (in parentheses) results from training on a "reduced" subset of Dataset 2 obtained by random sampling.

Model Trained on Dataset 2	Performance on Training Set 2	Performance on Testing Set 2	Performance on Dataset 1 (all)
SVM	62.1%	57.39%	60.43% (53.89%)
k-NN	69.2%	54.9%	66.28% (54.19%)
DT	68.03%	55.04%	64.16% (52.27%)
RF	70.47%	55.07%	66.96% (55.66%)
MLP	50.51%	49.62%	48.19% (48.22%)

The performance of models trained on Dataset 1 varied from 53% for the MLP model up to 58.88% for the SVM (Table 1) these results being in-line with state-of-the-art work by England et al. [2] and Huang et al. [5]. Likewise, the models trained on the augmented Dataset 2 exhibit similar performance with the MLP architecture performing poorly with 49.62% accuracy and SVM obtaining up to 57.39% accuracy on the testing set (Table 2).

Evaluation on Respective Datasets: Model performance is quite promising and substantially better than random choice ($\approx 16.67\%$). However, given the bias of the original dataset (cf. Section 2.1), it is interesting to investigate the performance of models trained on Dataset 1 (the original MetiTarski dataset) and the newly produced Dataset 2, the latter a superset of Dataset 1. As illustrated in Table 1, there is a significant drop in classification accuracy for all models trained on Dataset 1, with more than 25% drop in some cases. Models trained on the "debiased" Dataset 2 retain good performance when evaluated on Dataset 1. We believe this is due to the training data being balanced and the model potentially seeing some of these samples during training, increasing its decision confidence. Interestingly, we also see good performance for models trained on a "reduced" version of Dataset 2 for which we select one random permutation per problem.

4 Conclusion

We have re-examined a classical dataset for ML-driven CAD variable ordering and observed issues of bias. To address this, we have applied symmetry-based data augmentation to create a debiased version and have shown this improves generalizability. We believe this phenomenon is quite general, and that debiasing with formula symmetries should be a standard tool for applications of ML in computer algebra, program verification, and other fields manipulating mathematical formulas. While this approach generalizes naturally to more variables, there is a bottleneck of exponential growth in the number of distinct orderings that must be considered as the dimension grows (e.g., for 6 variables we have 6! combinations). We intend to investigate variants where, instead of considering a full ordering up front, we consider partial solutions, e.g., the first k variables to project, etc. Nevertheless, an enormous number of RCF verification problems encountered in practice take place over $\mathbb{R}^3$, so even the classical focus on the 3 variable case is well motivated. We plan to extend this work into general-purpose tools and apply it to many problem domains (e.g., Gröbner bases, BDDs, SAT).

References

1. Akbarpour, B., Paulson, L.C.: MetiTarski: an automatic theorem prover for real-valued special functions. J. Autom. Reasoning **44**, 175–205 (2010)
2. England, M., Florescu, D.: Comparing machine learning models to choose the variable ordering for cylindrical algebraic decomposition. In: Kaliszyk, C., Brady, E., Kohlhase, A., Sacerdoti Coen, C. (eds.) CICM 2019. LNCS (LNAI), vol. 11617, pp. 93–108. Springer, Cham (2019). https://doi.org/10.1007/978-3-030-23250-4_7
3. Geirhos, R., Rubisch, P., Michaelis, C., Bethge, M., Wichmann, F.A., Brendel, W.: Imagenet-trained CNNs are biased towards texture; increasing shape bias improves accuracy and robustness. In: International Conference on Learning Representations (2019). https://openreview.net/forum?id=Bygh9j09KX
4. Geirhos, R., Temme, C.R., Rauber, J., Schütt, H.H., Bethge, M., Wichmann, F.A.: Generalisation in humans and deep neural networks. Adv. Neur. Inf. Proc. **31** (2018)

5. Huang, Z., England, M., Wilson, D.J., Bridge, J., Davenport, J.H., Paulson, L.C.: Using machine learning to improve CAD. Maths. in C.S. **13**(4), 461–488 (2019)
6. Kawaguchi, K., Kaelbling, L.P., Bengio, Y.: Generalization in deep learning. arXiv preprint arXiv:1710.05468 (2017)
7. Passmore, G.O., Paulson, L.C., de Moura, L.: Real algebraic strategies for metitarski proofs. In: Jeuring, J., et al. (eds.) CICM 2012. LNCS (LNAI), vol. 7362, pp. 358–370. Springer, Heidelberg (2012). https://doi.org/10.1007/978-3-642-31374-5_24
8. Scarselli, F., Gori, M., Tsoi, A.C., Hagenbuchner, M., Monfardini, G.: The graph neural network model. IEEE Trans. Neural Netw. **20**(1), 61–80 (2009)
9. Vaswani, A., et al.: Attention is all you need. In: Advances in Neural Information Processing Systems, vol. 30 (2017)

VizAR: Visualization of Automated Reasoning Proofs (System Description)

Jan Jakubův[1]([envelope])[iD] and Cezary Kaliszyk[2][iD]

[1] Czech Technical University in Prague, Prague, Czech Republic
jakubuv@gmail.com
[2] University of Innsbruck, Innsbruck, Austria and INDRC, Prague, Czech Republic
cezary.kaliszyk@uibk.ac.at

Abstract. We present a system for the visualization of proofs originating from Automated Theorem Provers for first-order logic. The system can hide uninteresting proof parts of proofs, such as type annotations, translate first-order terms to standard math syntax, and compactly display complex formulas. We demonstrate the system on several non-trivial automated proofs of statements from Mizar Mathematical Library translated to first-order logic, and we provide a web interface where curious users can browse and investigate the proofs.

Keywords: Proof Visualization · First-Order Logic · Automated Theorem Provers

1 Introduction

With the increasing power of *Automated Theorem Proving* systems (ATPs), the size and complexity of the proofs they output are also increasing. This additionally implies that analyzing such automatically generated proofs is becoming more daunting for users. This is of particular importance for proofs that originate from machine-learning-guided provers. The guided version of E, ENIGMA [6] can automatically find proofs of many theorems that have previously been provable only with long manual proofs. A large number of such proofs have been discussed in our recent work on machine learning for Mizar [5]. To allow users to inspect and analyze such proofs conveniently, we developed and present the VizAR system:

http://ai.ciirc.cvut.cz/vizar/

The system can hide uninteresting parts of proofs (such as Mizar soft type system annotations and reasoning about them), translate first-order terms to

---

Supported by ERC-CZ grant no. LL1902 POSTMAN and EU Regional Development Fund under the Czech project AI&Reasoning no. CZ.02.1.01/0.0/0.0/15_003/00004, and Cost Action CA20111 EuroProofNet.

C. Dubois and M. Kerber (Eds.): CICM 2023, LNAI 14101, pp. 303–308, 2023.
https://doi.org/10.1007/978-3-031-42753-4_22

standard math syntax (such as presenting Element(x, y) as $x \in y$), and compactly display complex formulas. The system provides several ways to visualize complex proofs. In the full proof view, the proof is displayed as an interactive SVG image. In order to simplify orientation in large proofs, the system features a conjecture-centered view which helps to identify essential proof steps. Finally, the proof step view allows the user to interactively browse individual proof steps and reveal the proof essence hidden in their symbols.

Related Work. There exist several tools for viewing general automatically found proofs. One of the first generally usable visual viewers for automatically found proofs was the LΩUI [7] viewer offered as part of the Omega system. TPTP tools include an interactive derivation viewer IDV [8] which allows users to focus on particular clauses in TPTP proofs and see their relation (distance) from the axioms and the conjecture. One of the most advanced viewers for proofs is PROOFTOOL [4] which allows viewing GAPT transformed proofs.

Urban et al. [10] have developed an online tool for Mizar that checks if particular subgoals are ATP-provable and if so views the premises (rather than proof details as our tool does). Visualizing proof search differs quite a lot from the presentation of complete proofs and has also been investigated [3]. Hammer systems use automated theorem provers to find proofs of conjectures in more complex logics. The reconstruction of such ATP proofs often requires presenting them in a more complex logic including mechanisms able to transform the conjecture to its positive form [2]. Finally, the most advanced tools for presenting non-ATP Mizar proofs are used to render Mizar Library articles in LaTeX for the Journal of Formalized Mathematics [1]. To our best knowledge, we are not aware of any proof visualization tool as advanced as VizAR.

2   VizAR: The Proof Navigator

VizAR can display an arbitrary proof in the TPTP language. In addition, it integrates extended support for proofs of Mizar statements coming from the MPTP [9] translation of Mizar to first-order logic. A large amount of MPTP proofs has been recently generated by ATPs (E and Vampire) with machine learning guidance [5]. Selected proofs can be investigated on the VizAR web page. VizAR shows the original Mizar statements for every conjecture and assumption, and it provides links to Mizar proofs and symbol definitions.

Symbol Translation. MPTP uses its own names for Mizar symbols. VizAR uses Unicode symbols to display terms and predicates in standard mathematical notation when possible. For example, the MPTP symbol m1_subset_1(X,Y) corresponds to Mizar symbol Element(X, Y) and in VizAR it is presented as $X \in Y$.[1] Another example is the MPTP symbol r2_wellord2(X,Y) corresponding to the Mizar symbol are_equipotent(X, Y) which is written as $|X| = |Y|$ in VizAR.

---

[1] We use LaTeX to typeset VizAR syntax in this paper. Unicode used in HTML/SVG looks fairly close to it, with the exception of better spacing and fonts in LaTeX.

The translation is implemented using simple templates to position arguments. For symbols without special VizAR translations, original Mizar symbol names are used. Mizar names are composed of various ASCII characters resembling the standard math notation, for example, c= stands for $\subseteq$.

Clause Visualization. ATP proofs consist of clauses with positive and negative literals. In the VizAR syntax, clauses are displayed as sequents in order to avoid the negation sign ($\sim$ in TPTP). For example, the clause $A \mid B \mid \sim C \mid \sim D$ is considered as the logically equivalent sequent $C, D \Rightarrow A, B$. The *antecedents* (left-hand side) are implicitly connected by logical *and*, while the *consequents* (right-hand side) are implicitly connected by logical *or*. The sequents are visualized as boxes with the content displayed vertically (top-down) as demonstrated in Fig. 1. Clauses without negative literals (for example, $A \mid B$) are displayed simply as A, B instead of $\top \Rightarrow A, B$. Clauses without positive literals (for example, $\sim C \mid \sim D$) are displayed as $C, D \Rightarrow \bot$. As an exception, a unit clause with one negative literal is displayed as $\neg A$ instead of $A \Rightarrow \bot$ to save space. This is the only case where the negation sign can be encountered in VizAR.

Clause Simplifications. MPTP first-order translations of Mizar statements typically use soft type guard predicates to specify types of variables. A typical clause (written as a sequent) looks as $\mathsf{natural}(X1), \mathsf{natural}(X2) \Rightarrow \mathsf{natural}(\mathsf{plus}(X1, X2))$. This states that the sum of two naturals is a natural number. To simplify the proof presentation, VizAR hides the type guards applied to variables, and introduces a different variable symbol for each type predicate, for example, N for natural numbers and R for real numbers. Hence the above sequent becomes just $\mathsf{natural}(\mathsf{plus}(N1, N2))$. In the VizAR syntax, this becomes simply $(N_1 + N_2) \in \mathbb{N}$ as VizAR uses Unicode subscript letters to typeset variable indices. This means that, for example, the VizAR statement $N_1 \in \mathbb{R}$ should be interpreted as "every natural number is a real number". As a second step, all negative occurrences of type guard predicates (even with a non-variable argument) are completely hidden. This is because they typically provide no interesting information from the human point of view. While the first simplification preserves all information in the clause, the second removes intuitively trivial literals but the original clause cannot be fully reconstructed.

Proof Transformations. Proofs considered by VizAR are proofs by contradiction because of the underlying ATP provers. The prover first negates the conjecture and then searches for the contradiction with other assumptions. An ATP proof in the TPTP language is a directed acyclic graph where the leaves correspond to assumptions and all the edges can be followed to the sink node representing the contradiction. Every inner node represents an inferred clause and the edges connect premises with the inference outcome. After symbol translations and clause simplifications, two consequent graph nodes might represent syntactically equal clauses. For example, the Mizar statements $\mathsf{Element}(X, \mathsf{NAT})$ and $\mathsf{natural}(X)$ are both represented as $X \in \mathbb{N}$ in VizAR. In these cases, to further simplify the proof

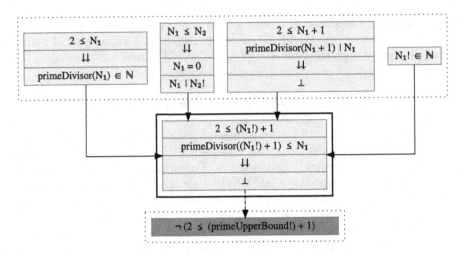

Fig. 1. Visualization of a proof step from the proof of MPTP theorem `t72_newton`.

graph, we unify consequent nodes labeled with the same VizAR expression and merge their respective source and destination edges.

Proof Visualizations. VizAR uses Graphviz to render proof graphs while the web interface is implemented by the static site generator Jekyll. VizAR web interface provides several ways to investigate ATP proofs. In the *full proof view*, the whole proof graph is displayed as an SVG image with hyperlinks. Graph leaves corresponding to assumptions are displayed in blue and all the nodes inferred from the negated conjecture are displayed in orange. Hence all non-orange nodes represent statements generally valid in Mizar. Clicking on any node takes the user to a detailed description of the corresponding proof step.

Since the full proof view might be very complex, VizAR features a *conjecture-centered view* where only the statements derived from the conjecture are displayed. This is a subgraph of the full proof view. Additionally, for every conjecture-related node, its non-conjecture premises used to derive this step are displayed. This view can help the user inspect how the negated conjecture is transformed into the contradiction. Thus, it is useful to identify the key steps of the proof.

In the *proof step view*, only a single proof graph node is displayed with its immediate parents and children. Additional information is provided about the symbols appearing in this proof step. Again, the user can click on any of the nodes to see the corresponding proof step view. Figure 1 shows an example proof step in VizAR. The ATP proved the Mizar theorem `t72_newton`, which states that there is no upper bound on the prime numbers. Proving this in one ATP run is rather impressive, so we inspect the key steps leading to the contradiction. The ATP inferred that when $n! + 1 \geq 2$ then $n! + 1$ has no prime divisors less or equal to n. We already see the instantiation found ($n! + 1$) and can inspect the key reasoning steps: In the later step, this is applied to the upper bound on primes assumed by the negated conjecture, which quickly leads to a contradiction since the upper bound must be greater than 2. For the sake of presentation, we display the ATP Skolem symbols (sk_i in VizAR) as primeDivisor and primeUpperBound and hide trivially false statements (primeDivisor(..) = 0, 1).

Skolem symbols are introduced by ATPs to eliminate existential quantifiers and they typically constitute an important part of the proof. Hence it is important to understand their meaning and, to help the user with that, VizAR displays their origin in the proof overview. Clicking on the axiom will take the user to the *axiom view* where they will also see the original formula that gave rise to them. The Skolem symbols are also displayed in the proof step view when some of them are included in the step claim.

3 Conclusions and Future Work

We have developed the VizAR ATP proof visualization system and we publish its web interface on GitHub pages with a custom domain redirect. The web interface currently features selected ATP proofs of MPTP statements. In the proof gallery, we present *featured proofs* with improved VizAR syntax for all relevant Mizar symbols. Moreover, the *other proofs* section of the page contains a large number of proofs where Mizar names are used for selected symbols.

The VizAR system can be enhanced in many ways. First, VizAR syntax can be provided for more Mizar symbols to display statements in standard math notations. Second, additional proof simplification rules can be applied, for example, to hide clauses like $A \Rightarrow A$ or $(s = t) \Rightarrow (t = s)$. Such simplification rules could also be detected automatically or provided interactively.

References

1. Bancerek, G., Naumowicz, A., Urban, J.: System description: XSL-based translator of Mizar to LaTeX. In: Rabe, F., Farmer, W.M., Passmore, G.O., Youssef, A. (eds.) CICM 2018. LNCS (LNAI), vol. 11006, pp. 1–6. Springer, Cham (2018). https://doi.org/10.1007/978-3-319-96812-4_1
2. Blanchette, J.C., Böhme, S., Fleury, M., Smolka, S.J., Steckermeier, A.: Semi-intelligible Isar proofs from machine-generated proofs. J. Autom. Reason. **56**(2), 155–200 (2015). https://doi.org/10.1007/s10817-015-9335-3
3. Byrnes, J., Buchanan, M., Ernst, M., Miller, P., Roberts, C., Keller, R.: Visualizing proof search for theorem prover development. In: UITP. ENTCS, vol. 226, pp. 23–38. Elsevier (2008). https://doi.org/10.1016/j.entcs.2008.12.095
4. Dunchev, C., et al.: PROOFTOOL: a GUI for the GAPT framework. In: UITP. EPTCS, vol. 118, pp. 1–14 (2012). https://doi.org/10.4204/EPTCS.118.1
5. Jakubův, J., et al.: MizAR 60 for Mizar 50. CoRR (2023). https://arxiv.org/abs/2303.06686
6. Jakubův, J., Chvalovský, K., Olšák, M., Piotrowski, B., Suda, M., Urban, J.: ENIGMA anonymous: symbol-independent inference guiding machine (system description). In: Peltier, N., Sofronie-Stokkermans, V. (eds.) IJCAR 2020. LNCS (LNAI), vol. 12167, pp. 448–463. Springer, Cham (2020). https://doi.org/10.1007/978-3-030-51054-1_29

7. Siekmann, J.H., et al.: LΩUI: Lovely Ωmega User Interface. Formal Aspects Comput. **11**(3), 326–342 (1999). https://doi.org/10.1007/s001650050053

8. Trac, S., Puzis, Y., Sutcliffe, G.: An interactive derivation viewer. In: UITP. ENTCS, vol. 174:2, pp. 109–123. Elsevier (2006)

9. Urban, J.: MPTP 0.2: design, implementation, and initial experiments. J. Autom. Reason. **37**(1–2), 21–43 (2006). https://doi.org/10.1007/s10817-006-9032-3

10. Urban, J., Rudnicki, P., Sutcliffe, G.: ATP and presentation service for Mizar formalizations. J. Autom. Reason. **50**(2), 229–241 (2013)

Extending Numeric Automation
for Number Theory Formalizations
in Mizar

Adam Naumowicz$^{(\boxtimes)}$ [iD]

Institute of Computer Science, University of Bialystok, Bialystok, Poland
adamn@math.uwb.edu.pl

Abstract. In this paper we present an experimental version of the Mizar proof checker equipped with new built-in routines for automating common numeric computations. This implementation has been directly motivated by recent formalizations of selected number theory topics that required extensive numeric calculations and proving numerical properties of specific numbers. The potential of automating parts of such proofs has been evaluated and, consequently, the Mizar checker has been extended with code that enabled refactoring the current contents of the Mizar Mathematical Library.

Keywords: Mizar · Numeric computation · Number theory formalization · Built-in knowledge

1   Introduction

Mizar is a proof assistant best known for its underlying proof language primarily designed to closely resemble the mathematical vernacular, as well as the pioneering long-term development of a repository of formalized mathematics, Mizar Mathematical Library (MML) [1], established in 1989. For several decades the development of MML has been conducted in parallel to the evolution of the proof checking system. The system was originally designed to be used by mathematicians, not programmers, and therefore the possibility of implementing its extensions by typical users is not provided. However, various features of the system have been implemented by the system developers in response to specific needs that emerged during the formalization of particular theories. One of recent formalization projects aims at encoding W. Sierpinski's book '250 Problems in Elementary Number Theory' [14]. The initial Mizar formalizations related to that effort were done in 2020 and the resulting dataset was presented at CICM 2020 [10]. To date, the joint formalization work resulted in developing a sequence

---

The processing and analysis of the Mizar library has been performed using the infrastructure of the University of Bialystok High Performance Computing Center (https://uco.uwb.edu.pl).

C. Dubois and M. Kerber (Eds.): CICM 2023, LNAI 14101, pp. 309–314, 2023.
https://doi.org/10.1007/978-3-031-42753-4_23

of Mizar articles submitted to MML [3,5–8,11] which cover almost 100 of the problems.

No deeper prior knowledge of the Mizar language and system should be needed to follow the next sections. However, readers who would like to learn more about Mizar are kindly referred to its brief description, 'Mizar in a Nutshell' [2]. The Mizar system distribution (containing executables and the contents of MML) can be downloaded from the Mizar website [9]. The code used for the work presented in the current paper is derived from the Mizar source code available on GitHub[1]. The pre-compiled experimental version of the Mizar checker as well as the changed source files mentioned in the paper can be downloaded from the Mizar website[2].

2 Number Theory Automations

The current version of the Mizar checker supports direct calculations on rational complex numbers (complex numbers with rational coefficients). Internally, the calculations are performed by the checker for arbitrarily big values represented as decimal-encoded strings. However, the code has not been designed to perform intensive calculations on par with optimized dedicated calculation tools, and so the numerals that can explicitly be input by the user cannot currently exceed the value of the maximal signed 32-bit integer. This restriction is as a compromise between typical user needs and the reasonable processing time of the verification system.

The functionality is switched on by inputting the, so called, requirements ARITHM directive [13] in the environ part of the Mizar text being developed. Then, the Mizar checker performs polynomial elimination and accepts numeric operations as obvious, so the users do not need to provide any justification for the parts of their proofs based on such computations. Once the underlying code was available in the checker, it offered the possibility to reuse some of its internal routines to shorten the process of writing proofs that involve simple number-theoretic reasoning. Some of such notions (div, mod, etc.) were identified as prospective additions to the checker's automation [12]. Their potential usefulness, however, was at that time limited by a small number of number theory developments in the Mizar library, and so the idea was not officially implemented in the Mizar distribution.

The situation changed considerably when there appeared more MML contributions devoted to number theory. The work on formalizing the aforementioned Sierpinski's textbook can serve as a good example here. In the course of formalizing numerous facts related to elementary number theory, the authors often needed to refer to, for instance, the basic divisibility properties of concrete (sometimes quite big) numbers, or to prove whether a particular number is prime or not. To facilitate writing such proofs on top of the current MML, A. Kornilowicz

---

[1] https://github.com/MizarProject/system.
[2] https://mizar.uwb.edu.pl/~softadm/int_d.

of the Mizar library committee generated a set of 'encyclopedic' articles identifying all prime numbers in the range up to 10,000[3]. These articles contain a handy set of referential facts that authors may potentially need when formalizing various theorems in number theory. However, the massive files (almost 800K lines of Mizar text in total) cause serious performance problems, especially when processing the whole library is required. Our extended automation is, therefore, devised to eliminate the users' need to directly reference facts from these articles by making them obvious for the Mizar checker. From the point of view of end users, the Mizar language is not complicated in any way by this extension, only the internal implementation changes. The implementation details presented in this work should be most useful to future developers who intend to create their own similar extensions of the Mizar system.

3 New Directive: requirements INT_D

All the presented automated notions have their definitions in two Mizar articles, (INT_1 and INT_2), so the corresponding new library file dubbed int_d.dre ('d' for divisibility) provides the following signature and links between respective MML constructors and the numbers of the built-in requirement type in the Mizar code:

```
<?xml version="1.0"?>
<Requirements>
<Signature>
<ArticleID name="HIDDEN"/>
<ArticleID name="INT_1"/>
<ArticleID name="INT_2"/>
</Signature>
<Requirement constrkind="K" constrnr="4" nr="35"/>
<Requirement constrkind="K" constrnr="5" nr="36"/>
<Requirement constrkind="R" constrnr="3" nr="37"/>
<Requirement constrkind="K" constrnr="7" nr="38"/>
<Requirement constrkind="K" constrnr="8" nr="39"/>
<Requirement constrkind="V" constrnr="3" nr="40"/>
</Requirements>
```

The values of the constrnr XML attributes represent the numbering derived from the imported MML signature, whereas the nr attributes refer to hard-coded requirements (in source file builtin.pas), c.f. [12].

3.1 Functors div and mod

The numeric constant calculations make use of simple routines that compute the div and mod operations. In order to reuse them in the checker's EQUALIZER module (file equalizer.pas in the source code) as a direct implementation of the MML notions, they must exactly match the semantics of the library definitions (including the floor operation for div and the mod 0 variant):

---

[3] These are MML articles XPRIMET1, XPRIMES0, XPRIMES1, and XPRIMES2 available in recent Mizar distributions.

```
definition
  let i1,i2 be Integer;
  func i1 div i2 -> Integer equals  ::  INT_1:def 9
  [\ i1 / i2 /];
  func i1 mod i2 -> Integer equals  ::  INT_1:def 10
  i1 - (i1 div i2) * i2 if i2 <> 0
  otherwise 0;
end;
```

3.2 Functors lcm and gcd

Similarly, two operations for calculating the least common multiple and the greatest common divisor of two integer values must match the general Mizar definitions:

```
definition
  let a,b be Integer;
  func a lcm b -> Nat means  ::  INT_2:def 1
  a divides it & b divides it &
  for m being Integer st a divides m & b divides m holds it divides m;
  func a gcd b -> Nat means  ::  INT_2:def 2
  it divides a & it divides b &
  for m being Integer st m divides a & m divides b holds m divides it;
end;
```

3.3 Predicate divides

The next automatized definition denotes the integer divisibility:

```
definition
  let i1,i2 be Integer;
  pred i1 divides i2 means  ::  INT_1:def 3
  ex i3 st i2 = i1 * i3;
end;
```

It should be noted that such predicative definitions can be automatized using definitional expansions [4], but then a typical proof context looks this way:

```
30 = 2*15;
then 2 divides 30;
```

Please note the lack of references in both proof steps, yet the first inference is necessary to provide the witness for the expansion of the divides definition. Our automation eliminates the need to input such intermediate steps whatsoever. Unlike in the case of the functor requirements mentioned before, the implementation here requires also providing code in the Mizar's UNIFIER module (file unifier.pas) to facilitate generating clause substitutions based on the divisibility of the available constants. In general, whenever the verifier tries to disprove some statement quantified over two numbers with the assumption that one is divided by the other, then any suitable pair of constants available in the inference can serve as the substitution for unification.

3.4 Attribute `prime`

The notion of primality is defined the standard way, but technically applicable to any integer number:

```
definition
  let p be Integer;
  attr p is prime means  :: INT_2:def 4
  p > 1 & for n being Nat st n divides p holds n = 1 or n = p;
end;
```

The implemented automation saves users from having to refer to the encyclopedic articles of the XPRIME* collection. It might still be worthwhile that the available proofs be maintained by the MML committee as a sort of low-level complete proof data or for regression testing purposes.

4 Conclusions

The proposed extension of the Mizar system and library can be used by a simple user import command in any Mizar text that develops a theory requiring extensive use of integer divisibility. The usefulness of its application is clear from the big number of automated proof steps in typical article-sized Mizar formalizations similar to the NUMBER* series. Standard Mizar utilities (e.g., `relprem`) equipped with the enhanced checker reveal hundreds of unnecessary references in the original scripts. Note, however, that just as with the other `requirements`, its use should not be imposed on the users, especially if the possibility of developing proofs in full detail may be beneficial, for instance, for didactic purposes.

References

1. Bancerek, G., et al.: The role of the Mizar Mathematical Library for interactive proof development in Mizar. J. Autom. Reason. **61**(1–4), 9–32 (2018)
2. Grabowski, A., Kornilowicz, A., Naumowicz, A.: Mizar in a nutshell. J. Formalized Reason. **3**(2), 153–245 (2010)
3. Grabowski, A.: Elementary number theory problems. Part VI. Formaliz. Math. **30**(3), 235–244 (2022)
4. Kornilowicz, A.: Definitional expansions in Mizar - In memoriam of Andrzej Trybulec, a pioneer of computerized formalization. J. Autom. Reason. **55**(3), 257–268 (2015)
5. Kornilowicz, A., Surowik, D.: Elementary number theory problems. Part II. Formaliz. Math. **29**(1), 63–68 (2021)
6. Kornilowicz, A.: Elementary number theory problems. Part III. Formaliz. Math. **30**(2), 135–158 (2022)
7. Kornilowicz, A.: Elementary number theory problems. Part IV. Formaliz. Math. **30**(3), 223–228 (2022)
8. Kornilowicz, A., Naumowicz, A.: Elementary number theory problems. Part V. Formaliz. Math. **30**(3), 229–234 (2022)
9. Mizar Homepage. https://mizar.uwb.edu.pl. Accessed 10 Apr 2023

10. Naumowicz, A.: Dataset description: formalization of elementary number theory in Mizar. In: Benzmüller, C., Miller, B. (eds.) CICM 2020. LNCS (LNAI), vol. 12236, pp. 303–308. Springer, Cham (2020). https://doi.org/10.1007/978-3-030-53518-6_22
11. Naumowicz, A.: Elementary number theory problems. Part I. Formaliz. Math. **28**(1), 115–120 (2020)
12. Naumowicz, A.: Evaluating prospective built-in elements of computer algebra in Mizar. In: Matuszewski, R. Zalewska, A. (eds.): From Insight to Proof: Festschrift in Honour of Andrzej Trybulec, Studies in Logic, Grammar and Rhetoric 10(23), 191–200 (2007)
13. Naumowicz, A., Byliński, C.: Improving Mizar Texts with *Properties* and *Requirements*. In: Asperti, A., Bancerek, G., Trybulec, A. (eds.) MKM 2004. LNCS, vol. 3119, pp. 290–301. Springer, Heidelberg (2004). https://doi.org/10.1007/978-3-540-27818-4_21
14. Sierpinski, W.: 250 Problems in Elementary Number Theory. Elsevier, Amsterdam (1970)

Extracting Theory Graphs
from Aldor Libraries

.

Florian Rabe[1(✉)] and Stephen M. Watt[2]

[1] Computer Science, University of Erlangen-Nuremberg, Erlangen, Germany
`florian.rabe@fau.de`
[2] David R. Cheriton School of Computer Science,
University of Waterloo, Waterloo, Canada
`smwatt@uwaterloo.ca`

Abstract. Aldor is a programming language for computer algebra that allows natural expression of algebraic objects while also allowing compilation to efficient code. Its language primitives, however, do not correspond exactly to those of modern proof assistants nor to those of data formats used in mathematical knowledge management. We discuss these difficulties and export the Aldor library as a diagram in the category of theories and theory morphisms, using a simplified model of the Aldor language that retains its essential expressivity. This allows us to capture a rich set of expert-designed interfaces for use in mathematical knowledge management settings.

1 Background

Aldor emerged from the Scratchpad II project at IBM Research, developed as a generalization of a language first described in [3] and known first as $A^\sharp$ [9], and the *Axiom Library Compiler* before its release as Aldor as an independent package. Types are run-time values, with run time *domains* providing abstract data types, and *categories* qualifying domains by requiring certain operations or properties. The application to symbolic mathematical computation influenced the design to use dependent types pervasively, conditional run-time category membership, and *ex post facto* type extension [7,8].

Theory graphs are categorical diagrams of theories using truth-preserving compositional interpretations as morphisms between theories. They are an important language-independent tool for high-level knowledge representation, interrelating diverse constructs, and modular theory development [2]. A critical choice in the design of formal languages for mathematics is whether theories and morphisms are provided by a meta-layer formalism (which is always possible and relatively straightforward) or built into the language as first-class objects (which greatly increases both expressivity and complexity). For mathematical knowledge, the *built-in* design is very appealing because it enables using theories as the types of mathematical structures, thus elegantly capturing mathematical practice. Thus, many systems choose it, including Aldor. But the *meta-layer*

C. Dubois and M. Kerber (Eds.): CICM 2023, LNAI 14101, pp. 315–320, 2023.
https://doi.org/10.1007/978-3-031-42753-4_24

design is superior for integrating developments across different languages, systems, and libraries because they can share the theory layer, which provides exactly the interfaces needed for interoperability. This poses a recurring challenge for the integration of mathematical software systems.

In this paper, we present (i) a system for translating Aldor libraries into the language-independent theory graph formalism provided by MMT [6], and (ii) the data obtained by translating the available Aldor libraries in this way. The result comprises 440 theories and morphisms. This is valuable because (i) it makes the (so far unpublished) Aldor libraries accessible to the general community and (ii) provides insights into the general issue of connecting the *built-in* and *meta-layer* design choices. In particular, our work can serve as a starting point for porting the Aldor library to or as an interface for integrating Aldor computations in other mathematical software systems.

2   Modeling Aldor in MMT

As a running example we use the definition in Fig. 1, based on $\sum^{it}$ [1]. Here the function `ResidueClassRing` takes two arguments R and p and returns a theory (called a *category* in Aldor).

Theories are used as types akin to record types, and their elements (called *domains* in Aldor) provide definitions for all abstract fields of the category. Each Aldor domain provides a representation type (written %), which corresponds to a carrier set. The name of a domain doubles as a reference to that representation type, mimicking the

```
define ResidueClassRing(
    R: CommutativeRing, p: R): Category  ==
CommutativeRing with {
    modularRep: R -> %;
    canonicalPreImage: % -> R;
    if R has EuclideanDomain then {
        symmetricPreImage: % -> R;
        if R has SourceOfPrimes then
            if prime? p then Field;
} }
```

Fig. 1. ResidueClassRing in Aldor

mathematical practice of using the same name for a structure and its carrier. Here R is a domain, typed by a previously defined category, and p is an element of the carrier of R.

The category is defined to extend the category `CommutativeRing` with several declarations. Critically, Aldor allows conditional declarations: if R additionally has category `EuclideanDomain` (an extension of `CommutativeRing`), then *ResidueClassRing* is defined to also declare symmetricPreImage, and if R additionally has category `SourceOfPrimes`, *ResidueClassRing* is defined to also include the category `Field`. For example, `ResidueClassRing(Integer, 7)` extends `Field` with all three listed operations because the domain `Integer` has those two categories.

Representing Aldor Primitives. We use a manually written MMT theory `Aldor` to declare the about 30 primitive operators of Aldor.[1] The theory `Aldor` occurs as the governing language (called *meta-theory* in MMT) of all theories we generate from Aldor libraries.

For simplicity, we have not formalized Aldor in a logical framework, instead we declare it directly as a primitive language in MMT. Therefore, the constants in `Aldor` are untyped and provide only notations (via the # symbol). For example, we declare an operator `Qualify # L1 $ 2` for Aldor's primitive operation `modularRep $ C` of accessing the field `modularRep` of some domain variable `C` of category `ResidueClassRing`. MMT's notation language is expressive enough to mimic many details of Aldor's concrete syntax such as the $-notation for qualified names. These MMT constants occur as the heads of the MMT expressions representing Aldor expressions. For example, we export the expression above as the following MMT object (here given in OpenMath XML syntax):

```
<OMA><OMS cd="aldor" name="Qualify"/>
    <OMS cd="ResidueClassRing" name="modularRep"/><OMV name="C"/></OMA>.
```

Interpreting Categories and Domains as Theories and Morphisms.
Category-valued Aldor functions become parametric theories in MMT. For example, Fig. 2 shows the HTML+MathML rendering produced by MMT from our export of our example theory. The two kinds of declarations in Aldor categories (typed constants and category extensions) can be directly represented using the analogous features of MMT.

If a domain is declared at top level, it can be seen as a theory morphism from its type (which must be a category and thus be represented as an MMT theory) to the empty theory, i.e., the MMT theory `Aldor`. More generally, a domain-returning function can be represented as a theory morphism into the anonymous MMT theory declaring the function's arguments. If the type of a domain is the union of some Aldor categories, the domain of the MMT morphism is the corresponding union of MMT theories. If the type is an anonymous category, we generate a name for it and add it to the MMT theory graph. Finally, Aldor allows domains typed by an anonymous category and no definiens; this is Aldor's way of grouping statically available constants. We represent such domains as MMT theories.

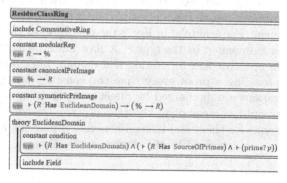

Fig. 2. ResidueClassRing in MMT

---

[1] This theory can be found at https://gl.mathhub.info/aldor/language/.

The Implicit Carrier Type. The type % is built into every Aldor category and treated specially by the system. We represent this in MMT by manually writing a special theory `Carrier` that declares only a type %. This theory is then included by every theory generated from an Aldor category. In Fig. 2, this include is not present explicitly because it is already inherited from `CommutativeRing` by composition of inclusions.

Each domain must define the name `Rep` to define the carrier set. In the language of theory graphs, this is simply the assignment to the constant %, and we translate it accordingly in the MMT theory morphism. To represent the Aldor type system correctly, we have to add a coercion rule that turns every use of an Aldor domain R in a position where a type is expected into the expression %$R.

Categories as Types. Contrary to Aldor categories, MMT theories cannot be meaningfully used as types directly. In fact, MMT does not impose any type system at all. Instead, it is the task of the meta-theory to declare appropriate constants and typing rules. We have previously presented a solution for using theories as types in [5], and we follow the same approach here: the constant *Category* of the theory `Aldor` serves as the type of categories, and we provide the rules

$$\frac{\text{theory } T \text{ includes } \texttt{Carrier}}{T : \texttt{Category}} \qquad \frac{c : \texttt{Category}}{c : \texttt{type}}$$

to turn each category (including those that are created dynamically) into a type. Thus, we can represent the type of the variable R in the running example simply as an OpenMath object referencing the theory `ResidueClassRing`.

Conditional Declarations. MMT does not allow for conditional declarations, and intentionally so because that makes it statically undecidable what the names provided by a theory are. We found two novel solutions to encode Aldor's conditional declarations that will have to be evaluated in the future.

First, we extend our representation of Aldor's type system with a propositions-as-types principle and represent the condition as an additional argument. For example, in Fig. 2 the condition of the constant `symmetricPreImage` is represented by the type ⊢ R Has EuclidenDomain (which uses Aldor's built-in operator `Has` for testing if a domain implements a category). This requires providing a proof every time the constant is used. In Aldor these proof obligations are discharged by direct computation, which amounts to a very simple sound-but-incomplete theorem prover. Therefore, we do not synthesize proof terms for them and instead generate a placeholder for an unknown subterm to be reconstructed by the reusing application.

This approach does not work for conditional includes though. Therefore, we developed a second solution that is more involved but would also be applicable to

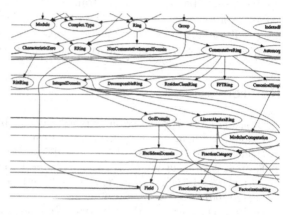

for every conditional declaration, we produce a nested theory that declares first the condition as an axiom and then the actual declaration. For example, in Fig. 2 the inclusion of Field is guarded by the conjunction of the two conditions in whose scope it occurs. We need to generate a name for this new theory, and we use some heuristics to pick a helpful name for it, in this case EuclideanDomain. Now given a proof of the condition, we can construct a theory morphism from the nested

Fig. 3. ResidueClassRing theory graph fragment

theory into its parent, via which the conditional declarations can be accessed.

Representing Aldor Libraries as MMT Theory Graphs. The Aldor distribution includes six libraries, but we focus on the two that have the most reuse value: the base library and the algebra library. We follow the best practice [4] of exporting a system-near export that is then imported into the target system using a general purpose data format (in our case: Lisp S-expressions) as an intermediate representation. We have adapted the Aldor compiler to produce the intermediate representation (as one .axy file for each of the 321 Aldor source files available), and we have written an MMT import tool that implements the representation described above. The (very verbose) intermediate representation makes up 360 MB (18 MB gzipped). This yields 440 MMT theories and morphisms, written out as OMDoc files totaling 0.5 MB, which is similar in size to the zipped Aldor sources. The import time is on the order of 1 minute on modern laptops. A fragment of the resulting theory graph is shown in Fig. 3. Here the conditional inclusion from our running example would appear as an edge from Field to ResidueClassRing/EuclideanDomain, which our theory graph layouting algorithm currently places it outside of the screenshot. We have also generated many smaller graphs representing individual parts of the library.We are able to release the generated .axy and OMDoc files and theory graphs. These are available at https://gl.mathhub.info/aldor/distribution and can be regenerated by running MMT.

3 Conclusions and Future Work

We have seen that the algebraic framework of the Aldor language and libraries carries over in a natural way to MMT theories. Certain language features, including conditional categories and *ex post facto* extensions appear to be useful more generally and we anticipate incorporating these in MMT.

References

1. Bronstein, M.: $\sum^{IT}$—a strongly-typed embeddable computer algebra library. In: Calmet, J., Limongelli, C. (eds.) DISCO 1996. LNCS, vol. 1128, pp. 22–33. Springer, Heidelberg (1996). https://doi.org/10.1007/3-540-61697-7_2
2. Farmer, W.M., Guttman, J.D., Javier Thayer, F.: Little theories. In: Kapur, D. (ed.) CADE 1992. LNCS, vol. 607, pp. 567–581. Springer, Heidelberg (1992). https://doi.org/10.1007/3-540-55602-8_192
3. Jenks, R.D., Trager, B.M.: A language for computational algebra. ACM SIGPLAN Not. **16**(11), 22–29 (1981)
4. Kohlhase, M., Rabe, F.: Experiences from exporting major proof assistant libraries. J. Autom. Reason. **65**(8), 1265–1298 (2021)
5. Müller, D., Rabe, F., Kohlhase, M.: Theories as types. In: Galmiche, D., Schulz, S., Sebastiani, R. (eds.) IJCAR 2018. LNCS (LNAI), vol. 10900, pp. 575–590. Springer, Cham (2018). https://doi.org/10.1007/978-3-319-94205-6_38
6. Rabe, F., Kohlhase, M.: A scalable module system. Inf. Comput. **230**(1), 1–54 (2013)
7. S.M. Watt. Handbook of Computer Algebra, chapter 4.1.3 Aldor, pp. 265–270. Springer, Cham (2003). https://doi.org/10.1007/978-3-642-55826-9_4
8. Watt, S.M.: Post facto type extension for mathematical programming. In: Proceedings of Domain-Specific Aspect Languages, pp. 26–31. SIGPLAN, ACM, October 2006
9. Watt, S.M., Broadbery, P.A., Dooley, S.S., Iglio, P., Steinbach, J.M., Sutor, R.S.: A first report on the $A^\sharp$ compiler. In: Proceedings of ISSAC, pp. 25–31. ACM, July 1994

System Entry

GeoGebra Discovery

Christopher W. Brown[1], Zoltán Kovács[2]([⊠]), Tomás Recio[3], Róbert Vajda[4], and M. Pilar Vélez[3]

[1] United States Naval Academy, Annapolis, USA
[2] PHDL Linz, Linz, Austria
zoltan@geogebra.org
[3] Nebrija University, Madrid, Spain
[4] JKU Linz, Linz, Austria

Description. GeoGebra is a dynamic mathematics software tool for all levels of education, that brings together geometry, algebra, spreadsheets, graphing, statistics and calculus. *GeoGebra Discovery* (GD) is an experimental version of GeoGebra, dealing with automated reasoning in elementary geometry. It contains some features that are under heavy development and therefore they are not yet included in the official GeoGebra version.

GD can be found at https://github.com/kovzol/geogebra-discovery.

Applications. Among other improvements, GD includes a set of either new or enhanced (w.r.t. the standard GeoGebra version) Automated Reasoning Tools for elementary geometry, which is a set of commands like ProveDetails, Prove, Compare, Relation, LocusEquation, Envelope, Discover, StepwiseDiscovery and Plot2D. These commands allow proving planar geometry statements via a portfolio of provers, and to visualize the locus or envelope equations. Also a point-based discovery is available, either in a casual run, or in a continuous setup. Planar curves can be (topologically) faithfully plotted, including them for real-time parametrized animations.

Changes from Previous Version. See [1] for a report on a former version. Now an updated implementation of the ProveDetails command is included which allows the user to mechanically prove, among others, geometric inequalities on a planar construction. GD exploits the free availability and comparable speed of the TARSKI software system to manipulate Tarski formulas (logical connectives of semi-algebraic formulas), in particular, the relevant case of those that contain only existential quantifiers. This facilitates the new version to consider a more delicate classification of truth can be obtained, similarly to the notion of "truth on parts" or "truth on components" in complex algebraic geometry.

Reference

1. Brown, C.W., Kovács, Z., Recio, T., Vajda, R., Pilar Vélez, M.: Is computer algebra ready for conjecturing and proving geometric inequalities in the classroom? Math. Comput. Sci. **16**, 31 (2022)

C. Dubois and M. Kerber (Eds.): CICM 2023, LNAI 14101, p. 323, 2023.
https://doi.org/10.1007/978-3-031-42753-4

Author Index

C. Dubois and M. Kerber (Eds.): CICM 2023, LNAI 14101, pp. 325–326, 2023.
https://doi.org/10.1007/978-3-031-42753-4

Printed in the United States
by Baker & Taylor Publisher Services